DEVIANT WOMEN

DEVIANT WOMEN

FEMALE CRIME
AND CRIMINOLOGY
IN REVOLUTIONARY
RUSSIA, 1880–1930

SHARON A. KOWALSKY

 NORTHERN ILLINOIS UNIVERSITY PRESS / DEKALB

© 2009 by Northern Illinois University Press

Published by the Northern Illinois University Press, DeKalb, Illinois   60115

Manufactured in the United States using postconsumer-recycled, FSC certified, acid-free paper.

Design by Julia Fauci

Library of Congress Cataloging-in-Publication Data

Kowalsky, Sharon A.

Deviant women : female crime and criminology in revolutionary Russia, 1880–1930 / Sharon A. Kowalsky.

   p.   cm.

Includes bibliographical references and index.

ISBN 978-0-87580-406-4 (clothbound : alk. paper)

1. Female offenders—Soviet Union—History. 2. Deviant behavior—Soviet Union—History. 3. Women—Soviet Union—Social conditions. 4. Crime—Soviet Union—History. 5. Criminologists—Soviet Union—History. I. Title.

HV6046.K69 2009

364.3'74094709041—dc22

To the memory of Florence Eisenberg

CONTENTS

LIST OF TABLES

ACKNOWLEDGMENTS

I would like to express my profound gratitude to the numerous institutions and individuals whose financial, intellectual, and moral support made the completion of this project possible. Generous grants from the University Center for International Studies (UCIS) at the University of North Carolina at Chapel Hill (UNC), the International Research and Exchanges Board (IREX) Individual Advanced Research Opportunities Program, the National Security Education Program (NSEP) David L. Boren Graduate International Fellowship, and the American Councils for International Education (ACIE/ACTR) Regional Scholar Exchange Program funded several research trips to Russia. Additional support from the UNC Graduate School and a Doris Quinn Fellowship from the UNC History Department enabled me to write the dissertation upon which this book is based. This work has also benefited from the comments, suggestions, and encouragement offered by conference participants at numerous meetings of the Southern Conference on Slavic Studies (SCSS) and the American Association for the Advancement of Slavic Studies (AAASS), as well as the Havighurst Center of Miami University of Ohio graduate student conference on "Social Norms and Social Deviance in the Soviet and Post-Soviet Era" (2001), where I presented my preliminary thoughts on the scope of the work.

Many people contributed to the evolution of this project over the years. My eternal gratitude and devotion belong, first and foremost, to Donald J. Raleigh, whose constant support, enthusiastic interest in my work, and ever-critical eye helped to move this project from concept to reality. Judith Bennett, Ron Bobroff, E. Willis Brooks, Jennie Burnet,

John Cox, Michael David-Fox, Marko Dumancic, Stuart Finkel, David M. Griffiths, Paul Hagenloh, Chris Hamner, Steve Harris, Dan Healey, Warren Lerner, Ann Livschiz, Rosa Magnusdottir, Paula Michaels, Martin A. Miller, Jackie Olich, Lynn Owens, Christine Ruane, Andrew Stickley, Paul Stronski, Kate Transchel, and Jon Wallace provided invaluable input and intellectual stimulation over the years that helped to shape, focus, and sharpen my ideas. The staffs of the granting institutions and the libraries and archives that I made use of in Moscow, St. Petersburg, Kazan, Saratov, and throughout the United States helped to make my research trips smooth and successful. Support and encouragement from colleagues at Georgetown University, the University of North Carolina at Chapel Hill, and Texas A&M University-Commerce made the completion of this work possible. I am extremely grateful to Betsy Hemenway, Dan Orlovsky, and Michael Learn for their willingness to devote time from their busy schedules to read parts of the manuscript. The detailed and insightful comments and suggestions I received from the press's two anonymous reviewers immensely improved the quality of the manuscript. My thanks go as well to the editorial staff at Northern Illinois University Press, Mary Lincoln, J. Alex Schwartz, Amy Farranto, and Susan Bean, for their unwavering support of the project and their commitment to it. Finally, I am indebted to my wonderful family for their encouragement and love— to my mom, who saw me through the many ups and downs of life; to the rest of my family, who understood better than most what I do and why; to my husband, Jorge, and his family, who warmly welcomed a scholar into their midst; and to my grandmother, Florence Eisenberg, who loved life, travel, and learning. It is to her memory that I dedicate this book.

Parts of this book have been published elsewhere. Elements and ideas from what are now chapters 3 and 5 appeared in "Who's Responsible for Female Crime? Gender, Deviance, and the Development of Soviet Social Norms in Revolutionary Russia," *The Russian Review* 62, no. 3 (July 2003): 366–86. An earlier and shorter version of chapter 5 was published as "Making Sense of the Murdering Mother: Soviet Criminologists and Infanticide in Revolutionary Russia," in *Killing Infants: Studies in the Worldwide Practice of Infanticide*, edited by Brigitte Bechtold and Donna Cooper Graves, 167–94 (Lewiston, NY: Edwin Mellen Press, 2006). I am grateful to the publishers for permission to include revised versions of these works here. Transliterations of Russian names and terms follow the Library of Congress system. Finally, of course, all errors and omissions in the book remain my own.

DEVIANT WOMEN

"On 1 October 1923 at seven in the morning, Nastia E., twenty-four years old, maimed her husband by amputating his penis." So begins psychologist A. E. Petrova's account of Nastia's crime, published in *Prestupnyi mir Moskvy* (*The Criminal World of Moscow*), a 1924 collection of essays about crime and criminals in Moscow edited by the eminent criminologist and Moscow State University law professor M. N. Gernet. As Petrova explained, in 1916 seventeen-year-old Nastia came to Moscow from a village in the Tambov region. After working as a domestic servant, she eventually found employment as a seamstress. Interested in bettering herself, she began to attend adult education classes and in 1919 enrolled in a course for workers, where she met her future husband. They became intimate in June 1922, but did not register their marriage until February 1923, by which time Nastia's licentious husband had infected her with venereal disease, leaving her unable to bear children. The day before the fateful incident, Nastia had visited her husband's mistress and had seen their child, whose appearance left no doubt about its father's identity. Although this child represented her husband's deceit, Nastia felt the strong pull of her maternal feelings as she held it. Unsure if she should confront her husband about his mistress and tormented by her own infertility, she entertained thoughts of suicide. That evening Nastia endured two incidents of forced intercourse with her husband, which caused her severe pain because of her illness and infection. Her distress and fever worsened during the night. Toward morning, delirious with pain, she saw her sleeping husband's exposed member and, near the bed on a table, a bread knife. Thinking "this is the cause of it all," she grabbed the knife and, without realizing what she was doing, quickly sliced off his penis.[1]

Delving into Nastia's psychological state at the moment she committed her crime, Petrova concluded that this case involved a *"primitive psyche which, on the path of prolonged, uninterrupted, and strenuous intellectual effort went beyond the bounds of its primitive level of development."*[2] In this analysis, Nastia's mental and physical stress caused her "primitive" psychological capabilities to "short circuit," leaving her temporarily insane at the moment she mutilated her husband.[3] Similarly, psychiatrist N. P. Brukhanskii, who included his own analysis of the case in his 1927 *Materialy po seksual'noi psikhopatologii* (*Materials on Sexual Psychopathology*), concluded that Nastia's "primitive origins" and "narrowness of consciousness" shaped her criminal behavior.[4] Both Petrova's and Brukhanskii's descriptions of Nastia's personality emphasized her peasant background, her lack of intellectual development, and her inability to fully engage in public life. Furthermore, they both stressed that Nastia's infertility, that is, her inability to achieve the proper reproductive outcome of her sexual activity, contributed to her mental instability. These factors led them to conclude that Nastia's "primitiveness," combined with the circumstances of her situation, particularly the severity of her venereal disease, created the context for her crime. As an expert medical examiner, Brukhanskii testified to this effect before the Moscow Regional Court (Gubsud) on 10 November 1924, and the court, agreeing, found that Nastia had acted in a state of temporary insanity and dismissed all criminal charges against her.[5]

Nastia's case became something of a cause célèbre within the Soviet criminological community of the 1920s. For us as well, this incident provides an appropriate starting point to discuss the analysis of female criminals, the nature of female crime, and the attitudes toward women in early Soviet society. Nastia's offense exhibited the basic features that Soviet criminologists associated with female crime: it occurred in connection with the domestic sphere, it involved female reproductive physiology (in this case infertility), and it reflected a level of primitive, violent, and emotional behavior usually associated with village life. These elements combined to create an image of the female criminal and the nature of female crime that criminologists used to make sense of women's deviance. Their interpretations linked female sexuality, physiology, and criminality, establishing the types of crimes women could commit and the motivations for their offenses. Criminologists' attitudes toward female offenders easily extended to all women, as the source of female crime emanated from women's common physiology. In this way, criminologists connected women to a potentially deviant sexuality and to the supposed backwardness and primitiveness of the countryside.[6] Their discussions of female crime suggested that women faced tremendous obstacles to becoming proper, conscious, and politically engaged Soviet citizens. These ways of thinking about female crime ascribed certain behaviors to women that reflected a divide between the ideals, expectations, and potential for revolutionary change and the realities that women faced in their everyday lives.

This book explores the nature of revolutionary transformation through the lens of criminology and female crime. During the transitional period between the October Revolution of 1917 and the rise of Stalinism in the early 1930s, Russians negotiated what it meant to be "Soviet." From the start, it was not entirely evident what this might involve. As Russians constructed and reconstructed their identities, adapting to the changing opportunities and restrictions imposed on them by Bolshevik ideological priorities, they contributed to the definition and establishment of new norms and practices of daily life.[7] Their attitudes, outlooks, and priorities, combined with and shaped by the harsh realities of everyday survival, helped to form some elements of Soviet social policy.

One arena where this process of negotiation emerged most clearly was in family law. As part of their vision of a society free of bourgeois exploitation, the Bolsheviks implemented a new family code in 1918, hoping to promote women's emancipation and undermine the traditional patriarchal family by liberalizing marriage and divorce laws: civil registration replaced church wedding; divorce could be obtained by either party without grounds; abortion was legalized; state guardianship of orphans eliminated the need for adoption; parents became responsible for child care in accordance with their means and regardless of their marital status. While the provisions of the family code sought to facilitate the eventual disappearance of the family, their implementation raised concerns among policymakers and observers about the destabilization of society as they tried to reconcile the idea of the newly liberated woman with older notions of female purity, compassion, weakness, and inferiority. They feared that radical policies such as easy divorce would lead to sexual promiscuity and irresponsibility, to the spread of disease, and to a breakdown in morals.[8] Such concerns helped fuel heated public debates about the family code and led to its first revision in 1926. The reworked code curtailed the law's authority over marriage by removing divorce from the courts and by recognizing common-law unions, but it also offered greater protections to women by extending alimony rights and it reaffirmed the importance of the family by legalizing adoption.[9]

By the late 1920s, the realities of the transitional period challenged the utopian goals of the Soviet regime's family policies, and the state's lack of resources prevented it from bearing the full social burden its early vision intended.[10] With Stalin's rise to power, the acceleration of industrialization, and the renewed drive to socialize the country that began in the late 1920s, the state increasingly looked to the traditional family as a source of stability that could fulfill the tasks the state would not or could not perform. A further revision of the family code in 1936 set forth a new view of society that ceded social responsibility to individuals and families, imposed restrictions on divorce, and recriminalized abortion. Urged to continue working while raising more children, women increasingly bore a double burden without the full measure of domestic assistance promised by the Bolsheviks.[11] By the mid-1930s, the utopian goal of abolishing the patriarchal family had given way to the reinforcement of a traditional form of the institution that would serve the needs of the Stalinist state. This abandonment of some of the more radical elements of the Bolshevik vision has been explained by the difficult circumstances the Soviet state faced in this period, the resistance to these changes from the Russian population, and the all-encompassing drive for industrial growth that called upon women both to produce in the workforce and to reproduce at home.[12] These factors all helped to shape the policy shifts, but the processes of negotiating what being "Soviet" meant that were reflected in the family law changes (and the reactions to them embodied in female crime) become clearer when these dynamics are considered in the context of a redefined and extended "cultural revolution."[13]

Scholars have employed the term "cultural revolution" as a key concept for understanding the shifts from the seemingly radical, utopian, and idealistic policies of Lenin to the conservatism and terror of Stalin. For the Bolsheviks and their fellow travelers, political change alone was insufficient; they sought to reshape behaviors and relationships by establishing cultural hegemony over all aspects of social life as well. In this context, "cultural revolution" refers to the transformations of social and cultural policies and practices in accordance with the Bolshevik ideological vision. The term "cultural revolution" has often been used to refer to a fundamental reorientation of Soviet policy as part of Stalin's drive toward socialism.[14] Indeed, the desire to separate the abuses of Stalinism from the utopianism of October has led some scholars to identify the points where Stalin supposedly diverged from the ideals of the revolution. Notably, Nicholas Timasheff, writing in 1946, discussed what he called the "Great Retreat," the seeming about-face in Soviet social policy that occurred in the mid-1930s. Timasheff posited that the Stalinist state abandoned its revolutionary goals in the face of the fascist threat from Nazi Germany and in an effort to bolster its popular support. Recently, historians have challenged this interpretation. Setting the Soviet system in the context of the development of the modern European surveillance state after World War I, these scholars argue that Stalin never turned his back on his revolutionary goals. Rather, he co-opted and adapted traditional cultural institutions in support of the socialist state precisely because he believed that socialism had been achieved. Stalinism in this interpretation thus represents a consolidation rather than a betrayal of revolution.[15]

"Cultural revolution," however, must also be considered as part of a larger and broader revolutionary transition. Michael David-Fox, for example, has suggested an understanding of cultural revolution as "an integral part of a broader vocabulary of transformation that encompassed everyday life, behavior, and the new Soviet person." In these terms, cultural revolution becomes inseparable from the Bolsheviks' drive to modernize Russia and traces its roots back to the very origins of the Bolsheviks' revolutionary efforts.[16] It embodies both radical and conservative elements, attempting to redefine society according to new terms while at the same time building on, preserving, and adapting the traditions of the past to suit the new conditions.

In this context, the family policy shifts in the mid-1930s represent not a retreat from socialist ideology but rather the culmination of an extended process of establishing Soviet values and the codification of long-standing social attitudes into Soviet policy. Throughout the transitional period, the shape and nature of the Soviet system and its family policies were very much up for negotiation. As the Bolsheviks set about constructing socialism in Russia, their understanding of social norms and their vision of society often clashed with the opportunities women had, the beliefs they held, and the realities they faced after the revolution. By examining representations of female criminal deviance, we can explore how the social continuities and dynamics of the transitional period worked to negotiate and define new norms of proper behavior, facilitating the eventual reversal of the family code's more radical policies as the regime set about determining exactly what it meant to be "Soviet."

The idea of an extended cultural revolution also suggests the importance of continuities during this period of transformation. Attitudes toward female crime and women expressed during the New Economic Policy (NEP) emerged from and were shaped by late-nineteenth-century pan-European intellectual currents, adapted to suit the needs of the post-World War I modernizing state. The development of the discipline of Soviet criminology itself reflects the application of these intellectual trends and suggests ways that professionals adapted to and worked with the Soviet regime.[17] Throughout the transitional period, a multidisciplinary cohort of sociologists, statisticians, psychiatrists, jurists, doctors, penologists, anthropologists, and forensic experts closely examined the dynamics of crime and the motives of offenders to determine the most effective means to eliminate crime from Soviet society. Together they established criminology as a legitimate professional scientific discipline, drawing on earlier western European developments in the field and their own fledgling efforts from before the revolution. Criminology as it emerged after the October Revolution preserved its prerevolutionary intellectual currents while at the same time defining itself as "Soviet." The central importance of these older ideas, particularly regarding female criminals, within Soviet criminology highlights the continuities between prerevolutionary and Soviet society. On one level, the progressive potential of socialist ideology came into constant conflict—as reflected in what the Soviet state determined was deviant behavior—with the persistent remnants of the past that the Bolsheviks attempted to destroy as they established new norms of proper "Soviet" behavior. Crime studies provided a way for observers to evaluate the population's progress toward socialism and the distance remaining to the successful construction of a socialist society. At the same time, criminology preserved deeper underlying attitudes persisting from before the revolution that contributed to shaping the course of Soviet socialist development.

These dynamics played out in criminologists' discussions of female crime. The explanations for female criminal deviance that criminologists provided throughout the 1920s emphasized the basic "primitiveness" and "backwardness" of women, their ignorance of socialist principles, and their inability, or unwillingness, to participate in public life to the same extent as men. If Soviet citizenship was defined by political activity and civic engagement, then, in the professionals' conception, women remained outside the boundaries of that citizenship, their distance from modern Soviet life resulting from their close connection to the rural and the domestic. By linking female deviance with the qualities associated with peasants and the countryside, criminologists suggested that ruralness was not merely the antithesis of the New Soviet Woman but her expected and natural manifestation.[18]

In their analyses of female crime, criminologists responded not only to the circumstances of the transitional period and their anxieties regarding the New Economic Policy and the building of socialism, but also to postwar pan-European concerns regarding modernity and the changing position of women in society.[19] Their interpretations of female deviance helped to alleviate fears about the chaos and uncertainty of the time by reinforcing a traditional patriarchal understanding of women's social position, which in combination with the realities of life in the transitional period, raised questions regarding both the new legal position of women after their emancipation and the effectiveness of the Bolsheviks' radical social and family policies for structuring the new socialist society. In effect, these attitudes, combining the intellectual currents of the prerevolutionary period with socialist ideology and the anxieties of the NEP, contributed to the creation of a gender hierarchy, paralleling the class hierarchy, that determined proper behavior and limited women's ability to become "Soviet."

Nastia's transgression thus provides a vivid introduction to the ways early Soviet criminologists discussed female crime. According to Bolshevik ideology, crime was supposed to disappear with the construction of socialism. Consequently, any crimes committed in the transitional period were manifestations of remnants of the "old way of life" that persisted in the "primitive" consciousness of the backward (and primarily peasant) Russian population. In Nastia's case, the analysts highlighted her "primitiveness"—a result of her social class origins—and her sexually induced mental infirmity as key factors in causing her crime. Nastia's personal trajectory—coming to Moscow from the provinces, becoming a worker, enrolling in workers' education courses—paralleled a journey both typical of the growing urban working population of the 1920s and encouraged by the Bolshevik regime. Yet despite following the appropriate paths to Soviet enlightenment, Nastia could not escape her peasant origins. She acted with the passion and violence that observers associated with the countryside and situated within the domestic realm that typically circumscribed women's crimes. Despite her best efforts, Nastia's rural "primitiveness" prevented her from overcoming her peasant backwardness to participate successfully in the challenges of modern, urban, public life.

Female physiology also influenced Nastia's criminal behavior: the analysts stressed that venereal disease and infertility contributed to her temporary insanity. Faced with the inability to have children, to fulfill her "natural" maternal instincts and reproductive functions, Nastia lashed out instinctively at what she perceived to be the cause of her misfortune. In this way, the specialists presented Nastia as driven by her sexual dysfunction and controlled by maternal instincts that could not be satisfied, unable to overcome the limitations of her diseased physiology to become a mother and thus a proper New Soviet Woman.

Class and sexuality shaped understandings of female crime in the transitional period, but they also acted as mitigating factors for determining women's punishments and for understanding the scope of women's crimes. In Nastia's case, the court found that her temporary insanity, heightened by her rural "primitiveness" and her physiological dysfunction, made her unaware of what she was doing and therefore not criminally responsible for her actions. In both scholarship and court practice, the confluence of women's reproductive roles and their social origins resulted in the perception that women remained backward and ignorant, at the mercy of their capricious sexuality, not able to take full responsibility for their actions, and consequently deserving of leniency. In their efforts to define proper behavior in the new Soviet state, criminologists and courts stressed that only by consistently applying compassion, understanding, and measures of cultural enlightenment and education—to make women aware of the benefits of socialism—could women even begin to become conscious, responsible, engaged members of modern Soviet society. At the same time, however, criminological studies emphasized the distance women remained from this goal and, as Nastia's inability to successfully better herself indicates, the possible limits of socialism's progressive potential with regard to women.

REVOLUTION AND SOVIET CRIMINAL LAW

The Bolshevik Revolution of 1917 and the Civil War that followed it were violent manifestations of the failures of the tsarist regime throughout the late Imperial period to implement political and social reforms. Instead of trying to change the existing political structure, the Bolsheviks seized the opportunity to establish a new system based on their understanding of Marxist principles of social equality. Calling for land reform, an end to Russia's involvement in World War I, and improved living conditions, the Bolsheviks appealed to a population worn out by fighting and to an intelligentsia frustrated by the slow pace of Russia's modernization. Over the course of the next decade, the Bolsheviks explored a variety of approaches to implement their social and political visions, consolidating power as they passed radical new laws that sought to restructure the very fabric of Russian society, abolish old beliefs, and create new social relationships.

In some ways, the Bolsheviks borrowed their approach to law from their tsarist predecessors. During the nineteenth century, Imperial reformers had tried to remove the arbitrariness of autocracy from the legal process. A major project to codify the laws got underway in the 1830s, but the culmination came with the 1864 Judicial Reforms that established independent courts and trials by jury. The new courts proved wildly successful, becoming forums for both dispute settlement and public opinion as crowds gathered to hear high-profile cases. The tsarist leadership, however, quickly found itself inconvenienced by the rule of law, particularly as the authorities dealt with a rising tide of terrorism in the early twentieth century. Imposing emergency measures and applying administrative sanctions, the tsarist regime abandoned certain elements of its legal reforms in the name of maintaining its political control.[20] Even more than did the tsars, the Bolsheviks exhibited a disdain for the law. They used the legal process as a transformative vehicle while adapting and manipulating it to facilitate the pursuit of their ideological goals.

During the Civil War, expediency and military needs shaped the nature of Bolshevik legal policies as the regime sought to secure its hold on power at the same time that it attempted to restructure Russian society. While passing laws and decrees designed to eliminate "bourgeois" exploitation, such as the 1918 family code, the Bolsheviks relied heavily on violence and coercion to enforce their policies.[21] The introduction of the New Economic Policy in 1921, however, initiated a different approach to the building of socialism and the role of the law. Intended by Lenin as a step back from the harsh policies of "War Communism," as the Bolsheviks' violent methods of expropriation during the Civil War came to be called, the NEP legalized market elements within the socialist economy to promote recovery after the devastation of the period 1914–1921. Although it was successful in stimulating economic growth, from the very beginning many Bolsheviks disapproved of the NEP economy. For Bolsheviks dedicated to the construction of a socialist state, the NEP, in restoring certain capitalist principles, strengthened social forces incompatible with socialism. To these Bolsheviks, it appeared that the drive toward socialism, which had seemingly made progress under the coercive policies of War Communism, had been totally abandoned.[22]

While economic policy during the NEP may have resembled capital-ism more than socialism, efforts proceeded apace on the cultural front to establish new, "proletarian" forms of cultural expression and new "social-ist" forms of social organization. During the NEP, the cultural revolution that began in earnest with the 1917 October Revolution continued to encourage cultural exploration, albeit within certain ideological limits. Experiments in music, theater, creative writing, and art embraced avant-garde and constructivist approaches that were supposed to bring ordinary people into the creative process and high cultural expression. Efforts to increase education and literacy rates also expanded across Russia as the Bolsheviks brought the message of the revolution to the countryside. Economic recovery and growing social stability during the NEP permitted a new Soviet culture to develop and to begin to spread among the Russian population.[23]

The NEP also ushered in a new period in Soviet law. Despite the distrac-tion of fighting the Civil War, the Bolsheviks had managed to abolish much of the tsarist legal structure. They revoked the old law codes but hesitated to implement new ones in their place, preferring instead to issue emergency decrees as circumstances arose. Bolshevik ideology contained an "antilaw" attitude that viewed the law as an exploitative bourgeois institution used to maintain a system of class oppression that, like the state, crime, and the family, would wither away with the achievement of socialism. This antilaw stance led to a reliance on the "revolutionary consciousness" of judges, or the judges' own individual sense of how best to apply revolutionary principles to the administration of justice, rather than on any standardized regulations, thus making the use and applica-tion of the law increasingly arbitrary and ideologically oriented.[24] By the start of the NEP, it had become clear that some legal standards would be required until socialism could be achieved. Legal specialists found that courts and judges needed guidance in their administration of criminal justice; their "revolutionary consciousness" proved too inconsistent (and sentences proved too lenient) to enforce the Bolsheviks' decrees.[25]

The new criminal code for the Russian Federation (RSFSR), introduced in 1922 and revised in 1926, signaled the importance of the law for establishing proper models of Soviet behavior during the NEP. Combin-ing provisions that addressed generally accepted definitions of criminal acts with articles directed against the regime's ideological "enemies," the criminal code provided guidelines for shaping social behavior and estab-lished uniformity in sentencing practices. The new code drew heavily from a 1903 draft code that had never been passed into law, but also integrated Bolshevik ideological principles and priorities in its provisions. Although it included sentencing guidelines, it continued to rely to a great extent on judicial discretion and the "revolutionary consciousness" of judges to determine appropriate punishments. In addition, the code incorporated a class bias that promised to protect workers from exploitation and recognized that mitigating circumstances, such as hunger or need, could inspire criminal action.[26] In this way, the criminal code allowed considerable leeway in the application of justice as well as flexibility in establishing a criminal's "social dangerousness" (*sotsial'naia opasnost'*), that is, the threat an offender posed to social stability, determined by the court according to the nature of the criminal act, the offender's awareness of its implications, and the class origins of the criminal.[27] Political revolutionary tribunals persisted in early Soviet society, particularly for the Bolsheviks' class enemies, but for ordinary criminals the courts, the criminal code, and the penal system became the primary venues for the administration of Soviet justice.

Soviet penal policy during the NEP also applied progressive penal theories to the Russian prison system. Widely embraced by western European penologists beginning in the late nineteenth century, progressivism emphasized that prisoners could be reformed and rehabilitated through corrective labor. In incarcerating criminals, it intended to punish them and to protect society while at the same time reforming offenders to prevent their return to crime. Soviet penologists stressed the goal of adjusting the criminal to a new life in Soviet society through compulsory labor, cultural enlightenment work, and education. All criminals, they emphasized, could be reformed; as one observer noted, Soviet power must give all offenders "the juridical possibility to return to an honest working life, to open for them an exit, to give them hope for rebirth. Only through such corrective penal politics does Soviet power acquire unity, fullness, and logical completeness."[28] The corrective benefits of the prison regime would be realized through individualized attention to the background, circumstances, and needs of each prisoner (making the study of crime and criminals a necessary element of penal policy), and this in turn would allow each prisoner, in theory, the chance to become a vital, contributing, and responsible member of Soviet society.[29]

While Soviet penal theory expressed the ideals and vision the Bolsheviks had for their new socialist society, the application of the criminal code's provisions reflected the underlying attitudes that shaped reactions to unacceptable behavior in the early Soviet period. The People's Commissariat of Justice (NKIu) exhorted its judges to act according to their "revolutionary consciousness," but inexperienced and poorly educated officials frequently relied on peasant customary law and traditional morality as they listened to the cases before them.[30] The gender, class, and social background of offenders became important factors in the application of the law and in the administration of Soviet justice as the determination of deviance and "consciousness" served to shape the very identity of offenders. For instance, professionals defined certain crimes as "male" or "female," "urban" or "rural," ascribing specific characteristics to the offenders that established their understanding of the motivation for and nature of the crimes. This served to categorize crimes according to the identity of the offender, making them natural, immutable, and, in many ways, resistant to the progressive reeducation efforts envisioned by Bolshevik penal policies. Although criminologists continually emphasized the role that socioeconomic factors, material circumstances, and the "old way of life" played in criminal offenses during the NEP, their basic understanding of the gender and class nature of criminality reflected beliefs that, while not necessarily incompatible with socialist ideology, raised questions about the long-term viability of Soviet social policies.

By the late 1920s, the NEP approach faced increasing criticism. Lenin's death in 1924 had left unresolved the question of leadership succession in the Communist Party and the direction that Soviet policy would take in the future. Debates within the party over NEP economic policies and the nature of the revolutionary project fed factions and the formation of alliances as prominent Bolshevik leaders vied for control of the party and the state. Stalin's emergence as leader and his consolidation of power during a period of sustained crisis brought about the end of the NEP. Rallying support around his idea of "socialism in one country," Stalin initiated a major push toward rapid industrialization accompanied by collectivization of agriculture with the First Five-Year Plan. At the same time, he created a loyal bureaucracy and new "Soviet" intelligentsia, solidified the policies that would determine the course of the country's future development, and curtailed the debates and exploration of other possible paths for building the socialist state, including the study of crime.[31] The law remained important in the new Stalinist state, but only to provide a veil of "socialist legality" that masked its increasingly arbitrary and ideologically based application. It is important to keep in mind, however, that while the First Five-Year Plan and the Stalinist system that emerged from it did signal a decisive change from what preceded it, the basic precepts that determined the course and shape of Soviet development had been established long before.

FEMALE CRIME AND CRIMINOLOGY

As the Bolsheviks attempted to remake society and the family in the socialist image, female crime exposed a point where old attitudes toward the family and women's position came into conflict with new Soviet ideals and state policies, and where continuities between the present and the past became clearly visible. Studying the margins of society, the points where social norms break down, has proved to be a particularly fruitful way to understand behavioral norms, cultural attitudes, and methods of social control.[32] Particularly in revolutionary contexts, the boundaries between normal and deviant become especially important as we seek to understand how societies refashion conceptions of proper behavior to fit a new social order.

While definitions of crime in general reflect the understanding of acceptable social norms, discussions of female crime in particular provide a way to assess the underlying and fundamental assumptions about the nature and structure of society. Late-nineteenth and early-twentieth-century analyses of female crime, in both Russia and western Europe, tended to link it more intimately to the family than male crime. Furthermore, female crime, while occurring less frequently than male crime, appeared to observers to be more disruptive to social stability precisely because of its close connection to the family. Female criminals behaved in ways contrary to those expected of women in their roles as mothers and nurturers. In this way, female criminals challenged the image of the morally pure woman and, by extension, the fundamental structure of society. Moreover, studies of female criminal deviance often directly connected women's criminal offenses to their sexual physiology, which needed to be monitored and controlled to ensure women acted within the boundaries of proper behavior.[33] In the context of Revolutionary Russia, analyses of women's deviance revealed the complex dynamics among family policy, socialist progress, and norms of proper behavior. Examining changes in female crime rates became a way for social scientists and communist bureaucrats to measure Russian society's progress toward socialism, the population's level of socialist consciousness, and the role the family played in Soviet society.

In the initial years after the revolution, the Bolsheviks paid considerable attention to liberating women from centuries of patriarchal oppression. Building on the Provisional Government's enfranchisement of women that occurred in June 1917, the Bolsheviks created a new constitution in 1918 that fully emancipated women, granting them political and juridical equality with men. They established the *zhenotdel*, the women's section of the Communist Party, to address the particular concerns and problems women faced and to raise women's awareness of the benefits of socialism. Furthermore, the Bolsheviks encouraged women to join the workforce, promising to establish nurseries and daycare facilities in factories, to increase maternity benefits, and to improve access to a variety of employment opportunities. Household labor and child care would be transferred to the public arena, removing women from the confines of the domestic sphere and freeing them to pursue other activities. As a result, some women served as elected representatives in the local and central government, participated in political meetings in the workplace, and obtained specialized training at higher educational and technical institutes. Encouraged by Bolshevik propaganda, during the 1920s and 1930s women took up all sorts of jobs, becoming chauffeurs, mechanics, pilots, and tractor drivers, among others—occupations that might have been considered "male" in different circumstances.[34]

While on the surface Bolshevik ideology promoted equality between men and women, representations of female crime by specialists revealed the deeper gender distinctions that shaped their understanding of the nature and scope of women's social position. Criminologists relied on socioeconomic interpretations of crime, but they also found psychology and biology compelling elements in their explanations for female crime. Women's physiological cycles, professionals argued, increased female susceptibility to criminal influences. Moreover, these influences had direct links to prerevolutionary morality and traditions that the Bolshevik Revolution had supposedly eliminated. In criminologists' analyses, female crime proved to be extremely resilient, retaining its traditional forms and nature in spite of the Bolsheviks' radical social changes and the new opportunities these policies potentially created for women to engage in public life. There was nothing particularly unique about female crime in early Soviet society; it followed patterns observed by prerevolutionary Russian professionals and by their counterparts elsewhere in Europe. Yet the revolution's particular ideology informed interpretations of female crime, determined the state's and the criminologists' responses to women's deviance, and provided a means to evaluate the transformation of Russian society by emphasizing the importance of educating women, the appropriate levels of punishment for female criminals, and the extent to which women could be held responsible for their criminal actions.

While a range of studies have focused on various aspects of crime and the law in the late tsarist period, historians have only recently begun to investigate criminal deviance in Soviet society before Stalin. Works on daily life by western and Russian scholars have touched on issues of crime, in particular hooliganism, in the 1920s, but the phenomenon of female crime remains relatively unexplored.[35] In the following discussion, I hope to fill this void by situating female criminal deviance within a broader context of revolution, modernization, and social development. Previous studies of female crime have sought to explain the variations in women's crime rates identified by criminologists in the 1920s.[36] In contrast, this project uses criminologists' interpretations of female deviance to explore the nature of social change and the creation of behavioral norms in early Soviet society.

CHAPTER OVERVIEW

In exploring early Soviet social norms and the position of women, this book engages with two main subjects: the development of Soviet criminology and criminologists' analyses of female crime. Part I focuses on the emergence of the discipline of criminology in the context of the modernizing state. Chapter 1 traces the evolution and development of criminological principles, and theories of female deviance in particular, situating them within the increasingly radical intellectual environment of late Imperial Russia. Chapter 2 examines the dynamics of criminology as a scientific discipline after the Bolshevik Revolution, exploring the relationship between the state and society as the professionals attempted to carve out some autonomy, through professional organizations, from a regime seeking to direct all aspects of social life.

Part II shifts the focus to the analyses by criminologists of female crime specifically and the attitudes of these criminologists toward women more generally. Chapter 3 concentrates on female sexuality and the ways in which women's physiological functions shaped criminologists' understanding of female crime. Tracing changes and continuities across the revolutionary divide, this chapter highlights tensions in criminological discourse between the idea that women's increased contact with what criminologists called the "struggle for existence" would push female crime to become more like male crime and the belief that the influence of women's physiological functions confined female deviance to the domestic sphere. Chapter 4 uses the concept of the "geography of crime" to show how class could be determined by the nature of the crime committed, regardless of the geographic location of the crime. The association of the words "rural" with "primitive" crimes and "urban" with "skilled" crimes linked women with the countryside and backwardness, and emphasized how far women remained from the ideals of the revolution. Chapter 5 ties the idea of sexuality and class together through a close examination of infanticide, the most "typical" and most disturbing crime committed by women. For criminologists, infanticide represented the ruralness of women, their physiological weaknesses, and their inability to embrace the new Soviet way of life. Professionals' discussions of infanticide offenders reveal most vividly the underlying social attitudes toward women, the importance of the family, the nature and goals of the cultural revolution, and the ways that proper Soviet behavior was understood and ascribed to both women and men during the transitional period.

Russian and Soviet criminologists drew their observations of female criminals from personal interviews with prisoners and from court, prison, and police statistics. When they wrote about crime, in journal articles, newspaper reports, and scholarly monographs, they often provided detailed personal histories of criminals, pointing to the individual childhood and family circumstances that shaped the offender and led her on the path toward crime. To gather this data they completed questionnaires of arrested offenders and in-depth psychiatric evaluations of prisoners under their supervision. Criminologists also relied on a wide variety of statistics to describe trends in crime rates. The Department of Moral Statistics, a division of the Central Statistical Administration (TsSU) established in 1918 and headed for a time by criminologist M. N. Gernet, compiled crime and suicide statistics from across the RSFSR and USSR.[37] Criminologists supplemented these official data with statistics taken from smaller sample groups collected by criminological organizations from local and regional courts and prisons. Sometimes the numbers were based on arrest rates, sometimes on trial and sentencing rates, and sometimes on prison populations. The incomplete, unsystematic, and variable nature of early Soviet statistics makes it impossible to rely on them to present an accurate picture of crime levels. What these statistics do reflect, however, are the trends in crime that criminologists identified and studied. In other words, the statistics reflect the ways criminologists understood the problems facing the Soviet state, and provided them with the scientific evidence they needed to confront these problems.

While some of the crime scholars that populate this study published widely and played prominent roles in Soviet society, most worked in relative obscurity. Beyond a short publication or two, little biographical information remains extant for them, making it difficult to determine the course of their careers in more than the broadest strokes. Moreover, the inherently interdisciplinary nature of criminology makes it impossible to establish a comprehensive intellectual orientation for the discipline. Ultimately, criminological scholars were products of their core disciplines. Wherever possible, the professional or bureaucratic designations of the scholars are indicated. If a specialist's educational background or official position could not be determined, however, the term "criminologist" is employed as a convenient label to situate that specialist within the broader criminological discourse. Moreover, the use of "criminologists" as a collective reference to those involved in crime studies is not intended to diminish or conflate the very real disciplinary and methodological differences among these professionals, but rather to place their professional endeavors within the scope of criminology as a general approach to the scientific study of society. Furthermore, while a vast majority of crime specialists were men, a small group of professional women also contributed to the criminological discourse. In the female criminologists' analyses, however, their gender did not overtly determine the results of their studies; their conclusions generally paralleled those of their male colleagues.[38] These determinations were particularly true in research on women's deviance. While disagreement among the diverse cohort of criminologists continued throughout the transitional period regarding the methods for and approaches to studying crime in general, professional analyses of female crime reflected a general cohesiveness above and beyond the general studies of crime. This reveals the pervasiveness, resilience, and homogeneity of attitudes toward women that persisted across disciplinary divides and within criminological debates.[39] In closely examining female crime, however, I do not mean to imply a radical difference in male and female motivation for crimes, or in the justifications offered by criminologists for them. Nor do I seek to explain women's motives for their criminal acts beyond those that criminologists suggested for them. Instead, I focus specifically on determining how criminologists' understandings of women's deviant actions in particular elucidate the processes of revolutionary transformation during the transitional period.

Thus, the following analysis takes its cues from the interests and orientation of criminologists themselves in their discussions of female crime. In most instances, when they analyzed women's deviance, professionals disregarded or minimized political ideology and politically defined offenses (such as counterrevolutionary crimes) and avoided attributing political motives to offenders. Female counterrevolutionaries may have been arrested, tried, and sentenced, but criminologists generally ignored these offenders, instead focusing their attention on "ordinary" female criminals committing traditionally "female" crimes connected with the domestic sphere. Such crimes, often perpetrated in moments of passion and in the absence of overt ideological motives, challenged the legitimacy of the Soviet government in more subtle ways. By raising questions regarding the effectiveness of social and family policies, women's crimes exposed faults in the structure of the Soviet system and in its ability to fulfill its promises of equality, revealing the implicit beliefs of criminologists about women, illustrating women's position in society, and describing the realities of life in the transitional period for both women and men.

The following discussion draws primarily on criminologists' publications to explore representations of female deviance. Consisting of a broad range of statistical, sociological, psychiatric, medical, and polemical works, these scholarly monographs, journal articles, and newspaper pieces provide a rich source base from which to evaluate criminologists' attitudes and interpretations of women criminals. I supplement the publications with archival sources from the central repositories in Moscow that elucidate the institutional development of criminology as a discipline and the dynamics of its relationship with the Soviet state. The nature of the available sources in each case, however, places limitations on the scope of this work. The publications of the criminologists, based on personal evaluations of individual criminals and statistical data, impose their interpretations on their subjects' actions, removing the offenders' own voices from this study and necessarily shaping the conclusions of this investigation. Likewise, the archival record illuminates the bureaucratic structure of criminology but not the actual experiences of the women who passed through the judicial system. Few detailed transcripts from court cases in the 1920s remain extant, and archival restrictions prevented access to those documents. Because of such limitations, I am unable to address directly the lives and experiences of the women who make up the subjects of this study. It is through criminologists' eyes, therefore, that I explore the broader attitudes that shaped criminological study and court practice during the transitional period, and the process of negotiation that occurred among the perceptions of women's social position, the ideological goals and priorities of the state, and the realities of everyday life.

PART ONE

THE DEVELOPMENT OF CRIMINOLOGY

ANTHROPOLOGY, SOCIOLOGY, AND FEMALE CRIME

The Origins of Criminology in Russia

Criminology as a discipline developed in Russia over the course of the nineteenth century in response to and as part of the process of modernization, emerging out of a growing interest among educated Russians in science and social studies as a way to improve society. For these professionals, criminology provided a conceptual framework for explaining, understanding, and categorizing the social transformations of fin-de-siècle Russia. While the first statistical examinations of Russian crime appeared as early as the 1820s, it was only after the Judicial Reforms of 1864 and the subsequent systematic compilation and publication of judicial statistics, beginning in 1873, that sufficient empirical foundations existed to support criminological studies. These bureaucratic and technological developments coincided with a growing concern among Russian elites about social disorder and rising crime rates, stimulated by increasing industrialization and urbanization in the second half of the nineteenth century and reinforced by the terrorism and violence in the aftermath of 1905. As they began their own scientific investigations, Russian jurists, statisticians, sociologists, and doctors interested in studying crime looked for guidance to the west, where statistical research on crime was by this time already well established.[1] They drew upon European criminological theories as well, adapting them to suit the specific Russian social and political conditions. Interest in criminology also paralleled the establishment of organized, systematic, and humane penal institutions, adapted from western models and intended to reform offenders through discipline and labor.[2] The development of Russian criminology in the nineteenth century shows that Russian social attitudes and visions of modernity rested on the same foundations as those in Europe while also highlighting the uniqueness of Russian circumstances.[3]

Nineteenth-century European criminology had its origins in Enlightenment philosophy.[4] Scholars frequently point to the publication in 1764 of *Dei delitti e elle pena* (*On Crimes and Punishments*) by the Italian, Cesare Bonesana, Marchese di Beccaria (1738–1794), as the beginning of modern criminology.[5] Beccaria embraced liberal Enlightenment ideas of individual freedom and reason. Interested in countering the arbitrariness of the absolutist ancien régime and committed to the rule of law, he believed that clearly established definitions of crimes and their corresponding punishments would serve as deterrents to criminal action. Beccaria understood the offender as a rational, reasoning individual who carefully weighed the consequences of his actions. By the early nineteenth century, Beccaria's position had developed into what has been called the "classical school" of criminal law, which dominated legal and penal practices for the next one hundred years.[6]

By the late nineteenth century, however, several new "schools" of criminology began to emerge in Europe. These loose associations of like-minded scholars, the most prominent of which included the criminal anthropological and the sociological schools,[7] responded to concerns about the rising crime rates that accompanied industrialization and the inadequacy of the classical school to explain this trend. Widespread fear of the "dangerous classes," the desire to separate criminals from normal society, and a growing interest in science and empiricism led European social scientists to seek explanations for crime based on "objective" statistical evidence. Moreover, increasing concerns about protecting society from dangerous individuals led these scholars to look to the personality of the offender—the personal, moral, physical, and environmental factors that influenced and shaped the individual—to explain crime and criminality. Inspired by Darwinian evolutionary theories, the Italian school of criminal anthropology, led by Cesare Lombroso, collected anthropometric data on offenders to explain why certain individuals became criminal. The Marxist-influenced sociological school, relying on theories postulated by Emile Durkheim (1858–1917) and Gabriel Tarde (1843–1904), emphasized social and environmental factors to explain the existence of crime in society.[8]

Many historians of criminology have observed that the development of the field of criminology has proceeded in a cumulative fashion, with each new school emerging out of previous approaches and incorporating older theories and methods.[9] Indeed, although their interpretations of crime differed and although they defined themselves in opposition to one another, both the criminal anthropological and sociological schools came out of the same context, built upon the same assumptions, shared a common interest in the practical application of criminological theories for social reform, and reached many of the same conclusions. Nowhere do the similarities between the two schools become more apparent, however, than in their studies of female deviance: scholars of both approaches placed emphasis on women's physiology as a central factor in female crime and found confirmation of women's proper social position in their discussions of female offenders.

Both the criminal anthropological and sociological schools found supporters in Russia who adapted the European theories to suit the Russian context. By the early twentieth century, however, the criminal anthropological school, critiqued for its reliance on theories of inherent deviance and on anthropometrical measurements of criminals' physical characteristics, had been thoroughly discredited, both in Russia and abroad. A "left wing" emerged out of the Russian sociological school that took a radical socialist view of crime and its causes. Influenced by the intelligentsia's concern for social reform, this group emphasized socioeconomic explanations of crime and argued that crime could be understood only by examining the impact of external influences on the offender. Such an approach would later prove to be compatible with Bolshevik ideology, allowing the left-wing criminologists to form the core of the Soviet criminological discipline after the 1917 October Revolution. Thus the course of criminology's development in nineteenth-century Russia provides the basis for understanding its successes in the early Soviet period.

The following discussion traces the theoretical developments in European criminology and their adaptation and application in late Imperial Russia, focusing in particular on Lombroso's theories of crime and Russian reactions to them. It reveals the strong influence late-nineteenth-century European criminologists had on the nascent discipline in Russia, but it also shows how the social and political context of the late Imperial period shaped Russian criminology. In addition, it explores the emergence of theories of female crime as postulated by Lombroso and interpreted by Russian criminologists in the late tsarist era, seeking to understand the factors and attitudes that shaped these scholars' understanding of women's criminality. Despite their general attraction to sociological explanations of crime and their rejection of criminal anthropology, Russian criminologists, like their European colleagues, incorporated elements of multiple approaches (including Lombroso's) into their interpretations of female crime. They emphasized the central importance of women's sexuality in defining female deviance, and their explanations confirmed for them the idea that women's traditional social position and reproductive functions shaped the nature of female criminality.

THE SCHOOL OF CRIMINAL ANTHROPOLOGY

One of the most influential and controversial figures in nineteenth-century criminology, Cesare Lombroso (1835–1909) founded what became known as the Italian school of criminal anthropology. Lombroso, a clinical psychiatrist and professor at the University of Turin, became interested in crime through his examinations of mental patients and insanity. In his work he emphasized the importance of experiment, investigation, and empiricism, employing an anthropological perspective and establishing "scientific" principles for the study of crime.[10] Lombroso set out his theories of crime in *L'Uomo delinquente* (*The Criminal Man*), first published in 1876. In developing his anthropological approach to crime, Lombroso conducted systematic investigations of male prisoners, measuring their physical characteristics and exploring their mental capacities. Through this work, Lombroso identified what was later termed a "born criminal" type, a person exhibiting what he considered to be atavistic, or primitive and innate, traits that made the born criminal genetically predisposed to commit criminal acts. For Lombroso, the born criminal embodied "a reemergence of the historical and evolutionary pasts in the present."[11] He described this born criminal, basically a primitive subspecies of man, as a "biological throwback" to an earlier evolutionary period, a person who would naturally act contrary to the laws and expectations of modern civilized society.[12] This approach differed dramatically from that of the classical school, which posited that criminals, and indeed all people, made rational choices and exercised free will. Denying the concept of free will and applying evolutionary principles, the school of criminal anthropology determined that a person had no choice in committing a criminal act—he was either a born criminal or a normal man.

Lombroso pinpointed the characteristics of the born criminal by taking anthropometric measurements of prisoners and deviants. In the long list of physiological anomalies Lombroso identified, however, not all could be attributed solely to atavism. In addition, therefore, he emphasized degeneracy—the effect of social diseases such as alcoholism, malnutrition, tuberculosis, and venereal disease on the mental and moral health of a person—as central to determining criminal proclivities.[13] For instance, Lombroso argued that epilepsy represented a pathological condition that prevented normal neurological development and led to a degeneracy similar to that of the born criminal. Although he maintained that the born criminal was a distinct anthropological type, Lombroso found that epileptics displayed similar traits. As a result, he classified them as degenerates and therefore potential criminals as well.

Lombroso eventually identified several types of criminals in addition to the born criminal and the epileptic: the criminal of passion, the insane criminal, the occasional criminal, the pseudocriminal, the criminaloid, and the habitual criminal. These categories reflected varying levels of atavism and degeneracy; some even implicitly recognized environmental influences and suggested that under extreme circumstances degeneracy could lead a "normal" person to crime. Lombroso remained committed, however, to the primacy of inborn individual factors, emphasizing the parallel roles of atavism and degeneracy in creating the criminal type.[14]

Lombroso's theories held considerable appeal for some late-nineteenth-century Russian intellectuals, particularly because of their "scientific" orientation. His method of measuring criminals' physical features provided an empirical basis for criminological study at a time when scientific principles were becoming increasingly important for legitimating the social sciences.[15] Many Russian professionals embraced criminal anthropology as a way to bring scientific methods into the field of jurisprudence that for decades had been dominated by the thinking of the classical school.[16] For instance, N. S. Lobas, a doctor who spent many years working among criminals in Russia's Sakhalin prison, noted with approval the "rise of the criminal anthropological school's scholarly-historical methods of study. From that moment the classical school of criminal law, which believed that the criminal's 'free will,' and therefore 'evil will,' caused his criminal activity, was given a death blow. This is the significant, immeasurable contribution of Lombroso that makes amends for all his mistakes."[17] The classical school of criminal law argued that evil will could be contained within the criminal, appearing when a person confused proper and improper behavior or when such a person proved incapable of understanding the difference between right and wrong. Lobas noted, however, that millions of people struggled to survive under less than ideal circumstances and yet did not commit crimes. Therefore, he concluded, "it is altogether natural to look for the causes of crime not only in the circumstances of the criminal's life, but also in the criminal himself, in his immature psychophysiological development, that *prevents* him from choosing the path that everyone else travels."[18] From this perspective, it was not free will that caused a person to commit a crime; rather, it was something in the basic constitution of the person, inherent in his or her physiology. Combining elements of Darwinian theories of evolution with "scientific" statistical data drawn from anthropometric measurements, criminal anthropology explained the persistence of criminal activity and the propensity of certain people to criminal activity. It provided a justification for the removal of criminals from society and suggested a way to protect society from criminal elements, particularly in the context of the increasing crime, violence, and terrorism that Russia faced in the first years of the twentieth century.[19]

Criminal anthropology helped its supporters to ground in science their concerns regarding the potential criminality of the masses. For instance, Praskov'ia N. Tarnovskaia (1848–1910) used criminal anthropology to call for social reform through biological improvement. A trained doctor and active participant in international criminological circles, Tarnovskaia, together with her husband physician V. M. Tarnovskii, ardently supported Lombroso. She even contributed to Lombroso's study of female offenders by providing him with anthropological data on Russian female murders. Tarnovskaia noted: "Criminal Anthropology seeks to clarify the destitution of the criminal by studying his physical and moral, acquired and hereditary insufficiencies and deviations."[20] She understood that the tasks of criminal anthropology were "to clarify the general biological foundations for the growing number of crimes; to identify the most probable causes leading to the appearance of people predisposed to criminality; . . . and to study measures to better prevent the tendency to commit crimes." Tarnovskaia focused in particular on the biological aspects of criminal anthropology, stressing that research into hereditary criminal traits formed only one part of the broader study of human development and evolution. Furthermore, Tarnovskaia saw the study of criminals as a fundamental element of social hygiene and the "primary task of this new branch of biology."[21] Thus, according to Tarnovskaia, the study of crime was an intricate part of the promotion of social hygiene and social welfare. Directly related to biology, criminal anthropology would elucidate the causes of crime and help to develop measures for its prevention, particularly by identifying those naturally predisposed to criminal activity, that is, born criminals. In this way, criminal anthropology became a social science, intimately linked to preserving the health of the social organism and society.

Even Lombroso's staunchest supporters, however, found it necessary to adapt criminal anthropology to suit Russian conditions. For instance, D. A. Dril' (1846–1910), an unwavering advocate of criminal anthropology, found Lombroso's theories useful only to a certain extent when considering both individual and environmental factors of crime. A prominent criminologist, jurist, and professor of Russian law, Dril' worked for some time as head of the department of correctional education in the tsarist Central Prison Administration and as legal counsel for the Ministry of Justice. He enjoyed a long career as an academic, teaching in the law faculty of Moscow University and at the Psycho-Neurological Institute in St. Petersburg, and publishing extensively on crime and criminality.[22] Although Dril' embraced theories of criminal anthropology, he remained critical of Lombroso's specific methods of studying criminals, emphasizing that a complete understanding of crime could be achieved only by examining the general social factors that influenced the criminal, in addition to his or her physiological characteristics. He stressed the importance of individual factors but also recognized the role of "external conditions" and the "milieu" of the individual in determining one's propensity to criminal activity.[23]

Dril' stressed that criminal anthropology as developed by Lombroso brought a scientific, systematic method to the study of crime. Before Lombroso, he argued, criminal law understood the criminal in abstract terms. Lombroso, in contrast, revealed the relationship between crime and the criminal, "not only in his reality but also in his heredity and individual physical and psychological past and in the various *social* conditions of his existence." Lombroso's criminal anthropology applied "specific methods of the natural sciences that have already achieved brilliant results in other fields of science and reworked them, thanks to which man continues to reveal the mysteries of nature, mastering her secrets and controlling her phenomena."[24] As Dril' saw it, criminal anthropology made the study of crime a part of science, employing methods based on statistics and empirical evidence to increase human understanding of the interaction between man and society. He emphasized that criminal anthropology would provide the tools for discovering the inner workings of the human mind and human psychology. This in turn would enable society to better understand and control the criminal.

While embracing criminal anthropology, Dril' nevertheless criticized Lombroso's obsession with the born or uncorrectable criminal, noting that this focus looked "not forward, but backward to the epoch of human barbarity."[25] He stressed that a more complete understanding of the criminal must examine both the individual characteristics of the offender *and* the overall social context in which the individual lives:

> We do not know man outside of society, and we do not know society without man and the surrounding cosmic environment. Therefore science, in its totality—and this includes the criminal anthropological school—cannot study crime and criminality as a result of only anthropological or sociological or cosmic factors. It must study them as the overall result of all three types of factors. Only then will the study be total, all-encompassing, and, consequently, scientific.[26]

Dril' approached crime as a "sickness of the social organism," the causes of which must be studied in their totality, as with any disease, if they were to be eliminated. He combined Lombrosian "scientific" methods of individual anatomical study with a broader perspective that considered the influence of social factors and the environment surrounding the criminal.

For Dril', and possibly for other Russian adherents of criminal anthropology, Lombroso's theories appealed not in terms of his conclusions per se, but because he applied specific "scientific" statistical methods to the study of criminals and crime. The centrality of empiricism—of experiment, measurement, and observation—in criminal anthropology attracted those interested in infusing criminology with science, seeking objective foundations for penal reform and applying such principles for social control. Particularly in the context of growing protests and violence in Russia, Lombroso's theories provided the justification for the removal of certain potential troublemakers from society. Nevertheless, the centrality of evolutionary principles in criminal anthropology located the impetus for crime within individuals. This adherence to innate causes undermined Lombroso's appeal for many criminologists interested in theories of positivism, social progress, and the influence that external factors, particularly the widespread violence of the early twentieth century, had on crime rates.

THE SOCIOLOGICAL SCHOOL OF CRIMINOLOGY

The success of criminal anthropology as a school of criminology was short-lived, both in Europe and in Russia, although elements of its theories remained compelling as explanations for crime in modern society and influential far into the twenty-first century.[27] While criminal anthropology did employ "scientific" methods, its "science"—based on the anatomical measurements of a small group of criminals—often appeared less than objective, not bringing a sufficiently rigorous empirical analysis to the study of society. Indeed, with its emphasis on atavism and degeneracy, criminal anthropology seemed anti-progressive and anti-modern to many observers. In Russia in particular, the intelligentsia's commitment to social reform and the improvement of the masses provided a strong counterbalance to Lombroso's claims of inherited criminality. Furthermore, for those Russians investigating crime, denouncing Lombroso became a way to define and shape their own criminological theories and their efforts to promote social reform and modernization. Although Lombroso continually revised his theories, by the 1890s asserting that nature "creates the basic, biological preconditions of crime, but society provides the conditions releasing the criminal inclinations of the born criminal,"[28] this recognition of social influences did not go far enough for many criminologists. These professionals generally rejected the biological determinism of Lombroso's ideas in favor of a more sociological approach that emphasized the primacy of social conditions and the influence of the social "milieu" over the role of "hereditary" factors.[29] While the sociological school's perspective of the criminal differed from Lombroso's, both drew upon similar intellectual currents. Indeed, the parallel development of sociological theories provided the groundwork for critiques of Lombroso's approach. One such response came from the socialist-leaning criminologists associated with the "positivist" school of criminology, in particular Lombroso's colleague and friend Enrico Ferri (1856–1929).

Ferri was the acknowledged leader of the positivist school from 1878 until his death in 1929. An accomplished trial lawyer and university professor who served for several decades in Italy's national parliament, Ferri, throughout his professional career, maintained a close association with Lombroso and is often credited with coining the term "born criminal" associated with Lombroso's criminal types.[30] Although Ferri's approach to crime studies resembled Lombroso's and reflected Lombrosian principles in many ways, Ferri incorporated a broader sociological "positivist" approach in his understanding of a criminal's motivation that reduced Ferri's reliance on inborn criminal traits.

"Positivism," a term first coined by French philosopher Auguste Comte (1798–1857), separated science from morality and placed priority on science. It saw sociology as the most "scientific" of the social sciences and examined man not as an individual but as a member of society.[31] The positivist school of criminology likewise sought to understand the criminal as a product of his social environment. In *Criminal Sociology* (*Sociologia criminale*), first published in 1884, Ferri stated that the purpose of the positivist school was "to study the natural genesis of criminality in the criminal, and in the physical and social conditions of his life, so as to apply the most effectual remedies to the various causes of crime."[32] He argued that the metaphysical concept of moral responsibility that the classical school advanced had to be replaced by the idea of legal or social responsibility. Sanctions for criminal offenses would no longer be retributive and based on the objective nature of the act, but would be determined on a scientific basis that took into account the danger the offender posed to society and his or her motivations for committing the offense.[33]

The positivist school also emphasized the scientific classification of criminals. Ferri himself identified five types that paralleled Lombroso's classification scheme: the born criminal, the insane criminal, the criminal of passion, the occasional criminal, and the habitual criminal.[34] Although it placed less emphasis on the physiological characteristics and focused more on sociological factors, Ferri's approach clearly had much in common with Lombroso's theories. Indeed, Russian psychiatrist Iu. V. Portugalov critiqued the positivist school for this, admonishing it to "stop relying on determinism as the central unshakable basis, for this doctrine, as an offspring of the lower natural sciences, has been significantly undermined in recent times and cannot support the serious study of crime."[35] Nevertheless, Ferri's focus on criminal law reform and the concept of legal responsibility—that punishments must correspond to the "dangerousness" of the offender and that the goal of punishment was the protection of society—appealed to Russian criminologists who sought to incorporate such principles into penal theories (and which would become an integral part of Soviet "progressive" penal policies). Ferri had strong socialist leanings and took a close interest in Russian socialists and revolutionaries. His major work on criminal sociology was translated into Russian, as were his thoughts on Soviet criminal law, and his principles of criminal law would influence the first Soviet legal codes and penal policy.[36]

Many Russian professionals studying crime before the Bolshevik Revolution also criticized Lombroso's theories, their more sociological approach to criminal studies in part inspired by Ferri's approach. For instance, S. V. Poznyshev (b. 1870), a pioneering forensic specialist and author of one of the first Russian textbooks on criminal law, argued that "crime is not some special biological phenomenon; its nature is social from the perspective that the groups of acts considered criminal at various moments are determined by social conditions and needs."[37] Lombroso, according to Poznyshev, erred because:

> [he] ignored the huge distinctions between the conditions of primitive life and contemporary society and thus the significant distinctions between then and now in the understanding of the permissible and impermissible . . . . In all of our contemporary anthropological knowledge about primitives, nothing leads to the view that the anomalies identified by Lombroso were the general rule among primitive people.[38]

Poznyshev continued, noting that:

> with the downfall of the idea of the born criminal also falls the anthropological school, the very possibility of criminal anthropology, because if there is no anthropological type of criminal, there cannot be any special science about him. . . . As so, there is no born criminal, and no uncorrectable criminal. No general anthropological type of criminal. This is a very important conclusion that will protect the study of the criminal from numerous mistakes.[39]

Advocating a positivist, sociological approach to criminology, Poznyshev argued that the classical school had separated individual criminals' circumstances from the crimes they committed and examined crime as a static phenomenon according to absolute categories. With a sociological approach, in contrast, there would be a greater awareness of the connection between the criminal and the crime, of the psychological orientation of the offender, and of the nature of his personality. The practitioners of the sociological approach dismissed the classical school's concepts of free will and moral guilt. Instead, they argued that the causes of crime could be found in society and socioeconomic conditions, and in individual and physiological factors. According to them, these factors determined the commission of crime and not free will or choice on the part of the criminal. Crime was no longer an abstract concept but instead an actual and real response to the specific conditions affecting the offender.[40] The school of criminal anthropology had taken a similar stand against the classical school, focusing as well on the relationship between the criminal and the crime. Although they both emerged in reaction to the classical school, criminal anthropology and criminal sociology differed in their views of the nature of the criminal. In contrast to the anthropological school, the sociological school located the factors of crime primarily in social conditions; certain people could not display innate deviant characteristics since notions of criminal behavior changed over time according to the needs of society.

In Russia, criminal sociology developed into the Russian sociological school of criminology. One of the founders of the Russian sociological school and one of the first criminologists to apply a sociological approach to criminal research in Russia was I. Ia. Foinitskii (1847–1913), a professor of law at St. Petersburg University and chairman of the Russian group of the International Union of Criminologists.[41] As early as 1873, Foinitskii began formulating his sociological theories of criminality. Examining crime statistics, he identified three distinct types of factors that caused crime: socioeconomic—unemployment, food prices, and poverty; physical—time of the year, climate, and air temperature; and individual—sex, age, and psychological make-up of the offender.[42] In his first major work, "The Influence of the Time of the Year on the Distribution of Crime," Foinitskii found that temperature changes affected the commission of property crimes and violent crimes. He linked the seasonal shifts in crime rates to the economic conditions of the poorer segments of the population, noting that colder temperatures exacerbated the situations of the poor.[43] By stressing the connections among environmental conditions, economics, and criminality, Foinitskii emphasized the importance of the external socioeconomic factors influencing criminal activity more than the physiological traits of the criminal.

Foinitskii's analysis of crime relied on much of the same terminology as a Lombrosian approach would, but interpreted the meaning of the terms in different ways. For instance, he found the role of "primitiveness" important in understanding an offender's actions. This "primitiveness," however, was not an innate and hereditary limitation but rather a product of the criminal's environment. The more complex and varied a person's surroundings were, Foinitskii argued, the more developed he became psychologically, causing "primitive" forms of intelligence and morality to mature and bringing the person to a higher level of "civilization."[44] In addition, in his studies Foinitskii stressed the importance of biology. The first step in understanding the personality of the offender, he wrote, lay in "biological theories of crime." Yet for Foinitskii, these biological theories had less to do with physiognomy and anthropological characteristics than with the psychological makeup of a criminal, and it was this approach that he believed was necessary to determine criminal responsibility.[45]

Foinitskii's attention to the bio-psychology of criminals reflected a growing interest in criminal psychiatry within the Russian sociological school in the late nineteenth century. Early psychiatric work had focused on insanity and the institutional treatment of those deemed insane. A noticeable preponderance of insanity among criminals and of criminals among the insane led early psychiatrists in Europe and Russia to postulate a link between insanity and crime.[46] This link between criminality and insanity emerged directly from concerns about the impact of the processes of modernization (industrialization, urbanization, poverty, and disease) on the masses. Indeed, Russian psychiatrist P. I. Kovalevskii (1849–1923), a professor at Khar'kov University and founder of Russia's first psychiatric journal, argued that because of increases in social stress and anxiety accompanying the rise in expectations in modern society, insanity was spreading in Russia, threatening the social order, and leading to increased criminality, especially among Russia's youth. He advocated preventative care to stop the development of mental disease, as well as confining the insane.[47] Kovalevskii's views reflected the idea that insanity bred criminality as a result of the disintegration (degeneration) of the social fabric. This approach focused the scientist's attention on the individual offender and his or her state of mind. Psychiatrist Iu. V. Portugalov also promoted the study of crime from the perspective of psychology, noting the importance of determining the "general moral direction of the psychological activities, the impulses, urges, and desires, that incite a person toward one or another action."[48] While he recognized that "criminality does have a sociological aspect which may alter itself, fluctuate, be passed on from generation to generation, disappear, and reappear anew," he stressed that "for the study of [crime's] etiology, economic and social moments are important, but for the analysis of its 'criminal statics and dynamics' . . . only psychology is important."[49]

European advances in criminal psychiatry facilitated the Russian sociological school's development. Notably, the work of German psychiatrist Gustav Aschaffenburg (1866–1944), a professor at the Academy of Medicine in Cologne, combined the individualistic approach taken by psychiatry with an understanding of the sociological causes of crime. In his influential 1903 monograph, *Crime and Its Repression*, published in Russian translation in 1906, Aschaffenburg argued that both social and individual factors affected crime rates. He maintained, for instance, that the rise in rates of property crime in Germany was a result of people's difficulty in adjusting their lives to the decreases in income that accompanied increased grain prices. In addition, he found that the social environment was responsible for crime because the squalor in which the working classes lived led to a "biological degeneration" that left them unable to compete in the "struggle for existence." According to Aschaffenburg, "social causes led to biological degeneration; the resulting biological abnormalities severely handicapped its victims in social life; and this inferior social position—rather than any 'moral defect' or 'criminal inclination'—led some of them to criminal behavior."[50] For practitioners of the sociological school, Aschaffenburg's theories effectively combined the need to examine the psychiatric condition of the individual criminal with the consideration of his or her social situation, highlighting the compatibility of criminal sociology and criminal psychiatry.

Aschaffenburg's psychiatric approach enabled the study of the individual criminal—a central focus of criminal anthropology—to develop within the Russian sociological school. In 1913, psychiatrist A. L. Shcheglov set out to clarify the position of psychiatry within sociological studies of crime. He noted that the sociological school saw crime as the "product of the social conditions in which we live," using statistical methods to uncover various factors that shed light on the nature and origins of criminality.[51] He stressed, however, that for psychiatrists individual factors were no less important than external factors in determining criminality. External social factors influenced everyone, yet relatively few people engaged in criminal activity. Therefore, Shcheglov argued, in addition to sociological factors it was essential to study the psycho-physiological mentality of the offender, focusing on an individual's predisposition to commit criminal activities.[52] Indeed, Shcheglov advocated the primacy of the psychiatric within sociological studies of criminality:

> Crime belongs to that liminal region between norms and pathologies, where it occupies a broad expanse of our subjective worries and inclinations. . . . Therefore, the study of the criminal must proceed, according to our view, not from the study of the particularities of his anatomy to the study of his physiology and psychology, but in the opposite direction, specifically: from the study of his psychological functions and the study of his neuro-physiological activities to the study of the particularities of his physiology.[53]

Shcheglov situated criminal psychiatry firmly within the practice of social medicine and social hygiene, comparing the exploration of the criminal mind to the study of public health issues such as venereal disease, alcoholism, and other epidemics. Thus, Shcheglov emphasized the need for a psychological-physiological analysis, in the name of public health, combined with a sociological analysis to identify the external influences that caused people to commit crimes as well as to determine what in their nature stimulated deviant activity.

As it developed, the Russian sociological school advocated both a sociological approach that sought the causes of crime in external environmental factors and a psychiatric approach that focused on understanding the criminal mentality. In contrast to criminal anthropology's definition of the criminal according to innate physical and atavistic characteristics, the sociological school focused on the external factors, the environment, and the criminal's psychological reaction to his surroundings. In Russia, the outlook of the sociological school complemented the general interest in social reform among the nineteenth-century intelligentsia, but for some it did not go far enough in explaining the causes of crime.

THE "LEFT WING" OF THE SOCIOLOGICAL SCHOOL

The social and political atmosphere of late-nineteenth-century Russia guided the direction in which the Russian sociological school of criminology developed. Russian educated elites, dissatisfied with the arbitrariness of the tsarist government and its inefficiencies, increasingly attempted to involve themselves in social reform projects. For instance, in the 1870s, idealistic students, believing the peasant commune held the key to Russia's future, went "to the people" to encourage them to revolt. Many peasants, distrusting the students, turned them over to the police. While the failure of this effort turned some young intellectuals into terrorists, it may also have convinced other young professionals and specialists that the best way to accomplish reforms and to improve the lives of the Russian people remained to work through state-approved channels. Indeed, the establishment of the *zemstvo* assemblies after 1864 created an outlet for these specialists to conduct practical work among the people, providing employment to doctors, teachers, statisticians, engineers, and agronomists who brought their professional services to the countryside and thus helped to spread modern knowledge among the peasantry.[54] The practical engagement in *zemstvo* work also served to radicalize many professionals as their daily efforts convinced them of the absolute necessity for rapid social reforms. It was in this spirit that criminologists examined crime, and this context that fostered the conditions for the development of criminology as a professional discipline in Russia.

I. Ia. Foinitskii, together with his colleagues M. V. Dukhovskii (1850–1903) and N. S. Tagantsev (1843–1923), formed the original core of the

Russian sociological school of criminology. Their research emphasized the sociological factors of crime, supported and confirmed with empirical data from crime statistics. By the early twentieth century, however, a sense of the urgent need for social reforms to modernize Russia, a growing interest in socialist thought among the intelligentsia, and increasing participation of educated elites (including some criminological scholars) in opposition activities, combined with the professionals' sense of social responsibility, sparked the emergence of a "left wing" (*levoe krylo*) within the Russian socio-logical school, led by M. N. Gernet (1874–1953), A. N. Trainin (1881–1949), A. A. Zhizhilenko (b. 1873), and E. N. Tarnovskii (1859–1936). Combining the sociological school's approach with radical socialist ideology, this new generation of jurists and statisticians focused their explanations of crime on socioeconomic factors. They looked for trends over time and emphasized the social and economic changes that affected criminal behavior, relying on statistics to support their findings and minimizing—but not completely disregarding—the role of individual factors in their interpretations to a greater extent than did Foinitskii and his cohort.[55]

For instance, Tarnovskii, a statistician employed by the Ministry of Justice and responsible for compiling and editing the *Svod statisticheskikh svedenii po delam ugolovnom* (*Collection of Statistical Information for Criminal Cases*), the official state compilation of crime statistics, explained the causes of property crime in economic and social terms. Correlating the price of grain with crime rates, Tarnovskii found that low bread prices and successful harvests were important for both the economic and moral well-being of society. He argued that the alleviation of economic need precisely at moments of crisis was a necessary measure in the fight against crime, and that by providing honest work for those in need, "society or the state could, with a clear conscience, send cases to court and subject criminals to punishment knowing that among them were not people who turned to crime out of inescapable need."[56] Tarnovskii's analysis, although certainly not new, stressed the influence of economic factors on crime rates. But he also raised the issue of the need for social reforms, and the importance of government assistance and social security, a conclusion that situated left-wing criminologists among those calling for the radical reform of Russian society according to socialist principles.

M. N. Gernet became the acknowledged leader of the left-wing crimi-nologists with the 1906 publication of his dissertation, *Obshchestvennye prichiny prestupnosti* (*The Social Causes of Crime*).[57] Born in 1874 in Ardatov, a city in the Volga province of Simbirsk (the birthplace of V. I. Lenin, later renamed Ulianovsk), Gernet entered Moscow University's law school in

1893, finishing his degree in 1897. In 1898, he began teaching at his alma mater while he pursued his doctoral studies. He made his first research trip to Europe in the years 1902–1904, a tour that included stops in all the major European centers of criminological study—Germany, France, Italy, and Switzerland.[58] In *The Social Causes of Crime*, Gernet noted the influence of European criminology on the Russian sociological school and particularly on the left-wing criminologists. Tracing the development of criminology through the western Enlightenment tradition (including in the works of Thomas More, Jean Jacques Rousseau, and Beccaria, among others), Gernet emphasized that the sociological school had emerged as a result of the progressive development of, interest in, and concern for controlling crime through social reform. Although the sociological school's adherents stressed the importance of social factors and the need for social reform, they still argued that the law would preserve the interests of the ruling class, and they failed to see that the exploitation of the working class was more dangerous and deadly than murder. This deficiency, according to Gernet, sparked the development of the sociological school's left wing, influenced in part by Enrico Ferri's positivist approach and other European socialist-leaning intellectuals, for instance Italian socialist Filippo Turati (1857–1932). Turati had argued for the importance of studying crime as a product of both political and social developments, emphasizing that social reform would be more effective than punishment in eliminating crime.[59] In the wake of the 1905 Revolution, in which Tsar Nicholas II made some concessions to the clamor for constitutional rights and representation, Gernet's *Social Causes of Crime* and the left wing's call for social reform dovetailed with the radical agenda of the emerging socialist political parties.[60] The left wing thus politicized the sociological school's concerns with the causes of crime and social reform, emphasizing the exploitation of the working class as a key factor in crime and the alleviation of its burden as a central method for crime prevention.

The left-wing criminologists of the sociological school examined crime not to serve the interests of the individual (although they considered individual factors of crime) but to serve the interests of the collective, to protect society from crime and the criminal.[61] They remained committed to social reform, using their studies of crime to call for greater changes and legal reforms. The atmosphere in Russia at the turn of the century, the growing popularity of socialist ideology, and the overwhelming sense that social change and social reform were absolutely crucial, provided the conditions that encouraged the emergence of the Russian sociological school and led to the adaptation of European (particularly Italian and German) criminal sociology and criminal psychiatry into a radical approach that brought politics into the analysis of crime. This fostered the development of a relationship between the left-wing criminologists and the socialist radicals of the late Imperial period, and indeed, many of those studying the dynamics of crime participated in oppositional activities (intellectual and otherwise) during the revolutionary era.[62]

Even within the sociological school's more radical left wing, however, there was no general consensus regarding the most appropriate methods for studying crime. Criminal sociologists and criminal psychiatrists coexisted uneasily, and would continue to do so throughout the first decade of the Soviet period. Indeed, Gernet himself suggested that a serious divide existed among members of the sociological school regarding approaches to interpreting crime. Fundamental differences separated sociologists from psychiatrists, for although both groups may have had similar political and social reform goals, they disagreed on how much focus should be directed toward the individual offender. This tension between the need to focus on the psychology of individual criminal personalities to understand trends in crime and the importance of studying the general social causes of crime would remain imbedded within Russian and Soviet criminology throughout the 1920s. Nevertheless, Gernet stressed that "these deep differences in the views of the criminalists-sociologists and other sides of the sociological approach on the basic causes of criminality and the methods for fighting it do not preclude the possibility, in some instances, of a unified solution to one or another question about the immediate factors of criminal acts."[63] One area where the various practitioners of the sociological school, and indeed adherents of other approaches as well, came together was in their discussions and explanations of female crime.

CRIMINOLOGICAL THEORIES OF FEMALE CRIME

Lombroso's publication in 1893 of *The Female Offender*, coauthored with colleague and son-in-law Guglielmo Ferrero, marked the first attempt to classify scientifically and systematically the phenomenon of female crime and to explain the differences between male and female criminality.[64] Social observers certainly had noticed earlier that women tended to commit specific types of crimes and usually committed fewer crimes than men. Discussions of female crime had been published periodically over the course of the nineteenth century. For example, several studies of infanticide had appeared in Russia as early as 1868; S. S. Shashkov explored the role of women in prostitution and infanticide in his 1871 work, *The Historical Fate of Women, Infanticide and Prostitution*; in the early and mid-1880s, a handful of Italian criminal anthropologists produced studies of female prisoners; an 1886 article by E. N. Tarnovskii examined criminal statistics for violent crimes according to sex, age, and family situation; and in 1891, D. A. Dril' published an anthropological study of female murderers.[65] Yet, despite this interest, no serious attempt was made before 1893 to develop specific theories that addressed the causes of women's deviance. Lombroso's work thus received worldwide attention and proved to have a lasting influence on studies of female crime throughout Europe and Russia. In the course of his research, Lombroso sought to determine a "born criminal" type for women as he had for men. His interpretations of the female offender, as with the criminal man, essentialized criminality and based it on seemingly natural biological characteristics. Although adherents of the sociological school criticized Lombroso's conclusions, instead locating the differences between male and female crime in women's social position, they nevertheless incorporated elements of the biological, or more accurately the physiological and sexual, nature of women into their explanations of female crime.

Lombroso's understanding of the female offender stressed women's "primitiveness." He noticed fewer deviations of mental and physical characteristics among normal and deviant women than among criminal and noncriminal men, and thus found it more difficult to identify a unique female born criminal. The lesser deviations in the female criminal meant that, for Lombroso, the nature of female crime was more hidden, subtler, and also more common than male crime, and that all women, precisely because of the lack of differentiation, possessed potentially criminal tendencies. When Lombroso was able to identify physiological deviations in women criminals, he found that these anomalies were much more significant than in men, making born criminal women more "ferocious" than male criminals, despite their lower overall numbers.[66]

Lombroso also found evidence of masculine traits among those few criminal women who possessed physiological deviations. According to Lombroso, the female born criminal possessed "masculine qualities which prevent the female criminal from being more than half a woman. . . . Her maternal sense is weak because psychologically and anthropologically she belongs more to the male than to the female sex."[67] This gender inversion further reified the normal woman. Indeed, in this formulation, any deviation in behavior from the ideal of the woman as mother would lead naturally to defeminization and consequently to criminality.[68] Lombroso argued that "what we look for most in the female is femininity, and when we find the opposite in her we conclude as a rule that there must be some anomaly."[69] Thus the born female criminal had to be masculine in her traits and behavior, since the definition of femininity did not permit any deviations.

In this analysis, the masculine female born criminal was driven by her deviant sexuality. The maternal instincts that served to restrain normal women's sexuality were declared absent in criminal women. Lombroso found:

> the moral physiognomy [i.e., sexuality] of the born female criminal approximates strongly to that of the male. The atavistic diminution of secondary sexual characters . . . shows itself once again in the psychology of the female criminal, who is excessively erotic, weak in maternal feelings . . . and dominates weaker beings sometimes by suggestion, at others by muscular force; while her love of violent exercise, her vices, and even her dress, increase her resemblance to the sterner sex.[70]

In equating born female criminals with men, Lombroso directly linked their behavior to their "abnormal" sexuality and their lack of the maternal feelings that "normal" women were supposed to possess and that defined their position in society. As such, female criminals stood outside of and posed a threat to social stability precisely because their actions ran counter to the behavior expected of normal women.

Furthermore, despite the masculine nature of the female born criminal, the relatively few physiognomical differences between female criminals and normal women led Lombroso to conclude that women overall were less "advanced" than men, whose born criminal type yielded greater variations and anomalies compared with normal men. Women tended to be more "conservative," leading more sedentary lives than men, due primarily, Lombroso noted, to the "immobility of the ovule compared with the zoosperm." Occupied with the family, women had less exposure to the "varying conditions of time and space." This hindered their natural evolution, making women into a "primitive type of the species" with less diversity in their characteristics and thus having less evolutionary development.[71] For Lombroso, this explained the similarities between normal and criminal women. Women were simply less advanced from an evolutionary perspective. He linked this primitiveness directly to women's sexuality, asserting that the "primitive woman was rarely a murderess; but she was always a prostitute."[72] He argued that prostitution, or sexual deviance, was the norm for women and that their criminality rested in their sexuality. The prostitute, for Lombroso, was the "genuine typical representative of criminality."[73] Female sexuality thus made all women prostitutes, and potential criminals.

Lombroso found that women's criminal tendencies, based as they were in women's sexuality, were held in check only by their timidity, weakness, and maternal instinct. Women's immaturity and inferiority, however, left them unable to control themselves when their sexual desires remained unsatisfied, and they needed only a small stimulus to cause an extreme reaction. When a woman's latent criminal instinct overcame her morality—her piety, sexual frigidity, maternity, and under-developed intelligence—she became doubly exceptional, as a criminal among noncriminals and as a woman among criminals, and as such the female offender was "consequently a monster" whose "wickedness must have been enormous before it could triumph over so many obstacles."[74] Lombroso concluded:

> when a morbid activity of the psychical centers intensifies the bad qualities of women, and induces them to seek relief in evil deeds; when piety and maternal sentiments are wanting, and in their place are strong passions and intensely erotic tendencies, much muscular strength and a superior intelligence for the conception and execution of evil, it is clear that the innocuous semi-criminal present in the normal woman must be transformed into a born criminal more terrible than any man.[75]

Thus all women possessed a latent criminal potential that manifested itself at moments of heightened physiological stress. This made the female criminal more threatening than the male criminal precisely because her criminal type was harder to identify and had the potential to emerge in all women. These arguments suggested the importance of controlling and protecting women, emphasizing the need for moral training and male supervision to prevent the unleashing of their inherent criminal tendencies.

Lombroso also found that women frequently committed crimes under the influence or suggestion of a third party. "Women—even bad women (and they are the most frequently hysterical)—have less strength and less capacity than men for deeds of violence and they are consequently . . . more subject to that auto-suggestion which incarnates an idea and transforms it into action."[76] Indeed, Lombroso and his colleagues understood that women deserved lighter punishments for their crimes precisely because they were weaker and more inclined to act under the influence of outside forces, particularly the suggestions of their husbands and lovers.[77]

While Lombroso's ideas, anthropological approach, and conclusions were certainly not new, his work did legitimate the scientific study of female criminality.[78] Despite being criticized, even by his own students and colleagues, for ignoring obvious social causes of both male and female criminality,[79] Lombroso provided the foundation for the development of a modern, empirically based approach to criminology through the systematic and methodical analysis of criminals' physical traits. His conclusions regarding female offenders emphasized women's biological, intellectual, and emotional inferiority and their passive, maternal, pious, and domestic qualities. Lombroso's views of female criminals reflected broader contemporary ideas of women as weaker, less developed than men, and more prone to hysteria and fits of passion linked to their sexuality.[80] In Lombroso's view, women were primarily domestic and maternal; they did not engage with the larger social world to the same extent as men. Their lesser anatomical differentiation made them the more primitive and less evolved sex, but also the more potentially disruptive to society. Women embodied a dangerous sexuality that could be held in check only by their maternal sense and piety; they needed to be constantly monitored to ensure that their potential criminality remained controlled.

Lombroso's interpretation of female criminality logically led to the bolstering of traditional views of women and their position in society. It provided "scientific" confirmation of women's proper roles, reinforcing contemporary notions of women's social position and timeless, eternal nature, and arguing for the importance of biology and evolution in determining the scope of female criminal activity.[81] In a recent critique of Lombroso, David Horn notes that Lombroso saw a woman "as both normal in her pathology and pathological in her normality. This construction not only removed all women from the domain of rights, duties, and politics, but also inscribed them in the domain of the social. It made women suitable objects of ongoing surveillance and corrective interventions that, in an effort to restrict 'opportunities' for criminality, blurred the lines between penal practices and social work."[82] Horn argues that Lombroso marked women as a pathological "other," more conservative than men and opposed to historical progress, by linking the evidence he found of lesser degeneration among criminal women to lesser variability, female weakness, and inferiority.[83] Likewise, Mary Gibson suggests that because Lombroso viewed female criminals as biologically inferior, less intelligent, and more primitive than men, he advocated a form of social Darwinism that promised that even greater sexual differentiation, and not equality, would come with evolution.[84]

Although the Russian sociological school and its "left wing" rejected biological determinism to the exclusion of other factors, their explanations of female crime retained elements of Lombrosian discourse, which they adapted to reflect the Russian context. For example, Foinitskii, in a lengthy analysis of female criminals published late in 1893, argued that women's social position, that is, their more domestic and sedentary lives, led women to commit crime less often than men. Biology, however, played a central role in determining the nature of female crime and the types of crimes women committed, even if it did not affect their crime rates. Foinitskii noted that "the best explanation of the differences in the relative criminality of men and women lies in the differences in the physical and psychological strengths of each sex, which explain also the preferred forms of each of their activities."[85] Physiology thus determined women's range of actions, while social position established their extent. For Foinitskii, as for Lombroso, explanations of female criminality served to bolster and reinforce traditional views of women and their position in society.[86]

Left-wing criminologists, in contrast, attempted to minimize the biological factors of female crime, taking the position that both the rates and nature of female deviance resulted from women's social position and their seclusion within the domestic sphere. Gernet, for one, challenged the link Lombroso identified between prostitution (i.e., female sexuality) and criminality, opting instead for an interpretation based solely on sociological factors. According to Gernet, Lombroso found a lower level of development in women when he examined their anatomy and biology, comparing them to children in their physical and mental capacities. This primitiveness meant that women should commit more crimes than men, who were more "advanced." However, because the criminal statistics did not support this conclusion, Lombroso located the criminality of women in their sexuality, finding that their deviant tendencies expressed themselves through prostitution (i.e., sexuality) instead of through crime.[87] Gernet presented an alternative explanation for the smaller number of female criminals that:

> refuses to search for the causes of female criminality in the particularities of women's anatomical construction, and in addition does not agree that women's nature inherently contains the forces that push her into depravity and criminality more than men. . . . The causes of this rest in the social situation: men spend more time outside the home than women, and lightning strikes more often out of doors. The sociological theory of female criminality

explains the smaller percentage of female offenders exclusively through the situation of women's lives. Her life is less frenetic and less varied than man's, not only in the past but also in the present. A woman remains chained to the family hearth. She participates less in the struggle for existence.[88]

While Lombroso's views of women centered on their "primitiveness," Gernet's sociological perspective linked female criminality directly to women's rights. "If a woman stood," he argued,

> on an equal level with men economically, she would stand equal to him in her incidence of criminality. But the history of women differs substantially from the history of men. The red thread [connecting factor] that passes through all the life of women is their humiliation and seclusion in the circle of domestic responsibilities. They became slaves before slavery existed. . . . The humiliating condition of women and the denial of their right to participate in the social life of their native land persist to the present day. . . . Their legal and political situation continues to bear the characteristic traits of the past and they still have a long struggle ahead to achieve complete equality with men.[89]

The Russian sociological school and the left-wing criminologists thus took Lombroso's basic physiological explanations for female criminality and incorporated them into their own theories of crime, adapting them to suit Russian conditions and attitudes toward the "woman question" and social reform. Educated women in Russian society had long pursued opportunities to contribute to society. Their efforts led to increasing recognition of the need for social reforms to improve women's legal position.[90] This reformist attitude was reflected in left-wing criminologists' attitudes toward female crime that emphasized the possibility and potential for women to break out of the traditional limitations and expand their criminality as they achieved equal rights and economic parity with men. Nevertheless, left-wing criminologists found that women's very biology and sexuality could be a hindrance to the achievement of this goal.

It is not surprising that Lombroso's analysis of female criminality came under criticism in turn-of-the-century Russia. Left-wing criminologists in particular emphasized that "the problem of female criminality appears as one of the main points of conflict between the anthropological and sociological schools of criminal law,"[91] for it reflected a fundamental difference in the understanding of contemporary society. In Gernet's view at least, the anthropological school emphasized primitiveness and stagnation while the sociological school stood for progress, modernization, and women's liberation. Gernet and his colleagues stressed the central importance of social factors in female criminality, but at the same time they found that explanations of women's criminality had to consider the influence of female physiology. The criminality of women was determined by their social position, yet that social position was in part defined and limited by their physiology and their sexuality.

Despite the criticisms they set forth, members of the Russian sociological school retained elements of Lombroso's approach in their analyses of female crime. Indeed, as Stephen Frank notes, "Russian criminologists comfortably mixed elements from various schools of thought precisely because each defined the criminal woman as having crossed moral, social, biological or environmental boundaries beyond which 'normal' women did not venture."[92] Turn-of-the-century criminologists, including Lombroso and Gernet, understood that female crime occurred as a result of the individual psychological characteristics emerging out of the inherent nature of all women.[93] Women's emotional responses to their natural biological cycles, criminologists argued, inclined them toward irrationality and potential violence. By analyzing the social, psychological, and physiological factors leading to female crime, including menstruation, pregnancy, maternity, and menopause, criminologists could understand both normal and deviant female characteristics, because female criminals were "like all women, only more so."[94]

CONCLUSION

Russian criminology emerged in direct dialogue with developments in the field in late-nineteenth-century Europe. Concerns regarding the effects of modernity—of urbanization and industrialization in particular—and the growing visibility of the urban working class stimulated discussions of methods of social control in both Europe and Russia. The desire to impose order on society and the need to explain the dislocations of modern life in rational and scientific terms led to the establishment of new interpretations of criminal activity and the formation of the criminal anthropological and sociological schools of thought. In practice, criminal anthropology and criminal sociology remained closely related. Both relied on the systematic scientific analysis of offenders (through anthropometric measurements, statistical analysis, or psychiatric evaluation). Both based their theories on broader social, cultural, and political developments. Both sought practical solutions for social and legal reform through criminological study. And both emerged in reaction to perceived shortcomings of the classical school. Despite these similarities, criminologists of the Russian sociological school, and particularly left-wing criminologists, defined themselves directly in opposition to criminal anthropology. They denounced Lombroso, emphatically arguing against his theories and discrediting his approach to establish the correctness of their own.

Studies of female crime, however, comfortably combined elements of the various criminological approaches. As we shall see, regardless of an observer's particular theoretical or ideological beliefs, analyses of female crime emphasized the deterministic role of female reproductive physiology in facilitating women's criminality. Although the Russian sociological school rejected Lombroso's theory that women were more "primitive" in their evolution than men in favor of a view that emphasized the crippling influence of women's traditional social position on their criminal offenses, women's sexuality remained a fundamental factor shaping and limiting the understanding of female criminality. Even left-wing criminologists, with their emphasis on progress and women's rights, recognized that the social position of women (and thus their criminality) was determined by their physiological and reproductive functions. Thus, while the Russian sociological school and its left wing emphasized the need for social reform, studies of female crime also served to reinforce and reaffirm the traditional position and role of women in Russian society. These attitudes persisted within Soviet criminology as it emerged as a scientific discipline after the Bolshevik Revolution.

PROFESSIONALS, SOCIAL SCIENCE, AND THE STATE

The Organization of Soviet Criminology

Russian criminology evolved considerably in the last years of the Imperial period, but it was the 1917 October Revolution and its accompanying transformations that created the context for criminology's emergence as a state-supported scientific discipline. The early Bolshevik interest in the study of social problems found expression in criminologists' interpretations of crime, particularly those coming from the sociological school's left wing. Compared to the tight central control over intellectual endeavors that characterized the Stalin years, an atmosphere of relative intellectual freedom and exploration pervaded the immediate postrevolutionary period and the New Economic Policy (NEP). Although in the early 1920s the Bolsheviks expelled hundreds of intellectuals, those who remained found room to pursue their intellectual activities within the framework of Soviet ideology.[1] In this context, the affinity between the criminologists' approaches and the Bolsheviks' objectives combined with the state's concern over growing crime rates to provide favorable conditions for the creation of a "Soviet" criminology. This Soviet criminology incorporated prerevolutionary specialists and their theories into its structure and outlook, integrating the professional interests of these specialists with the state's agenda to eliminate crime. The founding of criminological institutes, laboratories, and bureaus throughout the Russian Federation

(RSFSR) and the Soviet Union served to legitimize, systematize, professionalize, and institutionalize the study of crime in Soviet Russia. These organizations, by incorporating sociological, psychological, psychiatric, and biological methodologies into their basic structures, endorsed an interdisciplinary approach to crime studies. They encouraged practitioners to pursue multifaceted interpretations of deviance and to examine not only general statistical representations of crime rates and trends, but also the backgrounds and motivations of individual criminals. In this way, criminology's institutional structure facilitated its service to the Soviet state, but it also promoted the intellectual exploration, experimentation, and innovation that would eventually bring criminology into conflict with the regime.

Soviet criminology began to emerge during the Civil War, but it really came into its own as a discipline in 1922 with the founding of the first government-supported criminological organization in Saratov, and reached its pinnacle in 1925 with the establishment in Moscow of the State Institute for the Study of Crime and the Criminal (Gosudarstvennyi institut po izucheniiu prestupnosti i prestupnika) under the auspices of the People's Commissariat for Internal Affairs (NKVD). After 1928, changes in the Bolshevik leadership and the push toward rapid industrialization and collectivization shifted state interest away from studies of individual criminals and crime as a social phenomenon, effectively curtailing the practice of criminology until after Stalin's death.

The period from 1922 to 1928 can be considered the "golden age" of Soviet criminology, an era of growth and evolution in the discipline. For its practitioners, the study of crime and its causes was "at the center of attention of Soviet legal sciences."[2] The work conducted by criminologists at this time, and particularly the connections they made between criminal individuals and their social, political, and economic circumstances, reflected a level of innovation and sophistication not matched in the West until after World War II.[3] Furthermore, early Soviet criminologists, by establishing theories, approaches, and interpretations of crime, created solid foundations for criminological study that enabled the discipline to reemerge after Stalin's death and to reassert its independence after the collapse of the Soviet Union.[4]

During the period 1922–1928, criminology occupied a unique position within the Soviet intellectual community. A combination of prerevolutionary experts, students, Soviet bureaucrats, and court and prison employees participated in criminological research, all bringing their own perspectives to the study of crime. The prominence of prerevolutionary specialists in criminology paralleled developments in other professions during the 1920s.[5] Yet, the interinstitutional and interdisciplinary nature of criminology hindered the emergence of a coherent corporate identity often found among other professional cohorts. In addition, because the state supported the discipline and had a specific purpose for it, namely, to understand the causes of crime and to develop methods to hasten its elimination, criminology remained bound by the state's needs and dependent on the state for its existence. Without a cohesive professional identity, criminology became more susceptible to the shifts in the political atmosphere that affected all independent and autonomous scientific pursuits by the early 1930s. Indeed, criticisms of the discipline amid accompanying ideological pressures encouraged its practitioners to revert to their fundamental disciplines and abandon criminological research. Nevertheless, the diverse and amorphous nature of the discipline in the 1920s facilitated the application of a wider variety of methods, approaches, theories, and innovations in the study of crime than could have occurred under a more unified and established discipline.

The scope and practice of criminology in the 1920s shaped specialists' interpretations of female crime. Criminological organizations, by incorporating biological and physiological approaches into their very structures, preserved within Soviet criminology the same perspectives that had proved compelling in prerevolutionary analyses of female deviance. In addition, the prominence of psychiatry and psychiatrists in criminological studies during the 1920s ensured that physiological explanations of individual offenders remained central to analyses of female offenders. Understanding criminology as a discipline, therefore, provides the context for interpreting criminologists' analyses of female crime. To that end, this chapter investigates the emergence and development of criminology as a scientific discipline in NEP-era Russia, describing the institutionalization of criminology and the professionalization of the criminologists, and exploring the intellectual freedoms and limitations that shaped criminological studies in the 1920s.

SPECIALISTS AND THE STATE

Many of those involved with criminology in the 1920s, in particular the psychiatrists, psychologists, jurists, statisticians, penologists, forensic experts, and other professionally trained specialists, fit the category of "bourgeois specialists," the prerevolutionary professionals who had filled bureaucratic and institutional positions under the tsarist regime and on whose expertise the Soviet regime relied until new "Soviet" specialists could be trained.[6] As the Bolsheviks set about governing Russia, they found it necessary to utilize the expertise of these specialists, whose skills and knowledge proved crucial in running the country effectively. While some professionals condemned the Bolshevik government and fled Russia after the revolution, many others chose to remain in their positions, continuing with their work in the new political and intellectual climate of the Soviet state.

Professionalization played a key role in shaping the attitudes of these specialists. In the late Imperial period, professionals had begun to establish organizations that helped create a sense of independent corporate identity for them.[7] Professional organizations provided Russian specialists with a scholarly community that fostered and encouraged the pursuit of their professional goals and helped them link their work to the needs of society.[8] As Elizabeth Hachten argues, professional organizations and meetings "functioned as avenues not just for enhancing professional identity, but for contributing to the extension of autonomy and free speech in the public sphere."[9] In this way, prerevolutionary specialists created a space for the development of an identity and a service ethos independent of the state, establishing a nascent civil society that cultivated "an ethos of earnest service and usefulness" with a goal toward the mobilization of resources for national progress.[10] Yet, by the early twentieth century, many professionals had become frustrated by the repressiveness of the tsarist government and the limitations it placed on professional activities.[11] Those who joined the opposition movement, actively or passively, embraced the need for change that the revolution represented. Sympathizing with the Bolshevik project of social transformation, they now hoped to find in the Soviet system a respect for their professional expertise and an opportunity to implement their ideas for social reform.

These professionals occupied an ambiguous position within the new Soviet order. Although they had generally not been advocates of the tsarist regime, they were not necessarily Bolshevik supporters either. For those who did not join the Bolshevik party, their status as nonparty "bourgeois specialists" made them suspect to the new regime. Indeed, the nature of their professional identity—an identity shaped through their independence, autonomous organizations, and service ethos—clashed with the Bolsheviks' centralizing impulses and made the new regime wary of those it considered its potential enemies. On their part, nonparty specialists saw an opportunity to pursue their agendas by working with the new regime. They found the Bolsheviks' socialist goals compatible with their own service orientation and willingly took positions within the new government.[12]

By the beginning of the NEP, the Bolshevik government had set the tone for its relationship with nonparty specialists. As Stuart Finkel suggests, the regime viewed intellectuals as enemies whose potential harmfulness had to be neutralized. The intelligentsia's vigorous defense of their own autonomous spheres (university departments, voluntary associations, and independent journals) conflicted with the regime's interest in directing all aspects of revolutionary life. The state targeted in particular those intellectuals who lacked the practical skills necessary for reconstructing the country, and this promoted an atmosphere of suspicion that pervaded all arenas of intellectual and scientific activity. Within these limits, however, the regime cultivated a relationship, based on necessity, with nonparty specialists, particularly with those possessing technical expertise—whose research and labor concretely benefited the development of Soviet society (for example, agronomists and engineers). The Bolsheviks redefined the intelligentsia, no longer viewing them as critical thinkers but rather professional leaders whose "mental labor" would serve the interests of the proletariat.[13] It was in this new understanding of the category "intelligentsia" that criminologists found themselves, and it was in service to the state that they conducted their work.

While many specialists saw the ability to pursue their goals limited by Bolshevik priorities, others found the NEP atmosphere and the Bolsheviks' goals particularly suited to their professional and public service interests. As Susan Solomon's study of social hygiene illustrates, in the early 1920s hybrid fields such as social hygiene (and also eugenics, plant sociology, and even criminology), which combined the biological with the social, enjoyed considerable success. Social hygiene aimed to promote the well-being of the population by examining the social conditions that caused disease to spread and by promoting measures that would prevent disease. It emphasized the notion that health and disease were fundamentally social in nature. Practitioners of social hygiene worked within the state structure, conducting their research under the auspices and with the patronage of the People's Commissariat of Health (Narkomzdrav). Solomon suggests, however, that social hygienists, by highlighting specific social problems, potentially challenged the regime to fulfill its promises of social change. Social hygiene's dependence on its patron, its implicit criticism of social conditions, and the regime's decreasing interest in preventative health programs led to the curtailment of social hygiene by the early 1930s. While social hygiene was institutionalized, it failed to become a legitimate field of scientific inquiry, and the loss of its patron signaled its demise.[14]

Criminology followed a trajectory similar to that of social hygiene. As a discipline offering professional expertise, it acted as a vehicle through which its practitioners could serve the interests of the state while at the same time pursuing their own intellectual goals. It provided an outlet for performing the socially useful "mental labor" that the state would permit of the intelligentsia and the specialists, giving professionals theoretical and practical spheres in which to apply their expertise that fit within the confines of the state's ideological boundaries. However, criminology was bound to the state in a way that other professions were not, depending on it and its patrons for access to the subjects (prisoners) that were the basis and objects of its studies.[15]

The emergence and development of criminology in the early Soviet context reflects the continuation of both the prerevolutionary professionals' relationship with the state and the state's interest in controlling the autonomy of the public sphere. Indeed, criminologists sought to mediate their relationship with the state by founding professional organizations to serve as institutional intermediaries between criminologists and state bureaucracies while at the same time preserving some autonomous space for their research pursuits. To some extent, the Soviet state facilitated criminology's professionalization by encouraging the creation of specialized institutes and organizations for scientific inquiry.[16] The criminological organizations that emerged in the 1920s thus reflected broader trends in early Soviet society that enthusiastically embraced the potential of science and sought to establish semiautonomous venues for scientific study. These new organizations contributed to the professionalization of the discipline by creating the structure through which criminological research could be pursued. The dual nature of criminology as an "objective" empirical science and a state-sponsored endeavor, however, brought criminological scholars' research goals into potential conflict with the priorities and interests of the state, and complicated efforts to create and maintain a "Soviet" criminology. The course criminology took highlights the temporary compatibility of the Russian intellectual ethos with early Soviet interests, the willingness of professionals to work within the limits set by the Soviet state, the arenas of independence professionals found for themselves and their research within this framework, and the constraints the state placed on public, autonomous activity.

THE PROFESSIONALIZATION OF CRIMINOLOGY

Early crime statistics gathered in the immediate postrevolutionary period seemed to reveal continuous and growing levels of crime.[17] Indeed, according to one observer, crime rates were four times higher in 1917 than at the beginning of the century.[18] In connection with this perceived explosion of crime accompanying the uncertainties, dislocations, and difficulties of the early twentieth century, the new Bolshevik government expressed an increased interest in crime studies. Crime had become a serious issue as definitions of "criminal activity" changed, offense rates rose, and prisons became more overcrowded. The state's first impulse was to blame the remnants of the "old way of life" and the precarious nature of life during the war years for the continued crime problem. As the newspaper *Izvestiia* noted in early 1918:

> The old authorities [*vlast'*] and old laws have been overthrown. But the new power still has not had time to establish order and authority. The masses of people, accustomed during the Revolution to disregard all laws, have retained this habit even though the enemy is already vanquished. . . . . We should not forget, too, that within the triumphant revolutionary democracy, within its most enthusiastic intentions, . . . are always lurking various dark elements, people with criminal pasts who have committed more than one brutal crime. Even during the Revolution these elements continue to preserve their old customs and criminal habits.[19]

The state's concern regarding the extent and nature of crime spurred it to encourage investigation of the phenomenon to determine the most effective ways of dealing with criminal deviance, until the successful implementation of the new way of life would eliminate the problem altogether. As one observer later noted, "Soviet law stresses that crime is the result of the socioeconomic conditions of life, and therefore measures of social protection [i.e., criminal sanctions] must be applied to the criminal not to avenge him but to adapt him to the conditions of working life. Therefore, it is essential to study crime and the criminal in order to clarify how to liquidate crime and how to fight crime until its liquidation."[20] Because crime was supposed to wither away and disappear with the achievement of socialism, the analysis of crime rates would measure the progress toward that goal.

Taking advantage of the opportunities created by the Bolshevik Revolution and the new regime's encouragement of the creation of scientific institutes, scholars wasted little time in establishing new programs of study and new criminological institutions to conduct their research, and worried little about the methodologies they employed. The new Soviet criminological organizations provided an institutional structure that prerevolutionary Russian criminology had lacked. Although some prerevolutionary scholars had participated in the Russian group of the International Union of Criminologists,[21] and although the tsarist Ministry of Justice had supported criminological research by collecting crime and sentencing statistics,[22] no dedicated organizations existed to conduct and promote criminological scholarship before the revolution, nor was criminology a separate field of study in Russia's universities. Crime studies remained marginal within broader legal and social control interests.

The chaos that accompanied the Bolshevik Revolution and fueled the need to address the seeming explosion of crime fundamentally altered the structure and status of criminology. During the Civil War, local government organs from regional courts to prisons to health departments expressed interest in crime studies.[23] Indeed, these years saw the creation of several institutes and organizations to assess and evaluate the criminal population, including the establishment of psychiatric surveillance units in prisons and a Diagnostic Institute of Criminal Neurology and Psychiatry in Petrograd under the direction of psychiatrist L. G. Orshanskii (b. 1866) for the practical and scholarly study of the neurological and psychiatric condition of prison inmates.[24] The Moscow Psychoneurological Institute also established a department of criminal psychology for practical forensic psychiatric analysis, and the Central Penal Department organized a penitentiary museum and institute.[25]

Efforts were also made to integrate criminology into academic institutions. For example, in 1921, S. V. Poznyshev (b. 1870), a forensic expert and psychiatrist involved with the Moscow Psychoneurological Institute, proposed the creation of a criminological department as part of the Section of Court Law and Criminology (Sektsii sudebnogo prava i kriminologii) of the newly formed Institute of Soviet Law. This department was conceived for the "scholarly-practical" study of all aspects of crime and its repression, including the history of criminal law, criminal statistics, criminal anthropology, forensic psychiatry, forensic medicine, psychiatry, investigatory techniques, penitentiary problems, forensic expertise, and forensic photography. In addition to a museum and laboratories for practical work, the criminological department would establish autonomous divisions in major cities in the RSFSR, contributing to the laying of "a new path in the fight against crime . . . [by assessing] the fundamental criteria for determining the punishment of offenders dangerous to society."[26] The organization of these departments and institutions highlights the considerable interest in criminological studies among professionals, and particularly psychiatrists, as a means to assert the importance of their professional expertise for legal proceedings and penal practices, and reveals the strong connection between the emerging fields of psychiatry and criminology.

While efforts during the Civil War reflected the growing interest in criminology, it was not until after the start of the NEP that the first official autonomous scholarly organization devoted to criminological investigation appeared, in the Volga city of Saratov. Founded in 1922 under the auspices of the Saratov Prison Inspectorate by A. P. Shtess, a psychiatrist involved with prisoners' education, the Saratov Regional Bureau of Criminal Anthropology and Forensic-Psychiatric Expertise (Saratovskii gubernskii kabinet kriminal'noi antropologii i sudebno-psikhiatricheskoi ekspertizy) investigated the ethnology, pathology, pathogenesis, and personality of the criminal.[27] According to M. P. Kutanin, one of the Saratov Bureau's founders, this organization was established to develop scientific responses to the question of criminality and to determine new methods for fighting it. In focusing on life in the criminal world, the Saratov Bureau studied the mental state and the physical development of criminals as well as the nature of their environment. It also sought to work out scientific and rational measures for reeducating criminals that could be implemented in prisons.[28] Like the Petrograd Diagnostic Institute, the Saratov Bureau employed a distinct psychiatric approach in its study of crime and criminals. Its commitment to this approach and its seeming association with Lombrosian methods (because of the reference to criminal anthropology in the bureau's name) raised questions about its viability as a Soviet scientific institution by the late 1920s.

The Moscow Bureau for the Study of the Criminal Personality and Crime (Moskovskii kabinet po izucheniiu lichnosti prestupnika i prestupnosti) faced a similar situation. Created in June 1923 by the Moscow Soviet (Mossovet) and organized under the auspices of the Moscow Department of Criminal Investigation (MUUR) to conduct research and interviews among local prisoners, the Moscow Bureau sent students from Moscow State University into prisons to collect survey information.[29] This work resulted in the publication of *Prestupnyi mir Moskvy* (*The Criminal World of Moscow*), a collection of articles about crime and criminal trends in Moscow edited and introduced by the leading criminologist M. N. Gernet.[30] *Prestupnyi mir Moskvy* and the Moscow Bureau's work proved so successful that by late 1923 a permanent criminological clinic had been established in a Moscow prison. The clinic sought to study the criminal personality in a more practical environment using a psychological approach. It functioned as a sort of low-security prison where specific measures of correction could be determined on an individual basis, and a careful understanding of offenders' character, developmental level, and comprehension of socio-legal norms could be achieved.[31] As Gernet later observed, "if scholarly interest to continue this work [among prisoners] was, in the current understanding of the word, gathering momentum, so its clear results showed us that the significance of these new beginnings would continue to grow with the establishment of a permanent organization for the future collection and study of material."[32] In addition to the work of the criminological clinic, the Moscow Bureau published a yearly journal entitled *Prestupnik i prestupnost'* (*The Criminal and Crime*) and several special volumes that examined specific crimes of particular concern to Soviet social stability and socialist development, including murder, sex crimes, hooliganism, and poverty.[33] Its members held public meetings at regular intervals to present their current research, and compiled reports for use by local government authorities. The Moscow Bureau also had a practical orientation, working closely with the Moscow Regional Court (Gubsud) to provide its members' expertise to the court. The 1927 appointment of G. M. Segal, head of the Moscow Gubsud's criminal affairs division, as director of the bureau's sociological section formalized the relationship between the Moscow Bureau and the Moscow Gubsud.[34]

The Moscow Bureau approached the study of crime from a bio-psychological perspective, emphasizing the analysis of the offender's personality. Those involved with the Moscow Bureau understood that the individual character of the criminal rested at the center of the problem of criminality. The study of individual criminals would therefore expose the "roots of crime as a social disease."[35] This psychological orientation was in part the result of a change in the administrative organization of the bureau and its transfer from MUUR to the Moscow Regional Health Department (Moszdravotdel) soon after the department's creation.[36] The new patron encouraged its members to bridge the gap between medicine and sociology by emphasizing atavism, epilepsy, and pathology in their studies of criminal behavior.[37] Their work linked the external socioeconomic and cultural situation of offenders to their psychological constitution, considering both internal and external influences on criminals. The incorporation of such potentially "Lombrosian" elements into the work of the Moscow Bureau, compounded with the very name of the organization that placed "criminal personality" before "crime," gave the Moscow Bureau's work a distinctive psychological orientation that made it susceptible to criticism by the late 1920s as the political climate changed.

Criminological study in Leningrad differed slightly from that conducted in Saratov and Moscow. While the Saratov and Moscow bureaus originally focused on studying prisoners, the Leningrad Criminological Bureau (Leningradskii kriminologicheskii kabinet) worked in closer connection with the courts. The impetus for a criminological organization in Leningrad had emerged out of legal specialists' recognition that the courts needed clearer guidelines for sentencing criminals. This view was confirmed in the conclusions taken by the participants in the January 1924 All-Russian Conference on Pedagogy, Experimental Pedagogy, and Psychoneurology, which emphasized that criminal politics must be considered "on the level of a central government task," that all criminological research must be linked directly with correctional organs, and that it must provide psychiatric expertise to the courts.[38] The Leningrad Regional Court (Gubsud) began a systematic study of crime in 1923 and officially established the Leningrad Criminological Bureau in 1925 to address issues of forensic psychiatry and forensic medicine in court practice.[39] As one observer noted regarding the work of the Leningrad Bureau:

> Insofar as crime as a social phenomenon is generated by circumstances originating in economic conditions, and crime in its internal expressions (violation of the law) is linked with the personality of the criminal, the Soviet Court, having in mind the social reeducation of the criminal and his adjustment to collective life as the fundamental goal of our criminal politics, must set before itself this practical task: the multisided study of the criminal—in particular workers and peasants—and his surrounding social environment, while at the same time taking into account his individual attributes.[40]

Thus, sociologically based solutions to crime could only be determined by considering the individual particularities of the offender.

The Leningrad Bureau conducted its research in study circles (*kruzhki*), small groups of specialists who met regularly to discuss specific questions or problems regarding crime. Each circle examined its appointed question for a period of several months, after which it presented its findings to the bureau and began work on a new subject. Much of the circles' work concerned practical issues of court politics and methods of investigations, but a number of the study circles examined questions of criminal psychology, psychiatry, sexual life, alcoholism, hypnosis, suicide, juvenile delinquency, and eugenics, among other topics.[41] The Leningrad Bureau's practical nature as a court organization, and its leadership by psychiatrist L. G. Orshanskii—the head of the Diagnostic Institute—meant that in addition to clarifying the application of the law codes its work addressed the needs of the courts, specifically in determining the psychiatric health of prisoners and the most effective sentences for individual offenders according to their mental outlook. When considering the treatment of criminals, the Leningrad Bureau's work retained a clear psychiatric orientation.

The creation of criminological bureaus in Saratov, Moscow, and Leningrad highlights the relatively free atmosphere of the NEP, the initiative of local specialists to develop a practical understanding of criminal behavior, and the serious interest among regional judicial and administrative organs to study crime and criminals.[42] These early organizations generally embodied the interests, priorities, and approaches of the individuals who established them. In the first tumultuous years of Soviet power, government organs remained more concerned about dealing with the increasing numbers of offenders flooding the courts and prisons than with developing new "Soviet" criminological theories. Specialists working in the early criminological organizations therefore focused on practical matters and individual criminals, hoping to understand what motivated offenders' actions and the best way to correct their deviant behavior, in many ways putting into practice the ideas professionals had developed before the revolution. In their outlook and orientation, these professionals helped to establish the groundwork for the scope and direction of crime research in the early Soviet period.

Specialists' emphasis on the criminal personality reflected the considerable influence the development of criminal psychiatry in the West had on Russian criminology.[43] Psychiatric studies provided an effective approach to assess an individual's responses and behavior, and criminals appeared to be the ideal, captive subjects for such investigations. Studies of the individual offender's personality and motives, according to these specialists, also suggested concrete corrective measures and actions the state could take to reduce crime rates. Indeed, the prominent involvement of psychiatrists in the formation of the early institutes and bureaus indicates a concerted effort to promote psychiatric and forensic expertise, and to make their specialized knowledge available to the courts and prisons.[44] Thus the early criminological organizations served the practical needs of local and regional governmental organs while at the same time allowing specialists to pursue their scholarly objectives.

For local criminological specialists, the psychiatric study of criminals was not incompatible with the socioeconomic orientation of Soviet ideology. Placing economics at the center of their efforts to eliminate the exploitation of the proletariat, the Bolsheviks prioritized economic and material concerns above all else and infused all aspects of Soviet life with this ideology. Although during the NEP the socialist reconstruction of the country eased in favor of general economic recovery, attempts continued to remake daily life, culture, and social relationships according to ideological dictates.[45] For criminologists, such an orientation meant that they needed to explain crime in terms of socioeconomic conditions. This approach suited the left-wing criminologists who understood crime in sociological terms, and it also proved attractive to those employing a psychological approach in their studies. As one observer noted:

> we stand on the foundation of scientific determinism . . . considering that every one of our steps, every thought, is the result of complicated interacting influences, social and biological, on our organism. We cannot, of course, understand the criminal as the bearer of free evil will (from the point of view of the classical school of criminal law), but see him, in his personality [*lichnost'*] and acts, as a product of his surroundings, the conditions of his individual development, etc., which in sum are determined by the nature of socioeconomic relations.[46]

For these specialists, research into the criminal personality was equivalent to and inseparable from the study of the criminal's socioeconomic background.

The professionals working in the early criminological bureaus asserted that only by understanding the relationship between the individual criminal personality and socioeconomic conditions could crime be eliminated. While these scholars distanced themselves from Lombroso's anthropometric and born criminal theories, they emphasized the importance of the individual and the psychological study of criminals to clarify offenders' reactions to their environment, and they argued that one could not be studied without consideration of the other. This link between the socioeconomic and the psychological became particularly important when criminologists focused on female deviance. For instance, A. S. Zvonitskaia, a legal scholar associated with the Institute of People's Economy in Kiev, stressed the need to integrate both biological and sociological approaches into criminological study. Zvonitskaia defined crime as an antisocial activity, "appearing first of all as the violation of the normal typical structure of social life." Only by examining this structure could the concept of crime be understood as a "social upheaval, creating temporary deviations in the actions of an individual."[47] "Crime, as a social pathology, absolutely correlates to social norms," she continued:

> All typical cases of emotional trauma speak extremely clearly about social anxieties, indissolubly connected with the concrete conditions of the social environment. Even when, for example, theft has a direct connection with a false sexual stimulation tied to an emotional response, there exists a moment of secrecy and shame—this moment is of social and not biological origin. The social moment, intertwined in its specific form with concrete psychophysical organization, appears extraordinarily vividly in emotional conflicts.[48]

Zvonitskaia suggested that only an understanding of the criminal psychology of the female offender, combined with consideration of her physiology, could elucidate the specific sociological factors contributing to the crime.

For E. K. Krasnushkin, a psychiatrist participating in the work of the Moscow Bureau, the psychological state of offenders was inseparable from their socioeconomic conditions. Krasnushkin typifies the criminologist as prerevolutionary specialist who embraced the Soviet state. Born in 1885, he completed his medical training in 1910 and quickly became a leading psychiatrist and forensic expert in the years after the revolution. He was instrumental in the foundation of the Serbskii Institute of Forensic Psychiatry in 1921 and taught forensic psychiatry at Moscow State University. Between 1919 and 1931, Krasnushkin also served as a resident psychiatrist for Moscow prisons, working under the auspices of the Moscow Regional Health Department. This appointment gave him access to the prisoners among whom he conducted his psychiatric research, but it also positioned him to take a leading role in the foundation, organization, and activities of the Moscow Bureau.[49]

In his 1925 article "What Is a Criminal?" ("Chto takoe prestupnik?"), which introduced the first volume of the Moscow Bureau's annual journal, Krasnushkin set out the importance of psychiatric studies in criminology and thus established the scholarly orientation of the Moscow Bureau. He argued that while there was no Lombrosian born criminal type, insufficiencies in the psychological and physical development of an individual, in response to his or her social environment, led to criminality. He pointed to degeneracy, "in terms of [the criminal's] antisocial psychophysical structure, in terms of his inadequate aptitude for social adaptation," as a leading cause of criminality. Krasnushkin found that degenerates had "inferior personalities" that resulted from the "insufficient development of the cortex, this most fragile part of the brain and the carrier of the central apparatus of passive and active adaptation to the dynamics of the social sphere." This created the conditions in which "the structure of the [degenerates'] psyche parallels that of 'proletarian thugs,' replenishing their numbers and in large measure recruiting new criminals from their ranks." He argued that the degeneration he observed among criminals stemmed in large part from socioeconomic conditions that had caused an epidemic of infectious diseases. Furthermore, he emphasized that this connection between degeneration and criminality, and degeneracy itself, could be overcome only by improving the socioeconomic life of the population, a path, he concluded, down which Soviet Russia had already begun to proceed.[50] In this way, Krasnushkin linked the psychiatric abnormalities of criminals (for women, centered in their reproductive physiology) directly to offenders' socioeconomic situations, suggesting that as life improved, the conditions that caused mental degeneracy, and thus criminality, would disappear. Therefore, an understanding of criminals' personalities illuminated the specific social and economic factors that led to their degeneracy and their criminal activity.

The local criminological bureaus' psychiatric orientation and their practical work among prisoners represented the central impetus and focus of criminological study in the early 1920s. As Krasnushkin's biography reveals, criminology provided an attractive and effective environment for the pursuit of psychiatric research and the provision of psychiatric expertise to the courts. Specialists involved in this work were employed not only in university settings and medical institutions, but also in bureaucratic positions within local government organs (and particularly in prisons). From these positions, they were able to acquire support for their criminological studies and gain access to their subjects. The criminological bureaus—created by interested professionals working within local government agencies and supported because their goals advanced those of the government organs—legitimized the study of crime and gave it a purpose directly linked to the state.

The early criminological bureaus focused almost exclusively on the practical study of the criminal personality and crime. They gathered and analyzed crime statistics, interviewed prisoners, evaluated the mental health of offenders, and provided expert medical opinions in court. Specialists working in the bureaus found a direct relationship between the psychiatric understanding of the criminal personality and the socioeconomic factors that combined to cause crime, in many ways continuing the prerevolutionary debates on the direction and orientation of criminology. The emergence of these early criminological bureaus reflected both a serious interest among regional-level judicial and administrative organs to support the study of crime and criminals, as well as the initiative of the criminological professionals in creating organizations to further their research agendas, professional identities, and interests. Specialists successfully convinced local bureaucrats of the necessity of criminological study and its application to court practice, forming groups and obtaining resources that furthered their research needs while at the same time asserting their essential contribution to Soviet justice. In this way, criminologists provided valuable expertise to the courts and police organs, both promoting their professional security and fulfilling the needs of the state.

THE STATE INSTITUTE FOR THE STUDY OF CRIME AND THE CRIMINAL

While the early criminological organizations had been founded with the support of local soviets and government organizations, their local and regional orientation limited the scope of their work. By 1925, interest had developed among specialists and bureaucrats involved with crime studies in the creation of a centralized criminological institute that would shape and direct crime research throughout the Soviet Union, and promote the development of a more "Soviet" approach to crime study. The success of the regional criminological bureaus probably sparked the desire of similar specialists working in the central bureaucracies to create their own criminological organizations. In addition, interest in a centralized criminological organization reflected the growing tendency of the regime, even in the mid-1920s, to try to assert central state control over all aspects of Soviet public life, as well as a practical need to supply the courts with professional expertise.

According to its supporters, a central criminological organization would unify crime studies by bringing together work on the dynamics of crime throughout the Soviet Union. Such an organization would be better positioned to conduct multifaceted studies of crime in all its manifestations.[51] Furthermore, the proponents argued, situating criminological study within a centralized institution would legitimize criminology as a state-sponsored discipline and bring it into line with Bolshevik ideology. At the same time, it would serve to place crime research under the control, supervision, and approval of the state, eventually limiting the freedom of criminologists to explore and apply different methodologies and approaches in their work.

The foundation of the State Institute for the Study of Crime and the Criminal in 1925 represented the peak of criminology's professionalization in early Soviet Russia, and reflected the Bolsheviks' broader centralizing impulses. It legitimized the study of crime and established a hierarchical structure that placed the work conducted in Moscow at the apex, making it the most important and most "Soviet" criminological institution. Embodying the nature of Soviet criminological study, the State Institute provided a central location through which to conduct the systematic study of crime. But its organization under multiple government commissariats ensured that the work of the State Institute would be subject to state supervision and the whims of its patrons. The State Institute also incorporated the multidisciplinary nature of criminological study into its very organization by supporting both sociological and bio-psychological methods. While this multidisciplinary approach reflected the broader nature of the discipline as it was practiced at the time, it also planted the seeds for criminology's eventual destruction within its professional structure.

The State Institute was conceived by E. G. Shirvindt, head of the Main Prison Administration (GUMZ) of the NKVD, and N. N. Spasokukotskii, head of the prison medical-sanitary department of Narkomzdrav, possibly in consultation with criminologist M. N. Gernet, in early 1925.[52] Both Shirvindt and Spasokukotskii bridged the boundaries between specialists and bureaucrats. They served at high levels in the state bureaucracy, but had been chosen for their positions because of their specialized expertise and interest in penology. From the start they envisioned the State Institute as an interdepartmental organization devoted to studying all aspects of crime and criminality from "general biological (anthropological, psychiatric, psychological, biochemical) as well as socioeconomic points of view," drawing on the "scientific knowledge, practical experience and interests" of a wide range of people's commissariats, and supplying its expertise to "administrative, court, penal, economic, medical, statistical, and general Soviet social organizations."[53] Furthermore, Shirvindt emphasized, the State Institute would facilitate the "penetration of Marxist ideas" into Soviet jurisprudence by approaching the study of crime from a scientific perspective and from a socioeconomic orientation.[54] By February 1925, Shirvindt and Spasokukotskii had obtained support for their project from the heads of their respective commissariats, A. G. Beloborodov of the NKVD and N. A. Semashko of Narkomzdrav.[55]

Other commissariats, however, needed more convincing. For instance, a letter dated 27 February 1925 from Glavnauka[56] of the People's Commissariat of Enlightenment to GUMZ argued that although an organization such as the proposed State Institute was timely and necessary, its incorporation under GUMZ was "pointless" since as a result the institute would bear a "departmental [*vedomstvennyi*] character." By this the letter writer meant that establishing the State Institute under the auspices of the NKVD and Narkomzdrav would serve to limit its investigatory scope to the priorities and concerns of those commissariats. Instead, Glavnauka proposed that the tasks of the State Institute could be better carried out by utilizing its already existing scientific organizations, specifically the Institute of Soviet Law in Moscow State University's Faculty of Social Sciences (FON), whose staff of qualified scholars could work to increase their contact with GUMZ employees.[57]

Glavnauka's resistance to the NKVD's plan highlights the nature of bureaucratic conflict in the 1920s. In protesting the creation of the State Institute, Glavnauka emphasized that the type of research to be conducted by the proposed institute would repeat the work of other similar organizations already under its jurisdiction, and that the institute would be more effective in an academic, as opposed to governmental, setting, stressing what it saw as the primary task of the State Institute—the theoretical development of Soviet criminology. This protest highlights interinstitutional competition for control of limited resources and personnel and Glavnauka's desire to maintain all aspects of organized scientific inquiry under its authority. Glavnauka's argument reflects an effort on the part of the People's Commissariat of Enlightenment (Narkompros) to control the State Institute and criminological study by placing it within its own sphere of influence. This in turn reveals the struggles among various commissariats during the NEP, suggesting that the boundaries of responsibility between government agencies still remained unclear in the mid-1920s, that significant overlap of duties and concerns occurred, and that the bureaucracies competed for and fought over their perceived areas of jurisdiction.[58] Furthermore, the debate over the patronage structure for criminology suggests that the discipline was important to the state and was viewed as a priority, worth funding and controlling.

Indeed, the State Institute, in its very organizational structure and conceptual scope, depended on the patronage and support not only of the NKVD and Narkomzdrav, but also of the People's Commissariat of Justice (Narodnyi Komissariat Iustitsii, or NKIu) and Narkompros. The institute's proposed activities, including theoretical work on the causes of criminality, practical work developing methods of fighting crime, and educational work among prisoners and training cadres, necessarily crossed departmental boundaries and made cooperation among the agencies essential for its success. Despite Glavnauka's initial reservations, the People's Commissariat of Enlightenment soon came on board, and the NKVD's petition of 6 March to the Council of People's Commissars (Sovnarkom) indicated that all four commissariats supported the project.[59] The State Institute's executive board (*soviet*) consisted of representatives from each of the commissariats involved: initially Shirvindt, Spasokukotskii, F. K. Traskovich (from the NKIu), and I. I. Mesiatsev (from Narkompros, soon replaced by P. I. Karpov), with a fifth representative, M. N. Gernet, nominated from among the institute's general membership.[60]

Although the State Institute was conceived as an interdepartmental organization equally represented by the four commissariats, the NKVD took the lead, establishing the institute by its Order No. 97 on 1 July 1925. In turn, the State Institute fell under the primary auspices of the NKVD, obtained its funding from the NKVD, and was held accountable primarily to the NKVD.[61] The close relationship of the State Institute to the NKVD shaped its position within the Soviet state, linking criminology to the NKVD's social control functions (in contrast to the medical orientation of Narkomzdrav) and making it most dependent on the patronage of this commissariat.

According to NKVD Order No. 97, the State Institute had six tasks: 1) to clarify the causes and conditions for the growth of criminality and specific types of crimes; 2) to study the success of methods for fighting crime and specific measures of punishment; 3) to develop penal theories and policies; 4) to create a system and method for studying prisoners and correctional efforts among them; 5) to study individual prisoners in order to better understand the phenomenon of crime; and 6) to examine the impact of specific measures of correctional labor on prisoners.[62] To conduct this work, the State Institute was divided into four sections: socioeconomic, penitentiary, bio-psychological, and forensic. The socioeconomic section studied the socioeconomic causes of crime as well as changes in the levels and types of crime; the penitentiary division examined questions of general penal policies and measures of "social protection," or punishment; the bio-psychological section focused on the "mechanism of behavior and the character of the criminal, the psychopathological personality of the modern criminal, the relationship between psychopathology and criminality," and the role of psychiatry in penal policies; the forensic section studied methods of criminal investigation. Based on work conducted by researchers, statisticians, scientific personnel, bureaucrats, and students, the central task of the State Institute was to become a "scientific-practical organization" that would explore questions of "vital practical knowledge in all areas of criminal law, the resolution of which are connected to the successful struggle against crime."[63] The State Institute also disseminated its work through publication, sponsoring its own journal, *Problemy prestupnosti* (*The Problems of Criminality*), and issuing regular reports of its activities.[64]

The plans for the State Institute emphasized the collective and centralized nature of the organization. Not only did the institute depend on interdepartmental cooperation, but the work conducted by its members would be based on the collaboration of specialists from a variety of fields. As criminologist M. M. Grodzinskii noted:

> The State Institute for the study of criminals is an organization, the development and growth of which is of interest to both Soviet science and Soviet society, so that the end result of the institute's work, proceeding along the path toward the collective scientific development of the question of criminality, will bring us closer to its successful resolution.[65]

In addition, this "collectivism" included not only scientific collaboration in research and publication, but also "collective criticism of the work of individual members of the institute."[66] This would ensure not only rigorous scientific standards in the work produced by the institute's members, but also that their research fit the ideological requirements of the socialist regime.

The State Institute established four affiliated organizations in Moscow, Leningrad, Saratov, and Rostov-on-the-Don.[67] These affiliates were intended to focus on the local and regional dynamics of crime, while the central core of the State Institute in Moscow explored broader national and international crime trends. By conducting research at both the national and local levels, criminologists hoped the State Institute would act as a "barometer of criminality," making it easier to identify changes in the dynamics of crime as a social phenomenon.[68] Furthermore, by establishing affiliates in the very cities where independent, local criminological bureaus already existed, the State Institute asserted its dominance over the discipline and attempted to exercise central control over criminological research. In Saratov, for example, the State Institute co-opted the Saratov Bureau, reorganizing it into a filial institute, renaming it, and subordinating its work to the general plans of the central institution.[69]

Although the State Institute did not colonize the existing criminological bureaus in Moscow and Leningrad, it did attempt to direct the course of criminological research through its local affiliates.

Even though they were affiliates of the State Institute, local criminological bureaus retained a considerable amount of autonomy from the center. This independence frequently manifested itself in a local preference for the psychiatric evaluation of individual criminals.[70] The Rostov Bureau, headed by psychiatrist V. V. Brailovskii, in particular resisted adopting a more Marxist, or socioeconomic, approach to crime research. Called the Bureau for the Study of the Personality of the Offender (Kabinet po izucheniiu lichnosti pravonarushitelia), the Rostov Bureau was organized under the North Caucasus Regional Health Department. Its journal, *Voprosy izucheniia prestupnosti na Severnom Kavkaze* (*Questions on the Study of Crime in the North Caucasus*), published annually between 1926 and 1928, focused almost exclusively on the psychiatric analysis of offenders and their psychopathologies. In the lead article for the journal, Brailovskii argued, as Zvonitskaia had earlier, for the compatibility of the biological and sociological approaches to crime and the necessity of taking both perspectives into consideration. Setting the tone for the work of the Rostov Bureau, Brailovskii emphasized how psychological and biological approaches to crime would complement sociological studies:

> A hermit in the desert does not commit crime—for this he needs some sort of surroundings, a social environment; thousands of automatons and machines similarly do not commit crimes—for this living human organisms are necessary. To study the living organisms of criminals while ignoring their social conditions, and likewise the opposite, contributes a disastrous one-sidedness to the activity; to organize irrationally the spheres of competency for each of these related disciplines, and not to provide contact through methods, is unhealthy as well.[71]

Brailovskii advocated separate but complementary roles for sociologists and psychiatrists in criminological studies. By justifying the necessity of the biological perspective as unique but supplementing the sociological, Brailovskii sought to protect his professional interests and the psychiatric approach taken by the Rostov Bureau.

The continued embrace of the psychiatric perspective even as the State Institute advocated a more sociological approach reflected a deep ambivalence over methodologies within Soviet criminology. Shirvindt noted this, stating:

The establishment of the State Institute for the Study of Crime and the Criminal occurred in connection with a recognition in the Soviet republics of the decisive significance of the economics of socialism for liquidating the phenomenon of crime in the USSR. But such recognition did not narrow the multifaceted study of the criminal, criminality and methods for fighting against it. The very structure of the institute speaks to this.[72]

By creating a bio-psychological section as well as a sociological section, the State Institute acknowledged the important contributions of criminal psychiatrists to crime studies. In addition, the participation of Narkomzdrav as a founder of the State Institute ensured that its interests (in the psychiatric health of criminals and in forensic psychiatric expertise for court proceedings) would be represented in the institute's work. These factors established the acceptability of psychiatric analysis even as political pressures for more "Soviet" (i.e., more socioeconomic and less psychiatric) criminological research increased.

Despite their methodological variations, those involved with the State Institute emphasized the importance of practical and theoretical work in achieving the goals of socialism, namely, the elimination of crime. According to B. S. Utevskii (1887–1970), a professor and penologist who wrote extensively on juvenile crime, criminal law, and correctional labor law, the State Institute's tasks included examining crime from a scientific Marxist point of view "for the objective study of crime in the transition from capitalism to the socialist epoch." He noted that the State Institute's use of criminal statistics made trends and tendencies in criminal activity readily apparent for practical use by court and police organs.[73] In addition, Gernet observed that the State Institute differed from criminological organizations in western Europe and the Americas because it focused on the socioeconomic causes of crime as a social phenomenon (this included psychological and psychiatric, as well as social and economic), and not on the anthropological characteristics of individual offenders.[74] As Utevskii emphasized:

The wide application of its tasks, the scientific-practical character of its work, its Marxist methods, the tenets at the basis of its work—all this places the State Institute for the Study of Crime as the first and so far only organization of its kind not only in our union but in Europe and even in all of the civilized world. . . . The creation of the State Institute once more underlines that, despite restrictive financial resources, the Soviet state not only encourages scientific work in the union, but also founds new scientific-research organizations and gives them the possibility to engage in broad and productive activities.[75]

In addition to its stated tasks, the State Institute represented Soviet criminology on an international level. Many of its members had been active participants in international criminological organizations before the revolution and were heavily influenced by, and closely followed, developments in the field outside of Russia. Gernet argued that the creation of the State Institute would bolster Soviet criminology's international reputation, not only as the first organization to approach crime from a Marxist perspective, but also as the first to eliminate all associations with Lombroso's criminal anthropology. He stressed that printing errors in publications as well as unfortunate choices in naming other criminological organizations (especially the Saratov and Moscow bureaus) had led to some misconceptions about the nature of criminological study in the Soviet Union. As the sociologist-criminologist lamented:

> The Moscow Bureau for the Study of the Criminal Personality and Crime, by putting the study of the criminal personality first in its name, aroused the shameful assumption in the foreign press that it 'is continuing the work of Professor Lombroso,' that psychiatric investigations are its main concern. . . . Unfortunately, the Moscow Bureau gave even more fuel to this mistaken assumption, producing a brochure in the title of which the word 'criminality' was completely missing, and only the study of the criminal personality remained. Even less fortunate was the name of the analogous organization in Saratov 'the Bureau of Criminal Anthropology.' It speaks to an angle of work which in actuality does not exist.[76]

According to Gernet, because of the unfortunate names chosen for the early Soviet criminological bureaus, they acquired a reputation in the West that was antithetical to their actual work and to the very nature of criminological studies in the Soviet Union, that is, that these organizations were inadvertently associated with a Lombrosian approach that focused on the personality of the offender. In contrast, Gernet stressed, the State Institute, as was clear from its name, emphasized the study of crime and not criminals. Thus, the State Institute fulfilled the essential role of repairing the international reputation of Soviet criminology and presenting Soviet criminological principles to the world. Gernet's emphasis on the "correctness" of the State Institute also reveals tensions between the center and local criminological organizations in terms of the most appropriate methods and approaches to criminological study (sociological versus bio-psychological), as well as a continuing disagreement over the meaning of "Soviet" criminology.

The State Institute drew its membership from a wide variety of persons and organizations that expressed interest in criminology. Many of those who worked with the State Institute were professionals whose research involved crime or criminals. These specialists were trained before the revolution as doctors, psychiatrists, statisticians, sociologists, jurists, anthropologists, penologists, and forensic experts. They frequently held teaching or research appointments in universities and specialized institutes of higher learning.[77] Law students also participated in institute activities, eventually becoming leading members themselves. Others represented governmental organs or institutes directly involved with the legal system, prisoners, and mental health.[78] Indeed, the practical nature of criminology encouraged nonspecialists to participate in the State Institute's work, and the institute's relevance to pressing social policy issues led to the engagement of a wide array of bureaucrats and legal personnel in discussions of crime trends. These people worked outside the scope of scholarly criminological investigation, contributing less to the theoretical development of criminology than to its practical application. The wide variety of specialists, law enforcement, and prosecutorial personnel involved with the State Institute indicates the importance accorded the study of crime in the 1920s and the diversity of the discipline. Bringing together professionals and bureaucrats from a wide variety of backgrounds and specialties, the State Institute provided a forum for professional and cadre interaction in a way that had the potential to encourage an open exchange of ideas.

The State Institute rapidly became the central organization for conducting criminological research in the Soviet Union. Supported by four important commissariats, the institute enjoyed advantages other criminological organizations did not. Its broad mandate enabled its members to explore a wide range of causes and factors of crime from different perspectives, and its position as a centralized organization permitted it to extend its influence and draw on resources throughout the country. In addition, its endorsement of multiple approaches to criminological study reinforced the methodological diversity among its practitioners while at the same time advocating a "Soviet" approach to crime studies.

Nevertheless, the research conducted and the goals pursued by the State Institute remained at all times securely within the structure and confines of the Soviet state. The State Institute remained entirely dependent on the goodwill of the Soviet leadership and the patronage of its commissariats. Even as the State Institute and other criminological organizations created a sense of professional identity, the practical nature of criminological research and the disparate community of people involved in the study of crime prevented the development of criminology as a cohesive discipline, making it even more dependent on government patrons to justify its existence and increasing its vulnerability to changes in the state's ideological priorities. Ultimately, the incompatibility of the multiple approaches to criminology with Stalinist ideology, combined with changes in the make-up of the commissariats and shifts in the goals of the regime by the late 1920s, made the continued study of crime, as conceived by the State Institute, impossible.

CONCLUSION—CRIMINOLOGY AND CIVIL SOCIETY

By making criminology a part of the central state apparatus, the State Institute legitimized crime studies and signaled their validity. This encouraged professionals in other cities to establish official criminological organizations. In 1926, for instance, specialists in Kazan petitioned Sovnarkom to support the creation of a Tatar criminological bureau. Adapting the same language used to justify the State Institute's scope of activities, they stressed the importance of local as well as central crime studies. Acknowledging that the establishment of the State Institute had been essential for advancing the study of crime, the petition stressed that the level of scholarly work on crime in the Tatar Republic remained inadequate. Additionally, it argued, a criminological bureau in Kazan would assist the state, decreasing its financial burden for maintaining prisoners by devising more rational penal and criminal policies. The Kazan group went one step further, though, by noting that a criminological organization had already been established in Kazan by the NKVD of the Tatar Republic, in cooperation with the regional NKIu and representatives from the commissariats and universities, including local criminologist B. N. Zmiev, an active member of the State Institute. Indeed, the group emphasized that the work of the Kazan organization was already underway and only requested funding from Sovnarkom to increase and expand its ongoing projects.[79] The NKVD of the RSFSR supported the Kazan application, confirming that the State Institute had no plans to open an affiliate in Kazan, that the "national and living conditions in the Tatar Republic impose their mark on the character of crime," that the struggle against crime needed a multifaceted approach, that for the study of criminality "it is necessary to establish special, although not necessarily large, organizations created on the scheme of bureaus for the study of crime and criminals," and that the Tatar Republic's NKVD approved the plan.[80]

Although there is no evidence of the result of this application and little remains of the work conducted in Kazan,[81] the efforts to establish a Tatar criminological bureau highlight the importance of state approval and funding for the existence of the criminological organizations, as well as revealing criminologists' initiative in securing the patronage necessary to establish these bureaus. By constructing their arguments based on the State Institute and emphasizing their ties to it, Kazan criminologists linked their bureau directly to the goals and objectives of the central organization. Furthermore, crime specialists proved adept at navigating the Soviet bureaucracy and in carving out officially sanctioned space in which to pursue their professional interests. Indeed, by the mid-1920s, additional criminological organizations had been established in major cities throughout the Soviet republics, including Baku, Tbilisi, Kiev, Khar'kov, Odessa, and Minsk, and while these functioned with relative autonomy from the State Institute, they remained dependant on their sponsoring government organs.[82]

Criminologists' interests and intellectual sympathies generally coincided with state policies and ideological directives during the transitional period. By the early NEP years the Soviet state had established its relationship with its intellectuals. As long as they engaged in socially useful "mental labor" that benefited the proletarian dictatorship, intellectuals would be allowed to pursue their scholarly interests.[83] For a time, criminologists' work fell into that category. Their studies focused on explanations of deviance, a task the state deemed important in its efforts to remake Russian society. Moreover, criminology had practical applications for penal policies and court procedures. By studying crime these professionals not only engaged in scholarly research but also offered skills and knowledge the state found particularly useful for advancing its goals. In this way, criminology provided a relatively independent outlet for professionals' scholarly and intellectual activity while at the same time satisfying the state's needs and objectives. The multidisciplinary nature of criminology both contributed to the diversity of criminological research and hindered the development of a cohesive professional identity among the practitioners of criminology, as specialists applied their specific disciplinary approaches to their studies. Their unwillingness to embrace a unified "Soviet" criminological methodology, however, made it easier for criminologists to revert to their particular disciplines by the end of the decade, when criminology, like the other social sciences, increasingly came under criticism.

The criminological bureaus and institutes established in the 1920s provided a legitimate public arena for specialists to investigate social problems. These organizations, however, cannot be seen as a Soviet adaptation of the voluntary associations that had begun to emerge in the late Imperial period.[84] The organizations may have been created on the initiative of individual criminologists in search of a public space to conduct research, but they existed only with the approval of government organs. Furthermore, their members frequently held important positions within the Soviet bureaucracy, and their enthusiasm for and eagerness to cater to the needs of the state made them willing participants in their own eventual cooptation. Because they directly contributed to and were linked with the evolution of criminal court practice and penal policy, and thus the state's ability to direct Soviet social development, their activities cannot be considered independent manifestations of a Soviet "civil society." Indeed, the Bolsheviks' conception of public society (*obshchestvennost'*) did not include independent organizations that could potentially act in an alternative or oppositional manner to the state. Only within certain boundaries did the regime encourage active engagement with society and social work, in keeping with efforts during the NEP to eliminate the population's "backwardness" and bring about the new socialist society.[85]

Indeed, the establishment of criminological institutes and organizations represented not only the legitimization of criminology as a viable social science discipline but also its cooptation by the regime. In this regard, the evolution of Soviet criminology simultaneously reveals both the compatibility of the ideology of the modernizing state with the intellectual outlook of the liberal social scientists and the processes through which the Soviet state sought to assert an increasingly centralized grip over all facets of society. Part of the success of the criminological bureaus during the 1920s was that while they facilitated the exploration of social problems, their complete dependence on the state limited their scope and curtailed their independence, preventing them from offering a true alternative vision of Soviet society. Indeed, their reliance on the state, with its centralizing and colonizing tendencies, reflects the increasing limitations placed on the scientific study of Soviet society even by the mid-1920s. At the same time, the nature of criminological investigation raised questions about the effectiveness of Bolshevik policies and the ability of the regime to fulfill its promises of social reform, making criminology a potentially dangerous and subversive discipline for the state to sponsor.

While emphasizing the importance of studying the socioeconomic conditions and other factors that caused crime, many criminologists focused their research as well on the individual criminal personality, arguing for the compatibility of the two approaches. The interest of criminologists in psychological and biological studies of individual criminals was particularly evident in their research into female crime. The nature and organization of the criminological institutions of the 1920s encouraged criminologists to continue to explain women's deviance in terms of female physiology and sexuality, reinforcing the criminologists' traditional understanding of female crime and reconfirming their perceptions of the position of women in Soviet society.

PART TWO

ANALYZING FEMALE CRIME

THE WOMAN'S SPHERE

The Role of Sexuality in Female Deviance

CHAPTER THREE

Early Soviet criminologists focused a considerable amount of their attention on female crime. While they expected all crime to disappear with the successful construction of socialism, the persistence of female crime in the transitional period in particular came to reflect for them both the incompleteness of the socialist revolution during the New Economic Policy and the inability of women to participate fully in Soviet society. According to their understanding, women's traditional isolation in the domestic sphere had removed them from engagement with the difficult realities of public life and wage labor, the "struggle for existence" as criminologists called it.[1] They found that women were thus unprepared to shoulder the burdens and deal with the stresses they faced—in connection with the difficult circumstances of life during the war years and the changing legal situation created by the Bolsheviks' policies—as they emerged from the home and entered the workforce. Furthermore, criminologists emphasized that women's continued adherence to pre-revolutionary traditions, practices, and morality shaped their responses to life's problems. Specialists asserted, however, that when women engaged with the public sphere and the "struggle for existence" as equals with men, when their material situation improved, and when they embraced the new socialist morality of the Soviet state—all of which would occur with the achievement of socialism—female crime would disappear.

At the same time, criminologists highlighted the role female sexuality played in women's deviance. Centering women's sexuality in their reproductive physiology, professionals stressed that cycles of pregnancy, birth, menstruation, and menopause weakened women and made them more susceptible to the influence of "outdated" beliefs and external pressures. Indeed, specialists found that traditional notions of women's proper sexual roles and behaviors fueled the commission of certain crimes by women, for instance infanticide and spouse murder, as women attempted to reconcile community pressures with their personal experiences. In the context of early Soviet society, where belief in the progressive potential of socialism to transform the very nature of human behavior drove social reform efforts, physiologically based interpretations of female crime effectively explained the persistent anti-Soviet actions of certain women. Soviet criminologists adapted traditional understandings of women's deviance, based on the potentially disruptive nature of unregulated female sexuality, to the new circumstances of the transitional period, embracing socioeconomic interpretations that incorporated biological and psychological elements. While criminologists looked forward to seeing women become more like men in their criminality as they entered the public sphere and the "struggle for existence," they still found that a central factor in female crime was women's inability to control their actions and emotions at moments of acute physiological stress, usually associated with women's reproductive functions. Resisting the implication that because of their biology deviant women were inherently criminal, professionals instead argued that physiological influences weakened women and hindered their ability to react rationally to their problems. Women's reproductive nature complemented notions of female social "immaturity"—a result of their traditional isolation in the domestic sphere—and this provided criminologists with a plausible explanation for the continued existence of the "outdated" morality that drove women to commit crimes, as well as a rationale for the seeming inability of women to become active participants in Soviet public life. In this way, female sexuality remained central to explanations of women's crime, defining the nature of such deviance and shaping the scope of criminologists' investigations.

This chapter explores the relationship between the social position of women and their sexuality in prerevolutionary and Soviet criminological literature. It sets out attitudes toward female crime, women's sexuality, and women's involvement in public life before the Bolshevik Revolution, and then traces how criminologists evaluated female crime and the impact of the revolution on it after 1917, pointing to discussions of female recidivism and prostitution to illustrate the relationships among women's crime, physiology, sexuality, and the implementation of successful social reforms. Nineteenth-century observers found that women's isolation in the domestic sphere intensified their reactions to familial problems and made them more susceptible to community pressures and physiological influences. They called for social reforms to alleviate the conditions that led to abnormal sexuality, and consequently crime, among women. In contrast, Soviet criminologists pointed not to the lack of improvement in women's condition but to the resistance to change that women embodied. Despite the new opportunities provided by women's emancipation and the expectation that the revolution would bring women into the public sphere and the "struggle for existence" as equals with men, in criminologists' works female crime retained much of its prerevolutionary nature and characteristics. Criminologists explained this "conservativeness" in terms of women's social position, but incorporated into their analyses a reliance on physiological explanations of women's deviance that focused their attention on the relationship between crime and female sexuality and reinforced traditional perceptions of women. These perspectives limited professionals' ability to see any real transformation in the lives and activities of women.

Abnormal Sexuality—Early Marriage in Late Imperial Russia

Dorie Klein, in her study of the literature on female crime in the West, notes that "the specific characteristics ascribed to women's nature and those critical to theories of female criminality are uniformly *sexual* in their nature. Sexuality is seen as the root of female behavior and the problem of crime. Women are defined as sexual beings, as sexual capital in many cases, physiologically, psychologically, and socially."[2] This perception of the sexual nature of female crime developed out of the broader context of nineteenth-century attitudes toward women that increasingly understood women's social position and intellectual abilities in terms of their sexuality.[3] Indeed, nineteenth-century European and American intellectuals accepted the notion that "in males the intellectual propensities of the brain dominated, while the female's nervous system and emotions prevailed over her conscious and rational faculties."[4] Medical doctors connected the processes of women's reproductive system to their nervous system, finding that changes in one were reflected in the other and that "imbalances" in the reproductive system stimulated deviant or pathological behavior, which could manifest itself as hysteria or as other psychological aberrations.[5] Accordingly, they understood all women as "prisoners of the cyclical aspects of their bodies, of the great reproductive cycle bounded by puberty and menopause, and by the shorter but recurrent cycles of childbearing and menstruation." From this perspective, women's physiological cycles defined their sexuality, shaping their social role, their intellectual abilities, and their mental and physical health.[6]

Russian criminologists likewise emphasized the role of physiology and reproduction in their discussions of female crime. Similar to the portrait of women advanced by Lombroso and other contemporary western observers, Russian professionals understood women as nurturers and mothers whose lives focused on the domestic sphere and whose natural maternal and moral qualities held their potentially deviant sexuality in check. As jurist and criminologist I. Ia. Foinitskii put it, a woman's role was "as our mother, wife, sister or daughter, as the producer of the next generation, the preserver of tradition, the first and most important educator of a man and his greatest delight."[7] Traditional Russian culture emphasized the importance of marriage and family for women, thus defining their role and purpose according to their reproductive functions.[8] When women committed crimes, criminologists expected them to occur within this sphere, in reaction to the domestic problems that plagued women. At the same time, and particularly when women committed violent crimes against relatives, they acted in opposition to the proper behavior expected of them according to the ideals of motherhood, and because of this their actions had a potentially destabilizing influence on society. Thus, attitudes toward female deviance and women's social position remained inherently contradictory. Ironically, the same forces that were supposed to keep women "normal" also made them potential criminals. The sexuality of women (specifically their reproductive capacity) became both the source of their morality and the catalyst for their criminality. From this perspective, the traditional position of women created the specific pressures that led them to criminal activity, but it was also the traditional position of women—the constraints of morality—that kept their sexuality, and their criminality, under control.

For nineteenth-century criminologists, women fell under the influence of their sexuality more easily and to a greater degree than men precisely because of women's closer connection to the domestic sphere and the family. One observer noted:

As a result of women's narrower circle of activities overall, sexual feelings and the nervousness and paroxysms [*affekt*] associated with them play a greater role in their personal world than among men. . . . All spontaneous crimes result, for the most part, from one or another abnormality or difficulty of sexual and family life. The severity of these difficulties or deviations from the common, normal type have a much more noticeable effect on women, because they are more dependent than men and less capable of independent existence, thus increasing the probability of women committing serious crimes such as infanticide and murder of relatives, despite the fact that the overall criminality of women is significantly less than the criminality of men.[9]

According to this view, women's domestic isolation and the centrality of family intensified the role sexuality played in their lives. As a result, women experienced problems in this area much more intensely than men, making women more likely to react to them. These reactions stemmed not from any inherent deviance in female sexuality but from physiological abnormalities that emerged as a result of women's domestic isolation. While female sexuality made women more moral, abnormalities in their sexual or psychological functions led women to commit crimes.

Because of the importance of female sexuality in mitigating women's deviance, discussions of its proper development and maturation occupied a prominent place in late-nineteenth-century discourses on female crime. Many medical and legal experts believed that sexual activity before maturity, that is, before puberty, was harmful for both boys and girls. While boys might be drawn into the evils of masturbation, the effects of premature sexual activity on girls were potentially much more devastating.[10] Russian psychiatrists viewed puberty and menstruation as a "physical, a psychological, and a moral event" that had a profound influence on women's sexuality. They believed a powerful maternal instinct developed in women during puberty. If women became sexually active before puberty, they argued, it could have disastrous results, harming their health and potentially causing temporary insanity or violent criminal acts.[11]

Russian scholars connected premature sexual activity with female criminal deviance. For instance, doctor and criminal anthropologist P. N. Tarnovskaia focused specifically on this problem in an 1898 study of female murderers.[12] She observed that many peasant women sentenced for murder had married at a young age, either before full sexual maturity or just when such development was occurring. Peasant customs, she noted, encouraged marriage for women at around sixteen, yet she stressed that at this age peasant girls had only just begun to develop sexually, and being slow to grow, they frequently did not reach full sexual maturity until age nineteen or twenty, even as late as twenty-two in some cases. Early marriage, she argued, harmed peasant women's sexual, physical, and spiritual development, increasing the likelihood that these women would murder their children or husbands. In fact, Tarnovskaia emphasized that the greatest number of spouse murders were committed by women who entered into marriage "before complete sexual development." For such women, many of whom were forced into an early marriage, marital difficulties and the sense that they lacked a way out of a difficult familial situation culminated in the murder of their husbands.

Tarnovskaia noted that deviations from "the correct development of sexual feelings" most often expressed themselves in spouse murder. Such offenders frequently were indifferent to the sexual act, and this indifference, even if temporary, could lead them to hysteria and violence.[13] She found that these women led an "unhappy, underdeveloped existence, having the potential to live honest and compassionate lives, but with only one innate insufficiency—an absence of sexual feelings." This in and of itself was not a crime, Tarnovskaia argued. Although predisposed to criminal activity, these women would not have committed murder if their sexual balance had not been disturbed. In other words, without early marriage and premature sexual activity they would not have been pushed into becoming criminals.[14]

Tarnovskaia's analysis placed sexuality at the root of female criminality. "Sexual feelings in the life of every person play an unquestionably important role," she argued, but restraint in sexuality was an "important condition of culture and the elevation of the human personality."[15] By emphasizing the late age of sexual maturity among peasant women, compared to urban women who developed earlier, at age fourteen or fifteen, Tarnovskaia highlighted the "primitiveness" of rural women and their slowness to develop even their own natural physiological functions. She used peasant women's "primitive" sexuality as a way to explain the occurrence of violent crimes among these women and their deviations from "proper" female behavior. Since peasant women married before they reached sexual maturity, she concluded, their violence must have resulted from the premature demands placed on their bodies sexually and physiologically. This situated the responsibility for peasant women's violent crimes squarely with their sexuality, the "backward" custom of early marriage, and the "primitiveness" of peasant women.

Tarnovskaia also argued that premature sexual activity could have severe consequences on women's reproductive capabilities. Beyond the potential number of infanticide cases committed by young mothers, the very health of future generations was at stake when women married and became sexually active before sexual maturity. Taking her cue from biological and zoological studies, Tarnovskaia drew a parallel between animals and peasant women, noting that among animals young mothers produce "feeble, poorly developed, and weak offspring."[16] Similarly, she found that peasant women who married young and had not yet fully developed physiologically also produced weaker children and lacked the strength to care for them. This led to higher levels of infant mortality and a lower birth rate among the peasantry.[17] Biological studies showed Tarnovskaia that the offspring of well-developed, healthy, and strong women could overcome any biological (or genetic) insufficiencies that fathers might possess; however, the results of premature marriage and women's insufficient sexual development would always be reflected in the children of the peasant population.[18] Thus, early marriage was not only harmful to a woman by forcing her into sexual activity before she reached maturity, but it also contributed to the genetic deterioration of future generations. In this way, Tarnovskaia emphasized the vital role that women played in the progressive improvement of successive generations. She suggested that changes in marriage practices among the peasantry were necessary to eliminate women's premature sexual activity and to preserve the health and strength of their offspring.[19]

Writing at about the same time, political economist and professor I. Ozerov took a more sociological approach to the problem of early marriage and female criminality. Unlike Tarnovskaia, who focused on peasant women's sexual development, Ozerov concerned himself with the social environment in which young women in general found themselves in marriage. Women, he argued, often committed violent crimes against their family members—husbands, children, and relatives—because such victims were readily accessible in women's lives to bear the brunt of their frustrations. Ozerov suggested that certain "abnormalities" in women's marital situations encouraged severe reactions in them against family members, and like Tarnovskaia, he pointed specifically to the frequent practice of forcing young girls into marriage.[20] He stressed that this practice not only demoralized women, but also harmed the "moral instincts" of future generations. To prevent this damage special attention must be paid to the "sphere of women" to eliminate the "abnormal conditions of marriage and family."[21] Ozerov located the root causes of the crimes women committed against family members not in the degree of their sexual maturity but in their level of morality, in the extent to which they embraced their "natural" maternal role. When conditions in the family and marriage were not conducive to developing women's morality, both the family and society overall became destabilized. Thus, Ozerov emphasized, reforms were necessary to preserve women's moral role and to improve women's position in the family.

Furthermore, Ozerov believed that marriage created a boundary for women that kept them confined within the domestic sphere and narrowed the scope of their criminality. Women gained economic stability through marriage, for example, which decreased their stimulus to commit property crimes. This stability, however, "is purchased at too high a price for women—with the difficult conditions of their new family life . . . the criminal energy of married women decreases, . . . but it does not disappear completely, only partially, thanks to abnormal social conditions that focus her attention more closely on the members of her new marital union, where tensions are deflated through murder, poisoning, etc."[22] Marriage benefited women by providing them with social and economic stability, yet at the same time served to focus women's lives more intensely on the domestic sphere, producing situations in which women's potentially deviant sexuality could lead them to violent crime.

Although they approached the problem from different perspectives, both Tarnovskaia and Ozerov upheld the place of women in the home, arguing that it was the customs and laws surrounding marriage that needed reforming, and not necessarily women's position and role in society. As Dorie Klein suggests, this view of female crime "*reflects* and *reinforces* the economic position of women as reproductive and domestic workers."[23] Women are sexual: their purpose is to reproduce. If something interferes with the normal fulfillment of that role, for instance premature sexual activity, women's sexuality has the potential to turn them to violence. These interpretations of female sexuality limited observers' perceptions of women as able to act in response to the situations in which they found themselves and reaffirmed women's "proper" place in society within the domestic sphere.

Interestingly, what emerges from both Tarnovskaia's and Ozerov's discussions is a sense of the absolute necessity for social reform to improve the position of women in the family and eliminate the factors—unhappy marriages, premature marriages—that created situations conducive to women's violence. In their view, it was not women's sexuality in and of itself that caused female crime but rather the legal and social conditions that fostered abnormal sexuality. In this way, these studies of female crime can be seen as an attempt to create a public discussion about the position of women in Russian society and to call for social reform. The studies emphasized the importance of the family and the traditional role of women as educators of the next generation while at the same time highlighting the specific conditions within the domestic sphere that led women to commit criminal offenses. This revealed the need for change, and even suggested some benefits that would result from improvements in the status of women, but it also reinforced women's traditional position in society and the limits that women's physiology and "backwardness" might place on the modernization process. The observers' reform-mindedness did not call for a revolution in gender roles; rather, it emphasized the legal and marital practices that needed to be altered so that women could better fulfill their proper roles in society and in the family.

THE STRUGGLE FOR EXISTENCE

Calls for social reforms and the elimination of early marriage paralleled a growing interest in the "woman question" in late-nineteenth-century Russia. Both liberal and radical women found common ground at this time in their struggle for equal rights. In increasing numbers, educated women began entering the medical and teaching professions, fields that seemed compatible with women's traditional role as mothers yet brought women into greater contact with the public sphere and expanded their social involvement. Industrialization and urbanization also challenged traditional ideas of the proper employment for women as the large numbers of working-class women earning wages outside of the domestic sphere became more visible to observers.[24] Concerns about female crime emerged in response to these trends and the perception of women's growing presence in the public sphere.[25]

Russian criminologists fully expected female crime to diversify as women engaged more with public life and the "struggle for existence." They reasoned that the more opportunities women had, the more varied their crimes would become. Criminologists argued that the diversification of female crime would be a positive step bringing women closer to male levels and types of crime, and thus closer to progress and modernity. Their studies, however, suggested that female crime remained securely within its traditional sphere. In their analyses, criminologists focused predominantly on the crimes they considered typically female—crimes linked to women's sexuality and occurring in the domestic sphere—that were also the crimes most often committed by women. The adherence of criminologists to traditional conceptions of the boundaries of female crime served to undermine the potential progressiveness they believed would occur with women's growing involvement in the public sphere and reinforced women's traditional place in the home.

TABLE 1—Percentages of Total Crimes Committed by Women, 1874–1913

Year	Percentage	Year	Percentage
1874–1878	8.7	1902	11.7
1889–1893	12.0	1903	10.4
1894–1896	—	1904	9.6
1897	14.3	1905–1910	—
1898	13.9	1911	6.6
1899	13.9	1912	6.6
1900	13.7	1913	6.5
1901	14.0		

Source: *Itogi Russkoi ugolovnoi statistiki za 20 let*, 136; A. N. Trainin, "Prestupnost' goroda i derevni v Rossii," *Russkaia mysl'*, no. 7 (1909): 10; N. Visherskii, "Raspredelenie zakliuchennykh po polu i prestupleniiam," in *Sovremennaia prestupnost'*, 15. No data was available for 1894–1896 and 1905–1910.

Note: The elevated percentage of female crime in the 1880s and 1890s may have been a result of the significant involvement of women in the revolutionary and opposition movements of the time.

Criminal statistics indicated to observers that women's involvement in criminal activity remained comparatively low. Indeed, throughout the last decades of the nineteenth and the first decades of the twentieth century, women's participation in crime never exceeded 14 percent of the total crime rates (see Table 1). Criminologists emphasized that women's isolation in the domestic sphere contributed to lesser rates of crime compared to men. Traditionally, they asserted, the position of women in the home had curtailed their activities, permitting less involvement in public life and concentrating women's attention more on the "sphere of intimate relations."[26] Their greater morality and religiosity, and their roles as mothers and nurturers, kept women and their potentially dangerous sexuality locked within the family circle and focused their attention more closely on domestic problems. Furthermore, as one observer noted, the "attachment of women to the domestic hearth and their comparatively lesser mobility as a result of their weaker physical strength and energy is manifested in their lesser participation" in crimes that required engagement in the public sphere.[27] Women's domestic isolation, they argued, limited the extent and range of female crimes, even as changing social and economic conditions suggested that women's criminal activity might increase.

Criminologists also asserted that the concentration of female crime within the domestic sphere made women less susceptible to criminal influences. For instance, women had "less cause for violent outbreaks than men" because their isolation had prevented them from developing the decisiveness and wariness that men possessed.[28] Indeed, Ozerov noted that "in order to commit serious crimes it is necessary to have more strength of will, to participate more in life, so that the struggle for existence leaves a person in such a situation that the path of crime is unavoidable."[29] Because women did not participate fully in public life, they were less likely to fall under criminal influence. "A woman," Ozerov continued, "engages less in active life, more rarely fights for a piece of bread in the name of need, and better preserves her moral qualities, so that criminal instincts do not find in her such a fertile ground for development as in a man."[30]

Women's isolation, however, ensured that when women did enter public life they would more easily succumb to its pressures. Women, criminologists argued, tended to be less prepared to engage in the "struggle for existence." Although the difficulties of life and material need affected both male and female crime rates, the traditional isolation of women caused such external circumstances to act more intensively on them. This, Ozerov stressed:

> is explained by the greater instability of women, their weaker constitution: a woman's character is more childlike, youth-like; she quickly yields to all external influences, beneficial and not beneficial, without pondering them. In her, impressions operate like a whirlwind or a turbulent river, with a rapid current that she does not have the strength to handle, and like a rickety canoe she is quickly carried on the waves of social life; no current—and she stops. . . . And so we see that woman is a creature with a special mental build, and the crude reality of our economic life and the extreme abnormality of her family conditions operate on her just as disastrously as our fall frost on summer flowers.[31]

Thus while the traditional position of women served as a shield protecting them from criminal influences, it also increased their weakness and susceptibility to the difficulties of the "struggle for existence" and the criminal temptations that accompanied it.

Criminologists suggested, however, that women would overcome these weaknesses as they became more like men in their criminality. Foinitskii noted, for instance, that "the wider the circle of life and activities of women, the greater and more varied the sum of her material and spiritual needs, . . . the greater her criminality, the closer she comes to men."[32] Criminologist M. N. Gernet, too, argued that "as the life of women comes to resemble the life of men, so too their crime rates will approach those of men."[33] As Ozerov further confirmed, "everywhere that we see the more active participation of women in life, we see also an increase in their criminality."[34] Indeed, he noted, "the criminality of women under the influence of industrial development increases more rapidly than male crime."[35] Therefore, by entering the "struggle for existence," criminologists expected women would abandon the traditional criminological limits of their domestic isolation, increase their participation in public life, and thus more closely come to approximate male criminal behavior.[36]

Were criminologists justified in their impressions of the anticipated changes in female crime? Interestingly enough, the correlation between increased economic opportunities and female crime pervades the criminological literature on women's deviance.[37] Modernization theories of crime, for instance, have emphasized the link between industrialization and rising crime rates.[38] Evidence suggests, however, that expanding opportunities for women are not always accurate explanations for increased rates of female crime, nor do they always cause it to rise. Eric Johnson, in his study of nineteenth-century German crime, found that as women began to engage more in public life, as a result of industrialization and urbanization, their criminality did not necessarily increase but their chances of becoming crime victims did. He suggests that perhaps women's increased involvement in activities outside the home threatened the established male order and that men reacted more violently in response to this "threat" to their dominance.[39] Likewise, Helen Boritch and John Hagan's study of crime in turn-of-the-century Toronto reveals that women's entry into the workforce did not necessarily lead to any real rise in female criminality, but it may have sparked changes in arrest and prosecution rates, resulting in a perceived growth in female criminal activity. The circumstances that brought women into the workforce, Boritch and Hagan argue, "provided the impetus for changing formal state controls directed at women, as well as for creating and establishing a network of informal social controls."[40] Stephen Frank confirms that a similar phenomenon occurred in the Russian case as well, noting that "changing occupation patterns among women and an upsurge of paternalistic and moral concerns over such changes decisively affected the types of offenses for which women were prosecuted and convicted."[41] Thus, while Russian women probably did participate in a wide variety of offenses, they were most consistently and frequently charged for traditional "female" crimes, the offenses that most blatantly contradicted the perceived proper role of women as mothers.

Regardless of the potential impact of "modernization" on female crime, the statistics presented by Russian criminologists reaffirmed for them the traditional nature of female crime. According to their numbers, between 1874 and 1878 only 8.7 percent of offenders were women. By the years 1889–1893 that percentage had risen to 12 percent.[42] Despite this fairly significant increase, the types of crimes for which women were charged remained consistent. Between 1876 and 1886, women were convicted for 98.6 percent of all infanticide cases, 69.7 percent of poisonings, 41.6 percent of spouse murders, and 17 percent of domestic thefts, but only for 5.5 percent of counterfeiting and 2.9 percent of robbery cases. By the 1890s, women made up 98.5 percent of those convicted for infanticide, 68.7 percent for poisonings, 45 percent for spouse murder, 2.4 percent for forgery, and 3.3 percent for robbery.[43] These statistics reveal the continued reliance on traditional definitions of "female" crime among prosecutors and criminologists. Indeed, the rise in female crime rates, while the types of crimes committed remained the same, suggests that women were most often arrested and tried for traditional female crimes (infanticide, abortion, spouse murder, and so on), the very offenses that threatened social stability by challenging the role of women as mothers and nurturers. These numbers do not necessarily reflect the actual extent of female criminal activity, but rather the perceptions of the police and the courts regarding the nature of female crime and the types of activities in which women engaged.[44]

Foinitskii's analysis of working women's crime rates confirmed that women's social position remained central to criminologists' understanding of female crime. Women's traditional isolation in the home, he argued, brought greater dissatisfaction and placed more attention on those daily problems that led women to murder. Foinitskii believed, however, that wage labor served as a corrective to female criminality: "The domestic hearth, therefore, in no way protects women from crime, the best means against which, at least in the conditions of our contemporary life, turns out to be for them precisely labor."[45] Indeed, he found that industrial working women committed fewer crimes than did housewives. Some historians have argued that factory work helped women avoid falling into criminality by providing a community of support for them.[46]

What Foinitskii seems to suggest, in contrast, is that when women left the home and discarded their traditional social position they committed fewer traditionally "female" crimes—those bound directly to the domestic sphere—thus appearing to reduce rates of female crime. For him, an expansion in working women's crime types reflected the processes through which women could become more modern, more engaged in the "struggle for existence," and thus more like men in their criminality.

Foinitskii also pointed to the educational level of women as a key factor in understanding their deviance. He found that over 90 percent of female criminals were illiterate, a much higher percentage than for male criminals and a higher percentage than among the general population.[47] In addition, he noted that levels of female crime were greater among less-educated women and lower among more-educated women.[48] Education, he argued, acted as a "civilizing force," giving women new ideas, new awareness of the possibilities of life, and new strength. It prevented women from committing crimes by making them more "human," by increasing their awareness of the importance of life, and by raising their cultural level.[49] Thus, the education of women would complement their entry into public life by making them more aware of their surroundings and by better equipping them to deal with the "struggle for existence." Theoretically, understanding the broader context of their problems would deter women from reacting in their traditional violent fashion to the difficulties of family life.

Even as women's opportunities expanded and they engaged more with the "struggle for existence," criminologists' descriptions of female crime reconfirmed its limitations. As historian Stephen Frank observes:

> Russians who studied judicial statistics found ready evidence to support the image of women's crime as both static and timeless—an unchanging reflection of gender rather than economic and social factors, court structures and jurisdiction, or the very way in which crime was defined and culturally constructed. . . . These sources thus provided 'scientific' confirmation for a mythical portrait of the female criminal, thereby reifying the very narrative responsible for creating this myth.[50]

Although Russian criminologists believed in the progressive potential for women in joining the "struggle for existence," their understanding of the nature of female crime and their perspectives on female deviance kept women's criminal activity securely rooted in women's traditional position within the domestic sphere.

WAR, REVOLUTION, AND THE NEP

The years of world war, revolution, and civil war (1914–1921) seemingly provided the perfect context and circumstances for female crime to break out of its traditional patterns. Wartime conditions naturally forced more women to enter the "struggle for existence" to make ends meet as well as to fill the jobs left vacant by men sent to fight at the front. In addition, the February and October revolutions radically altered women's legal and political position in Russian society through female enfranchisement and the implementation of new policies governing family and social services. Criminologists fully expected these changes to be reflected in female crime and anticipated seeing an increase in the number and diversity of crimes committed by women as they were forced by circumstance and encouraged by legislation to engage in the "struggle for existence" like men. While female crime rates did rise during the war years, by the mid-1920s they had returned to levels comparable with the prerevolutionary period. Furthermore, criminologists did not find reflected in their statistics the expansion in women's criminal behavior they believed would occur as women became more involved in the public sphere. Nevertheless, female crime continued to intrigue early Soviet criminologists, possibly because it did not change in the ways they expected, and they devoted considerable attention to understanding the reasons for this. They stressed that women's physiological and reproductive nature, and closer connection to the family, prevented women from taking advantage of their newfound opportunities. For criminologists, this reflected the incompleteness of the revolution during the 1920s.

The war years made serious criminological study all but impossible, and Soviet crime scholarship did not begin in earnest until the foundation of the criminological organizations in the early 1920s, after the introduction of the New Economic Policy.[51] Thus, the context of the NEP shaped criminological discussions of the wartime period and contemporary society. Not only did the NEP inspire concern among some communists about the fate of the revolution, it also raised fears and heightened anxieties about sexuality. Some observers worried about the social morals of the youth, concerns compounded by new policies that seemed to promote sexual promiscuity. To counter this, young communists were encouraged to deny their sexual appetites and channel their sexual urges into productive socialist labor.[52] For others, it was the capitalism of the NEP that suggested decadence and corruption.[53] As one observer noted:

Before the New Economic Policy, the streets of large cities were characterized by seriousness and work, but in recent years their order has also become
polluted. All types of restaurants and cafes, cabarets and gambling clubs,
luxury store window displays, and masses of automobiles, cinemas, and
beer halls draw the envious and greedy glances of unstable boys and girls.
The seeming brilliance and fabulous streets blind them, and the weaker,
unstable natures are ready for everything, if only they themselves could be
part of that brilliance.[54]

Here, the NEP became a minefield of depravity and temptation that facilitated a young woman's fall into vice and crime. Images of the NEP such
as this reflected the "dangers" of capitalism, but they also suggested the
corrupting influence of the NEP on women, as it exposed innocent and
unsuspecting youth to bourgeois excesses, and thus created conditions
that undermined the values and ideals of Soviet society.

During the early NEP, criminologists looked back on the years of war
and revolution as a period that stimulated a significant transformation
of both women's engagement in the public sphere and women's criminality.[55] The material they compiled revealed that changing patterns of
female crime accompanied the unstable social and political environment.
Criminologists found the war had a particularly devastating effect on
women, leading them to commit more and diverse crimes. According to
M. N. Gernet, female crime never made up more than 20 percent of all
offenses before the war; in 1915, however, it reached 28.6 percent, increasing to 33.4 percent by 1916. In contrast, male crime levels dropped by 53
percent in 1916.[56] Statistician D. P. Rodin agreed, noting that, compared to
1913, female crime rose 13 percent by 1915 and 79 percent by 1916.[57] The
dynamics of wartime life clearly manifested themselves in these statistics.
Indeed, criminologists fully expected to see a decrease in male crime rates
during the war. As Gernet pointed out, "the conscription of a significant
percent of the able-bodied population of the age particularly inclined
toward criminal activity should bring about a decrease in crime among
men of that age. A decline in the intensity of industrial life and trade, and
enlistment into the army of people occupied in industry and trade, should
also bring in its wake a decrease in the number of crimes [committed by
men]."[58] With fewer civilian men available, the proportion of crimes committed by women rose. In addition, women took over many traditionally
"male" jobs, which, following the logic of the "struggle for existence,"
exposed women to situations more conducive to criminal activity as they
attempted to make ends meet. As Gernet noted, the world war:

placed demands on women workers to engage in activities that only a year earlier even the staunchest defenders of women's equality would not have considered possible, and women appeared as policers of city squares, tram drivers, chauffeurs, and firefighters. . . . These new spheres of labor also opened new possibilities for violating the law. Taking the place of men sent to the front, women joined in the struggle for existence, which became more difficult with every passing year, and began to take the place of men in crime.[59]

In terms of criminal activity, the war years liberated women from the confines of the domestic sphere and traditional offense patterns. Furthermore, demobilization after the Civil War created high levels of female unemployment. These factors contributed to the continued growth of female crime rates, forcefully bringing women into the engagement with the "struggle for existence" that prerevolutionary criminologists had long advocated.

In addition, criminologists expected that the radical changes initiated by the Bolsheviks and aimed at transforming Russia into a socialist state would further expand the range of female criminal activity. "The October Revolution," wrote jurist V. D. Men'shagin, "placed women on an equal footing with men."[60] Psychiatrist Iu. Khodakov observed: "with its emancipation of women and their introduction into public life, with its colossal restructuring of the juridical and moral norms that had previously dominated the lives of women, [the revolution] should seemingly eradicate that vicious circle [of domestic isolation] and this, in the first place, should be reflected in female crime."[61] Indeed, Gernet explained that, with the end of the Civil War and the shift to socialist construction and the NEP, an entire corpus of acts was passed that did not merely "reform" but rather "revolutionized" women's situation. Noting that "since the more women approach men in their criminality, the more they resemble men in their social situation," Gernet fully expected women to begin committing a wider variety of crimes as they gained social equality.[62] "This growing percentage of female crime should not disturb or frighten anyone," Gernet stressed. "It is an inevitable and unavoidable stage in the development of female criminality, as it was for male criminality when it, in its time and in accordance with the very tenor of social life, lost its primitive, monotonous character and with every day became more varied and 'richer' in its operation."[63]

Criminologists saw the expansion in women's criminal activity as a positive, progressive trend that brought women into greater contact with the outside world, made them more "civilized," and broadened their horizons, even if it did increase their levels and types of criminal behavior. Gernet noted that "the gradual achievement of women's rights and the widening of the area of employment of [women's] labor brings an increase in [women's] criminality. But it would be completely wrong to put forward this rise in criminality as an argument against the equality of women and men."[64] He thus implied that by encouraging women's greater participation in public life and consequently more "varied and richer" criminal activity, the Bolshevik emancipation could potentially overcome women's physiological limitations and domestic isolation, eventually enabling women to become modern Soviet citizens. In this way, female criminality acted as a marker against which criminologists could measure progress toward the achievement of socialism.

Examining female crime trends reported by the criminologists of the 1920s, Louise Shelley has suggested that the rise in women's offenses was the result of the "inadvertent criminological consequences of war and revolution . . . compounded by Soviet policies that deliberately intruded into what remained of the traditional female role in Russian society."[65] According to her analysis, women were unprepared for the violence and turmoil they experienced during the war years, as well as the financial responsibilities they were forced to accept. This, combined with a new awareness of their right to control their own lives (a result of Bolshevik emancipatory policies), led women to take matters into their own hands and resulted in a greater incidence of murder and other crimes committed by women. Shelley concludes that crime provided an outlet for women, some of whom turned to it as "their only recourse against their economically and emotionally precarious situation," while others used it as an opportunity "to vent their personal frustrations for years of oppression at the hands of men."[66]

Shelley's analysis of female crime in the immediate postrevolutionary years highlights the impact that the violence and insecurity of the revolutionary period, along with the changes in morality and social policy enacted by the Bolsheviks, had on women's lives. Shelley stresses the effects of increased social, economic, and political opportunities on women's offense patterns, echoing Soviet criminologists' expectations for changes in female criminal behavior. But she also points to the new regime's interest in women's issues as a central factor in explaining the growth of female criminality after the revolution. While the Bolsheviks did initiate policy changes that significantly altered the role and status of women in Russian society, these efforts were more in line with their general socialist ideology than any particular commitment to solving the "woman question."[67] Wartime dislocation, financial insecurity, and social change certainly affected female crime rates. Yet by focusing their studies on the traditional "female" crimes of the domestic sphere, criminologists emphasized the unchanging nature of women's deviance, revealing their assumptions of women's social role and their understanding of the revolution's impact on female crime.

In criminologists' analyses of crime after the revolution, the family and the domestic sphere remained central both in causing women to commit crimes and in determining the types of crimes women committed, and this served to link female crime directly to women's sexuality. For example, Gernet noticed a significant increase in the number of women sentenced for violent crimes during and after the war. He found that although women made up only about 15 percent of all those charged for crimes against the person, the number of women sentenced for such crimes increased over 59 percent between 1922 and 1924, compared with a more reasonable, but still significant, 15.5 percent rise for men.[68] Gernet emphasized that despite the expansion of contact with the public sphere experienced by women during and after the war years, the nature of their violent crimes retained prewar characteristics: abortion, infanticide, and child abandonment remained the most common offenses against the person committed by women.[69] The crime rates showed criminologists that women's close connection with "the family circle and the limitation of [women's] interests to the sexual sphere determine the attributes of female crime, decreasing its numbers and narrowing its qualitative distinction."[70] Accordingly, the continued occupation of women in the domestic sphere served to ground women's criminality firmly within the sexual realm, governed by their physiology and reproductive cycles. As one observer noted, a woman's "physical features and social conditions predetermine her lesser participation in crime in general and in more serious crimes in particular."[71]

Many observers relied on biological analyses of women's physiology to explain the prevalence of traditional "female" forms of crime among female offenders after the revolution. Endocrinologist A. V. Nemilov, in his controversial work *The Biological Tragedy of Women* (*Biologicheskaia tragediia zhenshchiny*), pointed out that biological differences between men and women had prevented much change in the status of women despite efforts to achieve equality between the sexes, and that "the life of women and the female soul can only be understood by starting from its biological basis."[72] Female crime should, therefore, be explained not only in socioeconomic terms but also in the context of the influence that women's physiological functions had on female behavior. As jurist A. A. Zhizhilenko stated, "Overall it must be noted that all phenomena closely connected with women's sexuality have an effect on [women's] criminality. The period of pregnancy, birth, the postpartum period, the period of menopause, as cessation is called—all this should be taken into consideration in the analysis of female crime."[73] V. L. Sanchov agreed, noting, "it has long been established that certain phases of sexual life (in particular among women—menstruation, pregnancy, giving birth, and menopause) specifically infuse the psyche of the individual and lead him [sic] to criminal activity."[74] Nemilov added that if in some women menstruation instigated capricious behavior, in others its influence took on a more pathological form that caused temporary insanity, completely irrational crimes, and even suicide.[75] In these analyses, physiology became central to interpreting female crime because although women's sexual functions were less understood than men's, the experiences of women tended to be more emotional and thus more directly linked to their psychology, which was influenced by their reproductive cycles.[76]

The difficulty with the biological theory of female crime in the 1920s rested in its determinism. If female sexuality could be held responsible for female crime, then such behavior could not be corrected or eliminated since it was inherent in a woman's physiological constitution. This brought the criminologists dangerously close to the Lombrosian view of the female born criminal that made every woman a potential offender. Such an interpretation of female criminality could not be tolerated in the Soviet context precisely because crime, as a product of socioeconomic conditions, was supposed to disappear with the achievement of socialism. In addition, the Soviet penal system focused on correcting criminal behavior through enlightenment and labor. A completely biological view of female crime would undermine the very principles of the Soviet project and make the rehabilitation of women criminals impossible.

Yet the biological approach held considerable appeal for most crime specialists, particularly doctors and psychiatrists, as the structure of criminological institutions reveals (see chapter 2). To some extent, the biological perspective may have served to express anxieties regarding the NEP. Fears of the potential failure of the socialist experiment could be focused on women as representatives of the old way of life and as biologically unable to transform themselves into Soviet citizens.[77] Often, however, criminologists saw the physiological as a contributing factor to criminal deviance and as an intrinsic element in their interpretations of crime. A. S. Zvonitskaia, for example, argued that understanding the physiological nature of the offender was essential to understanding the sociological causes of crime, and vice versa.[78] Zhizhilenko added that "we cannot deny . . . that sex shows up as an individual factor in determining instances."[79] For specialists, women's crime could be understood only by considering both physiological and socioeconomic circumstances.

Criminologists' examinations of female violent crimes in particular highlighted the inherent link specialists identified between the physiological responses of women and their social and material situation that caused them to lash out against those closest to them—family members. For criminologists, violent crimes against relatives stood out as typical offenses committed by women. They understood female biological and physiological cycles as facilitating the commission of crimes by playing on women's emotional reactions, causing women to respond violently to those around them. According to criminologist S. Ukshe's statistics, women made up only about 15.5 percent of all prisoners in Moscow jails in 1923, but were 36.3 percent of the murderers.[80] Ukshe stressed that murder, particularly of spouses and relatives, was committed by women "isolated in the family circle" more often than all other kinds of violent crime except acts against children.[81]

In a 1926 study of female spouse murder, Ukshe emphasized the emotional characteristics of female crime and the role of marriage and jealousy in sparking such crimes. One case Ukshe examined was that of D., a twenty-year-old woman from an educated St. Petersburg banking family. Left with no relatives after the death of her mother and the emigration of her father, D. went to Pskov and joined the Komsomol (Communist youth organization) there, where she met and married a Communist functionary from the working class. A year after the wedding, D. learned that her husband had a mistress. Six months later her husband moved out, saying they needed to get divorced because married life interfered with his party work. At the time D. was four months pregnant. Still in love with her husband, she took to waiting outside his building after work and grew jealous after his landlady showed her a love letter from his mistress. One day she purchased a gun. On 12 April 1924, D. went to her husband and gave him an ultimatum—either live with her or she would kill herself. After a long talk in which she asked him at least to give her some money to live on and he responded that she should sell her coat instead, she took out the gun and shot him.[82]

In analyzing the crime, Ukshe emphasized the physiological and emotional influences acting on D. at the moment of the murder:

> The crime was committed under the influence of a strong paroxysm [*affekt*], of gradually aroused irritation directed against her husband, of jealousy, of sleepless nights, and of the clearly expressed desire of her husband to abandon her at that very moment when she was particularly in need of his support and attention. It goes without saying that her pregnancy should have an effect on the strength of the paroxysm.[83]

Although material need may have pushed D. over the edge, Ukshe's analysis indicated that D. committed her crime as a direct result of her emotional situation, compounded by the physiological influences of the pregnancy. Ukshe concluded that female spouse murder could be explained "not as much by social factors as by mental illness aroused due to the betrayal by a loved one."[84]

The reliance of criminologists on physiological and psychological explanations for female violent crimes related to the domestic sphere was consistent with their understanding of women's nature and women's close connection to the family circle. What is more surprising, however, is their focus on physiology even when women committed typically "male" crimes. Since women were supposed to become more like men as they entered the public sphere and the "struggle for existence," the attention to female physiology in explanations of women's nontraditional crimes—for example, embezzlement—highlights the persistence among professionals of traditional views of women. According to criminologists' theories, an increase in female participation in crimes like embezzlement (*rastrata*) would provide evidence of the progressive expansion of female criminality. Overall, convictions for embezzlement increased from 29.2 percent of all white-collar (*dolzhnostnye*) crimes in 1924 to 49.1 percent in 1925.[85] Among embezzlers, criminologists found that in 1924, 16.8 percent were women, up slightly from 12.6 percent in 1922.[86] While convictions for work-related crimes in general nearly tripled by 1926 compared to 1922, embezzlement increased fourfold, and establishing a working understanding of the causes and nature of *rastrata* became a priority in criminological studies by the mid-1920s.[87]

The explanations criminologists offered for women who embezzled focused not on material need, educational level, or increased involvement in public life, but on female physiology, sexuality, and pathological impulses. In one telling case reported by psychiatrist A. N. Terent'eva, S., a fifty-year-old woman, was found guilty of embezzling funds from her employer and gambling away the money in a casino. According to Terent'eva, at the time of her arrest S. worked as a secretary in the Moscow office of the Chechen Republic, and her duties included safeguarding the office cash. Because the office was not secure, S. often took the cash home with her. In October 1925, she received 200 rubles of her salary and also took 1,500 rubles home from the cash box. That day she went straight to a casino after work to play cards. S. quickly lost her own 200 rubles and then, little by little, all the money from the office. She left the casino and returned home in a state of panic, tearing her hair and beating her head against the wall. Soon, however, one desire overtook her—to play cards and forget everything else. Her "unpleasant feelings of fear and horror somehow quickly transformed into feelings of sexual excitement," and while riding the tram, some small bumps in the road fed her sexual arousal, which she had never felt so strongly, and caused her to experience an orgasm. She told no one about losing the money and began spending every night at the casino. She lost her shame, her honesty, and her self-respect, sold all her belongings, took on odd jobs, and gambled away all the money. To feed her compulsion, she turned to theft. While her boss was away she stole an additional 8,500 rubles from the office, which she also squandered at the casino. She was eventually arrested and sentenced to three years in prison.

Terent'eva found S. to have a schizophrenic temperament similar to impulsive psychopaths, and a pathologically heightened sexual drive with sadistic elements. She argued that a variety of misfortunes in life, including the loss of a beloved husband and a long period of illness, weakened S.'s constitution and resulted in her impulsiveness. However, sexuality played a central role, for "as her passion for cards grew, so did her pathologically heightened sexual excitement." Terent'eva concluded that this crime was caused by an extreme pathological sexuality and that "menopause, which in a fifty-year-old woman is not far away, will mark the end of her sexual drive and her social dangerousness."[88] Therefore, the rehabilitation of S. would be possible once her reproductive capability ended. Terent'eva's testimony at S.'s trial emphasized the defendant's pathological personality. A report of the trial that appeared in *Proletarskii sud* (*Proletarian Court*), a journal for court employees, focused, however, on the culpability of S.'s employer, who hired a woman he met in a casino and frequently left her unsupervised.[89] In both accounts of the crime, female sexuality emerged as the primary culprit, centered in the deviant sexual pathology of the unsupervised woman in public. Even when women committed crimes made possible because of their greater involvement in the "struggle for existence," criminologists relied on explanations for female deviance that removed responsibility from women by emphasizing their physiological and sexual nature and the uncontrollable passions that drove them to commit criminal acts.

RECIDIVIST WOMEN

Women's recidivism rates provided vivid confirmation for criminologists of the relationship between female crime, women's physiology, and the ability to participate in the "struggle for existence." Women's lack of experience with the realities of public life and isolation in the domestic sphere prevented women from engaging in criminal activity to the same extent as men; however, when women did enter the criminal world criminologists found they had more difficulty returning to honest life. That the proportion of female repeat offenders was always statistically higher than among men indicated to criminologists that women's "weaker" nature, "inherent" criminal tendencies, and social position made reforming female criminals, and bringing women into full participation in Soviet society, much more difficult.

Recidivism remained a concern for the criminologists and the courts throughout the 1920s because it represented a failure of the Soviet penal system to successfully reform all prisoners. Based on theories of progressivism, the Soviet penal system sought to rehabilitate offenders through corrective labor and cultural enlightenment.[90] Recidivism rates reflected the inadequacies of the penal system and the difficulties of transforming criminals into honest citizens. But at the same time recidivism levels suggested that certain offenders embodied a greater level of "social dangerousness," making them deserving of harsher measures of repression. According to criminologists' statistics, while the vast majority of criminals in early Soviet society were first-time offenders, between 10 and 20 percent of prisoners had already spent time in prison. Among these, approximately 25 percent had two or more previous convictions.[91] Repeat offenders tended to receive fewer short prison sentences and more long prison terms (see Table 2). The differences in punishments for recidivists and first-time offenders, however, remained minimal. In the sentencing for murderers committing multiple offenses, for example, the difference in prison terms becomes visible only for the severest punishments, with nearly 25 percent of offenders receiving terms of 8–10 years, compared to fewer than 10 percent for first-time offenders (see Table 3).

TABLE 2—Length of Sentence by Number of Convictions and Gender, 1926

	MEN			WOMEN		
	First-time offender	One previous offense	Multiple offenses	First-time offender	One previous offense	Multiple offenses
Up to 6 months	35.0	26.3	20.0	45.1	34.3	26.6
6 months to 1 year	15.6	18.8	23.1	19.2	29.2	30.7
1–2 years	13.9	18.8	22.8	11.0	17.8	22.3
2–3 years	11.5	11.1	11.8	8.4	9.3	9.5
3–5 years	11.2	11.1	9.8	7.3	3.9	4.4
5–8 years	6.4	7.2	6.1	4.6	1.4	1.6
8–10 years	4.2	5.0	5.5	1.8	2.1	1.6
Unknown	2.2	1.7	0.9	2.6	2.0	3.3

Source: M. Kessler, "Imushchestvennye prestupleniia po dannym perepisi 1926 g.," in *Sovremennaia prestupnost'*, 54.

TABLE 3—Prison Sentences for Murder According to Recidivism and Gender, 1926

	FIRST-TIME OFFENDERS		REPEAT OFFENDERS	
	Men	Women	Men	Women
3 months	0.3	0.9	0.4	1.8
3–6 months	0.8	4.9	0.5	—
6 months to 1 year	3.6	9.0	1.2	3.6
1–2 years	9.8	15.0	3.2	10.9
2–3 years	19.2	14.1	15.8	10.9
3–5 years	26.8	26.1	19.4	23.6
5–8 years	30.6	23.3	36.1	25.6
8–10 years	8.9	6.7	23.2	23.6

Source: A. Shestakova, "Prestupleniia protiv lichnosti," in *Sovremennaia prestupnost'*, 64–65.

Several criminologists attributed high recidivist rates to the preponderance of short prison terms handed out by the courts. According to penologist B. S. Utevskii, short prison terms merely disrupted a convict's life without giving him or her enough time to benefit from the prison's rehabilitation regime. Data from the 1926 prison census indicated that over 50 percent of prisoners spent less than one year in jail (with 5.3 percent spending less than one month), a period that Utevskii believed was long enough for them to lose their jobs and thus become strong candidates for committing future crimes, but not long enough for them to be reformed into responsible Soviet citizens. He recommended increasing the use of fines and alternative measures of punishment in place of short prison terms.[92] This paralleled the general goal among penal policymakers to institute more progressive principles of punishment and the growing interest in the use of compulsory labor, fines, and other alternative administrative sanctions instead of prison terms.[93] Despite the desire to reduce the number of convicted offenders sent to prison, criminologists did see some positive impact of the prison rehabilitation program, specifically in literacy rates and in particular among repeat offenders. Utevskii noted that 83 percent of prisoners in 1926 were literate, a significantly higher percentage than among the general population, and that for repeat offenders literacy reached 86 percent, even rising as high as 95.4 percent among certain criminal groups.[94]

What caught criminologists' attention even more than the literacy rates of repeat offenders, however, were the levels of female recidivism. While the overall percentage of female crime after the revolution remained small compared to male crime, criminologists found that women returned to prison at a significantly higher rate than men. Indeed, in 1924, the percentage of women with two or more convictions exceeded the proportion of men, and in 1926 women's recidivism rates were greater than those of men nearly universally (see Table 4).[95] Furthermore, of imprisoned recidivist women in 1926, 61 percent had two previous convictions, 23 percent had three earlier arrests, and 14 percent had been in prison four or more times, significant proportions among such a small percentage of the prison population (Table 5 shows similar rates for 1924).[96] In seeking to understand these data, criminologists looked beyond the difficult social and economic circumstances in which women found themselves during the transitional period, and beyond the possible failures of the prison regime's corrective enlightenment, to explain female recidivism in terms of women's inherent proclivity toward criminal activity shaped by their social position and their physiology.

TABLE 4—Rates of Recidivism for Men and Women, 1922 and 1926

	1922		1926	
	Men	*Women*	*Men*	*Women*
Counterrevolution	—	—	9.6	11.4
Abuse of office	—	—	9.6	12.2
Crimes against the person	—	—	12.4	13.1
Crimes against administrative order	—	—	19.4	31.8
Property crimes	—	—	40.5	43.2
FOR SPECIFIC CRIMES				
Murder	25.9	9.0	6.7	7.7
Robbery	34.0	23.5	7.5	16.0
Embezzlement	—	—	11.0	6.6
Forgery	36.1	0.0	15.9	27.1
Illicit vodka production	18.3	26.6	47.6	69.0
Theft	41.3	48.7	71.9	67.5

Source: B. S. Utevskii, "Sovremennaia prestupnost' po dannym perepisi mest zakliucheniia," *Administrativnyi vestnik*, no. 1 (1928): 41; Utevskii, "Prestupnost' i retsidiv," in *Sovremennaia prestupnost'* (1927), 42; Utevskii, "Vozrast i gramotnost' retsidivistov," in *Sovremennaia prestupnost'*, vol. 2 (1930), 83; V. I. Kufaev, "Retsidivisty (Povtorno-obviniaemye)," in *Prestupnyi mir Moskvy*, 106.

TABLE 5—Repeat Offenders, 1924

(In Percentages)

	RURAL		URBAN	
	Men	*Women*	*Men*	*Women*
No prior convictions	80.2	78.8	68.1	72.3
Prior convictions	9.7	11.1	19.5	18.8
Unknown	10.1	10.1	12.4	8.9
OF THOSE WITH PRIOR CONVICTIONS				
One prior conviction	82.4	74.4	76.9	73.3
2–3 prior convictions	15.3	25.6	20.0	25.2
4 or more prior convictions	2.3	—	3.1	1.5

Source: E. N. Tarnovskii, "Osnovnye cherty sovremennoi prestupnosti," *Administrativnyi vestnik*, no. 11 (1925): 53.

Utevskii examined the 1926 prison census data on female recidivism in two articles published in 1927 and 1928, emphasizing that "a woman more quickly becomes a habitual criminal."[97] He argued that the higher rates of recidivism among women indicated that once women entered the criminal world, they had a harder time leaving it than men.[98] M. Kessler confirmed this trend, noting that it had long been recognized that "declassed" women had great difficulty reintegrating into honest society.[99] Utevskii further suggested that women easily became accustomed to the criminal lifestyle, and having few options after release from prison, quickly returned to their old habits. For this reason, he stressed, women needed the influence of an expanded correctional regime while in prison and increased assistance after their release.[100] Another observer agreed, emphasizing the influence of female physiology on women's criminality and thus women's need for paternal control, much like children:

> Under current conditions, women, once falling onto the path of crime, have more difficulty leaving it than men. If we add to that the passivity of the female psyche that developed over a thousand years and the high percentage of female criminals . . . who were seriously impaired by alcoholism and abnormal sexual lives, so it becomes clear that any reduction in the scope of correctional efforts with regard to women is just as irrational as with regard to juveniles.[101]

Despite acknowledging the difficult social and economic conditions that previously convicted women faced, criminologists linked female recidivism directly to women's psychological and physiological nature, suggesting that female offenders were inherently unreformable. In discussing recidivism rates for banditry and robbery, for example, Utevskii noted that while men repeated these offenses at a rate of 45.9 percent, women's recidivism for the crimes reached an astonishing 55.8 percent. Amazed, Utevskii wrote, "Even in cases of robbery and banditry, offenses assumed to be without doubt male crimes in which one needs strength and risk, fearlessness and cruelty, the ability to use weapons and calmly spill a victim's blood, women are ahead of men. . . . Truly, this reflects the capricious play of female psychology, combining extreme gentleness with extreme cruelty and mercilessness."[102] Utevskii concluded:

> At the same time women's participation in crime is often less than among men, [women's] tendency toward repeat offenses is significantly higher. The cause of this can be seen in two factors: in the specificities of the female

psyche on the one hand, and in the surrounding milieu on the other. A woman less easily enters onto the path of crime, but once started on it, it is more difficult for her to leave this path. Strength of habits and conservativeness of the psyche are more characteristic of women than of men, so that bad influences find in the gentle passive female psyche a more fertile soil. Furthermore, women committing crimes and landing in prison have more difficulty reintegrating themselves in society, more difficulty obtaining the possibility of earning an honest living. Resistance to change and the prejudice of narrow-minded persons stigmatize prison terms more strongly for women than men. . . . Men can disregard the call of social opinion; women are forced to submit to it.[103]

For the criminologists, women's high rates of recidivism compared to men's indicated women's inability to fully embrace the new way of life offered by the Soviet system. Women's traditional isolation in the domestic sphere and the broad influence of female physiology, criminologists found, prevented women from adapting to the changing conditions of life and their increased involvement with the "struggle for existence," drawing them more easily into a life of crime and making their rehabilitation more difficult. Although criminologists were aware of the social and financial obstacles facing former convicts, compounded by the difficult circumstances of life in general in the transitional period, their analyses of female recidivism nevertheless emphasized the weaker nature of women and their physiological limitations. These explanations reflected and preserved within criminological discourse traditional understandings of women's social position and the need for paternal controls, reinforcing criminologists' perceptions of the "backwardness" of women.

THE PROSTITUTE AS CRIMINAL

While female recidivism revealed the intransigence of women, prostitution provided the most visible and public link between crime and female sexuality. For criminologists and other social activists, prostitution embodied the "primitiveness" they associated with women. Its connection to female sexuality seemed to suggest a proclivity toward prostitution that reinforced the idea of women's inherent backwardness. In addition, prostitution represented the persistence of the old way of life within Soviet society and an element of bourgeois capitalist exploitation that appeared to be thriving during the NEP. For many communists and observers, prostitution and its public display of female sexuality reflected the worst elements of the New Economic Policy. Lying at the intersection of sexuality, capitalism, and crime, prostitution revealed to Soviet social observers both the inadequacies of the NEP experiment and the ultimate failure of women to overcome their physiological limitations.

Prostitution occupied an anomalous position in early Soviet society. Upon coming to power, the Bolsheviks abolished the tsarist system that regulated prostitution. In the late nineteenth century the regulation regime had come under considerable attack. Many social activists, including socialists, opposed the inherent double standard in the Imperial regulation system. Ostensibly intended to protect public health, regulation subjected prostitutes, but not their clients, to regular health inspections and thus did little to address the spread of venereal disease.[104] In addition, some critics condemned the regulation system for encouraging immorality. For example, social activist Maria Pokrovskaia argued that the living conditions of prostitutes made the women into alcoholics. Brothel keepers kept control of these young women through drink, and the women themselves turned to alcohol to dull the pain of their existence and the humiliation of medical checkups. Pokrovskaia also linked prostitution to male depravity, arguing that prostitutes would get men drunk to obtain more money from them. She concluded, "This patronizing system of trade in ignorant and defenseless young girls turns a blind eye to the cruder instincts of the population, encourages the spread of alcoholism, provides young people with corrupt morals, and is ruining the future of the country." The fight against prostitution, she added, could only begin once the regulation system was abolished.[105] Activists from across the political spectrum from liberal to radical agreed that the regulation of prostitution needed significant reform. Thus, the Bolsheviks had considerable support for their decision to abolish the system.[106]

Once in power, however, Bolshevik leaders hesitated to issue any new laws to regulate, legalize, or outlaw prostitution. They asserted that prostitution, like the state, the law, and crime itself, would disappear with the establishment of socialism. Nevertheless, prostitution remained a serious concern, and in 1919 the People's Commissariat of Social Welfare sponsored the creation of an Interdepartmental Commission on the Fight against Prostitution to address the issue. Representatives of the commission proposed various strategies based on their institutional jurisdictions and priorities, ranging from detention and incarceration of prostitutes to medical examinations of the general population to creating "model homes" for youth. While the commission did not arrive at a solution to the problem of prostitution, it did conclude that prostitutes should not be punished but rather rehabilitated into a life of productive labor.[107] The commission's work helped shape thinking on prostitution during the NEP and the ways in which the police and judicial systems dealt with the problem.

For most social observers and Bolshevik sympathizers during the NEP, prostitution represented an outdated institution of capitalist exploitation that had no place in the new socialist society. Its continued presence raised anxieties about the revolutionary transformation of sexual relations, providing direct evidence of the decadence of the NEP and the persistence of capitalist elements and class enemies in Soviet society. Indeed, as Petrograd Soviet leader B. G. Kaplun argued, professional prostitution was not a part of communist thought. The notion of prostitution as a person's profession did not exist. Therefore, he concluded, "there is no such thing as a struggle against prostitution; rather, the government must fight against those women who have no definite occupation."[108] In addition, Bolshevik observers believed the emancipation of women that accompanied the revolution would increase women's economic opportunities and discourage them from engaging in the activity. The continued existence of prostitution during the NEP thus suggested to these observers that many people retained their "bourgeois" sensibilities and that material conditions had still not improved sufficiently to deter women from entering the profession in the first place. Finally, criminologists linked the "parasitic," "capitalist," and sexual nature of prostitution with female crime, emphasizing the connections between women's criminal "primitiveness," sexuality, and prostitution.

It is perhaps no surprise that Soviet criminologists connected the prostitute with the criminal. The relationship between prostitution and the criminal underworld had been well established in Europe and Russia before the 1917 Bolshevik Revolution.[109] Indeed, some nineteenth-century criminologists, including Cesare Lombroso, had emphasized the connection between female criminality and prostitution.[110] Russian specialists generally rejected interpretations of female sexual deviance that presumed prostitution to be a natural and fundamental female activity. Nevertheless, they found embodied in the prostitute and her connection to the criminal world a duality that lay at the heart of their understanding of female crime itself. Elizabeth Waters has argued that early Soviet observers' views of the prostitute changed over time. During the Civil War and the First Five-Year Plan, prostitutes were depicted as "villains," parasites, class enemies, and saboteurs of socialist construction. In contrast, the political and economic circumstances of the NEP led observers to view prostitutes as downtrodden and exploited "victims" of circumstances.[111] Even as they understood the prostitute to be a victim during the NEP, however, criminologists also focused attention on the negative and criminal behaviors associated with the profession, emphasizing the incompatibility of prostitution with proper Soviet behavior and socialist morality. This victim/villain duality allowed criminologists to view the prostitute as both a hopeless criminal deserving of punishment and a helpless victim of social circumstances and the depravity of the NEP.

For Soviet criminologists and social scientists, prostitution and prostitutes provided a vivid reminder that the old way of life was alive and well in the NEP. In many ways, early Soviet observers linked prostitution with what was considered "bourgeois," labeling it as parasitic, as a "social anomaly left over from the old order."[112] Capitalism in particular created the conditions for prostitution; as one observer noted, "Only social inequality with its exploitation of man by man, with its unequal distribution of material goods, with its legal inequality of the sexes . . . could beget such an awful phenomenon as selling one's body—prostitution."[113] Prostitution, criminologists asserted, resulted directly from the socioeconomic conditions and moral depravity of capitalism and continued to exist in Soviet society due to the slow pace of socialist construction. These observers pointed specifically to unemployment as the chief socioeconomic factor causing prostitution,[114] but emphasized that only the establishment of socialist principles would curtail the profession. Criminologist and law professor P. I. Liublinskii argued:

> Correct sexual education, the protection of women and the creation of free employment for [women], free marriage, the understanding of the individual value of every person—all this should bring about the extinction of prostitution in all its disgraceful forms, as it existed in the epoch of capitalism and as it is still partially preserved. . . . It is necessary to approach prostitution not with the slogan of complete freedom from it, but with measures of social politics directed toward the removal of all that enables prostitution and toward an understanding of the responsibility of the individual engaging in prostitution and of the dangerousness that [s]he brings to society.[115]

This dangerousness was located specifically in the nonproductivity of the prostitute as well as in her sexuality and criminality. As another observer agreed: "Prostitution, as a profession, is . . . without a doubt a crime, as this profession, not creating or contributing any real economic benefit, has no social value. . . . Such a profession is a crime against [Bolshevik] ideals and the entire social system and as such, like crime, prostitution under Soviet power cannot not be punished."[116] For these observers, prostitution was not solely a vice, but also provided clear evidence for the persistence of capitalist remnants and the presence of class enemies within NEP society.

Although criminologists understood that the NEP and the continued existence of the old way of life created the conditions that drew women into prostitution, they also emphasized that such women were victims of their circumstances and deserving of sympathy, not punishment. As criminologist A. A. Zhizhilenko noted, "Prostitution appears as an immoral trade, but the prostitute is not liable for punishment just for engaging in this trade."[117] Sociologist L. M. Vasilevskii agreed, explaining that "our law does not punish [the prostitute] because it would be extremely unjust to punish her for engaging in depravity while the man who buys her remains unpunished."[118] Instead, Soviet law called for the prosecution of those who exploited the helpless position of women by facilitating prostitution. Specifically, enforcement efforts focused on the brothel keeper who, criminologists argued, sought to gain financially from the exploitation of others. As one jurist pointed out, "The law, considering prostitution a serious social evil, forgoes the struggle against it through the application of measures of repression against those persons engaging in prostitution. All persons who, out of selfish interest, facilitate prostitution are subjected to all the severity of legal repression for the crime."[119] Thus, in the NEP environment the brothel keeper became the "capitalist" exploiter, the enemy of socialism, the cause of the continued persistence of old patterns of behavior, and the source of social depravity, and the brothel keeper bore the brunt of legal repression for prostitution.[120] This served to remove responsibility for prostitution from both the women who engaged in it and the men who purchased their services.

At the same time that criminologists removed blame and criminal responsibility from prostitutes themselves, they found fault with women's behavior as prostitutes. Vasilevskii noted, for instance, that the prostitute was a social parasite and a dangerous element.[121] Prostitution, criminologists asserted, brought a woman into close contact with criminal elements and initiated her into a life of depravity. Zhizhilenko, noting that "[p]rostitution was from its origins an outlet for the depravity of women," argued:

> [Prostitution] dulls a woman's moral feelings and leads her slowly toward mental degeneration. . . . The dangerous closeness of the profession of prostitution to the profession of theft undoubtedly makes prostitutes concealers of others' crimes, and together with that often accomplices to them as well.

> Finally, one mustn't forget that the very nature of prostitution creates an
> easy path to property crime, particularly to theft.[122]

For Zhizhilenko and others, a very fine line existed between the prostitute
as a victim of circumstances and as a criminal deserving of social repression. As one criminologist emphasized, "There is no profession darker
and more socially dangerous than selling the female body."[123]

The relationship among the prostitute, the criminal, and sexuality
becomes particularly evident in criminologists' discussions of hooliganism. Hooliganism as a phenomenon drew the attention and concern
of criminologists, particularly during the later years of the NEP. In part
this derived from concerns regarding male public behavior, especially in
the wake of the 1926 Chubarov Alley case, in which a large group of
drunken workers gang-raped a young woman right off a main street in
Leningrad.[124] For the social observers, this high-profile case in particular
illuminated both the degeneracy of the NEP and the continued persistence of the old way of life within Soviet society. As psychiatrist L. G.
Orshanskii noted, clearly "contemporary man is far from the high ideals
of the revolution."[125]

In contrast to male hooliganism, however, female hooliganism itself
barely raised the eyebrows of the criminologists. In fact, criminologists
Rapoport and Kharlamova, in one of the few studies that addressed female
hooliganism, stressed the complete lack of social danger female hooligans
posed, noting that most women who disturbed the public order did not
act like male hooligans—in an organized manner under the influence of
alcohol. Rather, women's "hooliganism" manifested itself through insults
and fights connected with domestic disputes, jealousy, revenge, avoiding
arrest, hysteria, and so on. Female hooliganism was directly linked with
women's traditional social position in the domestic sphere and thus was
less threatening to the social order than male hooliganism, causing concern only when private conflicts spilled over into public spaces. Rapoport
and Kharlamova went further, however, by equating female hooliganism
with prostitution. Of the seventy-five female hooligans examined in their
study, the authors found that twenty, or 26.7 percent, were prostitutes,
by far the most represented "profession."[126] Moreover, the authors argued
that for the most part only women already involved in the criminal world
engaged in hooliganism, and that this criminal element made up a more
significant segment among female hooligans than among male offenders.
According to their statistics, 26.7 percent of female hooligans had previous
convictions for hooliganism, 22.7 percent had records for hooliganism

and other crimes, 12 percent had committed other crimes only, and 38.7 percent had no prior convictions.[127] Compared to statistics for male hooliganism, women were more likely to have prior arrests and convictions, both for hooliganism and for other crimes, than men. While Rapoport and Kharlamova presented male hooliganism as a temporary behavioral problem associated with alcohol consumption, they saw female hooliganism as a lifestyle choice intimately connected to prostitution. Female hooligans, they argued, tended to maintain connections to the criminal world.[128] From this perspective, hooliganism became the expected behavior for prostitutes, a result of the "constant and unavoidable companions of their unfortunate lives, of vodka, cocaine, swearing, scandals, [and] fights." "Prostitutes," Rapoport and Kharlamova concluded, "cannot conduct themselves in a civilized manner."[129] For these criminologists, prostitution and criminality remained inseparable, and prostitution naturally, logically, and inevitably led women to criminal behavior.

The relationships among female hooliganism, crime, and prostitution linked socioeconomic explanations of female deviance directly to women's sexuality. They provided stark evidence that elements of the "old way of life" persisted in NEP society, but also suggested that women themselves remained unwilling and unable to embrace the new social order. For criminologists, women's deviance revealed and reflected the traditional position of women, centered in the domestic sphere and shaped by female sexuality. Mary Louise Roberts, in her study of gender in interwar France, argues that observers made sense of their anxieties regarding the "modern woman" by emphasizing the traditional female characteristics of domesticity and motherhood in the new postwar context.[130] As Soviet criminologists attempted to interpret and understand the radical changes that accompanied the revolution, they also drew on models of women's traditional roles to assuage anxieties about female sexuality and NEP policies. The Bolshevik emancipation (theoretically) created new and exciting possibilities for women to engage in society. By emphasizing the connections between prostitution and criminality, however, criminologists argued that female deviance remained sexual and oriented around the domestic sphere. Focused on the "traditional" nature of female criminal and sexual deviance, criminologists' interpretations of female crime and prostitution served to dispel the anxieties that accompanied women's emancipation, suggesting that women remained "backward," tied to the hearth, at the mercy of their sexuality, and thus incapable of participating on an equal basis in the new socialist society.

Even as female deviance outlined the limits of women's roles in Soviet society, the NEP itself contributed to criminologists' understanding of prostitution and female crime not as social problems for which solutions must be devised but as by-products of an incomplete revolution, as left-over remnants of the old way of life that had not yet disappeared. Anxiety regarding the NEP, the successful construction of socialism, and the persisting remnants of bourgeois capitalism made the link between prostitution and crime much more insidious, disruptive, and threatening to the social order. Prostitution and crime provided measures of the distance that Soviet society remained from the ideals of the revolution, and called into question the very success or potential of success of the socialist experiment. By uniting both unregulated female sexuality and anti-socialist market forces, prostitution embodied the anxieties and fears that Soviet professionals expressed regarding the future of the socialist society.

CONCLUSION

In reviewing the literature on female criminality in the West, Dorie Klein concludes that "biological explanations have *always* been prevalent; every writer has made assumptions about anatomy as destiny."[131] For Russian and Soviet criminologists, the perception that female physiology played a central role in women's crime shaped their understanding of the position of women in Russian society. Indeed, the victim/villain duality that social observers identified in the NEP-era prostitute reflected their broader interpretations of female crime. For them, women's sexuality both removed responsibility from women for their actions but also inherently influenced their behavior and reactions to external events. Women were, in terms of their criminality, victims of their social position and the precociousness of their sexuality. Yet, criminologists found that the same physiology that was supposed to embody the morality of women and keep them from committing crimes actually helped facilitate their entry into the criminal world and made it more difficult for them to abandon it.

Despite attributing a positive meaning to increases in female crime rates—as a result of increased engagement with the "struggle for existence"—criminologists failed to find any significant change in the nature of female deviance. In their discussions, professionals implied that the "struggle for existence" had the potential to erase the distinctions between men and women, at least in terms of their deviance. Indeed, these professionals fully expected that socialism would someday eradicate the "old way of life," suggesting that the socioeconomic could triumph over the biological. Yet they found women uniquely unprepared to engage in that struggle. Furthermore, NEP anxieties regarding sexuality and the fate of the revolution attracted observers to physiological explanations of female crime, and their commitment to the analysis of the individual criminal personality reinforced it. Throughout the 1920s, criminologists adhered to the idea of female crime as oriented around the domestic sphere and defined by female physiology. Even when women did break out of the traditional mold, specialists still explained the actions of women as deriving from their sexuality. In this way, criminologists essentialized women's experiences, taking the social position of a woman as a natural phenomenon directly linked to her reproductive functions. This reinforced the preconceived ideas of criminologists regarding the position of women and the nature of female crime, and limited their understanding of the Bolshevik Revolution's full impact on women's lives. For criminologists, war and revolution may have altered women's relationship with crime, but emancipation did not necessarily lead to increased or diversified female criminal activity.

THE GEOGRAPHY

OF CRIME

City, Countryside,

and Trends in CHAPTER FOUR

Female Criminality

In his introduction to the 1924 volume *Prestupnyi mir Moskvy* (*The Criminal World of Moscow*), leading criminologist and law professor M. N. Gernet vividly called to mind the characteristics of the urban atmosphere that encouraged criminality:

> Here specifically, on the expanse of noisy streets, bustling squares, multi-storied buildings, crowded theaters, movie houses, race tracks, and restaurants, . . . [crime] reveals its multifaceted forms. . . . Streets bursting with people, customers cramming stores, theaters, tram stops, omnibuses, ships, underpasses, and train cars; all this creates favorable conditions for pickpocketers. The growth of large cities as commercial centers, with their labor exchanges, colossal stores, constant street trade, and assorted markets, encourages an atmosphere of speculation that promotes fraud. . . . Containing numerous administrative organizations with many thousands of employees, large cities become places for increased corruption. Finally, they also foster the growth of sexual crimes: masses of transient elements, overcrowded apartments of the poor, open and hidden prostitution, the satiation of all types of vice and dissolute living—all this inevitably increases sexual crimes in the modern-day Babylon, Sodom, and Gomorrah.[1]

Criminologists of the 1920s saw urban crime as a troubling phenomenon linked to the rapid urbanization that began in the late Imperial period and brought growing numbers of people to the cities in search of work. The anonymity and atmosphere of large cities facilitated the commission of crimes and made solving them more complicated. One observer noted that cities, as the "main breeding grounds of crime, possess a particular magnetic power for criminals: in cities it is easier for them to hide and get rid of their loot, easier to find accomplices for theft, robbery, and fraud."[2] With urban crime rates more than two and a half times greater than rural rates, criminologists' concerns about the criminal nature of cities seemed well founded. At the same time, specialists noticed that certain crimes occurred more frequently in the cities, giving such offenses an "urban" nature. The specific types of crimes criminologists identified as "urban"—fraud, forgery, and embezzlement, among others—appeared to these observers as more professional, more specialized, more skilled, and less violent, and this reflected their belief in the progressiveness and higher "cultural level" of Soviet cities. Rural crimes, in contrast, remained violent and fueled by emotion, connected to the "primitive" impulses in human nature, and encouraged by what the criminologists saw as the "backwardness and ignorance" of the peasantry.

This urban/rural dichotomy was particularly true in considerations of female crime. Here, criminologists identified a divide between urban and rural, linking female crime directly to the peasantry and the countryside. They observed that typically "female" crimes—infanticide, spouse murder, domestic theft, and *samogon* (homebrew) production, for instance—generally embodied the nature of "rural" criminality, where crime was an outcome of the peasantry's "primitive" impulses fed by outdated traditions. Even when women committed crimes in urban areas, criminologists highlighted the rural character of women's actions. By equating "female" with "rural" and "peasant," criminologists replicated the hierarchical class and gender divisions of Soviet society, emphasizing that women remained inherently backward and ignorant, influenced by the old way of life, and insufficiently prepared to take on the obligations and responsibilities of Soviet citizenship.

This chapter employs the concept of the "geography of crime" to explore criminologists' understanding of female crime in the 1920s as "rural" and "primitive." Since the emergence of criminological study in the early nineteenth century, criminologists and social observers worldwide have relied on urban and rural differences to explain crime rates. In recent years, geographers and criminologists have used the "geography of crime" as a way to explore crime in its spatial context, discussing variations in criminality according to place as well as to how place changes the focus of law enforcement.[3] In the Soviet case, for example, criminologist Louise Shelley has examined the impact of the passport registration system on the geographical distribution of crime in the Soviet Union after World War II, arguing that limits on migration to major urban centers altered the dynamics of Soviet crime by forcing it into newly established peripheral cities.[4] This sort of analysis looks at social factors to explain changes in crime rates in different parts of the country and the underlying social or policy shifts that affected where crimes were committed.

Approaching the 1920s studies of female crime from a spatial perspective provides an analytical framework for tracing criminologists' categorizations of criminal activity. Here, geography and gender played a role in the processes of negotiating identity and citizenship, because the nature of crimes committed reflected the class consciousness of offenders and defined their social class.[5] Because of the way criminologists understood modernization and progress, where a crime was committed physically was often less important than its conceptual categorization as "urban" or "rural." In this context, social class and gender became markers of urban and rural, and thus of progress and backwardness. By "ruralizing" female deviance, criminologists marked geographical differences and the identity of offenders not by physical location but according to behavior. At the same time, criminal behavior indicated social class and class consciousness. Thus, female crime was rural, "rural" criminals were backward, and "backward" criminals were not aware of their rights and duties as Soviet citizens. In this way, the geography of female crime suggests a complex and shifting relationship between class and gender, reflecting the influences both of socialist ideology and traditional notions of female crime in criminologists' underlying assumptions about the position of women, the "modernity" of the city, and the progress of socialism during the transitional period.

The following discussion outlines criminologists' views of the differences between urban and rural crime and the place of women within this geography. Exploring the impact of urbanization and "modernization" on views of female crime, the chapter suggests that criminologists retained their perceptions of women's backwardness and "ruralness" despite what they saw as the potentially progressive influence of the city. It focuses on how criminologists' conception of urban and rural crime differences contributed to the ascription of class and the nature of punishment. In addition, it discusses the importance criminologists placed on education and enlightenment for eliminating crime, particularly among peasant women, and how this reveals the tensions between the perceived inherent backwardness of rural women and the potentially modernizing and progressive impact of the Bolshevik Revolution. Finally, using the example of the anti-samogon (homebrew) campaign during the NEP, the chapter illustrates how the intersection of place, class, and sex preserved criminologists' images of women as rural, backward, ignorant, and primitive.

THE URBAN/RURAL DIVIDE

The classification of crimes as "urban" or "rural" shaped criminologists' perceptions of the nature of the city and the countryside. While criminologists saw the city as a "breeding ground" for crime, full of vice, deception, and danger, they also understood it as a bastion of modernity and progress. The countryside, in contrast, remained pure and untainted by the realities of modern life. This meant that compared to the more "advanced" crimes of the cities involving deception and skill, crimes committed in the countryside reflected a more "primitive" and simplistic quality based on the primacy of peasants' emotional reactions. In many ways, criminologists of the 1920s retained from their prerevolutionary intelligentsia heritage a romanticized view of the countryside and the peasantry. Nineteenth-century Russian elites saw the peasants as pure and simple, while at the same time finding them primitive, ignorant, and prone to violence.[6] After the revolution, such views continued to shape professionals' understanding of deviance. For criminologists, crime in Soviet Russia preserved its distinctly "rural" nature, stemming from the fact that 85 percent of the population lived in the countryside.[7] Criminologists often focused on the question of rural crime, and this was reflected in their discussions of female criminality: women embodied the ignorance of the countryside and the peasantry in the types of crimes they committed, despite the social changes that criminologists believed should have encouraged women to expand their criminal repertoire.

In absolute numbers, three-fourths of all crimes committed in the Soviet Union in 1924 occurred in rural areas.[8] Crime rates, however, remained higher in the cities. A small sample analyzed by statistician E. N. Tarnovskii revealed that while 69 percent of crimes occurred in rural areas and only 31 percent in urban centers, the smaller proportion of city residents (given as 15.4 percent of the total population in March 1924) made urban crime rates more than twice as high compared to rural rates

TABLE 6—Comparison of Urban and Rural Crime Rates
for Men and Women, 1922–1924

	1 9 2 2		*1 9 2 3*		*1 9 2 4*	
	Male	*Female*	*Male*	*Female*	*Male*	*Female*
Urban	16.5	33.4	28.8	41.4	20.9	34.1
Rural	82.0	64.8	67.1	54.9	77.7	64.9
Unknown	1.5	1.8	4.1	3.7	1.4	1.0

Source: G. Manns, "Derevenskie ubiistva i ubiitsy," *Problemy prestupnosti*, no. 2 (1927): 27; M. N. Gernet and D. P. Rodin, "Statistika osuzhdennykh v 1922 g. i statistika samoubiistv v 1922–23 gg.," *Biulleten' Tsentral'nogo Statisticheskogo Upravleniia*, no. 84 (1924): 117; M. N. Gernet, "Statistika gorodskoi i sel'skoi prestupnosti," *Problemy prestupnosti*, no. 2 (1927): 18.

of crime.[9] Female crime rates paralleled these overall levels, with 34.1 percent of the crimes committed by women occurring in the cities and 64.9 percent in the countryside (see Table 6).[10]

Higher urban crime rates, criminologists argued, resulted from the nature of the city and its anonymity, whereas people were more likely to know their neighbors in the countryside. "Naturally," Gernet noted, "crime in the cities is still higher than the figures show us, since the conditions of urban life and especially of large cities make it even easier for the criminal to remain hidden."[11] Urban criminals were "able to conceal themselves more easily, destroying the traces of their crime and so on, than the inexperienced rural novices of the criminal world."[12] In contrast, Gernet emphasized, in the villages "crime becomes an event that draws the community's attention. Here a murderer does not have sufficient concealed places to wipe the blood from his hands. The thief cannot find a reliable market for his stolen goods, making it difficult for him to take full advantage of the fruits of his crime."[13] In Gernet's view, not only could crimes be committed more easily and with less chance of detection in the cities, but urban criminals had greater levels of sophistication than rural ones, suggesting the progressive nature of the cities compared to the countryside.

The criminologists also found that specific types of crimes occurred more readily in urban areas. They characterized cities as centers of theft, deception, and speculation, and the countryside as a place of violence. As criminologist G. Manns emphasized, "If crime in cities is characterized by the predominance of fraud, theft (except horse theft) and offenses against state authority, then *inflicting bodily injury, murder (particularly infanticide), and arson are more common in the countryside.*"[14] Gernet reiterated the countryside's violent nature: "the city abounds in crimes against property, while the countryside is rich in crimes against the person. In the city, the hand of the criminal, hidden and unseen, uses various methods to remove the property of another. In the countryside, it most often openly deprives another of life."[15] Indeed, figures from the years 1924–1925 indicated that while nearly 50 percent of urban crimes consisted of theft (excluding horse theft), fraud, forgery, and embezzlement, such crimes made up only 25 to 30 percent of rural crimes. In contrast, abuse of authority, distillation and sale of samogon, murder, serious bodily injury, banditry, robbery, horse theft, arson, and extortion made up more than 40 percent of all crimes committed in the countryside but only 20 percent of urban crimes.[16]

In their analyses, criminologists found that urban crime tended to pose a danger to society (*sotsial'no-opasnyi*) while rural crime was more dangerous to the individual (*lichno-opasnyi*).[17] For the Bolsheviks, activities posing a "danger to society" encompassed all behavior that threatened the economic and political well-being of the Soviet state. This included, among other things, counterrevolution, speculation, abuse of authority, misuse of natural resources, and recidivism. In many instances, however, intent became the central factor in determining an individual's potential threat: a person had to possess some awareness of the dangerous nature of his or her offense. Thus, for example, repeat offenders posed a greater danger to society for persisting in their anti-social behavior, and because of their refusal to reform, recidivists often received more severe punishments for subsequent offenses.

A central difference in the nature of urban and rural crime was located in an offender's level of consciousness, or her awareness of the "danger" her act posed for Soviet social stability. The criminologists argued that the "ignorance [*temnota*] and backwardness [*otstalost'*] of the countryside . . . or remnants of the old way of life [*byt*]" led to higher rates of violent crime in rural areas.[18] They emphasized that the backwardness and lack of culture of rural residents, and their adherence to past traditions, made them more willing to turn to violence in response to their problems, unlike city residents who had "long ago abandoned the primitive impulses in their nature."[19] As statistician D. P. Rodin stressed, "If urban crime is directed against property and can be explained by . . . socioeconomic conditions, [then] rural crime is directed against the person and can be explained by the coarseness and ignorance of the countryside."[20] Gernet added that "murder is more likely a rural crime than an urban one and is centered in the unequal balance of force with the degree of cultural development."[21] As the peasantry came to embrace the new Soviet way of life, criminologists emphasized, they would turn away from the use of force. Violence would therefore remain the norm in the villages and the countryside until the peasantry's cultural level reached that of the city.

Crimes that criminologists characterized as typically rural also carried less danger to society, since their perpetrators were backward, ignorant, and lacked the capacity to understand the inappropriateness of their actions, and their actions were directed more often at individuals. For instance, Leningrad psychologist L. G. Orshanskii argued, "The rural murderer, far removed from modernity and often childishly cruel and simple, rarely contains the characteristics of actual social dangerousness. . . . [The] rural murderer usually has not yet engaged with modern cultural life. The urban murderer is already out-dated or is a rapidly dying-out breed."[22] Even the means to commit crimes remained more "primitive" in the countryside, as Manns pointed out: "If in the city the instrument of murder is usually a revolver or dagger, in the countryside above all it is the ax, that is, an object that is always within reach in the peasant household. After the ax, the most common instruments of rural murder are logs, bricks and heavy stones, stakes from a fence, and knives."[23] By emphasizing the "primitiveness" of rural criminals, the criminologists highlighted the criminals' distance from modernity, drawing a sharp line between the city and the countryside. Differences in urban and rural crime showed criminologists that the countryside remained mired in the past while the city was more modern and advanced. In this way, urban and rural criminality were defined as much by the nature and method of the crimes as by the geographical location in which they were committed.

URBANIZATION, MODERNIZATION, AND CRIME

Rapid urbanization came together with industrialization throughout Europe in the late nineteenth and early twentieth centuries, and the growing working-class populations of cities raised concerns about increased urban criminality. This trend both troubled and fascinated European social observers, who often linked rising crime rates to the expansion of the working class.[24] These observers found compelling the "modernization" theory of criminality, which posits that as a society progresses, presumably through industrialization and its accompanying urbanization, property crimes tend to increase while violent crimes decrease. Recent research on the links between crime rates and urbanization has found that this is not necessarily the case. Eric Johnson and David Cohen, for example, argue that urban growth and population growth themselves do not cause crime, except by contributing indirectly to the spread of other socioeconomic factors, such as poverty and unemployment, that relate more directly to crime.[25] While it is important to understand the impact urbanization had on crime rates and criminality, the perceptions of social observers just as effectively reveal the ways in which they understood their world and the process of modernization. From this perspective, the differences between urban and rural crime take on an important meaning, helping to define and track the rates of urbanization and, consequently, modernization and revolutionary success.

Historians of urbanization in Russia have highlighted the fluidity of movement between the countryside and the city. Most urban migrants retained close ties with their native villages, and this slowed the process of assimilation and the creation of an urban identity for new residents.[26] Additionally, many peasants came to the cities looking for temporary work, returning periodically to their families in the countryside to help with the harvest and perform other agricultural tasks. More to the point, urban migrants often could not find stable employment and lived in unsanitary, overcrowded rooms, conditions that fostered among observers such as Gernet a sense of the city as a "breeding ground" for criminality. The fluidity of the borders between urban and rural complicated discussions of criminality, contributing to the categorization of crime by social class and sex as well as by place. For criminologists, crime contained certain characteristics that defined it as "rural" or "urban," regardless of where and by whom it was committed.

The differences between urban and rural crime also became a measure of the process of modernization and the progress toward socialism in Soviet Russia. According to Bolshevik ideology, crime would wither away and disappear with the achievement of socialism. Trends in criminality thus reflected the extent to which the party had succeeded in creating a socialist system and the degree to which the population had accepted the new socialist values.[27] Criminologists found that the modernization theories of their western colleagues complemented their own sense of social progress and integrated easily with Bolshevik ideology. They argued that cities, as centers of revolutionary consciousness, were naturally more progressive than the countryside, and crime there would likewise be more "modern" and more "advanced." As cities grew and their populations became more "conscious," their criminality would move away from typical "rural" crimes and come to embody a more "urban" character.

Indeed, statistician M. Zamengof recognized this trend even before the revolution, noting: "The larger the city, the fewer cases of murder and bodily injury. Increasing criminality of an urban character, the growth of cities in and of itself decreases crimes of a rural nature—serious forms of crimes against the person."[28]

Criminologists stressed that urban residents engaged in a "struggle for existence" that rural dwellers did not, and they argued that this struggle contributed to the higher levels of crime in cities. As Manns noted, the atmosphere of the city created temptations "for unstable and weak-willed people, drawing them along the path of crime first through various property crimes (theft, fraud), with which they figure to obtain the necessary means for survival."[29] Low salaries, high unemployment, overcrowded and inadequate housing, and periodic food shortages all contributed to higher rates of urban crime. In contrast, rural residents could take advantage of the countryside's natural resources and had less cause to commit such offenses. As one observer noted, in the countryside, "where every resident's daily needs are satisfied, where almost every peasant has his own hut, his garden plot, and piece of land, there, naturally, the conditions of the struggle for existence do not stand in such sharp relief as in the city."[30] In the perhaps overly idealistic view of criminologists, rural life was simpler and more straightforward than urban life, and this made it more "primitive." Even if the urban atmosphere encouraged greater criminality, the nature of crime in the cities, that is, its more direct relationship to economic life, made it more "progressive" than rural crime.

Criminologists situated the urban/rural divide within a public/private dichotomy when discussing female crime. For them, women's traditional sphere of influence was in the family where "the homemaker, wife, and mother frequently found herself as if chained to hearth and cradle."[31] Naturally, she would react more intensely to family problems, venting her anger and frustration within the limits of her reach. Statistics seemed to support this, indicating that before World War I women committed only 3.4 percent of all murders, but 27.9 percent of the murders of spouses and relatives.[32] As previously noted, criminologists found that women's seclusion within the family minimized their rates of crime and limited the types of offenses women committed. The old patriarchal traditions that gave a husband complete control over his wife further restricted a woman's interaction in public life and thus limited her range of criminal activity.[33] In the nature of their deviance, therefore, women remained isolated in the private sphere, and thus "rural" in their criminality.

With the revolution, criminologists expected the variety of crimes women committed to expand as they engaged more with the public sphere and the "struggle for existence."[34] Indeed, criminologists attributed a brief rise in urban female crime rates during the war to this phenomenon as women entered the workforce to replace men sent to the front.[35] Women, Gernet wrote, took on all sorts of new roles in society during the war, including policing the streets, driving trams, and fighting fires. These new jobs "created new possibilities for violating the law."[36] Criminologists argued that the more women appeared in the urban labor market and the public sphere, the more they would be "compelled to clash with the law."[37] Crime statistics reflected this dynamic: in 1922, 33.4 percent of convicted women in the RSFSR committed their crimes in urban areas, rising to 41.4 percent by 1923.[38] Increasing rates of female urban crime thus suggested that women's participation in the "struggle for existence" would make female deviance more "urban" and more modern.

Although they expected female crime to take on a "progressive" nature in the cities, criminologists' statistics nevertheless confirmed that female crime retained its "rural" and domestic character. As one criminologist noted, "the basic sphere of criminal activity of the modern Russian woman, as much as she is still removed from broad social activity, are such crimes that are closely connected with life in the narrow family circle: [brewing] samogon, crimes against the person (fights, arguments, and so on), arson, and socially dangerous destruction of property out of jealousy."[39] These "female" crimes were defined by their primitive "rural" qualities, shaped by violence, emotion, and lack of skill. By 1928, more than ten years after the revolution had eliminated legal inequality between the sexes, criminologists still found that women lagged behind men in their criminality; as penologist B. S. Utevskii bluntly stated: "To this day, women are frequently housewives who do not participate significantly in the struggle for existence, who do not stand as equals with men in economic or public life."[40] Women continued to commit typically "female" and "rural" crimes, stubbornly retaining their backwardness in the face of progress. Although they expected women's emancipation to alter female criminality and make it more "modern" and "urban," criminologists focused their attention almost exclusively on the primitive, "rural" nature of female crime. Thus, in terms of female crime, the emancipation of women that came with the revolution ultimately failed to "urbanize" and consequently "modernize" women's deviance.

Criminologists' conception of female crime as "rural" and thus women as backward denied the very influence of women's "struggle for existence" in the cities. But women did engage in the "struggle for existence," even though female crime did not seem to take on the new forms the professionals expected. The prevalence of "traditional" crimes of the domestic sphere might suggest that the revolution and the NEP did not in fact significantly increase opportunities for women to interact with men as equals in the public sphere. Or it may reflect an unwillingness on the part of specialists to look beyond their established notions of the nature of female deviance. Regardless, by seeing the lack of diversification in female criminality not as a failure of emancipatory equality but as evidence of the continued backwardness and primitiveness of women, criminologists linked female urban crime directly to "rural" criminality and reinforced the image of women as ignorant, isolated from public life, attached to the domestic sphere, and disengaged from modern Soviet society.

Specialists' adherence to this view of the female criminal reinforced the social hierarchies between urban and rural, man and woman, and worker and peasant. Although criminologists viewed the process of women becoming more "urban" in their criminality as a positive measure of socialist advancement, their continued reliance on the image of the "rural" female criminal suggests some anxiety over the more public roles that women could play in Soviet society, as well as the limited ability women actually had, because of the nature of life in the transitional period, to take advantage of their new opportunities. By emphasizing that female crimes were "rural" crimes, criminologists shifted the focus of their explanations away from concrete socioeconomic factors and toward an abstract and timeless concept of female crime that obscured the realities women faced in the years after the revolution.

ASCRIBING CRIME

Historian Sheila Fitzpatrick has argued that the Bolsheviks created a "virtual class society," a statistically imagined division of society into class categories in which membership was ascribed according to social background. At least during the NEP and until the reintroduction of internal passports in 1932, the boundaries and assignment of these categories remained fluid and mutable, based by varying degrees on parents' social background, former (prerevolutionary) activities, and current occupation.[41] The geographic labeling of criminal behavior by specialists was part of this process of class creation. In this conception of a "virtual class society," "urban" and "rural" became categories for ascribing class and determining appropriate punishments for offenders. Identifying specific types of crimes as "urban" or "rural" implied that certain people would commit such crimes. Peasants, for instance, engaged in "rural" criminal activity, so "rural" crimes were committed by "peasants." Furthermore, the type of crime committed reflected an offender's level of "consciousness," setting out his or her position in the class hierarchy. Again, "rural" crimes reflected less "consciousness" than "urban" crimes. In this way, criminologists helped to shape a definition of class that was not based purely on social and economic categories but rather was determined by behavior, political identity, and state priorities.

One area where behavior determined class was in the arrest and prosecution of women for crimes against state authority (*prestuplenie protiv poriadka upravleniia*). This category encompassed all offenses that threatened the Bolsheviks' socialist vision but did not warrant the death penalty, including public disruptions, anti-Soviet agitation, failure to pay taxes, forgery, counterfeiting, avoiding military service, hooliganism, misuse of natural resources, vigilantism, failure to cooperate with the police, speculating in apartment sales, and preparation and sale of liquor and drugs, among others.[42] Offenses considered crimes against state authority involved specifically anti-Soviet behavior rather than antisocial behavior.

According to official criminal statistics for 1923 and 1924, women committed more crimes against state authority than any other type of criminal offense.[43] Within this category, the nature of female crime remained predominantly rural: that is, criminologists found that women committed more crimes in the countryside, and even when such crimes occurred in the cities, they were committed more often by women from nonproletarian backgrounds. Moreover, criminologists emphasized that the crimes women did commit retained a rural quality, generally involving an emotional response and requiring a low level of skill to carry out. For example, in 1923, nearly one-fourth of all women arrested for nonpayment of taxes in urban areas were peasants, as were over 80 percent in rural areas. Similarly, although only about half of the women sentenced for contempt of authorities (*oskorblenie vlasti*) resided in the countryside, four-fifths of those arrested were peasants. In contrast, other than their minimal involvement in producing and selling samogon, urban female factory workers committed relatively few crimes against state authority.[44]

These urban/rural dynamics highlight the class-based nature of crime and punishment in the early Soviet Union. The police and the courts expressed greater interest in pursuing people of certain (undesirable) social backgrounds for anti-Soviet behavior, and were more likely to find such people committing these offenses than the more "conscious" proletariat (who happened to be less numerous as well). Moreover, the large proportion of women involved in anti-Soviet crimes reflected a sense among legal professionals that women, particularly peasant women, resisted the changes brought about by the Bolshevik Revolution.

The very act of committing certain crimes revealed an offender's social background. Rural crimes, for instance, could only be committed by peasants. In this way, social background and place of residence (and sex for female criminals) intersected as criminal behavior became a means to define class identity. The sentencing of criminals reflected this process of class ascription. Place and gender played central roles in determining the severity of punishment an offender received from the courts. Peasants, and peasant women in particular, frequently received more lenient sentences because they were seen as less "conscious" and therefore less responsible for their actions. By making punishment contingent on perceptions of a person's awareness of the harmfulness of an action to Soviet social stability, the courts helped to formulate a sense of class based on behavior: the type of crime committed determined "consciousness," which in turn established class identity. In this way, sentencing practices shaped and reinforced criminologists' conceptions of the differences in and the nature of urban and rural crime.

Differences in urban and rural sentencing statistics also reveal Soviet courts' understanding of women's level of "consciousness" and thus the extent of their criminal responsibility. According to official statistics, in

TABLE 7—Types of Punishments for Men and Women by Location, 1923–1924
(In Percentages)

	1 9 2 3				1 9 2 4			
	URBAN		*RURAL*		*URBAN*		*RURAL*	
	Male	*Female*	*Male*	*Female*	*Male*	*Female*	*Male*	*Female*
Suspended sentence	15.1	21.5	7.1	14.2	19.6	24.0	10.4	17.3
Prison terms	30.9	23.4	15.1	13.3	31.8	20.4	13.3	9.4
Compulsory labor	17.1	19.0	21.7	23.0	11.5	9.9	15.4	10.8
Confiscation of property	22.8	24.6	37.7	34.0	29.4	36.4	52.2	52.8
Other punishments	14.1	11.5	18.4	15.5	7.7	9.3	8.7	9.7

Source: *Statistika osuzhdennykh v SSSR 1923–1924* (Moscow: Izdanie TsSU SSSR, 1927), 32–33, 122–23.

1923 women committed 40.2 percent of their crimes in the cities and 58.4 percent in the countryside. In 1924 this had fallen to 34.1 percent in the cities and 64.9 percent in the countryside.[45] In 1923, 34.6 percent of female offenders were sentenced to terms of imprisonment, decreasing to 32.8 percent for 1924. However, only 17.4 percent in 1923 (over 50 percent of those sentenced) and 13.2 percent in 1924 (only about 40 percent of those sentenced) of all female criminals actually spent time in prison (see Table 7). Most women received suspended sentences—49.6 percent in 1923 and 59.7 percent in 1924. In contrast, suspended sentences made up about 32 percent of punishments for male criminals in 1923, rising to 42 percent in 1924.[46]

Urban women also went to jail more often than rural women. In 1923, 54 percent of women sent to prison lived in the cities and 44.6 percent in the countryside (1.4 percent unknown); by 1924 that number had decreased slightly to 52.6 percent for the cities and 46.4 percent for the countryside (1.0 percent unknown). Prison sentences themselves tended to be short for women, however, and even shorter for rural women. For example, in 1923, 40.3 percent of rural women sentenced to prison served terms of less than six months, compared to 34.6 percent for urban women. Women also received shorter sentences compared to male criminals: for example, only 1.2 percent of urban female criminals spent more than five years in prison, while 4 percent of male criminals served sentences of this length.[47] Thus women received shorter and lighter sentences than men, and peasant women spent less time in jail than their urban counterparts.

TABLE 8—Lengths of Sentences by Gender, 1924 and 1926

(In Percentages)

| | OCT.-DEC. 1924 | | 1926 | |
	Men	*Women*	*Men*	*Women*
Up to 6 months	19.9	26.6	68.9	75.9
6 months to 1 year	21.8	32.7	13.9	13.0
1–2 years	18.6	17.1	8.0	6.2
2–3 years	13.4	11.5	4.1	2.6
3–5 years	13.3	7.3	3.0	1.4
5–10 years	13.0	4.8	2.1	0.9

Source: *Statisticheskii obzor deiatel'nosti mestnykh administrativnykh organov NKVD RSFSR* (Moscow: Izdatel'stvo NKVD, 1925), 55; *Statistika osuzhdennykh v SSSR v 1925, 1926 i 1927 gg.* (Moscow: Izdanie TsSU SSSR, 1930), 55.

As Rodin noted, "suspended prison sentences, reprimands, and other such light types of repression are more often applied to women than men for the very same crimes and places committing them (city, countryside). Just the opposite, men are more often sentenced to capital punishment and strict isolation."[48]

The lighter levels of punishment women, and particularly rural women, received suggest that courts often found women to be less "socially dangerous" and therefore less responsible for their crimes than men. Although the leniency shown to women for the most part resulted from less female involvement in serious crimes, or their role as accomplices in more serious crimes, the trend in the courts to sentence women to shorter prison terms also reflected the notion that the crimes women committed and the offenders themselves presented less of a danger to society than similar actions committed by men.[49] Indeed, penologist V. R. Iakubson noted that one of the reasons women tended to receive shorter prison sentences was the "milder attitude of the courts toward women."[50] In general, this "milder attitude" came from traditional views of women as weaker and less criminal than men; however, a part of it emerged from perceptions that women remained backward and ignorant, unaware of their rights as Soviet citizens, and therefore unable to bear full responsibility for their actions.

Furthermore, Iakubson argued, imprisonment did not have the same reformative effect on women that it did on men, and could even be detrimental to them and the goals of Soviet penal policy. Iakubson found that, because of a stronger connection to their families, incarceration had a harsher impact on women, so that even short prison sentences carried greater severity of repression than for men. While Iakubson believed that this discrepancy would diminish as women became more involved in public life and more equal with men, he emphasized that for now imprisonment for women was a less effective measure for eliminating their criminal activity because of women's "social position, closer connection to the family, [and] less social adaptability to changes in residence."[51]

Soviet courts followed this advice, frequently imposing suspended sentences on female criminals, but they also made use of alternative noncustodial measures of punishment including compulsory labor and confiscation of property. Of all convicted women in 1923, only 17.4 percent actually spent time in prison, about 17 percent received suspended sentences, 21.4 percent had to perform forced labor, and over 30 percent had property confiscated. (For men, 20.5 percent had compulsory labor, 33.7 percent had property confiscated, 19.3 percent spent time in prison,

TABLE 9—Percentages by Gender for Different Punishments, 1926

	Overall	Men	Women
Execution	0.1	0.1	0.005
Suspended Sentence	14.4	12.5	25.5
Imprisonment	39.0	41.7	28.4
Compulsory Labor	13.9	14.4	15.3
Confiscation of Property	—	29.0	27.0
Reprimand	—	1.2	3.1
Others	32.6	1.1	0.7

Source: Statistika osuzhdennykh v SSSR v 1925, 1926 i 1927 (Moscow: Izdanie TsSU SSSR, 1930), 55; A. A. Gertsenzon, "Bor'ba s prestupnost'iu v RSFSR," Sovetskoe pravo, no. 3 (1929): 104.

but only just over 9 percent received suspended sentences.) In 1924, forced labor made up 10.5 percent of the punishments women received, but confiscation of property rose to make up 47 percent (Table 9 gives similar figures for 1926). In the countryside, 52.8 percent of women's punishments involved confiscation of property, while in the city it made up a smaller 36.4 percent.[52] The differences in punishments applied to female criminals in the city and the countryside probably reflected the economic situation of women as much as their social position. Urban women generally had less property to confiscate. The significant disparity in rates of suspended sentences for men and women, however, indicates that female crime required less severe punishment than male crime, and that the courts adhered to the notion that, for women, prison was less effective as a corrective measure than cultural enlightenment efforts.

The high rates of alternative measures of punishment reveal several trends in the early 1920s. First, space in prisons had become extremely scarce. The Bolsheviks inherited the tsarist prison system, and many of the facilities were outdated, in poor condition, and overcrowded. By 1924 the courts had already become interested in alternatives to prison sentences. This found reflection in the lower number of prison sentences handed out, the generally short length of the terms, the growing number of suspended sentences, and the reliance on fines and compulsory labor. Second, the high rates of property confiscation by 1924 reflected a shift in police and court activity to focus on the fight against samogon producers (discussed below). This campaign brought large numbers of people, both men and women, into the courts and prisons, and forced the legal system to turn to alternative measures of "social protection" in the face of an exponentially growing criminal population. Finally, and perhaps more important for the Bolsheviks, court emphasis on alternative punishments put into practice progressive penal theories, which emphasized that imprisonment and repression in and of themselves were insufficient as deterrents to criminal activity, and that education and enlightenment would make more effective weapons in the fight against crime.[53]

The prevalence of suspended and short prison terms, and alternative punishments as the 1920s wore on, was a reflection of the circumstances of the NEP and the limited resources of the Soviet state to make incarceration on a wide scale an effective tool of socialist reeducation.[54] Believing that many criminals acted as a result of the difficult material circumstances in which they found themselves, criminologists recognized that incarceration often only strained the already precarious economic situation of offenders and thus increased the rates of recidivism. While the actual impact of alternative punishments on offenders is difficult to assess, penalties such as property confiscation most likely made life more difficult for peasant offenders, although it did provide an effective way for the state to redistribute wealth (at least away from those it saw as kulaks or bourgeois). The high rates of alternative sentences do reveal, however, that the Bolsheviks understood that reeducation and cultural enlightenment work among the Russian population needed to occur using the courts and the criminal code as a system of deterrents as well as outside the legal system via the educational efforts and agitational work of party cells and cadres throughout the countryside and in the workplace.[55] Soviet socialism would not be built solely on the legitimacy of the law but through party work, the results of which would be secured by the courts and the law according to a class-based understanding of anti-Soviet behavior. This would set a dangerous precedent for later developments.

Two Worlds Collide—Ignorance versus Enlightenment

For criminologists, differences between urban and rural criminality embodied the disparity between the old way of life and the new socialist order. In the nature of urban and rural crime, Gernet observed, "we can see the collision of two worlds, the old and the new."[56] Rural residents, he argued,

> lag significantly behind urban ones in cultural attitudes and development, resulting from the fact that the most varied superstitions continue to thrive in peasants' consciousness and allow disputes with neighbors to become

court sessions resolved by the strength of one's own fist, in contrast with city residents who long ago abandoned the primitive impulses in their nature.

So it has been for hundreds of years. And the new world view that brought our revolution must follow the same uneven road that the peasant travels to the city: here there is no direct route, no straight path.[57]

Just as the peasant did not easily assimilate into the urban environment, the new revolutionary order had difficulty penetrating the countryside. Criminologists emphasized the importance of education and enlightenment that would raise the peasantry's level of consciousness and lead to the elimination of crime. This would be achieved by increasing the peasantry's (and women's) level of literacy and by creating greater awareness of the benefits of the socialist state.

The Bolsheviks made education a priority in their efforts to modernize Russia. Although literacy levels grew throughout the late Imperial period, when the Bolsheviks came to power only about 44 percent of the population was able to read and write.[58] Rising literacy levels, however, may have fostered the development of the atmosphere of revolution. Indeed, as Gregory Guroff and S. Frederick Starr have argued, in the years leading to 1917, literacy was seen as a way to improve one's social position, and the failure of political changes to keep pace with growing literacy levels made some sort of conflict inevitable.[59] The Bolsheviks believed that improving the political literacy of the population was essential to achieving their revolutionary objectives and increasing their base of support throughout the country. In addition to building their mandate, the Bolsheviks pursued a modernizing agenda that sought to remake the Russian mentality according to socialist principles.[60] They believed that when the people understood the benefits of socialism, they would rally behind the revolution and the Bolshevik program. For the Bolsheviks, basic literacy was the first step toward political literacy, and literacy taught through propaganda would indoctrinate peasants and workers while teaching them the skills necessary for their participation in the new system.[61] As penologist Iu. Iu. Bekhterev confirmed, "the industrialization of the country and the intensification of agriculture are unthinkable without a general improvement in the cultural level of the population."[62]

In the pursuit of their goals of social change and reform, criminologists embraced the Bolsheviks' emphasis on literacy, and the struggle against crime necessarily paralleled and drew upon elements of the campaign against illiteracy. The criminologists' objective was not necessarily to garner support for the revolution, however, but to raise the level of "civilization" of criminals. They believed that through enlightenment, the backward traditions that persisted in the countryside, and criminality, would be abandoned in favor of rational socialist ideals.

TABLE 10—Educational Level of Offenders, 1924

(In Percentages)

	URBAN		RURAL	
	Male	*Female*	*Male*	*Female*
Illiterate	8.8	42.3	19.8	64.3
Read only	4.2	2.1	4.0	2.3
Read and Write	82.3	51.6	71.3	28.6
Unknown	4.7	4.0	4.9	4.8

Source: Iu. B., "Prestupnost' goroda i derevni v 1924 g.," *Administrativnyi vestnik*, no. 6 (1925): 27; E. N. Tarnovskii, "Osnovnye cherty sovremennoi prestupnosti," *Administrativnyi vestnik*, no. 11 (1925): 48.

According to criminologists, ignorance remained one of the most significant factors that perpetuated rural criminality, particularly among women. Overall, only about one-fourth of rural women were literate, compared to two-thirds of urban women.[63] More urban criminals were literate than rural criminals, but women generally tended to be less educated than their male counterparts. In 1924, for example, among offenders in urban areas, 42.3 percent of women and 8.8 percent of men were illiterate, while among rural offenders, 64.3 percent of women and 19.8 percent of men were illiterate (see Table 10).[64] Overall, significantly more female criminals were illiterate than male criminals, and rural residents of both sexes tended to be less educated than their urban counterparts. As P. V. Verkhovskii observed, one of the most important factors in the continuation of crime was the "low cultural level" of the countryside. He stressed the need to improve cultural awareness in the villages, particularly among youths, using schools and other such institutions to set a good example of honest work and productive behavior so that young people would not fall into criminal ways.[65]

Criminologists saw increased literacy as a preventative step in their struggle against crime that would slowly bring awareness to the countryside of the benefits of modern Soviet life. One L. Artimenkov argued, for instance, that while the countryside remained enveloped in ignorance, the peasantry had, little by little, begun to follow the new political path. The task for everyone was to extend help to the peasantry under the banner of fighting illiteracy.[66] Psychiatrist A. Shestakova also highlighted the importance of education in eliminating crime and the old mentality in the countryside: "Increasing the cultural level of the peasantry, by encouraging the development of the younger generation and by extinguishing the last remnants of the old way of life through systematic measures of prevention, undoubtedly brings about the decline of [crimes against the person] and ideally leads to its complete disappearance."[67] The "old way of life" and even "rural" crimes would thus disappear as the peasantry became literate.

Likewise, in an analysis of urban and rural crime, Bekhterev emphasized that rural-type crimes persisted as:

> a result of the lower level of culture among the rural population, the villagers' insufficient understanding of the essence of the Soviet state system, its laws, and their responsibilities as citizens of the Soviet state. After all, there, in the blind corners of our state, where the traditions of the past, darkness and ignorance, various superstitions, and other prejudices still reign, where instinct still dominates over reason, favorable conditions naturally exist for the commission of such crimes.[68]

The peasantry's failure to completely embrace the principles of the socialist state thus explained the continued existence of rural crime. As Bekhterev argued, "the basic causes of contemporary crime in the city and countryside are socioeconomic conditions. And only by improving the economic welfare of the masses, liquidating among them general and political illiteracy, and teaching the younger generation in the spirit of the struggle for strengthening and achieving communism will the state be able to eliminate crime."[69] Thus, criminologists firmly believed that only through enlightenment could the ignorance that fed the rural nature of crime among the peasantry be replaced by modern socialist consciousness.

Criminological professionals remained particularly concerned about the education and enlightenment of rural female criminals. For example, among infanticide offenders, a typically "rural" crime with primarily female perpetrators, 88 percent were illiterate in 1917. Although this dropped significantly to roughly 23 percent by 1926, comparatively, only 12.3 percent of offenders for other types of murder were illiterate.[70] For criminologists, despite clear evidence of successes in the literacy campaign, these rates revealed the persistent backwardness of peasant women. Even in 1930, specialists continued to emphasize this problem: the differences between levels of male and female education had deep roots in the past, but as Bekhterev noted, "only in Soviet Russia, where women are equal with men in the social and cultural life of the country, the literacy of women quickly grows, thanks to which the former disproportion between female and male literacy also decreases."[71] He stressed that illiteracy occurred more often among women in the countryside and among those committing crimes against state authority, the person, and property.[72] By highlighting the higher levels of illiteracy among the offenders of these particular categories of crimes, Bekhterev reinforced the perceptions of these crimes, and the people who committed them, as typically "rural." Here illiteracy and ignorance were intrinsically linked with women, the peasantry, and rural-type crimes. The countryside remained trapped in the old way of life, and peasant women retained their traditional position within that world.

Criminologists' emphasis on the education and enlightenment of offenders as measures leading toward the eradication of crime contributed to the aims of the NEP, which sought alternatives and experimentation in the process of remaking the Russian peasantry into Soviet citizens.[73] Consistent with progressive penal policy, educational efforts were pursued throughout the 1920s as an innovative way to reform criminals without long periods of incarceration, and to remake offenders into contributing members of society. These efforts, however, also highlighted the patronizing relationship between Soviet power and peasant women. By emphasizing the links among illiteracy, women, and the countryside, criminologists implied that the ignorance of these offenders prevented them from understanding the nature of their actions. Only through enlightenment, by raising their "cultural level" and their awareness, would peasant women even begin to overcome their backwardness so they could join as equal partners with men in the construction of the Soviet socialist state.

THE ANTI-SAMOGON CAMPAIGN

Within the context of the struggle against crime and the struggle for literacy, the anti-samogon campaign of the NEP provides an interesting example of the intersection of place, sex, and social background, revealing criminologists' conceptions of urban and rural, views of women, and understanding of class. By emphasizing the "rural" nature of samogon offenses—although the campaign focused on the production of samogon and its sale in urban areas—and the significant level of female participation in the crime, criminologists confirmed the overwhelming "rural" nature of female crime itself.

After the revolution, the Bolsheviks sought to control what they saw as excessive alcohol production and consumption in the cities. They eventually reinstated the tsarist government's vodka monopoly, but first they outlawed samogon production and focused considerable police attention on offenders. Beginning in 1922 and continuing through the end of 1926, the Bolsheviks conducted a massive campaign against the illegal production and sale of alcoholic beverages that brought this crime to the forefront of urban crime statistics and criminological analysis.[74] Even *Prestupnyi mir Moskvy*, the 1924 study of criminals in Moscow prisons, included an article on *samogonshchiki* (bootleggers) among its other studies of "urban" crime.[75] Intense police focus on samogon offenses meant that the number of arrests vastly exceeded those for any other crime. Because women were often involved with the production and sale of illegal spirits, the anti-samogon campaign also brought large numbers of women into contact with the police and the criminal justice system. Thus, the ways criminologists dealt with samogon offenses helps to reveal the dynamics of urban and rural crime as well as male and female crime that help explain professionals' attitudes toward women, crime, place, and class.

The Soviet government became interested in curtailing the production of samogon for a variety of reasons in the early years of the NEP. Concerned about the food supply as the country recovered from a severe famine, Soviet leaders worried that too much grain was being turned into alcohol. Indeed, because of low prices and high transportation costs, it was actually more profitable for peasants to sell the finished product than unprocessed grain.[76] In addition, the Bolsheviks distrusted the growing market for spirits, fearing the sale of samogon was contributing to a rise in commercial activity that, while officially tolerated during the NEP, remained anathema to their socialist vision. Nevertheless, they couched their efforts in terms of public health and in late 1922 launched their campaign against the production and sale of samogon, which they saw as having reached "a large scale, inflicting harm on public health and causing pointless squandering and damage of grain and similar food products."[77]

The 1922 RSFSR criminal code categorized offenses involving samogon as economic crimes. Article 140 stated: "The preparation and sale of wine,

vodka, and alcoholic beverages and alcoholic products in general without proper permission or with alcohol content stronger than permitted
by law, and also the illegal storage of such beverages and products, is
punishable by forced labor for up to one year and partial confiscation
of property."[78] Already by September 1922, it was clear to Soviet officials
that the code's provisions against samogon production were having little
effect. The crackdown against those selling samogon had been too lenient,
argued People's Commissar of Justice and RSFSR Prosecutor D. I. Kurskii.
Courts often handed out suspended sentences and small fines without
sufficient cause for such reduced sanctions. Kurskii recommended that
the full force of article 140 be applied against those guilty of producing
samogon and that repeat offenders be considered "socially dangerous," a
qualification that brought increased punishments of up to three years in
exile.[79] In November 1922, not even six months after the implementation
of the criminal code, the fourth session of the eleventh meeting of the
All-Union Central Control Commission (VTsIK) approved an amended
version of article 140 along the lines suggested by Kurskii. The new
version prescribed imprisonment for not less than one year and partial
confiscation of property for samogon crimes, and included a separate section addressing "socially dangerous" repeat offenders.[80]

For the Bolsheviks, the battle against samogon production involved
more than just the confiscation of property and the arrest of samogonshchiki; it was also a fight to establish a new way of life, to abolish the old,
and to improve public health.[81] The Bolsheviks believed that victory could
be achieved only if the struggle proceeded relentlessly. The Commissars
of Justice (Kurskii) and Health (N. A. Semashko) combined forces in this
task, issuing a joint circular in early June 1923 to focus the anti-samogon
campaign primarily "in the *volost* and *uezd* towns where this process
might have an agitational meaning among the peasant population, who
are the most highly involved in samogon preparation." This campaign
would be directed by experts employed by the local health departments,
bringing the fight against samogon production out of the limited arena
of the courtroom and into the broader sphere of public health, although
in cooperation with and supported by the legal system.[82]

By 1923 the anti-samogon campaign was well underway. According
to D. Kniazev, a member of a special committee of the Moscow People's
Court created to hear samogon cases, in the first two months of the committee's existence it heard 1,735 cases and confiscated property worth
193,073 rubles.[83] In 1922 alone, another observer noted, 15,406 people
were found guilty of crimes under article 140, and between 1921 and

1923 arrests for samogon offenses in the RSFSR increased 535 percent.[84] While only 5 percent of cases tried in Moscow's people's courts in 1920 were for samogon offenses, by 1923 they made up nearly 95 percent of all economic crimes.[85] The numbers of people prosecuted for samogon offenses in the early 1920s grew faster than any other criminal offense in the RSFSR. Indeed, criminologist A. Uchevatov's statistics indicated that samogon offenses made up 4.5 percent of all crimes in 1921, rising to 25.2 percent in 1923.[86] Furthermore, 55.7 percent of all crimes investigated by the police in 1923 were crimes against the state authority, and 65 percent of those involved the production and sale of samogon.[87] Between April and June 1924 alone, RSFSR police processed 69,328 cases of samogon offenses, or 47 percent of all crimes registered during that period.[88] This represented a significant dedication of resources to the anti-samogon campaign. Official statistics for 1924 indicated that convictions for samogon offenses made up 40.4 percent of all economic crimes and 29.3 percent of the overall total number of convictions in the Soviet Union.[89] Of course, as Tarnovskii noted, these increases were not necessarily due to a rise in the number of people producing and selling samogon, but to the effective efforts of Soviet power in fighting this crime.[90]

The overwhelming success of the campaign, as evidenced by the large numbers of convicted offenders, led to its reassessment in early 1924 and to a further revision of article 140, possibly in response to the system's inability to process so many offenders. The revision allowed for mitigated punishments of short periods of compulsory labor in cases where the criminal's motive was material need.[91] The state also reestablished its monopoly over alcohol production and sales in late 1925. By making large amounts of cheap vodka readily available, the state dealt a severe blow to the samogonshchiki, basically eliminating the market for home-brew in the cities. These successes led to a further reevaluation of the laws against samogon production and to amendments to the criminal code in early 1927 that removed samogon offenses from criminal prosecution and brought the anti-samogon campaign to an end.[92]

How did criminologists understand the samogonshchiki who poured into the prisons during the anti-samogon campaign? Despite finding that violent crimes occurred more often in the countryside, criminologists classified samogon crimes as "rural," as crimes that did not involve any sort of force or violence yet occurred "primarily in the countryside."[93] That samogon production required little or no skill cemented its connection to typically "rural" crimes. Official statistics confirmed this, indicating that 79.9 percent of samogon cases in 1924 were linked to the countryside.[94]

Furthermore, the high number of peasant samogon offenders prosecuted gave criminal activity in general an overwhelmingly rural character.[95] S. Krylov, discussing the progress of the anti-samogon campaign in 1925, commented that most samogonshchiki were peasants or kulaks who had begun moving their operations from the cities to the countryside, where it was easier to hide their activities.[96] An evaluation of a small sample of rural samogonshchiki led one V. Mokeev to conclude that the peasantry remained rooted in an outdated mind-set that required celebrations to involve drinking. Poor peasants, he argued, made samogon because they wanted to celebrate a wedding or festival but could not afford to buy vodka. Only cultural enlightenment work in the villages and the economic stimulation of the countryside would combat this mind-set where "the ignorance, lack of culture, and general backwardness of our peasantry become indicators of offenses directed against life, health, freedom, and personal dignity."[97]

Criminologists also found that a significant proportion of women engaged in the illegal production of samogon, which further confirmed the "rural" nature of the offense. As Uchevatov observed, the number of women involved in the distillation and sale of spirits increased significantly in the space of just a few years.[98] In 1922, for example, 41.5 percent of all female criminals committed samogon offenses and 26.6 percent of female recidivists returned to prison for this crime, compared to only 18.3 percent for men.[99] In 1923, while 6.3 percent of all criminals were convicted for samogon offenses, nearly 60 percent of all imprisoned women had been sentenced under article 140 but just over 23 percent of men.[100] At the height of the anti-samogon campaign in 1924, about 40 percent of all women sentenced for criminal activities were in jail for samogon crimes, compared to only 15 percent for men.[101] Indeed, the 1926 prison census indicated that women made up 48.3 percent of all samogon offenders, the highest representation of women for any single crime, and 21.5 percent of all female prisoners had been sentenced for samogon-related offenses.[102] The high levels of female participation in this crime contributed to making the illegal production and sale of spirits a typically "female" crime.

According to criminologists, distilling and selling spirits was a relatively easy way for women to make ends meet. The statistics confirmed that "samogon production is an activity committed primarily by women . . . to increase their meager incomes."[103] In the years 1924–1925, 51 percent of housewives sentenced for crimes had committed samogon offenses, and together with property crimes, this made up 84 percent of housewives' crimes.[104] Uchevatov also noted that half of all unemployed women in prison had committed samogon offenses.[105] Furthermore, most samogonshchiki had two or more children to support, and a large percentage were widows. No other crime involved such a high proportion of widows, a result, criminologist B. Zmiev argued, of the war, when many men died at the front.[106] Women were also more frequent repeat offenders of samogon crimes. Data from the 1926 prison census indicated that among repeat offenders, 18.8 percent of men and 31.6 percent of women were sentenced for samogon offenses. Utevskii explained the higher levels of female recidivism for producing samogon because it was "primarily a female crime" that required few skills.[107] Statistician Rodin agreed, noting that samogon offenses characterized female crime and most women involved were first-time offenders who had turned to samogon production as an easy way to make money.[108] Criminologist V. D. Men'shagin went further by stressing that samogon offenses were stepping stones to further criminal activities, particularly brothel keeping and prostitution, other relatively easy ways for women to make money that did not require any special skills or physical strength.[109]

Criminologists also highlighted the differences in the numbers of female samogon offenders in the cities versus the countryside. Although overall levels of samogon offenses remained higher in the countryside, the statistics showed criminologists that women committed fewer samogon crimes in the countryside and more in the cities compared to men.[110] For example, in 1924, 44.5 percent of all women sentenced for crimes in urban areas committed samogon crimes, but only 40.4 percent of rural women, compared to 8.7 percent of urban and 11.5 percent of rural men.[111] In Moscow alone, between 1924 and the first half of 1926, samogon offenses represented 52.2 percent of all cases for crimes against state authority; in Moscow *uezd* the proportion was only 26.7 percent. Women made up nearly 60 percent of samogon offenders in Moscow, but only just over 30 percent in the countryside.[112] Of course, these differences may have resulted from the primarily urban focus of the campaign. Nevertheless, the higher offense rates of this "rural" crime occurring in the cities emphasized for criminologists the continued "primitiveness" of women in urban areas and the difficulties they experienced when forced to engage in the "struggle for existence."

Educational levels reinforced criminologists' interpretations of urban female samogon offenders. A. M. Aronovich, in his analysis of the samogonshchiki for *Prestupnyi mir Moskvy*, found that most samogon offenders from peasant backgrounds were illiterate. While only 33.2 percent of all offenders were illiterate, 55 percent of female samogon offenders had no education, compared to only 9.9 percent of men. Female samogon offenders also had less education overall than women committing other types of crimes.[113] From these figures Aronovich concluded that samogon offenses represented the sort of activity typical of and easily committed by illiterate, ignorant, peasant women.

Perhaps because of the large proportion of "ignorant" women involved in samogon production, criminologists emphasized the general harmlessness of the offense and the need for cultural enlightenment rather than repression to fight the crime. For Aronovich, samogonshchiki, who came mainly from the peasantry, did not constitute "class enemies of the proletarian republic."[114] Rather, these offenders, most of whom were women, suffered from poor preparation for the "struggle for existence. . . . Their weak intellectual development cannot recognize the difference between selling samogon and selling legal goods. They lack any comprehension of the harmfulness of samogon. Their awareness of this extends only to the same level as understanding that smoking is not healthy."[115] Thus the ignorance of women and their lack of preparation for the difficulties of daily life preserved the "rural" character of their offenses.

Women also received lighter sentences for samogon offenses. The low level of "consciousness" of most of the women involved with producing samogon and the day-to-day (*bytovoe*) nature, or domestic character, of the crime led the courts to impose less severe sanctions on these offenders than on those committing other crimes. In early 1925, for example, the most common punishment for samogon crimes in Moscow was partial confiscation of property, followed by suspended sentences and short prison terms.[116] M. Solov'ev, a member of the people's court in the Eniseiskii region, stressed that the 1924 revisions to article 140 prescribing mitigated punishments when the crime was motivated by need allowed the courts to act more in accordance with class principles and to engage more fully in the effort to bring enlightenment to the rural population. He argued that education and agitation helped the peasants understand Soviet power, and that the anti-samogon campaign went hand in hand with the fight against illiteracy, both efforts working to eliminate the backwardness and ignorance of the countryside and the peasantry through education.[117] Gernet also emphasized that severe repression of samogonshchiki only "hits a man when he's lying down [*b'et lezhachego*]." Long periods of exile and imprisonment would place the samogonshchik's family in a desperate situation that exacerbated the reasons for the crime's commission in the first place.[118] As Aronovich noted, "repression

. . . itself becomes a factor in the crime either because the confiscation of property ruins the well-being of the family already in dire straits and as a result gives birth to pauperism, or because exile from Moscow creates from the younger members of the family new ranks of homeless children [*besprizornye*] and new candidates to become criminals."[119]

Despite the Soviet government's commitment to the anti-samogon campaign, professionals emphasized the ineffectiveness of repression against this particular crime. Part of their hesitation to recommend prison terms might have come from the court system being overwhelmed by arrested samogonshchiki, but criminologists were also influenced by their understanding of female crime. They perceived samogon crimes to be committed by ignorant women who were ill-prepared for the "struggle for existence" and who lacked sufficient awareness to recognize that their activities were in fact illegal. Labeling samogon as a typically "female" crime, and the demand for samogon as typically "peasant," criminologists linked it to the ignorance and lack of culture they perceived in the countryside and emphasized the need for education and enlightenment among the peasantry, and peasant women in particular, to effectively combat the problem.

CONCLUSION

In his introduction to *Prestupnyi mir Moskvy*, Gernet argued that crime trends in Moscow showed it to be the most modern and advanced city in Russia. Over time, he noted, the "typical characteristics of metropolitan crime became more and more prominent in Moscow and gradually smoothed over features more representative of the village than the capital."[120] Even compared to the former Imperial capital, Leningrad, Moscow was more urban in its criminality. Moscow, Gernet emphasized, had fewer violent crimes than Leningrad, even before World War I and the revolution. In addition, Moscow recorded higher rates of work-related crime, another indicator that the residents of Moscow had become more civilized, more modern, and more urban than their northern counterparts.[121] Boasting of Moscow's "unique physiognomy," Gernet emphasized the progressiveness of the new Russian capital and the clear distinction that could be seen in terms of criminality between this metropolitan center and the rest of the country. Yet this "positive" view of Moscow's criminal world obscured the presence, in the capital and the rest of the country, of a population with strong rural ties attempting to make the difficult transition into a modern socialist society.

Criminologists recognized certain features that characterized urban and rural crime and separated one from the other. They believed urban residents were more conscious and progressive than the peasantry, who remained tied to tradition and outdated modes of thinking, and thus more likely to commit certain types of crimes. At the same time, the city was seen as full of vice, deception, and danger while the country-side retained a pure and untainted character, distant from the impact of modern life. In this dichotomy, women remained particularly backward and ignorant, firmly entrenched in the old way of life and the patriarchal structures of the peasant family. In the cities, women were supposed to engage more intensively in the "struggle for existence" and thus become more varied in their criminality, more modern, and more "urban." But women's participation in typically "female" and "rural" crimes remained high, supporting the notion of the inherent backwardness of women and their lack of progress along the path of modernization, whether residing in the city or the countryside. By emphasizing that female crimes were "rural" crimes, criminologists reinforced a patriarchal view of women that limited their understanding of women's participation in modern socialist society and revealed the distance women remained from the ideals of the Bolshevik Revolution.

Criminologists also emphasized the disparity between the old way of life associated with the countryside and the progress toward the new way of life during the transitional period. The old social structures, the Bolshe-viks claimed, had been destroyed, but the new ones had not yet been built. The Bolsheviks relied therefore on cultural enlightenment and literacy to educate the people and quicken the pace of socialist transformation. By focusing on the need for cultural enlightenment and not repression against female crime, criminologists underscored the backwardness and ignorance of women criminals. Repression would only exacerbate the problem among a group that had an insufficient understanding of the very notion that its activities were criminal. Although criminologists believed in the importance of cultural enlightenment in fighting female crime, their emphasis on the backwardness and primitiveness of women suggested that this goal could not easily be achieved.

What criminologists' discussions of female crime reveal is not just a perception of the "lagging tempo of development of the new culture,"[122] but an understanding of the persistence of the "old way of life" among women. In the end, what mattered most was not the strict geographical location of the crime but the nature of the offense and the social background and gender of the criminal: peasant women committed "rural" crimes even if they were longtime residents of the cities; the type of crime determined its geography. Women's lack of "progress" regarding criminality convinced criminologists that socialist ideals and modern life had still not penetrated the countryside or the female mentality, and that women remained a backward, "rural" element in Soviet society. This led them to continue to focus on the "traditional" characteristics of female crime and the retention of its domestic, rural, and backward qualities, a preoccupation that becomes even more evident in their discussions of infanticide.

A REMNANT

OF THE OLD

WAY OF LIFE

Infanticide | CHAPTER FIVE

in Theory

and Practice

In 1928, the Moscow Bureau for the Study of the Criminal Personality and Crime published a collection of ten articles analyzing murder and murderers in Moscow. Along with chapters on the psychopathology of murderers, murder in Russia and abroad, and court practice, among others, the volume contained three articles that specifically examined infanticide.[1] At the time infanticide made up fewer than one-sixth of all murder convictions in the Russian Republic (RSFSR), so the book's disproportionate focus on the crime reflects criminologists' lively interest in it. Moreover, while roughly 16 percent of all those convicted for crimes against the person were women, nearly 90 percent of infanticides were committed by women, making this a distinctly "female" offense.[2] For Soviet observers of the 1920s, infanticide represented the persistence of the outdated beliefs and morality that the 1917 Bolshevik Revolution had sought to destroy, and it embodied all the elements—female sexuality, physiology, primitiveness, ruralness, and ignorance—that defined female crime. The Bolsheviks hoped that their new socialist morality would eliminate the "backwardness" they believed caused crimes such as infanticide. Despite the efforts to transform Russia and Russians, however, some women continued to kill their children, and the phenomenon remained a serious concern for the Soviet criminologists, psychologists, and sociologists studying crime in the transitional period.

Infanticide occupied a central position in criminologists' studies in the 1920s, yet scholarly interest in the crime was not new. Tsarist judicial reforms, increased concern for the value of human life, changing perceptions of women's "natural" role as mothers and nurturers, and growing interest in the "woman question" by the mid-nineteenth century led observers to address the question of infanticide even before the systematic scholarly study of crime began.[3] Russian observers borrowed from western Enlightenment traditions and recent European trends in setting out their views of infanticide. Debates about infanticide in Victorian England, for example, typically focused on the act as a crime committed by poor unmarried women against their illegitimate children, highlighting what was perceived as an absence of "natural" maternal instincts among women committing the crime but recognizing that in some ways both mothers and infants were victims of poverty and betrayal.[4] Russian authors also took a compassionate view of the infanticide perpetrator. Writer S. S. Shashkov, in his 1871 work *The Historical Fate of Women, Infanticide and Prostitution*, criticized the historically harsh treatment of infanticide offenders, arguing against the effectiveness of severe punishments for the crime and for a more sympathetic approach that fully considered the circumstances of the mother.[5] Criminologist M. N. Gernet continued this trend in his 1911 sociological study of infanticide, *Detoubiistvo (Infanticide)*, examining infanticide statistics and comparing trends, rates, factors, and laws in European countries and Russia. Like Shashkov, Gernet emphasized the need for compassion and leniency in infanticide cases. Focusing primarily on sociological factors, he argued that infanticide and abortion represented opposing dynamics of social development. As abortion rates increased, he found, infanticide rates correspondingly decreased.[6] Since they viewed abortion as a modern, rational, and urban solution to unwanted pregnancies, Gernet and other social observers of the late Imperial period saw in high infanticide rates a direct reflection of the Russian population's low level of modernity and civilization, and a compelling justification for the call to legalize abortion. Infanticide rates provided clear evidence of the distance the peasantry, and women, remained from modern life and rational thought.

For these observers during the last days of the empire, infanticide also represented a breakdown of women's "natural" maternal instincts when faced with the social stigma of illegitimacy. Specialists highlighted the role of material conditions (such as marital status, economic resources, and community pressures) and the impact of female physiology (the strain of unattended childbirth) in the commission of the crime, emphasizing the need for compassion and leniency toward the "victims" of it. The same views persisted after the revolution, but Soviet ideology put a different twist on the understanding of the crime. In early Soviet criminologists' analyses, infanticide became not merely evidence of women's difficult circumstances but a clear signifier of women's cultural backwardness. Representing the ignorance and lack of social consciousness of its perpetrators, its occurrence also reflected the selfishness of placing personal interests above social and communal concerns. In the commission of infanticide, therefore, offenders revealed their lack of "consciousness" and their failure to wholly embrace the ideals of the Bolshevik Revolution.

To be sure, Soviet criminologists' discussions of infanticide reflected their overall understanding of female crime, embodying the "backwardness and ignorance" of women and their "ruralness." Infanticide revealed the influence and impact of women's physiology and psychology on their deviance. It represented the continued existence of the "old way of life" within the socialist state and reconfirmed criminologists' perceptions of women's position in society. Exploring the legal understanding of infanticide in early Soviet Russia and criminological analyses of the crime, this chapter highlights the role that class and gender categories played in interpretations of the nature of infanticide and the explanations for its persistence after the revolution. As the most "typical" of female crimes and as the act that most vividly undermined women's "natural" maternal role, infanticide became, for criminologists, the ultimate measure of the modernity of Soviet society and the socialist consciousness of Soviet citizens.

INFANTICIDE AND THE LAW

Historically, laws against infanticide linked it directly to sexual morality. In the ancient world, infanticide had been an acceptable and widely practiced method for controlling the size of the family. With the advent of Christianity, however, infanticide came to be condemned as an immoral act associated with illicit sexual activity and illegitimacy.[7] Early modern Russian law reflected these principles, categorizing the deliberate death of an illegitimate infant as a crime and judging offenders for their lack of morality not in the infant's death per se, but in the circumstances that led up to it. The Russian law code (*Ulozhenie*) of 1649 provided that any person killing an infant born "in sin" or out of "lust" would be condemned to death. In all other instances, however, the punishment for infant death was much less severe—imprisonment for one year. Indeed, the law expressly forbade the application of the death penalty against properly married parents guilty of murdering their own infants. The Ulozhenie thus distinguished between infanticide cases committed for "selfish reasons," such as hiding a premarital affair, and those committed because the mother lacked the resources to care for her child or chose to limit family size. It based the determination of the crime on the nature of the sexual liaison that resulted in the child's birth, with a view toward preventing fornication. The Ulozhenie's proscriptions paralleled the view of infanticide as a sexual crime upheld by the Russian Orthodox Church. An illegitimate birth provided clear evidence of illicit (and immoral) sexual conduct that called for harsh sanctions against the mother.[8] In this way, the Russian Orthodox Church and the Ulozhenie established a vision of sexual morality that reinforced patriarchal relationships and emphasized the importance of marriage and legitimate sexual behavior for women.

Beyond the punishments set out in the law for infanticide, the tsarist state sometimes provided women with alternatives to child murder. Eighteenth-century reformers, for example, addressed infanticide as part of their state-building goals. The pro-natalist policies of Peter I, intended to increase his supply of workers and soldiers, prompted him to establish foundling hospitals in the capitals to care for "children of shame," so that "their mothers would not compound the sin of illegitimacy by committing the greater sin of murder."[9] Catherine II, influenced by western Enlightenment ideas, further expanded the system of foundling homes as a way to mold and engineer educated, enlightened, and civic-minded citizens.[10] Although the foundling homes provided a place for those women who lived in close proximity to the capitals to dispose of unwanted infants, it is unlikely they did much to alter the rates of infanticide or the judicial or social reactions to offenders.

By the mid-nineteenth century, evolving attitudes toward women prompted a shift in the understanding of infanticide in Russia. A growing concern for human welfare, the changing views among the elite of women's position in society, and expanding medical interest in the physiological and psychological state of women during and after birth contributed to the belief that specific conditions encouraged the commission of infanticide and necessitated leniency in certain cases.[11] This more compassionate outlook in Russia borrowed from changes in western European attitudes toward women and infanticide. Across Europe in the seventeenth and eighteenth centuries, women had been punished severely for murdering their children, frequently by death, out of fears that infanticide represented the breakdown of the traditional social order. By the late eighteenth and early nineteenth centuries, however, the influence of Enlightenment and Romantic ideals inspired European judges and legal reformers to take a more ambivalent attitude toward women who committed infanticide, seeing such women as weak and feeble, to be pitied and treated with compassion.[12]

Similar developments occurred in the Russian treatment of infanticide offenders. In the early part of the nineteenth century, the tsarist government began to reform the country's legal system and codify Russian laws. The resulting criminal code, implemented in 1845, included a definition of infanticide that reduced punishments compared with other forms of murder when an unmarried mother killed her illegitimate child immediately after birth "out of shame or fear."[13] Lesser related crimes included concealment of a stillbirth and child abandonment, both punishable by one and a half years in prison.[14] By setting out these specific conditions for infanticide, the Russian criminal code made illegitimacy "not an aggravating but a mitigating factor in cases of infanticide."[15] This narrow definition of infanticide acknowledged that the primary cause of the crime was the same condemnation of illegitimacy that had shaped early modern laws. The 1845 code, however, embodied a different set of values. Instead of condemning women for fornication, the code espoused relative compassion for the predicament they were in by sentencing first-time offenders to shorter prison terms or exile. This change reflected Enlightenment ideals that sympathized with and sought protection for the unwed mother, and a growing awareness of the influence of "natural" female physiological reactions—centered in women's reproductive cycle—and the community's sense of morality on infanticide.[16]

By focusing on the "shame or fear" of young, ignorant women as the central factor in infanticide, the 1845 criminal code highlighted the need for a more lenient approach to punishing offenders. Furthermore, by establishing even more reduced punishments for concealment and child abandonment, it permitted alternative explanations of an infant's untimely death that spared women from infanticide convictions. For instance, when investigators had difficulty determining the infant's state at birth, the lesser charges could be applied. Yet, the criminal code's narrow legal understanding of infanticide as a crime committed specifically by unmarried women against their illegitimate children suggests that infanticide charges remained a way for the state to regulate sexual behavior, and that a dead infant's body was still the best evidence of an illicit affair. Nevertheless, the comparatively lenient punishments the code prescribed for the crime reflected the view that unmarried mothers should be considered as much the victims of community morality and their own physiological weaknesses as their murdered infants.

Many prerevolutionary observers objected to the criminal code's limited definition of infanticide, which not only excluded the possibility that multiple factors motivated infanticide, but also failed to take into account the circumstances surrounding the offense. Indeed, Gernet stressed in his 1911 monograph *Detoubiistvo* that the law privileged infanticide only when committed under the abnormal conditions of an illegitimate birth. Given this logic, he wondered why women could only commit murder in such instances. Wouldn't the psychological influence of the birth still affect a woman who, for instance, steals to feed her baby? In addition, he noted that factors other than shame or fear sometimes motivated women to commit the crime. Gernet pointed out that a woman's desire to rid herself of additional concerns, a fear of losing her position, or a wish to save her child from a life of poverty might lead her to kill her infant as well. Finally, the definition of the crime failed to take into consideration the social circumstances of the offending mothers. While most women tried for infanticide came from the working or peasant classes, Gernet did not rule out the possibility that an upper-class woman could be released from punishment under this law. "Imagine a case of infant murder," he speculated, "committed by a young girl of sufficient means, even wealthy, who does not hide her pregnancy, gives birth assisted by a midwife, and is not afraid of shame or poverty, but out of selfishness does not wish to burden herself with the added worries of a child. Can we call such a murder . . . of an illegitimate child infanticide?" Among the well-to-do, the motive for infanticide became selfishness, not poverty or shame, and in Gernet's eyes this made the crime equivalent to murder. Thus, Gernet's criticism of Russian law on infanticide emphasized the scope of the provisions that excused some by seeing their crimes as less serious offenses while at the same time excluding others whose actions should have been considered infanticide. Overall, Gernet believed the law did not adequately address the social and economic circumstances surrounding the crime.[17]

Tsarist legal interpretations of infanticide often failed to reflect the realities of its practice as well. Certainly, the patriarchal structure of the Russian peasant family played some role in cases of infanticide, as did economic considerations and the lack of alternative options.[18] But while the law defined infanticide as a crime committed by single women out of shame or fear, in the countryside married women frequently relied on infanticide to control family size. According to ethnographer Ol'ga Semenova Tian-Shanskaia's observations of late-nineteenth-century

Russian peasant village life, married women often committed infanticide for contraception by "rolling over" their newborn infants and smothering them while they slept. She also noted that most women guilty of infanticide acted in a conscious and deliberate manner. That relatively few women were arrested, tried, or sentenced for the crime suggests both that high rates of infant mortality commonly occurred and that the practice of infanticide as a contraceptive method was accepted among the prerevolutionary Russian peasantry, reflecting the wide gulf between actual practice and the provisions of the law.[19]

After the 1917 October Revolution, the Bolsheviks attempted to eradicate the conditions—material need and patriarchal morality—that they believed caused infanticide. Legal scholars and criminologists, such as Gernet, took advantage of the new opportunity to reshape the laws on infanticide they had considered inadequate under the tsarist regime. For them, infanticide was a backward crime committed out of ignorance of alternative options and under the influence of an outdated morality that condemned illegitimacy. In the new socialist society, they emphasized, legal abortions would eliminate the need to murder an unwanted child, while state support and alimony payments would provide single mothers with sufficient means to care for their children. Furthermore, the 1918 family code abolished illegitimacy as a social designation, making all children, regardless of their parents' marital status, legitimate in the eyes of the state. For the Bolsheviks and the criminologists, these measures were the first steps in the creation of a new moral order and a modern society that would eradicate the conditions that caused infanticide.

Because Soviet social policies supposedly abolished the conditions that led women to commit infanticide, it became unnecessary to acknowledge infanticide as a separate crime. Thus, the 1922 RSFSR criminal code eliminated all specific references to infanticide. Infanticide now fell into the broad category of crimes against the person (*prestupleniia protiv lichnosti*) and was considered a form of premeditated murder, punishable by a sentence of up to eight years in prison. Child abandonment remained a separate offense carrying a prison term of up to three years.[20] By characterizing infanticide as a type of murder, the criminal code attempted to end the "privileging" of the crime that excused women from severe punishment because they acted "out of shame or fear." In explaining the change, the authors of the criminal code assumed that Soviet family laws—abolishing illegitimacy, providing alimony, and legalizing abortion—would bring an end to infanticide. Thus, under the Soviet system women would no longer have to fear the financial burden of single motherhood or feel shame as unmarried mothers. Since Soviet law eliminated the specific conditions that caused infanticide, it would be unnecessary to mitigate punishment in any way. The commission of infanticide equaled the commission of murder.

The differences between the prerevolutionary and the early Soviet understanding of infanticide lay primarily in the implications of the crime: in prerevolutionary law a woman deserved leniency for infanticide because of the moral "shame or fear" that she faced with an illegitimate child; for the Bolsheviks, that "shame or fear" directly reflected the ignorance of women, their slowness to accept the benefits of the revolution, and their inability to overcome their "backwardness" to become conscious Soviet citizens. As such, the commission of infanticide revealed the continued cultural divide between the offender's actions and the state's efforts to modernize the country.

Despite the shift in the legal understanding of the crime after the revolution, Soviet courts continued to look with leniency upon women, and particularly peasant women, who murdered their children. Judges, frequently peasants themselves, still believed that unmarried women killed their illegitimate infants immediately after birth "out of shame or fear." The courts remained reluctant to punish these women harshly for a crime they committed out of desperation and ignorance. Despite the strict provisions of the law for murder, women found guilty of infanticide frequently received reduced sentences, their punishments mitigated with regard to their tenuous socioeconomic situation, their unstable mental state, their low educational level, and their minimal "danger" to society.[21] Indeed, the Moscow Regional Court applied suspended sentences to a majority of infanticide offenders.[22] Furthermore, out of 536 cases of infanticide surveyed by Gernet, only in 14 instances did the perpetrators receive the maximum eight-year prison sentence.[23]

Some Soviet criminologists, however, lamented the fact that the criminal code did not contain an article specifically addressing infanticide. Although they were pleased that the code's interpretation of the crime as murder extended beyond the narrow prerevolutionary legal boundaries, they believed a separate article on infanticide would better protect the interests of unmarried women and of Soviet society.[24] Criminologist B. N. Zmiev, for instance, noted that while infanticide as a type of murder was punishable by eight years in prison, most infanticides occurred when the mother was in a state of mental instability, a qualification that mitigated punishments to prison terms of up to three years. He argued that an article specifically addressing the unique circumstances surrounding infanticide would ensure offenders received sentences reflecting the nature of their crimes.[25] In 1928, Ia. L. Leibovich, the head forensic inspector for the People's Commissariat of Health (Narkomzdrav), actually proposed the insertion of an article on infanticide into the criminal code. His draft article defined infanticide as the murder of a newborn by its mother, but it also considered situations in which a father's abandonment of a mother led her to kill the infant.[26] Likewise, criminologist B. S. Man'kovskii argued for an article in the criminal code on infanticide that would protect pregnant women in de facto marriages and provide stricter punishments, particularly for fathers involved in the crime.[27]

Although the RSFSR criminal code never recognized infanticide as a criminal act distinct from murder, the courts remained concerned with the appropriate sentencing for the crime. In 1926, the Criminal Appeals Division of the RSFSR Supreme Court set out its understanding of infanticide and made its sentencing recommendations. The Supreme Court's definition of infanticide highlighted three major causes: serious material need on the part of the mother that would place the child in extreme poverty; strong feelings of shame, as a result of pressure from her "ignorant" community, that would make life unbearable for mother and child; and mental illness occurring in association with giving birth, particularly when the birth occurred in secret and without assistance. In the Supreme Court's opinion, these factors compelled a mother to overcome her natural maternal instincts and commit the crime. Because of the extreme circumstances in which infanticide occurred, the court argued that "severe punishments to protect society from these crimes do not provide any results. The struggle against this phenomenon must proceed not through criminal repression but by improving the material well-being of single women and making obsolete the centuries of prejudice that still have deep roots among the peasant masses."[28] This understanding of infanticide transformed traditional interpretations of the offense to fit the new Soviet conditions, emphasizing women's psychological reactions to birth and the continued "backwardness" of the rural population.

The Supreme Court's support of enlightenment over criminal repression, however, applied only in certain cases. Leniency could be employed if the circumstances of the crime matched the court's definition and then "only in cases of the extremely low cultural level of the mother."[29] In such instances, the criminal code provided that lengthy prison terms could be mitigated to suspended sentences.[30] If the required circumstances were not present, however, the Supreme Court advocated the imposition of the strict punishments provided in the code for murder. For instance, a woman with a sufficient "cultural level" or a comfortable material situation would not receive leniency from the courts. Infanticides committed with particular cruelty or by repeat offenders were likewise ineligible for suspended sentences, since this "testified to the increased social dangerousness of the mother who commits such a murder." Furthermore, leniency could not be applied to anyone other than the mother: "Persons instigating a mother to kill her child, as well as accomplices to the crime, particularly when acting for selfish reasons, should be considered by the court to have committed premeditated murder, with all its ensuing consequences."[31] In this way, the Supreme Court reaffirmed its understanding of infanticide as a crime that could only be committed by young, backward, and ignorant women.

Punishments for infanticide handed out by the courts reflected the Supreme Court's guidelines. According to one sample from the Moscow Regional Court (Gubsud), lenient sentencing increased significantly between 1926 and 1927. The percentage of infanticide offenders sent to prison for terms of one year decreased from 28 percent in 1926 to only 3.5 percent in 1927. At the same time, suspended sentences for the crime increased from 40 percent to 70 percent.[32] These rates illustrate how general interest among penal policymakers for the use of noncustodial measures of punishment found ready application in infanticide cases.

Many of those concerned about infanticide agreed with the Supreme Court's assessment of the crime and the increased leniency of sentencing for it. Jurist M. Andreev, for example, argued that the imprisonment of young women guilty of infanticide would only ruin the lives of these women, and would not alter their morality. In contrast, he believed severe sentences should be imposed on fathers who encouraged women to kill their children and on those who benefited financially from an infant's death.[33] Man'kovskii agreed, stressing that the Supreme Court's interpretation of infanticide upheld the basic principles of Soviet penal theory, which determined punishments according to the "social danger" of the offender as well as the crime. This implied that infanticide committed by a woman was less threatening to society than infanticide instigated by a man.[34] Psychiatrist A. Shestakova also noted that in instances where a married woman committed infanticide, the courts often considered her partner an accomplice, even when the woman acted alone in carrying out the actual murder.[35] In one case, for example, nineteen-year-old Aleksandra Gugina gave birth without assistance, killed her newborn, and concealed its body because her fiancé, Pavel Kiselev, would only marry her if she got rid of the infant. Recognizing Kiselev's role in inducing

Gugina to murder, the court sent him to prison while eventually free-ing Gugina from punishment altogether.[36] In this and other cases, the Soviet courts acknowledged the role that male influence could exert in infanticide cases and assigned fathers a greater level of responsibility for their participation in infanticide.

Andreev found that infanticide by fathers was a relatively new phe-nomenon that reflected the enforcement of Soviet laws regarding child support. To escape making alimony payments, men often encouraged their wives or girlfriends to terminate their pregnancies or commit infan-ticide.[37] More troubling, criminologists noticed a willingness among women to commit infanticide at the urging of a husband or lover. For instance, psychiatrist V. V. Brailovskii described a case in which Anna I. decided several months before she gave birth to murder her infant because she understood that her lover would only marry her if she got rid of the child.[38] Indeed, the fact that women were willing to kill their children at the request of their lovers and for the promise of marriage highlights the severe shortage of eligible men in the years after the war and the difficulty women had finding husbands. In addition, it demonstrates the continued importance of marriage in early Soviet society on a practical, if not legal, level. Women's desire for marriage reflected not only the economic neces-sity of the family in the Soviet Union and women's financial dependence, but also the continued cultural importance of the institution and the popular resistance to its elimination. Despite the early socialist reform efforts, marriage and the family remained essential social structures, a reality that the state acknowledged in 1936 with the adoption of a new family code that strengthened marriage, discouraged divorce, criminal-ized abortion, and ceded more social responsibility to the family.[39]

In 1928, the RSFSR Supreme Court issued instructions to clarify the responsibility of fathers in infanticide cases. Emphasizing that the purpose of leniency in infanticide sentencing was not only to advance cultural enlightenment but also to bolster economic and social order, the court argued that a father was "socially dangerous" when he refused to assist a mother in need. The Supreme Court determined that when a father was involved as an accomplice in the crime he should be tried for premeditated murder and given a sufficiently severe sentence to reflect that the weight of "social dangerousness" lay with him and not with the mother who actually committed the crime. Furthermore, the Supreme Court argued that a father who had the financial means to support a child but denied the mother's direct request for assistance should be found guilty of child abandonment.[40]

Court practice reflected the Supreme Court's interpretation of infanticide. According to statistics from the Moscow Gubsud, men consistently received more severe punishments than women for infanticide. Only 17.6 percent of men found guilty of the crime were sent to prison for less than two years, compared to 39.2 percent of women. While 58.6 percent of women received suspended sentences, the same was true for just 11.7 percent of men. Likewise, 23.7 percent of men served terms of eight to ten years, but no women received such lengthy sentences.[41] Men, the criminologists argued, generally committed infanticide to avoid making alimony payments. Although in many cases the father could not afford the payments, criminologists nevertheless believed these men acted for selfish reasons. In one case, for example, a father poisoned his infant daughter to avoid paying alimony to his wife, whom he had decided to divorce.[42] Clearly, the courts understood that men who resorted to killing an infant were not fulfilling their duties as good Soviet citizens. Man'kovskii concluded that in such cases, "the force of repression should be just as severe as sentencing for other types of murder."[43] For instance, the Moscow courts sentenced one S., a Komsomol member, to serve three years in prison for encouraging his girlfriend to throw her newborn baby into a river, while she received a lenient one-year suspended sentence.[44] By assuming that men, particularly Communist men, were more conscious of their obligations under Soviet law, the courts emphasized the need for male responsibility over women's actions, leaving women as passive participants who could not be held liable for their own conduct and therefore reinforcing patriarchal values in Soviet social norms.

Thus, infanticide became a gender and cultural issue in the Soviet Union of the 1920s. The law did not recognize the crime as distinct from other types of murder, but in practice the courts showed leniency toward those offenders—specifically women—who remained "mired in the ways of the past" and who lacked the "consciousness" to understand their rights under Soviet law. In court practice, the application of leniency in infanticide cases established a hierarchy of "social dangerousness" for the crime, punishing those whose assumed awareness of the law and consciousness of social responsibility—by virtue of their sex—made their disregard of that responsibility all the more threatening to social stability. For those who could not be held to such standards, due to their "backwardness and ignorance," the courts mitigated punishment, instead imposing measures of education and enlightenment to bring this "backward" segment of the population into line with the rest of society. In this way, under Soviet law and in Soviet court practice, a charge of infanticide equaled leniency and reduced punishment applied according to gender-based assumptions regarding the cultural level of the offender.

DISCOVERING INFANTICIDE—FORENSIC INVESTIGATION

For Soviet courts, a baby's dead body provided the primary evidence for infanticide. Concealment of a corpse or its improper disposal raised suspicions of infant murder, regardless of whether the child had been born alive or dead. Investigators found infant bodies buried in sheds and yards, left on riverbanks and in bathhouses, thrown in trash receptacles and along railway lines, and hidden in fields, storerooms, and attics.[45] In one case from 1927, a twenty-four-year-old unmarried peasant woman, V., came to Moscow to give birth. Upon her release from the hospital, she went directly to the train station to return home, tossing her baby into the Iauza River on the way. A policeman found the body the next morning, with its hospital bracelet still intact identifying the mother.[46] In another case, K., a twenty-nine-year-old widow who worked as a cook, gave birth to twins one night in the kitchen. The bodies were found cut up in a pail the next morning.[47] A third case found eighteen-year-old M. guilty of tossing her (still living, according to the forensic examiner) newborn baby from the window of a moving train.[48]

While the circumstances surrounding some cases clearly pointed investigators toward murder, often the cause of death was more difficult to determine. High rates of child mortality complicated the identification of infanticide cases and allowed some parents to conceal their intentions to dispose of a child under the cover of natural death. For instance, in one case N., 27 years old, unmarried, and unemployed, gave birth to a healthy baby. Within a month the child had died. The forensic examiner found that the infant had lost 0.68 kilos of its birth weight and concluded the child was intentionally deprived of food. Moreover, witnesses testified that N. never properly cared for the child or showed any maternal affection toward him, allowing him to cry constantly and giving him only rags soaked in sugar water to keep him quiet. Apparently N. had already lost two previous children to undernourishment, but she categorically denied her guilt, emphasizing that her material situation forced her to leave the baby alone while she looked for work. The court sentenced her to prison for one year.[49]

Women employed a variety of methods to get rid of unwanted babies, including poisoning, exposure, drowning, stabbing, and starvation, but in most cases they suffocated their children.[50] According to P. A. Aliav-din, the state forensic medical examiner in Ivanovo-Voznesensk, women favored suffocation because it left little evidence of foul play and the mothers believed their crimes would not be uncovered.[51] Women giving birth alone, I. Ia. Bychkov noted, often covered the mouth of the infant with their hands, fearing that its cries would reveal their secret.[52] In other instances, as Semenova Tian-Shanskaia observed among the prerevolu-tionary peasantry, women would "roll over" a child, suffocating it in its sleep.[53] For instance, in early February 1927 one Anna G. gave birth to a healthy baby. A week later, her husband applied to the doctor for permission to bury the infant, whom, he said, his wife had accidentally smothered in her sleep. The doctor found no problem with the request and issued the necessary documents. The couple quietly buried the child, but their neighbors learned of the infant's death and called the police, reporting that this was the couple's second child to die in this way. When the body was exhumed, the forensic examiner found fingernail marks suggestive of suffocation. In addition to the expert testimony presented at the trial, neighbors offered evidence of Anna's dislike of children.[54] In this case, the combination of circumstantial evidence, character wit-nesses, and expert testimony convinced the court of Anna's guilt.

In infanticide cases, forensic investigation was central to obtaining an admission of guilt from a suspect. Forensic examiners took into consid-eration where the infant's body was found, as well as indications that it had been born alive, such as hair and nail growth, and evidence of violence, such as cuts or bruising. Aliavdin emphasized that a woman would be more likely to confess to her actions when faced with irrefut-able evidence of murder. Furthermore, in cases where the suspect claimed to have lost her senses during birth, forensic evidence would reveal the nature of the infant's death, thus determining if a murder charge should be pursued.[55] Indeed, medical testimony often proved more convincing to the court than a woman's assertions, as in one case where despite the woman's protestations that the child in question was not hers, the court found her guilty on the basis of the forensic expert's testimony.[56] Forensic evidence that a child had been born alive was often sufficient to convince judges of foul play, even if the causes of death were "natural"—exposure, malnourishment, disease, and the like.

Forensic analysis of the dead infant's body helped to establish the validity of the infanticide charge, but early Soviet courts relied as much on the evaluation of the psychological state of the mother and the physi-ological functions of her body to assess the nature of the offense. "Mental insufficiency is the characteristic sign of the mother-infanticide," Bychkov stated in his in-depth analysis of infanticide. "The impact of the physiological paroxysms of birth on the mental insufficiencies of the mother," he continued, "can call up within her a primitive reaction, resulting in the murder of the newborn." Bychkov argued that because an individual's responsibility at the moment of committing a crime was central to determining the appropriate punishment for that crime, expert examination by a forensic psychiatrist was essential to evaluate infanticide cases. The forensic psychiatrist would thus consider the personality of the offender and the bio-psychiatric factors of the crime, in combination with the circumstances of the case, to determine if the accused had indeed committed infanticide, and the level of responsibility she should bear for her actions.[57]

Forensic experts, by determining the state of both the infant and the mother at the time of birth, established a woman's level of responsibility for the offense. Their testimonies in court represented the application of science, order, and modernity to what would otherwise have been imprecise circumstantial evidence of the nature of the crime. In addition, their evaluations helped establish the mental state of the infanticide offender, often concluding diminished capacity due to the circumstances surrounding the birth. By linking infant murder to a mother's reduced mental capacity, even if temporary, forensic analysis reinforced the criminologists' and the courts' view of the necessity for leniency in infanticide cases and of the nature of female criminality. Thus, in the Soviet understanding, a dead infant's body signified not sexual immorality, but social irresponsibility. How criminologists explained social irresponsibility—in terms of rural "backwardness" and female physiology—reflected their understanding of women's position in Soviet society and the distance women remained from embracing the new socialist order.

ERADICATING THE "OLD WAY OF LIFE"

Criminologists looked forward to the transformation of Russia and the disappearance of crime that would come with the building of socialism. In many ways, however, Russian society proved resistant to the radical changes initiated by the Bolsheviks. While portions of the population did begin to embrace the new order, educated observers found that the peasantry retained its traditional beliefs and morality even as elements of the socialist revolution slowly seeped into the countryside. The tremendous growth of infanticide in the early twentieth century signaled to criminologists that the Russian population remained distant from the goals of the revolution. According to observers, the number of child murders increased 160 percent between 1913 and 1916. While this might be explained as a consequence of the war, infanticide rates continued to climb after the revolution. By 1927, infanticide made up 16 percent of all murder cases and 20 percent of those cases with female perpetrators. Moreover, while the number of women sentenced for crimes against the person rose only 17.7 percent between 1924 and 1925, infanticide increased 106.8 percent.[58] For criminologists of the 1920s, the visible expansion of infanticide reflected the persistent backwardness among the Russian population. As the courts looked with leniency on certain infanticide perpetrators, finding that such offenders lacked the ability and awareness to act in a modern rational fashion, studies of infanticide reaffirmed traditional understandings of both the role of the peasantry and the nature of women.

Throughout the transitional period, criminologists explained infanticide as a rural phenomenon. Criminal statistics revealed that between 1896 and 1906, 86.5 percent of infanticides occurred in rural areas. In the years 1924–1925, 87.7 percent took place in the countryside.[59] The geography of infanticide suggested to criminologists that rural dwellers remained mired in backward traditions that led them to seek violent solutions to their problems. As psychiatrist A. O. Edel'shtein explained, "infanticide is an offense characteristic of a primitive level of human culture. So it is not surprising that the countryside, where cultural development is several centuries behind that of the city, accounts for almost 90 percent of infanticides."[60] Infanticide thus typified criminologists' understanding of rural morality, female crime, and the characteristics of peasant women offenders.

In their discussions of infanticide, criminologists focused in particular on the "backward" peasant morality, which condemned illegitimacy, as a significant factor in infanticide cases. Although the 1918 family code recognized the legality of all unions and their offspring, criminologists found that in the countryside the shame of premarital sex continued to play a major role in motivating infanticide. As criminologist B. N. Zmiev explained, infanticide was "that bloody sacrifice made by weak women (ignorant and without material means), in the name of preserving the steadfastness and sanctity of absurdly primitive opinions of out-of-wedlock pregnancy, views which to this day still retain their strength and meaning in our way of life and which fall in all of their severity upon the unmarried mother."[61] According to criminologist B. S. Man'kovskii, 60.2 percent of all those convicted of infanticide gave their motive as shame (*styd*); among peasant women the rate reached 82.8 percent.[62] Zmiev also noted that a peasant woman's desire to hide an affair and to protect her child from the shame of illegitimacy encouraged her to commit infanticide as a "protective reaction on the part of the unwed mother." An infant's cries would alert the community to her disgrace, so "to save her life, her freedom, her social position, and her tenderness, the unmarried mother, troubled by fear of punishment and afraid of social condemnation, violently ends the life that has only just begun."[63] For example, in January 1927, nineteen-year-old E. Cherina gave birth alone and in secret in her family's hut. After the birth, Cherina suffocated the child. Leaving the infant's body outside, she cleaned the hut and then buried the frozen body in the shed. At her trial, Cherina explained to the court that she acted out of shame and fear of the community's reaction to her disgrace.[64] Such attitudes, Zmiev emphasized, emerged from the poverty and backwardness of the countryside, developing long before the revolution and continuing to the present. Indeed, M. N. Gernet argued that infanticide rates reflected social attitudes toward premarital sex and pregnancy, so that in communities that condemned illegitimacy, infanticide occurred more readily.[65]

Criminologists also found that peasant attitudes toward family relationships encouraged the commission of infanticide. Jurist M. Andreev, for instance, explained the relationship among illegitimacy, rural morality, and infanticide in economic terms. Marriage, he argued, brought an additional worker into the peasant family, whereas an illegitimate child only created another mouth to feed. This "backward" economic system perpetuated the "shame" in illegitimacy and therefore the existence of infanticide. Andreev concluded that only with changes in rural morality and an increase in women's economic independence—similar to what he believed had already occurred in urban areas—would infanticide be eliminated from the countryside.[66] Likewise, V. Khonin observed that infanticide in Soviet society resulted from the tenacity of traditional "bourgeois" attitudes toward family, marriage, and "female honor" among the peasantry that ran counter to the gains of the revolution. He suggested the need for increased propaganda among the masses that emphasized the validity of de facto marriages and the lack of shame in unmarried motherhood.[67] Thus infanticide would only disappear when rural residents discarded their outdated beliefs and embraced the Soviet policies designed to support single mothers through alimony payments and socialized childcare.

Infanticide highlighted the clash between the new socialist morality and traditional rural values. Criminologists observed that a loosening of sexual morality resulted in more unwanted pregnancies and thus the continued existence of infanticide in the countryside, "where the old way of life remains particularly strong, as a result of the slower pace of socialist reconstruction of rural culture."[68] New attitudes toward sex had led to the emergence of a "frivolous outlook toward sexual relations,"[69] and while criminologists believed that sexual relations had become more liberal in the countryside, the economic structures and the morality governing them remained unchanged. Indeed, as Gernet noted, the countryside, "looks on out-of-wedlock pregnancy with a completely different view from the large cities; here the young mother carries on herself the inordinate weight of the condemnation of village social opinion and seeks escape in infanticide."[70] Accordingly, unmarried pregnant peasant women were isolated and alone, ashamed of their situation, and unable to ask anyone for advice or assistance. In contrast, urban women could draw on the experience and knowledge of their friends, in addition to the resources of the city designated to help poor single mothers. Thus, criminologists concluded that rural women turned to infanticide while urban women found their solutions in the more rational and modern alternatives of abortion and foundling homes.[71]

In understanding infanticide as the result of peasant women's "backwardness and ignorance," criminologists focused on the transformative potential of the socialist system. Soviet ideology stated that crime, a remainder of the "old way of life," would disappear with the successful construction of socialism. For criminologists, infanticide represented the persistence of outdated morality and beliefs among the peasantry and especially among women. Its continued existence reflected peasant women's slow embrace of the reforms the Bolsheviks had implemented to assist women. They did not see this as a failure of the Bolsheviks' reforms, however, but as a sign of the tenacity of the old beliefs, an indication that more work needed to be conducted to educate women about their rights and to make them conscious, responsible Soviet citizens.

It was not only the lack of education and awareness that brought women to infanticide. Criminologists indicated that female physiology exacerbated the impact of the old morality on women. Backwardness, shame, fear, and ignorance provided the social conditions for infanticide, but women's biological cycles, strained by the stress of childbirth, triggered a pathological reaction that led some women to react violently against their newborns. Traditionally seen as mothers and nurturers whose natural social role was reproduction, women who committed infanticide flouted that role by striking out against the very being they were designed to nurture. Criminologists explained this reaction by stressing that the physiological cycles of pregnancy, birth, and menstruation made women more susceptible to the external influences and social pressures that encouraged infanticide. According to this interpretation, the "primitive human forces" that inspired criminal activity were exaggerated in women.[72] Intellectually underdeveloped and driven by uncontrollable emotions, women's very nature led them to commit infanticide. As the nineteenth-century writer S. S. Shashkov observed:

> Pregnant women experience nausea, vomiting, headaches, ceasing of menstruation. Even just abnormal menstruation can subject women to hypochondria, melancholy, insanity, hysteria. . . . In addition, we must remember that very often unmarried women are forced to hide their pregnancies and give birth in some isolated spot, in an outhouse, in a pigsty, on the street, exposed to wind or cold, without any assistance. This further intensifies those pathological fits to which women are prone during birth. Fear, shame, the struggle between personal need and maternal love, the constant concern with hiding her situation, sleepless nights, a torturous birth, physical weakness and nervous disorder afterward,—all this makes the psychological condition of the unmarried infanticide exclusively pathological.[73]

In this view, the shame of illegitimacy and the fear of condemnation exacerbated the inherent pathological tendencies women experienced during pregnancy and birth. Their pathological physiology, combined with the pressures of community morality, led women to commit infanticide.[74]

Despite the revolution's socialist rhetoric, which prioritized socioeconomic factors and the equality of men and women, physiological differences between the sexes continued to shape criminological discourses. Early Soviet criminologists stressed that female sexuality complicated the situation single mothers faced. Combined with difficult social circumstances there was also added the "biological factor—the influence of birth on the organism."[75] Unmarried women frequently gave birth alone and unassisted, afraid of social condemnation, and ashamed of their situation. Under such pressures, the strain of childbirth encouraged a pathological reaction that could overcome their natural maternal instincts and result in infanticide. As jurist A. A. Zhizhilenko noted, "this condition is characteristic *only* of women because of the particulars of their physical organism."[76]

Infanticide also confirmed observers' perceptions of the backwardness of the peasantry in general. In his analysis of the psychopathology of infanticide, for instance, psychiatrist A. O. Edel'shtein observed that women's "primitive psyches and insufficient mental capacities" led them to kill their infants at birth, a moment of great biological stress. Noting that almost all cases of infanticide occurred in the countryside, Edel'shtein concluded that the strain of childbirth combined with the intellectual "backwardness" of peasant women caused them to kill their infants.[77] Similarly, psychiatrist V. A. Vnukov emphasized that traditional peasant morality led women to commit infanticide to hide their social transgressions, particularly illicit sexual relations. He claimed this reflected the "social weakness" of women, on whom "the pressures of society exert greater influence than on a man."[78] Responding to social values and needs, women committed infanticide out of a physiological weakness inherent in their nature. He noted:

> menstruation, pregnancy, childbirth, lactation, orgasms—all of these are open channels along which harmful external influences pass freely. This biological instability, specific only to women, can and does contribute to the distinctive way in which women process and assimilate their experiences and their reactions to personal problems. . . . Biological data all speak about one immutable fact: its manifestation in a woman, under the influence of specific social pressures, is more physiological than in a man.[79]

Women's natural biological cycles made them more vulnerable to the harmful influences that could lead to criminal activity. Vnukov argued that women's reactions to these influences were more emotional and subconscious than in men, who were more rational. Thus, because of her physiology, a woman's susceptibility to social pressures increased when she gave birth, affecting her instinctive reactions and her ability to deal effectively with the trauma of the birth, and potentially causing her to murder her child. At such moments an otherwise normal woman could be transformed into a criminal.

According to criminologists, female physiology and reproductive cycles shaped women's criminal behavior, increasing their susceptibility to external influences such as poverty and social customs. From this point of view, infanticide became a crime inherent in women's nature. By incorporating physiological factors into their explanations of infanticide, criminologists highlighted both the "naturalness" of the crime and the fundamental "primitiveness" of women. In so doing, they unconsciously cast doubt on the ability of the socialist project to eliminate the conditions that contributed to criminal activity, implying that women's crime was natural, rooted in biology, and thus immutable.

The unresolved tension between the progressive potential of socialism and the essential "backwardness" of peasant women, however, did not trouble criminologists, and they easily reconciled the sociological and bio-psychological elements of their understanding of infanticide. Despite identifying the "natural" physiological limitations of women, they argued that infanticide could be eliminated from Soviet society. Female physiology did not cause women to commit infanticide, they stressed; it merely made women more susceptible to the social and economic factors that led them to see it as the only solution to their problems, thus facilitating the commission of the crime. Once those conditions had been eliminated, once socialism had been achieved, the "backward" influences of the "old way of life" would no longer be present to exploit women's physiological weaknesses.

Education, Alimony, Abortion—Creating Alternatives to Infanticide

Criminologists emphasized that peasant women's ignorance of their rights under Soviet law and their lack of awareness of the alternatives to child murder exacerbated the desperate situation unmarried mothers faced. Women's physiological cycles may have made them susceptible to community pressures and stigmas that could overpower their natural maternal feelings, they stressed, but it was ignorance of alternatives that drove women to infanticide. Efforts to eliminate infanticide emerged out of the pro-natalist and pro-motherhood model established in Soviet family policy. Notably, Alexandra Kollontai emphasized the importance of motherhood as a natural duty of all women, as a contribution to the collective, and as a social concern.[80] In this regard, Soviet family laws sought to promote motherhood by promising childcare assistance and the protection of women's health. Women could petition the courts for alimony regardless of their marital status. In addition, the establishment of legal abortions would provide alternatives for women to terminate an unwanted pregnancy; the creation of birth homes would offer a safe, clean environment for women to give birth; and organizations such as the Society for the Protection of Motherhood and Childhood would make material assistance available to needy mothers.[81] These laws and services, observers asserted, would eliminate the "abnormal" conditions—material need and shame—that led women to commit infanticide, once women knew about and embraced them.

Professionals emphasized that the education and cultural enlightenment of peasant women were the most effective means to bring about changes in the rural morality that allowed the continued existence of infanticide. They found that while literacy had spread, nearly half of those charged with infanticide remained illiterate and ignorant of the benefits socialist law provided for them.[82] Women remained "the most backward members of our society."[83] As one scholar observed, peasant women "absolutely do not know the laws that Soviet power created to protect mothers and their children. . . . Not legal measures of repression but cultural steps must be undertaken in the fight against this crime."[84] "With legal measures in the struggle against infanticide," another observer noted,

> it is necessary to be extremely careful applying suspended sentences, but the main focus must be devoted to cultural enlightenment work in our countryside, in particular among peasant women. . . . Only by understanding women's consciousness, by understanding their cultural level, can we achieve the decline and maybe also the complete elimination of crime, namely infanticide.[85]

The socialist state would eradicate the conditions that led to infanticide, thus overcoming women's natural physiological limitations. As criminologist I. Ia. Bychkov emphasized:

> The defeat of indolence and ignorance, pushed aside by the tractors of Soviet construction in the countryside . . . as we sow the seeds of the new culture, of the new way of life, will with every harvest, with every sprout of these seeds, decrease the number of infanticides. The cultural and economic revival of the countryside is the absolute guarantee of the decrease of crime in general, and infanticide in particular, as a specific consequence of poverty and backwardness.[86]

Accordingly, once women were educated and aware of their rights and benefits as Soviet citizens, once socialist equality had been achieved, they would stop killing their children. Only through cultural enlightenment, therefore, would the Soviet state succeed in eliminating the tenacious conditions that caused infanticide.

The Bolsheviks and the criminologists firmly believed that the "backward and ignorant" Russian masses would come to embrace the new, superior, way of life being offered to them. By increasing awareness of the alternatives to infanticide and the repercussions for committing the crime, the Bolsheviks hoped to convince women to take advantage of their rights under Soviet law, particularly their right to alimony. These messages were presented in popular journals aimed at the newly literate population of Russia's rapidly expanding cities. The journals *Rabotnitsa* (*Woman Worker*) and *Rabotnitsa i krest'ianka* (*Woman Worker and Peasant Woman*), for instance, frequently ran short summaries of court cases. Targeting recent urban immigrants and factory workers, these stories were designed to illustrate the principles of Soviet justice and women's rights before the courts. By highlighting women's legal successes, the Bolsheviks hoped to provide their audience with examples of the proper behavior of Soviet citizens, male and female alike.[87]

For their readers, the journals presented cases that illustrated the compassion, justice, and equality of the Soviet system, emphasizing the seriousness of infanticide. For instance, in a 1926 issue, *Rabotnitsa* reported a case of infanticide by twenty-year-old Galina Volyntseva, a village priest's unmarried daughter. According to the report, Galina, fearing ridicule from the community, decided to hide her illegitimate pregnancy. Although the entire village was aware of her condition and heard the baby's cries when it was born, no one saw the mother strangle the child or dispose of the body on the riverbank, where it was later discovered. The article reported that, when asked about the child in court, Galina first asserted the child was not hers, denying she had ever been pregnant. Upon further questioning, Galina then argued she had not strangled the infant found by the river, and that her own child had been stillborn. The expert testimony of a forensic medical examiner confirmed, however, that the child in question had been born alive and healthy, and based upon that evidence the court found Volyntseva guilty and sentenced her to eight years in prison, reducing her punishment to a three-year term in light of her youth.[88] In a similar case, *Rabotnitsa* reported that Kostineva, a young peasant woman, told the court that she fell in love with Vasia Bakhchovan, who promised to marry her but abandoned her after she got pregnant. Vasia's mother also refused to help, so Kostineva decided to kill the child. The court sentenced Kostineva, Bakhchovan, and his mother to eight years in prison each. Taking into consideration the circumstances of the crime, the court reduced Kostineva's sentence to one year, Bakhchovan's to one and a half years, and the mother's to a three-year suspended sentence.[89] In a third story, Klavdiia Logova, a young peasant woman seduced and abandoned by her lover, frightened of her parents' reaction to her disgrace, and without financial resources to support her child, told the court that she would never have strangled her infant if she had known about Soviet alimony and paternity laws. In view of her youth and ignorance, the court commuted her eight-year prison term to a three-year suspended sentence.[90]

In each of these cases the reports emphasized the difficult circumstances and the ignorance of the offenders that led them to their actions. The reports highlighted the severity of the offense—the courts routinely handed out the eight-year prison sentences mandated for murder in the 1926 criminal code—but they also stressed the compassion and fairness of the judicial system. The sentences in each case were reduced in consideration of the perpetrator's youth and the circumstances of the crime. In this way the Bolsheviks tried to impress upon their audience the seriousness of infanticide and the alternatives to it. Indeed, that the mother of an abandoning lover could be prosecuted for her son's girlfriend's actions reflects the strictness with which the courts considered infanticide cases and the example to others they were intended to make. Yet the consistent show of leniency toward infanticide offenders, particularly when those accused of the crime were young, unmarried peasant women, reveals the courts' understanding of the crime as a holdover of the old way of life and its offenders as deserving of sympathy, compassion, and assistance rather than punishment and repression.[91]

Reports of successful alimony requests provided positive reinforcement of the alternatives to infanticide that bolstered the educational quality of these stories. *Rabotnitsa's* summaries of alimony cases emphasized the rights women and their children had to expect material support from fathers and encouraged women to pursue their claims through the courts. For instance, one article recounted the process through which Pelageia Abramova made the decision to seek alimony. After many years of marriage, Pelageia's husband Filipp left her for another woman, abandoning their children as well. She complained to a neighbor who advised her to go to court. "You yourself know," Pelageia answered, "that he trades in the market. What does he have to take? That's possible only for workers or state employees. No, I'm better off sorting this out myself." Her frustration and anger, however, changed her mind. In court, Filipp refused to pay alimony, saying the children should live with him. But a witness testified that the situation with the new wife was not conducive to raising children, and the court awarded custody to Pelageia, along with alimony payments of fifteen rubles per child per month.[92] In another case, after the father of her child refused to make his alimony payments, one Kondrat'eva went to see a lawyer who told her that the father's relatives could be held accountable for child support. The court found that while the father had no property, the grandfather, Petr Grachev, owned a two-story house, two cows, and an orchard. The court ordered Grachev to pay Kondrat'eva five rubles a month for the maintenance of his grandson.[93] These stories emphasized the victories of women who turned to the courts for alimony awards. In this way the Bolshevik press sought to educate women about their rights, emphasizing alimony as a viable alternative to infanticide.

Alimony awards were a central weapon in the Bolsheviks' struggle against the "old way of life" and infanticide. The Soviet family code envisioned an equal distribution of parental responsibility for offspring regardless of marital status. An unmarried or divorced mother could register the father of her child at the local registration office (ZAGS), after which the father would become legally obliged to share in the maintenance of the child. The courts would step in to establish the proportion of the financial expenses to be assumed by each parent if the parents could not come to an agreement themselves.[94] The code's provision of child support was in keeping with the goals of Soviet law to protect the weak and prevent the exploitation of those unable to defend themselves.[95] Mandating financial assistance from fathers for single mothers in this way would ensure that women had sufficient resources to care for their children. Child support laws also sought to diminish the stigma of illegitimacy by making all mothers eligible for alimony, not just divorced women. Thus, in advocating alimony, Soviet law and Soviet courts put forth a new vision of family relationships that held parents equally responsible for the well-being of their children, separating the institution of marriage from the family and parental responsibilities.[96] Although the state envisioned a time when it would provide the resources necessary for the care of children, the laws make it clear that the state never intended to replace parental involvement when it was available. In addition, the state's severe lack of resources during the transitional period hindered its ability to provide assistance for families and forced it to cede most of the burden to parents.

While the Bolsheviks hoped that educating unmarried mothers about their right to alimony would deter infanticide by providing women with financial security, awareness of child support laws and the desire to avoid payments sometimes sparked child murder. In a 1928 study, psychiatrist S. V. Poznyshev systematically explored the relationship between crime and alimony. He found that "the prospect of having to pay alimony not infrequently leads to crime by men, while the refusal of alimony support—by women."[97] The fear of having to pay alimony, he observed, often drove men to commit crimes against women who named them in paternity claims, and even against their own children. For example, Mikhail V., a twenty-two-year-old peasant, had an illegitimate daughter with Aleksandra Sokolova, who was awarded alimony payments of ten rubles a month. He asked her to take five rubles a month instead, but she refused. Deciding to rid himself of this burden, Mikhail convinced Aleksandra to move to the countryside with him. She agreed, but as they walked through the woods from the train station on their way to the village, with Aleksandra and the now one-year-old child in front, Mikhail took out a sledgehammer and killed both mother and daughter. The bodies were found six months later, and Mikhail was imprisoned for ten years with a loss of rights.[98]

While the desire to avoid the financial expense of child support payments motivated some offenders, others acted out of the conviction that the child in question was not theirs. As Poznyshev explained, "sometimes a woman's behavior is suspicious or straightforwardly dissolute, and her liaison with the particular person on whom she makes the demand for alimony is so short-lived that the man cannot believe that any sort of financial contributions can make him the father of the child."[99] Poznyshev emphasized the emotional nature of these crimes, particularly feelings of "vengeance, hatred, smoldering malice, or jealousy." When Vasilii K., a poor peasant from the Kaluzhskaia region, for instance, learned that his wife's healthy baby was born two months premature, he concluded the child was not his. He became jealous and began drinking heavily. One day when his wife left him alone with the infant he cut off its head with a knife, left the body in the cradle, and went off to drink with his friends.[100]

Many men, Poznyshev argued, expressed little concern for their illegitimate children, and worried only about hiding extramarital liaisons. The prospect of paying alimony would destroy that secrecy and so provided the impulse to criminal activity. For Poznyshev, this tendency warranted attention and the application of educational measures to increase men's understanding of their parental responsibilities and to improve the situation of the children.[101] While the criminal statistics do not permit a close correlation between infanticide cases involving male perpetrators and punishments, sentencing trends suggest that the courts determined the best means to reinforce paternal responsibility was through severe measures of repression. For instance, Moscow Gubsud statistics indicated that 23.7 percent of men sentenced for infanticide received prison terms of eight to ten years, while in contrast only 2.2 percent of women spent more than two years in custody.[102] The Supreme Court's mandate of harsher punishments against men who committed murder to avoid alimony payments reflected the attitude that men, as men and as "conscious" Soviet citizens, bore more responsibility for their children and their actions. In addition, this sentencing pattern reinforced the definition of infanticide as a female crime. While women acted out of "shame or fear," men murdered their infants for the "selfish" reason of not wanting to pay alimony. Not only could men's actions not be understood as a result of the physiological effects of the birth process (indeed, in most cases men committed the murder significantly after the child was born), but the "selfishness" of such men increased the "social dangerousness" of their acts. Alimony threats and claims proved to be an aggravating factor when men murdered their children.

Poznyshev also found that while men were likely to murder to avoid paying alimony, women committed criminal acts in reaction to a refusal of child support. One case involved Agrafina M., a twenty-five-year-old peasant woman from the Tula region. At seventeen she had married and had two children with her husband. In 1924 he moved to Moscow and began living with another woman; several months later he sent Agrafina notice of their divorce. Devastated and confused, Agrafina went to see her now ex-husband to ask about providing for the children and then applied to the court for alimony. The court awarded her child support, but her ex-husband made only one payment. Because of her difficult financial circumstances, Agrafina moved to Moscow and found work as a nanny. She frequently quarreled with her ex-husband and his lover, and took to carrying vitriol with her. One day in May 1926 she saw her ex-husband and his lover walking down the street. She crossed over to them and threw the vitriol right into his lover's face. For this, Agrafina was sentenced to three years' imprisonment. Although it seems distant from the crime, Poznyshev stressed that alimony was "the most important ingredient in the sum of circumstances that provoked this attempt. Agrafina is not a weak woman, sufficiently decisive, but nevertheless poorly equipped to sufficiently successfully orient herself in the circumstances and find a good way out of her accumulated difficulties."[103] Poznyshev also pointed to other cases where women committed infanticide because their lovers failed to pay them alimony. In one case, for instance, a peasant woman suffocated her newborn baby because the father refused to marry her or give her child support. In another, G., a domestic servant who became pregnant by her employer, together with her brother and mother decided to kill the baby, and when it was born she threw it into a hot stove.[104]

According to Poznyshev, failure to receive alimony turned women into criminals, but the fear of paying alimony made both women and children victims. Often, just the threat of alimony was enough to stimulate a violent reaction, as in one case from the Gomel region in 1926. Praskov'ia Gordeishchikova wanted to marry her lover Iakov G., a twenty-two-year-old peasant from the same village. They had slept together but his father opposed the marriage, so Praskov'ia started to see other people. One night Iakov and Praskov'ia met up at a party. Iakov, knowing Praskov'ia was pregnant, refused to marry her, and she threatened to request alimony through the court. Hearing her threat, he got scared and suffocated her with his hands. When asked why he refused to marry her, Iakov replied that he didn't know if the child was his.[105] Although Iakov protested that no one had ever paid alimony in his village, by 1926 the right to request alimony and women's willingness to do so seems to have penetrated into rural Russia.[106] In another case, twenty-year-old Maxim killed his pregnant girlfriend Irina because she "impudently nagged" him either to marry her or to pay alimony. Contemplating the results of his actions—a prison sentence of eight years—Maxim thought that perhaps it might have been better to let Irina take him to court for alimony before killing her. After all, he mused, the court might not have made an award.[107] Despite the clear risk, these accounts indicate that women were willing to secure their rights through the courts and to use those rights to try to obtain what they needed.

Criminologists expected the alimony provisions in the family code to decrease the incidence of infanticide. They believed that child support, by providing unmarried mothers with sufficient material resources, would diminish many of the factors that led to infant murder. Alimony awards, however, most likely failed to improve significantly the material situation of most women. Although a considerable number of women turned to the courts for alimony during the 1920s (in 1925 alimony cases made up 7.7 percent of all civil court cases heard in the city of Moscow and 12.6 percent in the region),[108] in many cases women never received the sums granted to them. Low wages and unemployment prevented alimony from becoming a significant source of income for single mothers, since fathers often lacked the means to make their payments. Many men became involved in new relationships and barely managed to support one family on their meager salaries, let alone two or more. In addition, men frequently disappeared, moving to another city or changing addresses, and this made the collection of alimony almost impossible.[109] Thus the difficulties of implementing and enforcing child support laws often outweighed the potential benefits. Furthermore, the very possibility and widespread application of alimony payments may have destabilized traditional relationships and created more crime victims, among both mothers and infants. Women's willingness to turn to the courts to secure their rights exposed them and their children to the violent reactions of fathers, and the relationship between alimony and murder raised sufficient interest and concern that the RSFSR Supreme Court found it necessary to take a stance regarding the role of fathers and their parental (and social) responsibility.

The Bolsheviks also hoped that legal abortions would provide an alternative to infanticide by creating a safe means for women to terminate an unwanted pregnancy. Prerevolutionary social reformers had long called for the elimination of laws against abortion (which carried punishments similar to those for infanticide) as a measure to protect women's health, a moral issue, and a means to curtail infanticide. They argued that legal abortions were a necessary evil that would keep women from turning to the unlicensed, unsanitary "babki" and the dangerous home remedies that sent large numbers of women to hospitals from complications and blood poisoning. According to Gernet, botched abortions accounted for 41.8 percent of hospital patients in Moscow in 1913, with even higher rates in St. Petersburg.[110] Furthermore, in the late nineteenth century, as socialist ideas gained support and interest in the "woman question" increased, the debate about abortion rights came to symbolize the very position of women in Russian society and their ability to control their bodies and make personal choices.[111] Although Russian social observers remained reluctant to relinquish social control over women, some, such as I. B. Fuks, recognized the need to allow women that freedom of choice: "Women alone carry all the burdens and suffering of childbirth, all the difficulties of raising children, and therefore the right to decide the question regarding the number of her children should be granted to her alone."[112] As he concluded, "the abolition of laws against abortion will undoubtedly have an effect in decreasing the numbers of infanticides."[113]

Abortion law reform became one element of the Bolsheviks' emancipation of women and their struggle against infanticide. On 18 November 1920, the Commissariat of Justice (NKIu) took the "gigantic, revolutionarily daring and significant socially justifiable step" when it legalized abortion, permitting the procedure if performed with consent by a doctor in a hospital and creating a commission to approve abortion requests.[114] A further decree issued 3 November 1924 established a hierarchy, based on Bolshevik ideological considerations, for determining who could receive free legal abortions. Priority was given to women workers and wives of workers who already had children.[115] Statistics of denials indicate the abortion commission's emphasis on social position in permitting abortions. Figures from 1925 show that urban abortion commissions denied abortion requests for 16.2 percent of single women but only 6.8 percent of married women. In rural areas 15.4 percent of single and 12.2 percent of married women were refused state abortions. Furthermore, the number of children a woman had significantly contributed to her chances of obtaining an abortion. While 18.1 percent of women with no children were refused an abortion, the requests of only 5.4 percent of women with four or more children were turned down (See Table 11).[116] Accordingly, in Soviet Russia abortion was envisioned as a form of birth control intended for married women who already had children, and not a means to provide women with the right to make personal choices.[117] Indeed, as jurist A. A. Piontkovskii pointed out, Soviet law classified (illegal) abortion as a crime against the health of the person, viewing the pregnant woman (and not the fetus, as was the case in many western law codes) as the victim.[118] Thus the legalization of abortion followed the Soviet legal principle of protecting the weak from exploitation. It offered some women the chance to avoid unwanted children, keeping them out of hospitals and prisons, but the legal limits imposed on abortion, and the practical obstacles to receiving them, ensured that the new regulations would not lead to a broad revision of women's social position or to a curtailment of infanticide.

Abortion policy contained a class element as well, particularly when criminologists considered it alongside infanticide. In his prerevolutionary work, Gernet had categorized abortion as an upper-class solution to unwanted pregnancies, while working-class women turned to infanticide. When women of the propertied classes did not want to have a baby,

TABLE 11—Percentage of Denials for Abortion in 1925

	Major cities	Other cities	Rural areas
Unmarried	16.2	9.7	15.4
Married	6.8	13.6	12.2
No children	18.1	16.5	19.1
One child	9.9	15.2	15.7
Two children	9.8	14.2	14.1
Three children	7.4	8.7	9.2
Four or more children	5.4	6.4	8.7

Source: A. F., "Aborty v gubernskikh gorodakh, prochikh gorodakh, i sel'skikh mestnostakh," in *Aborty v 1925 godu* (Moscow: Izdanie TsSU SSSR, 1927), 61–62.

he argued, they "turn to douches and to various internal remedies to promote miscarriage, but representatives of the unpropertied population commit infanticide."[119] State abortion, he argued, would eliminate such socioeconomic inequality by making this alternative available to those who could not otherwise afford it. Historian Laura Engelstein has pointed out that in the nineteenth century, class issues in the abortion debate had more to do with resource availability than income differentiation. Urban women chose to terminate their pregnancies early while peasant women disposed of unwanted children after they were born.[120] Soviet criminologists noticed a similar division, emphasizing that abortion was an urban phenomenon, while "in the Russian countryside [women] find their solutions in infanticide,"[121] reflecting the low cultural level of rural residents. Indeed, even when rural women sought abortions, they remained motivated by the same influences that led their sisters to commit infanticide. As one observer noted, both urban and rural women sought abortions out of material need, but shame, fear, and the desire to conceal a pregnancy played more significant roles among peasant women. For example, while 66.4 percent of women seeking abortions in large cities and 58.2 percent in rural areas cited their motives as material need, only 1.6 percent of abortions in urban areas were motivated by the desire to hide a pregnancy, compared to 7.3 percent in the countryside.[122] Abortion thus came to symbolize the modernity of the cities while infanticide reflected the continued backwardness of the countryside.

Although abortion was not legalized specifically to fight infanticide, it was expected that because the conditions leading women to abortion and infanticide were similar (and identical methods had to be employed to eliminate both), abortion would provide an alternative for women who might otherwise murder their infants and would thus result in a decrease in the incidence of infanticide.[123] Legal abortions, however, remained elusive, particularly for single rural women. The state abortion commission's priorities did not always coincide with the segment of the population most likely to commit infanticide. Moreover, analyses of abortion rates and the impact of abortion policy were directly shaped by the abortion commission's political priorities. While criminologists understood that infanticide was a crime committed by poor, unmarried, peasant women, legal abortion approvals privileged married, urban working women. This forced many women to turn to illegal abortions (performed by midwives outside hospitals), home remedies, or infanticide. Severe shortages of doctors and hospital beds outside the capitals further ensured that legal abortions remained nearly inaccessible for peasant women. Indeed,

Gernet observed that infanticide occurred more often in the countryside precisely because abortions were so difficult to obtain.[124]

In their struggle against infanticide, the Bolsheviks emphasized educating women on the alternatives to child murder. Efforts to improve women's awareness of beneficial Soviet social policies highlighted the courts' compassionate treatment of infanticide offenders, even as they sought to stress the seriousness of the crime and the availability of alternatives to it. The Bolsheviks and the criminologists had high hopes that alimony awards and legal abortions would lead to a decrease in infanticide, but the nature of the policies themselves and the circumstances of life in the transitional period prevented these alternatives from making their desired impact. Although many women turned to the courts to secure child support, the persistence of prerevolutionary attitudes toward illegitimacy and high levels of unemployment made alimony awards ineffective in providing sufficient resources for single mothers, and likely created additional crime victims. Similarly, the limits placed on legal abortions meant that, while effective as a method of birth control for women with families, safe abortions were not readily available to the segment of the population most likely to commit infanticide. The state's lack of resources in the 1920s prevented it from assuming responsibility for unwanted children and forced it to abdicate child care to parents whose needs, abilities, values, and beliefs often differed from the Bolshevik vision of Soviet society. In the end, the "old way of life" proved extremely difficult to eradicate.

URBAN INFANTICIDE

The educational and enlightenment measures pursued during the transitional period appear to have had little effect as criminologists continued to observe growing infanticide rates. In the Moscow region alone, for example, infanticide made up 21 percent of murder cases tried in 1926, rising to 28 percent by 1927.[125] As psychiatrist Brailovskii noted, "revolutionary life, penetrating into the mass of the peasant population, it would seem, should exert its influence by decreasing the number of those giving birth to unwanted 'illegitimate' children. . . . But the realization of all these desires did not give the slightest tangible decrease in the number of infanticides."[126] In attempting to explain the persistence of a crime that should have disappeared as the population came to embrace Soviet policies, criminologists found that infanticide remained rooted in the countryside, in the persistence of the old prerevolutionary peasant morality, and in the backwardness and ignorance of peasant women.

This realization shaped their analyses as they distinguished between rural peasant and urban worker and made class-based geographical origins the primary indicator and explanation for infanticide.

In the mid-1920s, however, criminologists noticed an increase in urban infanticide cases. Before the revolution, rural infanticides generally made up close to 90 percent of the cases.[127] According to Man'kovskii, 73.1 percent of infanticides in 1925 occurred in the countryside and 26.9 percent in the cities. By 1927, rural infanticides made up only 52.2 percent of the total while urban infanticides had reached 47.8 percent.[128] Criminologists blamed the growth of urban infanticides on the influx of peasant women who brought their backwardness with them to the cities and whose traditional beliefs continued to influence them in their new surroundings.[129] These urban migrants frequently found positions as domestic servants. Indeed, Man'kovskii noted that as the proportion of rural women convicted of infanticide dropped (from 62.3 percent in 1925 to 50 percent in 1927), the percentage of domestic servants found guilty of the crime increased (from 13.2 percent in 1925 to 36.4 percent in 1927).[130] Moreover, when infanticide was committed in the cities, domestic servants were the perpetrators in 65.5 percent of the cases. Man'kovskii argued that since most domestic servants had recently arrived in the cities, they could still be considered peasants, making urban infanticide an overwhelmingly "rural" crime. He concluded, "the growth of [infanticide] in the city comes as a result of domestic servants, in other words not from the native urban population but because of immigrants from the countryside."[131]

Domestic servants in the cities exhibited the characteristics criminologists identified among peasant women who committed infanticide. They were generally poor, uneducated, single, and young. Their motivation for infanticide, however, stemmed mainly from the desire to keep their jobs, rather than from the "shame" of illegitimacy or disgrace in the eyes of their community. In one case, P., a domestic servant, hid her pregnancy from her employers and gave birth at night alone in the washroom. Taking a knife from the kitchen, P. chopped the baby's body into small pieces and dumped them down the toilet. She thoroughly cleaned the washroom, removing all traces of the birth and her crime. Unfortunately for her, the pipes clogged and a worker found the body parts in the plumbing.[132] For domestic servants like P., an illegitimate child often meant dismissal, and thus financial considerations provided the major impetus for their actions. Man'kovskii indicated that while 60.2 percent of all those convicted of infanticide acted out of shame, only 5.3 percent of domestic servants gave shame as their motivation. He concluded that material need characterized the crime in the cities while shame played a greater role in the countryside.[133] Although this suggests that something in a woman's situation changed significantly when she moved from the countryside to the city, criminologists simply equated domestic servants' need to keep their jobs with peasant women's shame before their communities. Both emanated from illicit sex and the stigma of illegitimacy, and both displayed a "backwardness" of morality and an ignorance of Soviet laws designed to protect women's interests.

Criminologists recognized a difference between these new rural transplants and the urban working woman. In contrast to peasant women, proletarian women did not commit infanticide, because they knew their rights under the family code and had access to legal abortions, foundling homes, and charitable organizations.[134] If a working woman committed infanticide, criminologists suggested, it could only be the result of pressure from a husband or lover. Indeed, according to criminologists' statistics, proletarian women committed infanticide at rates significantly below those of peasant women and domestic servants. As infanticide among domestic servants increased, it dropped among women workers from 11.3 percent of the total in 1925 to only 9 percent in 1927.[135] Although many factors may have contributed to female industrial workers' lower infanticide rates—for instance, worker solidarity, comradeship, economic stability, or greater autonomy in urban areas—criminologists emphasized the modern morality and social awareness of this class of women, in contrast to the backwardness and ignorance associated with rural women.[136] They believed that working women, by virtue of their class "consciousness" did not commit infanticide, so if urban women committed the crime it was because they retained their former peasant "ruralness." Once the economic independence of urban women workers was transferred to the countryside, they argued, infanticide would disappear there as well. Changes in the rural economic situation, the position of women, and their morality would lead to the elimination of infanticide and, eventually, the liquidation of murder in general.[137] Thus, criminologists understood infanticide offenders in terms of class. They ascribed certain class characteristics to women who killed their children regardless of where the crimes took place or what social class the women occupied.

For criminologists, infanticide in the cities resulted not from the difficulties of urban life, but because a rural phenomenon manifested itself in an urban setting. This view attributed urban infanticide to poor, unassimilated, peasant women acting out of shame, desperation, or fear, because infanticide was a backward crime that could not occur in the progressive socialist city where alternatives, such as legal abortions, foundling homes and other social support services, existed. The belief of criminologists in the ability of social services to reduce infanticide rates revealed not only their socialist idealism, but also their naive view of the chance poor peasant women had to use such benefits, even when they migrated to the cities. Lack of consumer goods, food rationing, high female unemployment rates, and insignificant alimony payments contributed to the difficult life women faced in the years after the revolution. In addition, complex bureaucratic procedures, together with a shortage of doctors and hospitals, decreased most women's opportunities to take advantage of the limited social services the Soviet state was able to provide. The lack of alternative contraceptive methods and the continued stigma of illegitimacy (in practice if not in law) only served to exacerbate their situation.[138] In the end, the social policies implemented in the early 1920s failed to improve the lives of the majority of rural and urban women in Russia, particularly in relation to childbirth and contraception, leading some to resort instead to the "backward" solution of infanticide. For criminologists, infanticide remained firmly situated in the countryside, its occurrence in urban areas explained in ideological terms that prevented them from seeing the realities that Soviet women faced during the transitional period.

CONCLUSION

Criminologists of the 1920s saw infanticide as embodying the very nature and duality they identified in female crime in general. In one sense, women committing infanticide were "villains," deviants who acted in ways that challenged and undermined women's proper reproductive, nurturing role and thus threatened social stability. At the same time, these women were "victims" of outdated rural morality, of material conditions, of their male partners, of their own backwardness and lack of consciousness, and of their own physiology. As such, they deserved compassion, leniency, and enlightenment. By linking women's "ignorance" of their rights in Soviet society to their physiological condition, the courts and the criminologists ascribed certain characteristics to female offenders that reinforced a traditional understanding of women's position in society and questioned women's ability to participate fully in Soviet society. That women continued to kill their children at increasing rates indicated to criminologists that the measures intended to educate the population, especially women, had not achieved the desired results. Moreover, the realities of the NEP forced the Bolsheviks to place more of the burden of social support on individuals and families, leaving women few ways to escape the community pressures and morality that encouraged infanticide.

Soviet court practice reinforced criminologist's understanding of infanticide by awarding reduced or suspended sentences to female offenders and by placing greater responsibility, through harsher measures of repression, on the husbands and lovers who acted as accomplices, encouraged women to kill their infants, or refused to provide child support. This transfer of responsibility reflected the courts' view that women remained backward and had not accepted socialist morality. Infanticide offenders simply did not understand the benefits that socialism provided for them, and this lack of "consciousness" translated into diminished responsibility and reduced punishments. While the emphasis on male participation reflected the Soviet legal interest in preventing the exploitation of a weaker party, this policy contained an inherent gender bias that, in the face of increasing infanticide rates, sought to hold men responsible for their wives and girlfriends, and reinforced traditional patriarchal attitudes within Soviet policy.

For criminologists of the 1920s, infanticide embodied the gulf between urban and rural, modern and backward, proletariat and peasant, and male and female. It became a measure of socialist progress, revealing the extent to which the peasantry remained distant from the ideals of the revolution and modern Soviet society, and emphasizing the need for cultural enlightenment work among them. It exposed the backwardness of peasant women, their lack of socialist consciousness, and the durability of traditional peasant culture and morality. Infanticide showed criminologists that the Soviet government's measures designed to protect women and children—for instance, those set out in the 1918 family code—clashed with persistent but outdated notions of female honor, purity, and disgrace. These differences created a gulf that separated the peasantry, and women, from the rest of Soviet society.

Criminologists' emphasis on class differences and gender distinctions reflected the ideological priorities and class hierarchies of the Soviet system. In defining infanticide as a crime committed by backward peasant women and selfish fathers, criminologists and courts established the boundaries of proper behavior expected of honest responsible Soviet citizens. In their explanations of infanticide, criminologists found confirmation of their view of Soviet society, an outlook that combined both Bolshevik ideological priorities and a traditional understanding of social and gender hierarchies. These attitudes resonated with broader trends in Soviet society and helped to shape the course of Soviet development as the NEP period came to an end. In practice, however, women's actual motives for infanticide did not always match criminologists' understanding of the crime. Furthermore, Soviet laws promoted a vision of morality that the Russian population did not necessarily share. The continued existence of infanticide in early Soviet Russia reflected the tenacity of old values in the face of the new ideology, the importance of traditional relationships for social stability, the expression of personal interests over state desires, and the difficult conditions that women, and men, experienced and endured after the Bolshevik Revolution.

CONCLUSION

Female crime has long fascinated those who study criminality precisely because it is in many ways more troubling and more disruptive to social norms and ideals of proper behavior than male crime. Women's deviance often appears more "monstrous" to observers, is more frequently directed against family members, and seems more in contradiction to women's perceived natural maternal qualities. Because female deviance is so closely linked to women's position in the family, scholars have found confirmation of women's traditional social roles in the types of crimes women commit.[1] In the early Soviet case, this reaffirmation of women's social position also served to reinforce the notion that women's behavior was defined by female physiology and that women possessed an inherent backwardness that prevented them from participating fully in modern Soviet life.

Early Soviet criminologists' interpretations of female offenders reveal a picture of a society deeply influenced by its past traditions while at the same time struggling to define itself in a new light. Not surprisingly, despite the changes introduced by the Bolsheviks in 1918—the radical social and family legislation designed to abolish the old ways of living and thinking—most Russian citizens continued to exist as they had before the revolution. Indeed, the realities of life in the transitional period often failed to coincide with the social vision presented in Soviet policies. Social problems, exacerbated by the war years, persisted throughout the 1920s, resisting Soviet reform efforts and influencing the direction of social policies. By the end of the NEP, serious financial constraints and political priorities that stressed industrial growth and workforce expansion, as well as resistance from a population that remained attached to the "old way of life," pushed the state to cede greater social responsibility to families at the same time it moved forward with its plans for rapid industrialization and collectivization. Legislation passed in 1936 codified these shifts, making divorce more difficult, prohibiting abortions, and encouraging women to continue working while increasing the number of children they bore. Such measures placed an ever-expanding double burden on women and at the same time reaffirmed the importance of the family as an institution in Soviet society. Moreover, efforts to increase the birth rate by criminalizing abortion and rewarding mothers of large families, combined with the failure to socialize household labor, ensured that the family would not "wither away" as socialist ideology had predicted, but would instead become an essential element of the Soviet system.[2]

Underlying the social and political dynamics of the transitional period, however, were deeper continuities in attitudes toward women and their social role. While the state's cooptation of the traditional family reflected a continuous push to build communism, it also revealed a broader process of "cultural revolution" through which prerevolutionary values were transformed to fit Soviet priorities. Criminologists' analyses and interpretations of female crime during the transitional period incorporated and preserved traditional notions that women's crime and women's life were centered in the female reproductive capacity. Even as they emphasized the socioeconomic causes of female crime and envisaged its expansion, criminologists highlighted female physiology, and reproductive functions in particular, as a contributing or exacerbating factor in women's deviance. Such continuities, combined with political expediency and economic needs, helped to create a gender hierarchy that preserved the "traditional" patriarchal attitudes toward women in Soviet discourse and that shaped the understanding of women's proper position in Soviet society and, indeed, the proper behavior expected of all Soviet citizens.

Criminologists' attitudes toward women reflected and contributed to the broader Soviet understanding of society and social relationships. In particular, the link criminologists made between the "primitive" (i.e., physiologically driven) criminal woman and the "backwardness" of the countryside provided a concrete focus for Bolshevik antipathy toward the peasantry. Ascribing "ruralness" to female crime, criminologists helped to "feminize" the countryside, reinforcing hierarchies of gender and class in Soviet society. Scholars have pointed to this process in Soviet political propaganda. For instance, Victoria Bonnell notes that the image of the *kolkhoznitsa* (female collective farm worker) had displaced the male peasant as the representative of the countryside by the early 1930s. Bonnell states that this was "indicative of a new gendered discourse about the countryside [that] feminized the image of the peasantry as a social category."[3] Criminological analyses of female crime suggest that such attitudes toward the peasantry and women extended beyond propaganda. The "feminization" of the countryside formed a central element of criminological discourse, even before the revolution, and had become a convenient way for professionals to explain the persistent differences they observed in the crime rates of men and women. It served to distance the peasantry (and women) from modern Soviet life, and it showed observers that decisive measures (manifested in collectivization policies) needed to be taken to transform this resistant population. While criminologists probably preferred education and enlightenment to violence and repression, their attitudes nevertheless helped to pave the way for the Stalinist assault on the countryside that began in earnest in the late 1920s.

The emphasis criminologists placed on the "ruralness" and "primitiveness" of female criminals also suggests that they defined women's place in society according to traditional notions of female sexual and reproductive functions. The continued focus on women's "backwardness" and their inability to fully engage in the "struggle for existence" reflected some anxiety over the more public roles that women were invited to play in Soviet society. By stressing that female crimes were "rural" or "primitive" crimes, criminologists removed women from engagement with modern (i.e., urban) Soviet life, shifting the orientation of their explanations away from concrete socioeconomic factors and toward an abstract conception of female crime that obscured the realities women faced in the years after the revolution. This gender hierarchy reinforced a patriarchal view of women that denied them full participation in Soviet society and diminished the potentially progressive, modernizing impact of the Bolshevik Revolution on women. As Michael David-Fox notes, efforts to overcome Russian backwardness remained a central element in the Bolsheviks' extended "cultural revolution."[4] Yet, persisting notions of female crime as inherently "rural" and "primitive" within the rhetoric of socialist transformation suggest not only that the idea of female backwardness was deeply ingrained in criminologists' worldview, but also that gender differentiation served a real purpose in the state's efforts to make Russians "Soviet," establishing a hierarchy that placed maleness at the center of the revolutionary struggle.

The irony of the conception of female crime as "rural" and thus women as backward is that it denied the very influence of the "struggle for existence" criminologists found so positive. In fact, women continually engaged with the "struggle for existence," committing infanticide to preserve their employment opportunities in the case of domestic servants or, in the case of female samogonshchiki, turning to the production and sale of homebrew to supplement their incomes, as criminologists themselves pointed out. Also, when it suited their needs and to the best of their ability, women took advantage of the new social and family policies the Bolsheviks instituted, for example, obtaining abortions to limit family size and seeking alimony payments from delinquent husbands and lovers. Yet in their analyses, criminologists seemed not to notice these developments, failing to find any significant departure from the traditional boundaries of female deviance. If we take their statistics and arguments at face value, this lack of transformation suggests that the revolution did not in fact increase women's opportunities for interacting with men as equals in public life. But this also raises the possibility that women and men experienced the "struggle for existence" and the socialist transformation in radically different ways during the transitional period, ways that criminologists' analyses of female deviance did not discern. Nevertheless, by seeing the lack of diversification in female crime not as a failure of emancipatory equality but as evidence of the continued backwardness and primitiveness of women, criminologists linked female crime to the countryside and reinforced the image of women as ignorant, isolated from public life, and lacking the consciousness to participate as equals with men in Soviet society. Such explanations of female crime removed agency from women for their actions, often placing the blame instead on their husbands or lovers. This bolstered the notion of women as weak, in need of protection, and victims of their circumstances and their sexuality, preserving and reinforcing patriarchal attitudes toward women within Soviet criminal justice.

In locating the responsibility for female crime beyond the control of the offenders themselves, criminologists of the 1920s employed a rhetoric of progress and backwardness in their studies that placed deviant women in a subservient position where they were inherently "primitive," possibly unreformable, and certainly not responsible for their actions. Such attitudes coexisted alongside socialist ideals of sexual equality; however, these attitudes did not undermine the Bolshevik project. Rather, the continued presence of more customary views of women within the radical ideology of socialism facilitated the reversal of some of the more untenable and unrealistic social policies that occurred in the mid-1930s and was a crucial element in the overall process of the development of social norms of the Stalinist state and the establishment of "Soviet" socialist society.

THE FATE
OF SOVIET
CRIMINOLOGY

EPILOGUE

In concluding this study of how criminologists' interpretations of female crime helped to shape the transformation of early Soviet society, it is important to examine the fate of criminology in the early Stalinist era. The course criminology followed during the transitional period paralleled that of other professional disciplines, particularly in the social sciences. In the case of criminology, the intersection of the sociological and the biological that pervaded criminologists' discussions of female crime in the 1920s directly contributed to criminology's demise in the early 1930s. The two approaches combined most comfortably in the psychiatric analyses of individual criminals, and this remained the preferred methodology for crime studies throughout the 1920s, especially within the local criminological bureaus. Even the State Institute for the Study of Crime and the Criminal preserved the physiological orientation and psychiatric focus of crime studies within its institutional structure as it tried to create a centralized "Soviet" criminology. The end of the New Economic Policy and the start of agricultural collectivization and rapid industrialization that accompanied Stalin's First Five-Year Plan, however, radically changed the environment for Soviet social studies, making the psychiatric approach politically unacceptable. A renewed emphasis on the collective and adherence to strict socialist ideological principles led to a widespread reevaluation of social and professional engagement in all spheres of activity and produced calls for more "Soviet" scholarship, particularly in the "hybrid" social sciences, such as social hygiene, eugenics, and criminology, that combined social studies with biological elements.[1]

The need to place newly trained Soviet cadres in professional and bureaucratic positions also stimulated a redistribution of personnel and the replacement of those "bourgeois specialists" considered potentially harmful to the Soviet project.[2] Like specialists in other disciplines, criminologists increasingly came under fire for "errors" in their work, for not sufficiently incorporating Marxist-Leninist principles into their research.[3] A new generation of Soviet legal scholars, particularly those employed by the Communist Academy,[4] came to dominate the field. They conducted a purge, turning their criticisms on the more "individually" oriented professionals and accusing them of "neolombrosianism," that is, of preserving the "anti-sociological" and "individualistic" elements of Cesare Lombroso's criminal anthropological approach in their interpretations of crime and its causes. Confronted with accusations of their ideological and methodological errors, most professionals quickly and willingly curtailed their research into the causes of crime and the motives of offenders, and returned to a focus on their core disciplinary interests.

The attack on criminology began with an article published in the January 1929 issue of the Communist Academy's legal journal, *Revoliutsiia prava* (*Revolution of Law*), by S. Ia. Bulatov, recent graduate of the Institute of Soviet Law and researcher at the Communist Academy.[5] Bulatov charged criminologists in general, and the Moscow Bureau for the Study of the Criminal Personality and Crime specifically, with neolombrosianism. He argued that, particularly among psychiatrists studying crime, the tendency to link crime and mental illness, as well as the focus on atavistic traits, preserved elements of Lombroso's theories within Soviet criminological studies. Although he noted that the scholars in question had dismissed Lombroso's theories as unscientific, Bulatov nevertheless stressed that their studies clearly revealed a Lombrosian outlook. Their mistake, according to Bulatov, consisted of seeing crime as a result of the "psycho-physical inferiority of the criminal." Psychological interpretations of crime highlighted the criminal's insanity or mental illness, taking a social phenomenon and turning it into a medical one. In contrast, Bulatov emphasized, a true Marxist approach considered each offender as a representative of a certain class, and only in this way could the correct characterization of the criminal be determined.[6]

Bulatov's criticisms of criminology led the Communist Academy's Department of State and Law to convene a discussion in March 1929 on the proper methods and approaches to studying crime in the socialist state.[7] Despite the ostensible efforts of the State Institute to make crime studies more "Marxist," according to the charges leveled during this "dispute," criminology had not become "Soviet" enough. The Communist Academy dispute became the forum to point out the shortcomings of criminological research and to establish a unified method and approach that would shape Soviet criminology in the future. According to B. S. Man'kovskii, a criminologist himself and a recent graduate of Moscow State University, it was the task of the Communist Academy "to fight against deviations that reflect petty-bourgeois socialist ideology within Soviet criminology."[8] For the participants in the Communist Academy dispute, accusations of neolombrosianism provided a convenient way to identify what was not "Soviet" in criminology at a time when it was becoming politically important to do so. As Louise Shelley has suggested, these scholars may not have figured out precisely what was "Marxist" or "Soviet" about criminology, so that labeling what was not "Soviet" helped establish what was, much as defining deviance helped to determine proper behavioral norms.[9] In this dispute, the Communist Academy's members acted as the arbiters of criminology's future. They condemned the criminological research conducted during the 1920s as unacceptably anti-Soviet and called for the complete restructuring of crime studies.

A. Ia. Estrin, a leading legal scholar and law professor at Moscow State University, launched the dispute, arguing that examining the criminal as an individual had no place in Soviet scholarship. Studying crime was necessary, he continued, but "we must, first and foremost, investigate those forms of crime that characterize the present moment in our political life. We must study the multiple phenomena, the various crimes, with regard to the political tasks and the political precepts set out by our party and, above all else, in light of the class struggle, the struggle for socialist construction."[10] Psychiatrist G. M. Segal, a longtime member of the State Institute, head of the Moscow Regional Court's criminal affairs division, and law professor at Moscow State University, also criticized the state of criminological research. He agreed with other dispute participants that the study of individual criminals was absolutely necessary, but only for the practical purposes of penal administration. Segal emphasized that Soviet criminology had two tasks: first, to develop preventative measures against crime; and second, to establish comprehensive methods for

reforming criminals. Only by refocusing the orientation of crime studies, he argued, could the "insufficient correlation between theory and
practice" that haunted criminology be overcome.[11] Despite efforts from
penologist E. G. Shirvindt and jurist A. A. Piontkovskii, among others,
to defend criminological work, the Communist Academy membership
overwhelmingly condemned the scope and direction of criminology as it
had been conducted in the 1920s. Instead, they set a new course for crime
studies that aimed to eliminate all "neolombrosian" elements in favor of
a more homogenous, Marxist-Leninist orientation that focused solely on
socioeconomic factors. The outcome of the dispute clearly signaled that
psychiatric study had no place in "Soviet" criminology. This new orientation confined criminal psychiatry to a purely forensic role in criminal
analysis, and this led, over time, to a simplified understanding of crime as
a reaction to external socioeconomic conditions and cultural influences
caused solely by "remnants of the old way of life."[12]

The criticism of criminology presented at the Communist Academy
dispute had severe repercussions for the discipline. It affected the manner
and extent of criminological research, reorienting such research toward
penal studies and ending discussions of the gendered dimensions of
crime, as well as providing justification for the subsequent reorganization
and disbanding of the criminological organizations. The professionals
denounced in the dispute, however, did not necessarily become victims of
Stalin's violent repression in the 1930s.[13] Many scholars and bureaucrats
active in the criminological organizations, particularly those belonging
to the Communist Party, ended up in prisons and camps, including
bureaucrats E. G. Shirvindt and A. G. Beloborodov.[14] Others, however,
notably M. N. Gernet and A. N. Trainin, managed to continue with
their careers despite the accusations leveled against their work. Partially
because criminologists never developed a true corporate identity, because
they remained first and foremost members of their own scholarly disciplines, the restructuring of criminology did not destroy their professional
identities. Instead, these specialists were able, by shifting the focus of
their studies to fit the appropriate ideological framework, to continue
to advance their scholarly agendas even after criminological research as
conducted in the 1920s could no longer be pursued.[15]

The 1929 Communist Academy dispute initiated significant changes
in the structure and practice of criminology. First, it led to a shift in the
leadership and approach to crime studies. Soviet legal scholars, particularly younger cadres dedicated to the principles of Marxism-Leninism like

Bulatov, took control of the debate and established the discipline's new orientation. In this way, the Communist Academy dispute occurred along the same vein as other "purges" in Soviet society—the new communist-educated specialists took the initiative to purge their professional groups of the old "bourgeois specialists." Furthermore, arguments against criminology focused specifically on its methodological approaches, emphasizing that criminology itself was a sound Marxist discipline except for the mistakes of some of its members, whose errors simply had to be rectified for studies to proceed. The criticisms of neolombrosianism leveled against some criminologists meant that they could no longer investigate crime as they had during the transitional period, but not that crime could no longer be studied. Instead, criminology would have to minimize the study of individual offenders while focusing more closely on corrective measures and explaining crime in terms of socialist and class principles, class enemies, and outdated beliefs. The interdisciplinary nature of criminology and the lack of agreement among criminologists regarding methodology that had made crime studies so diverse and innovative in the 1920s had become unacceptable by 1929. Criminology's resistance to homogenization, which had enabled it to negotiate successfully the Soviet bureaucratic structure, in the end contributed to its downfall.

The liquidation and subsequent reorganization in 1931 of the People's Commissariat of Internal Affairs (NKVD), the State Institute's main patron, further curtailed the role and scope of criminology. Local criminological bureaus were disbanded, and the State Institute was transferred to the auspices of the People's Commissariat of Justice (NKIu). In its new capacity, the State Institute was to study only penal law and correctional labor. In 1934, the State Institute itself was reorganized to focus specifically on practical questions regarding the punishment and rehabilitation of offenders, without considering their psychology or physiology.[16] This move brought to an end the study of the criminal individual, and the innovative work conducted during the transitional period.

The history of criminology in Soviet Russia was shaped both by its reformist goals and the influence of socialist ideology. Early practitioners attempted, through the establishment of professional criminological organizations, to systematize the study of crime according to their commitment to social reform and scientific investigation, fulfilling as well the state's need to understand and eliminate crime. During the NEP, these goals proved to be compatible, but after 1930 the scope of criminological study as it had been practiced became potentially too subversive to be allowed to exist in the ideologically charged environment of Stalinism. The discipline of criminology could not, in the end, provide an autonomous forum for professionals to question the process of socialist construction or to offer alternative visions of the socialist future. Indeed, by exposing the points where the state's social goals and policies came into conflict with the behavior of its citizens, criminologists potentially threatened the stability of the very norms they were trying to institute. Under Stalin, the state lost its interest in analyzing crime as a barometer of the progress of socialist construction. Crime studies instead confirmed the persistence of crime and undercut the sense of progress toward socialism being made during the First Five-Year Plan. Since, according to Stalinist logic, the conditions that caused crime had been eradicated under socialism, any deviance that continued to occur could only be explained as remnants of the "old way of life" persisting among small pockets of unenlightened peasants such as kulaks or "enemies of the people," who still had not come to embrace the new order. In this way, crime became a reflection of resistance or a sign of opposition rather than a response to socioeconomic conditions. Moreover, a shift in penal policy from the correction of prisoners to the state's exploitation of them as a labor force further reduced the regime's interest in determining the motives and characteristics of offenders and working toward their rehabilitation.[17] Of course, crime persisted in Soviet Russia, but without the pursuit of a nuanced understanding of its causes and remedies.

LOOKING BACK—THE PERSISTING INFLUENCE OF EARLY SOVIET CRIMINOLOGY

Criminology revived in the 1950s and 1960s in connection with the de-Stalinization of society that began in earnest following N. S. Khrushchev's "Secret Speech" to the Twentieth Party Congress in 1956 in which he first acknowledged the abuses of the Stalinist system. The call for renewed "Leninist norms" in Soviet policy inspired legal scholars to look back to the early Soviet period and the formation of legislation as a basis from which to recreate Soviet law.[18] The new post-Stalin criminology, however, had to be "Leninist" as well, which meant a strict adherence to the principles of Marxism-Leninism in its theory and practice. While the post-Stalin criminologists sought to rebuild their discipline on the foundations their predecessors had established during the 1920s, they found it necessary to distance themselves from the "mistakes" of the past, specifically the focus on the criminal personality as identified in the Communist Academy dispute, and to draw a sharp distinction between the methodologies of the early period and their own more "Soviet" approach.

A. A. Gertsenzon, a legal scholar who as a young graduate of Moscow State University's Institute of Soviet Law in the mid-1920s had been involved in the activities of the criminological organizations and had published articles on various aspects of criminological research, led the efforts to revive criminology and reorient the discipline along Marxist-Leninist lines after 1956.[19] Participating in the Communist Academy dispute in 1929, Gertsenzon had argued that "the study of the criminal personality . . . cannot in any way effectively answer the question of the causes of crime."[20] Although he had contributed to the criticisms of the discipline, especially its condemnation of the psychiatric approach, he remained committed to the basic principles of criminological study. As early as 1945, in a call for the reinstatement of criminological research, Gertsenzon emphasized that a primary reason for the liquidation of criminology had been its "incorrect theoretical position regarding the nature of crime." He suggested, however, that such deficiencies did not detract from the importance of studying crime, but instead pointed to the need to reorganize crime studies in accordance with the "principles of the socialist science of criminal law."[21] The new criminology Gertsenzon envisioned would be a more "Soviet" one than had existed in the 1920s.

As he worked to reestablish criminology in the 1950s and 1960s, Gertsenzon identified the limitations of the early Soviet approaches to crime studies. One of the problems criminology had faced in the 1920s, he argued, was that "bourgeois influences" affected the Soviet legal sciences too strongly and prevented the full development of Marxist-Leninist theories of criminal law. Furthermore, he stressed, a rudimentary understanding of the sociological causes of crime had allowed "neolombrosian" theories to flourish within criminological studies.[22] The worst errors, he pointed out, had occurred because "the methods of studying crime and its causes did not follow a sufficiently deep and multifaceted Marxist-Leninist theoretical development."[23] In the new Soviet criminology, however, "there is not the slightest basis for reexamining the general conceptions of the causes of crime or for making even the least concession to biological or biosocial theories."[24] In contrast to the "neolombrosianism" of early Soviet criminology, the new criminology would study the criminal personality only to determine "how much a person was infected with remnants of the past in his consciousness, how much these remnants determined the antisocial behavior of this person, which conditions contributed to this, and what preventative steps should be taken to ensure the correction and reeducation of this person."[25]

Gertsenzon's reworked vision of criminology stressed the basic usefulness of the criminological work conducted in the 1920s but emphasized its fundamental ideological "mistakes." He sought to build upon the traditions of criminological research in Russia while distancing the new Soviet criminology from the errors of the past. Indeed, post-Stalin criminologists emphasized the isolated nature of these past methodological "flaws" as occurring solely within "the framework of individual theoretical works."[26] By admitting the mistakes of the past, criminology could proceed along the "correct" path of Marxist-Leninist development, and its post-Stalin practitioners situated it firmly within the ideological context of their time.[27]

By the mid-1970s criminology had been sufficiently reestablished as a "Soviet" social science that a more nuanced evaluation of criminology in the 1920s could occur. I. S. Noi, a legal scholar and criminologist from Saratov, suggested that the 1920s criminologists "understood that a person's consciousness is a product of society" and never argued otherwise in their studies. Early criminological research reflected the complexity of studying criminals and the need to consider social, psychological, and physiological characteristics to determine the causes of crime. Noi emphasized that a primary contribution of the 1920s criminologists was the creativity of the solutions they proposed to solve the problem of crime.[28] Criminological study in the 1920s, Noi asserted, was relatively free of the "abstract-deductive (ideological) methods" that came to dominate it after 1931. The legal scholars who took over criminological work after 1931, Noi stressed, were well aware of the sociological factors of crime but poorly acquainted with the psychophysiological characteristics of criminals. This prevented them from conducting the sort of penetrating studies carried out in the 1920s, hindered the development of new knowledge about crime, and forced criminological study to rely increasingly on simplistic explanations of crime that centered on "remnants of capitalism in the consciousness of people and the influence of capitalist encirclement."[29]

Noi's rehabilitation of early Soviet criminological methodology coincided with the beginnings of a shift in Soviet criminology. After 1976, criminologists again began including discussions of biological characteristics in their studies of crime, bringing sex, age, and psychological function back into crime analyses.[30] One must wonder, however, if the link Soviet authorities identified between dissidence and mental illness contributed to the rehabilitation of the biological perspective in criminology at this junction. Late Soviet criminologists ignored this potentially negative application of their discipline as they hoped the expansion of criminological methodologies begun in the 1970s and solidified under the policies of *glasnost'* in the 1980s signaled a new objectivity and autonomy in the science of crime and a new role for criminology in the post-Soviet era.[31]

NOTES

Introduction

1. A. E. Petrova, "Sluchai izuvecheniia muzha," in *Prestupnyi mir Moskvy. Sbornik statei*, ed. M. N. Gernet (Moscow: "Pravo i zhizn'," 1924), 82–83. Petrova indicated that the penis was cut off three-quarters of a centimeter from its base. Bacteriological analysis revealed the presence of severe gonorrhea in the amputated member. After several attempts, the severed penis was reattached and eventually regained its normal functions.

2. Ibid., 84.

3. Ibid., 83.

4. N. P. Brukhanskii, *Materialy po seksual'noi psikhopatologii. Psikhiatricheskie ekspertizy* (Moscow: M. & S. Sabashnikovykh, 1927), 14.

5. Ibid., 17. Eric Naiman, *Sex in Public: The Incarnation of Early Soviet Ideology* (Princeton, NJ: Princeton University Press, 1997), 124–26, discusses Brukhanskii's analysis of Nastia's crime as symbolic of the need to "castrate" the diseased elements of society introduced by the New Economic Policy (i.e., capitalism) in order to remove such corruption from Soviet life.

6. The connection among women, the countryside, and backwardness has been identified by several scholars. Political propaganda posters provide the clearest example of the dichotomy between woman-rural and men-urban. See Victoria Bonnell, "The Representation of Women in Early Soviet Political Art," *The Russian Review* 50, no. 3 (1991): 267–89; and Bonnell, "The Peasant Woman in Stalinist Political Art of the 1930s," *American Historical Review* 98, no. 1 (1993): 55–82.

7. A growing historical scholarship explores issues of identity in early Soviet Russia, framed both in terms of the construction of identity as a mechanism to negotiate daily life and also in the ways that citizenship and belonging were defined. See, among others, Golfo Alexopoulos, *Stalin's Outcasts: Aliens, Citizens, and the Soviet State, 1926–1936* (Ithaca, NY: Cornell University Press, 2003); Sheila Fitzpatrick, *Tear Off the Masks! Identity and Imposture in Twentieth-Century Russia* (Princeton, NJ: Princeton University Press, 2005); Igal Halfin, *From Darkness to Light: Class, Consciousness, and Salvation in Revolutionary Russia* (Pittsburgh, PA: University of Pittsburgh Press, 2000); Jochen Hellbeck, *Revolution on My Mind:*

Writing a Diary under Stalin (Cambridge: Harvard University Press, 2006); and Christina Kiaer and Eric Naiman, eds., *Everyday Life in Early Soviet Russia: Taking the Revolution Inside* (Bloomington: Indiana University Press, 2006).

8. On anxiety, sexuality, and social policy during the NEP, see Frances Bernstein, *The Dictatorship of Sex: Lifestyle Advice for the Soviet Masses* (DeKalb: Northern Illinois University Press, 2007); Gregory Carleton, *Sexual Revolution in Bolshevik Russia* (Pittsburgh, PA: University of Pittsburgh Press, 2005); Sheila Fitzpatrick, "Sex and Revolution: An Examination of Literary and Statistical Data on the Mores of Soviet Students in the 1920s," *Journal of Modern History* 50, no. 2 (June 1978): 252–78; Dan Healey, *Homosexual Desire in Revolutionary Russia: The Regulation of Sexual and Gender Dissent* (Chicago, IL: University of Chicago Press, 2001); Naiman, *Sex in Public*; and Tricia Starks, *The Body Soviet: Propaganda, Hygiene, and the Revolutionary State* (Madison: Universtiy of Wisconsin Press, 2008).

9. See Wendy Z. Goldman, *Women, the State, and Revolution: Soviet Family Policy and Social Life, 1917–1936* (Cambridge: Cambridge University Press, 1993), 185–253. Studies dealing with family policy in the Russian and Soviet context include, among others, Barbara Engel, *Women in Russia, 1700–2000* (Cambridge: Cambridge University Press, 2004), 140–85; David L. Hoffmann, "Stalinist Pronatalism in Its Pan-European Context," *Journal of Social History* 34, no. 1 (Fall 2000): 35–54; Douglas Northrop, "Subaltern Dialogues: Subversion and Resistance in Soviet Uzbek Family Law," in *Contending with Stalinism: Soviet Power and Popular Resistance in the 1930s*, ed. Lynn Viola (Ithaca, NY: Cornell University Press, 2002), 109–38; David Ransel, ed., *The Family in Imperial Russia: New Lines of Historical Research* (Urbana: University of Illinois Press, 1978); and Elizabeth Waters, "The Modernization of Russian Motherhood, 1917–1937," *Soviet Studies* 44, no. 1 (1992): 123–35.

10. For instance, the state's limited resources proved unable to solve the persistent and overwhelming problem of homeless children, or *besprizornye*. Even the legalization of adoption in the 1926 code, intended to ease the burden on the state to care for these children, did not significantly remedy the problem. See Alan Ball, *And Now My Soul Is Hardened: Abandoned Children in Soviet Russia, 1918–1930* (Berkeley: University of California Press, 1994). Elizabeth Wood also makes this observation: "leading Bolshevik policymakers sought to jettison state responsibility for all but the strongest parts of the economy, in the process undermining the social welfare goals of the revolution and bringing into question the commitment of the new rulers to their stated goal of emancipating women workers and peasants." Elizabeth Wood, *The Baba and the Comrade: Gender and Politics in Revolutionary Russia* (Bloomington: Indiana University Press, 1997), 124.

11. See Mary Buckley, *Women and Ideology in the Soviet Union* (Ann Arbor: University of Michigan Press, 1989); Janet Evans, "The Communist Party of the Soviet Union and the Women's Question: The Case of the 1936 Decree 'In Defense of Mother and Child,'" *Journal of Contemporary History* 16, no. 4 (October 1981): 757–75; Goldman, *Women, the State, and Revolution*; and David L. Hoffmann,

Stalinist Values: The Cultural Norms of Soviet Modernity, 1917–1941 (Ithaca, NY: Cornell University Press, 2003), 88–117.

12. See Goldman, *Women, the State, and Revolution*, 341–43.

13. As Katerina Clark calls it, a revolutionary "ecosystem" shaped and formed in reaction to developing circumstances. See her *Petersburg: Crucible of Cultural Revolution* (Cambridge: Harvard University Press, 1995).

14. See Sheila Fitzpatrick, ed., *Cultural Revolution in Russia, 1928–1931* (Bloomington: Indiana University Press, 1978). See also her work, *The Cultural Front: Power and Culture in Revolutionary Russia* (Ithaca, NY: Cornell University Press, 1992).

15. David Hoffmann discusses Timasheff's argument and compares it to Trotsky's similar vision of revolutionary betrayal. He argues, "Far from being a partial retreat or a return to the prerevolutionary past, Stalinism remained, for both Party leaders and the Soviet population, a system dedicated to socialist ideology and progress toward communism. . . . The achievement of socialism permitted the use of traditional institutions and culture to support and further the new order." David Hoffmann, *Stalinist Values*, 3–4. See also Stephen Kotkin, *Magnetic Mountain: Stalinism as Civilization* (Berkeley: University of California Press, 1995); and Peter Holquist, "Information Is the Alpha and Omega of Our Work: Bolshevik Surveillance in Its Pan-European Context," *Journal of Modern History* 69, no. 3 (1997): 415–50. Timasheff's thesis can be found in his work, *The Great Retreat: The Growth and Decline of Communism in Russia* (New York: E. P. Dutton, 1946).

16. Michael David-Fox, "What is Cultural Revolution?" *The Russian Review* 58, no. 2 (April 1999): 193. In this article, David-Fox challenges the "cultural revolution" paradigm first proposed in 1978 by Sheila Fitzpatrick in *Cultural Revolution in Russia, 1928–1931*. Some scholars, notably Katerina Clark and David Joravsky, have also identified a long Soviet "cultural revolution" extending as far back as World War I. See Clark, *Petersburg: Crucible of Cultural Revolution*; and Joravsky, "The Construction of the Stalinist Psyche," in *Cultural Revolution in Russia, 1928–1931*. Indeed, some historians have argued that we can find the roots of the Stalinist regime's nature in the wartime experiences of the Bolsheviks. Their ruthless willingness to use violence established dangerous precedents. Furthermore, the brutalization of the population during the extended wartime period (1914–1921), and their responses to the Bolsheviks' policies further enabled the course of events that followed. See Sheila Fitzpatrick, "The Civil War as a Formative Experience," in *Bolshevik Culture: Experiment and Order in the Russian Revolution*, ed. Abbott Gleason, Peter Kenez, and Richard Stites (Bloomington: Indiana University Press, 1985), 57–76; Peter Holquist, *Making War, Forging Revolution: Russia's Continuum of Crisis, 1914–1921* (Cambridge: Harvard University Press, 2002); Diane Koenker, William G. Rosenberg, and Ronald G. Suny, eds., *Party, State, and Society in the Russian Civil War* (Bloomington: Indiana University Press, 1989); Donald J. Raleigh, *Experiencing Russia's Civil War: Politics, Society, and Revolutionary Culture in Saratov, 1917–1922* (Princeton, NJ: Princeton University Press, 2002); and Kate Transchel,

Under the Influence: Working-Class Drinking, Temperance, and Cultural Revolution in Russia, 1895–1932 (Pittsburgh, PA: University of Pittsburgh Press, 2006).

17. Recent works on the relationship between the Soviet state and educated Russian society include James W. Heinzen, *Inventing a Soviet Countryside: Soviet State Power and the Transformation of Rural Russia, 1917–1929* (Pittsburgh, PA: University of Pittsburgh Press, 2004); Stuart Finkel, "Purging the Public Intellectual: The 1922 Expulsions from Soviet Russia," *The Russian Review* 62, no. 4 (October 2003): 589–613; Martin A. Miller, *Freud and the Bolsheviks: Psychoanalysis in Imperial Russia and the Soviet Union* (New Haven, CT: Yale University Press, 1998); and Amy Nelson, *Music for the Revolution: Musicians and Power in Early Soviet Russia* (University Park: Pennsylvania State University Press, 2004). On early Soviet criminology, see Louise Shelley, "Soviet Criminology: Its Birth and Demise, 1917–1936" (Ph.D. diss., University of Pennsylvania, 1977); Shelley, "The 1929 Dispute on Soviet Criminology," *Soviet Union* 6, no. 2 (1979): 175–85; Peter H. Solomon, Jr., *Soviet Criminologists and Criminal Policy: Specialists in Policy-Making* (New York: Columbia University Press, 1978); D. A. Shestakov, "K voprosu ob istorii sovetskoi kriminologii," *Vestnik Leningradskogo Universiteta*, seriia 6, *Istoriia KPSS, nauchnyi kommunizm, filosofiia, pravo*, no. 2 (1991): 74–81; and L. O. Ivanov and L. V. Il'ina, *Puti i sud'by otechestvennoi kriminologii* (Moscow: Nauka, 1991).

18. Elizabeth Wood argues that the ignorant rural woman, the "baba," served as a foil for defining the attributes of the New Soviet Woman. I would emphasize a much broader interpretation of the role that rural qualities played in perceptions of Soviet women. See Wood, *The Baba and the Comrade*. On the New Soviet Woman, see also Lynn Attwood, *Creating the New Soviet Woman: Women's Magazines as Engineers of Female Identity* (New York: St. Martin's Press, 1999); and Barbara Clements, "The Birth of the New Soviet Woman," in *Bolshevik Culture: Experiment and Order in the Russian Revolution*, ed. Abbott Gleason, Peter Kenez, and Richard Stites (Bloomington: Indiana University Press, 1985), 220–37.

19. For example, in her study of interwar France, Mary Louise Roberts argues that anxieties regarding the changing position of women could be dispelled by adapting the traditional female attributes of domesticity and motherhood to the new postwar context. See Roberts, *Civilization Without Sexes: Reconstructing Gender in Postwar France, 1917–1927* (Chicago, IL: University of Chicago Press, 1994).

20. See Anna Geifman, *Thou Shalt Kill: Revolutionary Terrorism in Russia, 1894–1917* (Princeton, NJ: Princeton University Press, 1993); and Richard Wortman, *The Development of a Russian Legal Consciousness* (Chicago, IL: University of Chicago Press, 1976).

21. On the Civil War, see, among others, Vladimir Brovkin, *Behind the Front Lines in the Civil War: Political Parties and Social Movements in Russia* (Princeton, NJ: Princeton University Press, 1994); Holquist, *Making War, Forging Revolution*; and Raleigh, *Experiencing Russia's Civil War*.

22. On the NEP, see, among others, Alan Ball, *Russia's Last Capitalists: The Nepmen, 1921–1929* (Berkeley: University of California Press, 1987); Vladimir

Brovkin, *Russia after Lenin: Politics, Culture, and Society, 1921–1929* (London: Routledge, 1998); Sheila Fitzpatrick, Alexander Rabinowitch, and Richard Stites, eds., *Russia in the Era of NEP: Explorations in Soviet Society and Culture* (Bloomington: Indiana University Press, 1991); and Roger Pethybridge, *One Step Backwards, Two Steps Forward: Soviet Society and Politics in the New Economic Policy* (Oxford: Clarendon Press, 1990).

23. On the Bolshevik cultural transformation, see, among others, Jeffrey Brooks, *Thank You Comrade Stalin: Soviet Public Culture from Revolution to Cold War* (Princeton, NJ: Princeton University Press, 2000); Abbott Gleason, Peter Kenez, and Richard Stites, eds., *Bolshevik Culture: Experiment and Order in the Russian Revolution* (Bloomington: Indiana University Press, 1985); Peter Kenez, "Liquidating Illiteracy in Revolutionary Russia," *Russian History* 9, nos. 2–3 (1982): 173–86; Lynn Mally, *Culture of the Future: The Proletkult Movement in Revolutionary Russia* (Berkeley: University of California Press, 1990); Amy Nelson, *Music for the Revolution*; William G. Rosenberg, *Bolshevik Visions: First Phase of the Cultural Revolution in Soviet Russia* (Ann Arbor: University of Michigan Press, 1990); Richard Stites, *Revolutionary Dreams: Utopian Vision and Experimental Life in the Russian Revolution* (Oxford: Oxford University Press, 1991); and James von Geldern, *Bolshevik Festivals, 1917–1920* (Berkeley: University of California Press, 1993).

24. On the Soviet view of law and crime, see Piers Beirne and Alan Hunt, "Lenin, Crime, and Penal Politics, 1917–1924," in *The Origins and Growth of Criminology: Essays in Intellectual History, 1760–1945*, ed. Piers Beirne (Aldershot, England: Dartmouth, 1994), 181–217; Robert Sharlet, "Pashukanis and the Withering Away of Law in the USSR," in *Cultural Revolution in Russia, 1928–1931*, ed. Sheila Fitzpatrick (Bloomington: Indiana University Press, 1978), 168–88; and Peter H. Solomon, Jr., *Soviet Criminal Justice under Stalin* (Cambridge: Cambridge University Press, 1996).

25. On the need for legal codes during the NEP, see Solomon, *Soviet Criminal Justice under Stalin*, 17–27.

26. Ibid., 27–33. See also V. P. Portnov and M. M. Slavin, "Iz istorii sovetskogo ugolovnogo prava (1917–1920 gg.)," in *Ugolovnoe pravo v bor'be s prestupnost'iu* (Moscow: Institut gosudarstva i prava Akademii nauk, 1981), 140–50. Many of those active in legal and criminological studies in the 1920s participated in drafting the 1903 code, as well as the later Soviet (1922 and 1926) versions.

27. Indeed, psychiatrist L. G. Orshanskii argued that there were many socially dangerous crimes, mostly stemming from the process of constructing the new way of life, but few socially dangerous criminals. See his "Chto takoe sotsial'naia opasnost'?" *Rabochii sud*, no. 7 (1927): 630–31. See also E. K. Krasnushkin, "Chto takoe prestupnik?" *Prestupnik i prestupnost'*, no. 1 (1926): 6; and N. Krylenko, "Criminal Law in the Soviet Union," *Communist* 2, no. 10 (1927): 173–80 and no. 11 (1927): 274–82. Krylenko noted that "the criminal code approaches every act designed against this order, and determines the measures of self-defense to be adopted by the new society, according to the degree of danger represented by the

said act. . . . The widespread powers given to the courts in defining the measure of social defense to be applied, . . . or the degree of social danger the culprit may represent, characterizes the fundamental attitude of Soviet criminal law toward the criminal" (180).

28. B. Ianchkovskii, "Prestuplenie i kara v Sovetskoi Rossii," *Proletarskaia revoliutsiia i pravo*, no. 15 (1921): 16.

29. The successful application of progressive penal theories in Soviet Russia was hindered by the poor physical conditions of prisons, shortages of trained personnel, financial constraints, and discrepancies in policy emphasis between the center and the local government and prison administrators. With the rise of Stalinism, the role of compulsory labor shifted from being a tool to rehabilitate the prisoner to serving the needs of the state. Cultural enlightenment and educational work, however, remained a central focus of penal policy throughout the 1920s and into the First Five-Year Plan period. Ellen Mary Wimberg, "'Replacing the Shackles': Soviet Penal Theory, Policy, and Practice, 1917–1930" (Ph.D. diss., University of Pittsburgh, 1996). See also Bruce F. Adams, *The Politics of Punishment: Prison Reform in Russia, 1863–1917* (DeKalb: Northern Illinois University Press, 1996); and Peter H. Solomon, Jr., "Soviet Penal Policy, 1917–1941: A Reinterpretation," *Slavic Review* 39, no. 2 (June 1980): 195–217.

30. On peasant customary law, see Moshe Lewin, "Customary Law and Russian Rural Society in the Post-Reform Era," *The Russian Review* 44, no. 1 (January 1985): 1–19; Stephen P. Frank, "Popular Justice, Community, and Culture among the Russian Peasantry, 1870–1900," *The Russian Review* 46, no. 3 (July 1987): 239–65; and Cathy Frierson, "Crime and Punishment in the Russian Village: Rural Concepts of Criminality at the End of the Nineteenth Century," *Slavic Review* 46, no. 1 (Spring 1987): 55–69. On the nature of judges in early Soviet courts, see Judah Zelich, *Soviet Administration of Criminal Law* (Philadelphia: University of Pennsylvania Press, 1931), 328.

31. See Sheila Fitzpatrick, "Stalin and the Making of a New Elite, 1925–1939," *Slavic Review* 38, no. 3 (1979): 377–402.

32. Scholars of the early modern period have used crime very effectively to reflect broader social attitudes. See, for instance, Edward Muir and Guido Ruggiero, eds., *History from Crime* (Baltimore, MD: Johns Hopkins University Press, 1994); Natalie Z. Davis, *The Return of Martin Guerre* (Cambridge: Harvard University Press, 1983); Carlo Ginzburg, *The Cheese and the Worms: The Cosmos of a Sixteenth-Century Miller*, trans. John and Anne Tedeschi (New York: Penguin Books, 1982); and Sarah Maza, *Private Lives and Public Affairs: The Causes Célèbres of Prerevolutionary France* (Berkeley: University of California Press, 1993).

33. See Clarice Feinman, *Women in the Criminal Justice System* (New York: Praeger, 1986), 3–4. Other contemporary analyses of female crime include Dorie Klein, "The Etiology of Female Crime: A Review of the Literature," in *The Origins and Growth of Criminology: Essays in Intellectual History, 1760–1945*, ed. Piers Beirne (Aldershot, England: Dartmouth, 1994); Ngaire Naffine, *Feminism and Criminology*

(Philadelphia, PA: Temple University Press, 1996); James W. Messerschmidt, *Capitalism, Patriarchy, and Crime: Toward a Socialist Feminist Criminology* (Totowa, NJ: Rowman & Littlefield, 1986); Rita Simon, "American Women and Crime," in *Readings in Comparative Criminology*, ed. Louise Shelley, 1–17 (Carbondale: Southern Illinois University Press, 1981); and Carol Smart, *Women, Crime, and Criminology: A Feminist Critique* (London: Routledge and K. Paul, 1977). See also Judith Walkowitz, *City of Dreadful Delight: Narratives of Sexual Danger in Late-Victorian London* (Chicago, IL: University of Chicago Press, 1992); and Ann-Louise Shapiro, *Breaking the Codes: Female Criminality in the Fin-de-Siècle* (Stanford, CA: Stanford University Press, 1996).

34. On women's emancipation and Bolshevik attitudes toward women, see Barbara Evans Clements, Barbara Alpern Engel, and Christine D. Worobec, eds., *Russia's Women: Accommodation, Resistance, Transformation* (Berkeley: University of California Press, 1991); Wendy Z. Goldman, *Women at the Gates: Gender and Industry in Stalin's Russia* (Cambridge: Cambridge University Press, 2002); Gregory J. Massell, *The Surrogate Proletariat: Moslem Women and Revolutionary Strategies in Soviet Central Asia, 1919–1929* (Princeton, NJ: Princeton University Press, 1974); Natalia Pushkareva, *Women in Russian History from the Tenth to the Twentieth Century*, trans. and ed. Eve Levin (Armonk, NY: M. E. Sharpe, 1997); Pushkareva, *Russkaia zhenshchina: Istoriia i sovremennost'* (Moscow: Ladomir, 2002); Richard Stites, *The Women's Liberation Movement in Russia: Feminism, Nihilism, and Bolshevism, 1860–1930* (Princeton, NJ: Princeton University Press, 1990); and Wood, *The Baba and the Comrade*. In *Iconography of Power: Soviet Political Posters under Lenin and Stalin* (Berkeley: University of California Press, 1997), Victoria Bonnell examines propaganda and the visual representation of women.

35. On crime in tsarist Russia, see Stephen P. Frank, *Crime, Cultural Conflict, and Justice in Rural Russia, 1856–1914* (Berkeley: University of California Press, 1999); Cathy A. Frierson, "Crime and Punishment in the Russian Village"; Joan Neuberger, *Hooliganism: Crime, Culture, and Power in St. Petersburg, 1900–1914* (Berkeley: University of California Press, 1993); and Richard Sutton, "Crime and Social Change in Russia after the Great Reforms: Laws, Courts, and Criminals, 1874–1894" (Ph.D. diss., Indiana University, 1984). Recent studies that deal with crime in the 1920s include Eric Naiman, "The Case of Chubarov Alley: Collective Rape, Utopian Desire, and the Mentality of NEP," *Russian History* 17, no. 1 (1990): 1–30; N. B. Lebina, *Povsednevnaia zhizn' sovetskogo goroda. Normy i anomalii 1920–1930 gody* (St. Petersburg: Zhurnal "Neva," 1999); Lebina and A. N. Chistikov, *Obyvateli i reformy. Kartiny povsednevnoi zhizni gorozhan v gody NEPa i Khrushchevskogo desiatiletiia* (St. Petersburg: Dmitrii Bulanin, 2003); and V. I. Musaev, *Prestupnost' v Petrograde v 1917–1921 gg.* (St. Petersburg: Dmitrii Bulanin, 2001). Scholarship on female crime in Russia and the Soviet Union includes Iu. M. Antonian, *Prestupnost' sredi zhenshchin* (Moscow: Rossiiskoe pravo, 1992); Stephen P. Frank, "Narratives within Numbers: Women, Crime, and Judicial Statistics in Imperial Russia, 1834–1913," *The Russian Review* 55, no. 4 (October 1996): 541–66;

Louise Shelley, "Female Criminality in the 1920s: A Consequence of Inadvertent and Deliberate Change," *Russian History* 9, nos. 2–3 (1982): 265–84; and O. A. Talysheva, "Sovetskie kriminologii o prestupnosti zhenshchin v 1920–1940–e gody," in *Voprosy sovershenstvovaniia zakonodatel'stva i pravoprimenitel'noi deiatel'nosti. Sbornik nauchnykh trudov*, 201–12 (Cheliabinsk: Cheliabinskii gosudarstvennyi universitet, 1998).

36. Shelley, "Female Criminality in the 1920s." Shelley asserts that the increase in female crime rates the criminologists observed after the revolution occurred as an unintended result of the social situation and the massive changes of the time.

37. On the role of the Department of Moral Statistics and the development of the statistical profession in late Imperial and early Soviet Russia, see Martine Mespoulet, *Statistique et révolution en Russie. Un compromis impossible (1880–1930)* (Rennes, France: Presses Universitaires de Rennes, 2001); S. S. Ostroumov, *Sovetskaia sudebnaia statistika* (Moscow: Gosudarstvennoe izdatel'stvo iuridicheskoi literatury, 1952); and Kenneth Pinnow, "Making Suicide Soviet: Medicine, Moral Statistics, and the Politics of Social Science in Bolshevik Russia, 1920–1930" (Ph.D. diss., Columbia University, 1998).

38. Women involved in criminology include: prerevolutionary doctor and criminal anthropologist P. N. Tarnovskaia, psychiatrist A. N. Teren'teva, psychiatrist Ts. M. Feinberg, economist A. S. Zvonitskaia, psychiatrist A. E. Petrova, A. Shestakova, S. A. Ukshe, and A. G. Kharlamova. From the professional training of this small group, it appears that women had more success in the discipline if they came from psychiatric or medical backgrounds than as legal scholars. One exception to the general rule that female criminologists came to the same conclusions regarding women criminals as male criminologists did can be found in T. Kremleva, "Vory i vorovki bol'shikh magazinov," *Problemy prestupnosti*, no. 4 (1929): 24–38. Kremleva examines shoplifting in Moscow and takes a completely socioeconomic view, arguing that women steal from stores because of material need and not out of hysteria or under the influence of their physiological cycles. Kremleva adamantly emphasizes that western literature on the sexually based nature of shoplifting is wrong. Her article, however, is the sole treatment of the subject in the Soviet context and thus her conclusions cannot be compared to those of a male counterpart.

39. Frances Bernstein also observes the homogeneity in professional discourse in her work on popular sex advice. See her work, *Dictatorship of Sex*, 16.

1—Anthropology, Sociology, and Female Crime

1. The *Svod statisticheskikh svedenii po delam ugolovnom*, the official compilation of Russian judicial statistics, was published annually between 1873 and 1915. In contrast, France began publishing official criminal statistics in 1827, and the first studies based on that information appeared in the early 1830s. See also Rich-

ard F. Wetzell, *Inventing the Criminal: A History of German Criminology, 1880–1945* (Chapel Hill: University of North Carolina Press, 2000), 21. On the tsarist Judicial Reforms, see Sergei M. Kazantsev, "The Judicial Reform of 1864 and the Procuracy in Russia," in *Reforming Justice in Russia, 1864–1996: Power, Culture, and the Limits of Legal Order*, ed. Peter H. Solomon, Jr. (Armonk, NY: M. E. Sharpe, 1997), 44–60; M. G. Korotkikh, "Sudebnaia reforma 1864 g. v Rossii," *Voprosy istorii*, no. 12 (1987): 20–34; and Wortman, *The Development of a Russian Legal Consciousness*. Concerns regarding the connections among urbanization, industrialization, and crime, and fears of the working classes, were well established in western European thought by the late nineteenth century. See, for instance, Eric Johnson, *Urbanization and Crime: Germany, 1871–1914* (Cambridge: Cambridge University Press, 1995; Gareth Jones, *Outcast London: A Study in the Relationship between Classes in Victorian Society* (Oxford: Clarendon Press, 1971); and Walkowitz, *City of Dreadful Delight*.

2. See Adams, *The Politics of Punishment*, 140–41; and Abby M. Schrader, *Languages of the Lash: Corporal Punishment and Identity in Imperial Russia* (DeKalb: Northern Illinois University Press, 2002).

3. Several scholars have recently linked the nature of the Russian and Soviet state, in terms of its projects and goals, both to the modernizing European states, particularly after the First World War, and to the Enlightenment project of rationality, seeing the Stalinist state in particular as a logical outcome of these processes. See Kotkin, *Magnetic Mountain*; Hoffman, *Stalinist Values*; and Holquist, *Making War, Forging Revolution*. On the development of Russian criminology, see also Daniel Beer, *Renovating Russia: The Human Sciences and the Fate of Liberal Modernity, 1880–1930* (Ithaca, NY: Cornell Universty Press, 2008); and Zygmunt Ronald Bialkowaski III, "The Transformation of Academic Criminal Jurisprudence into Criminology in Late Imperial Russia" (Ph.D. diss., Berkeley, 2007).

4. See, for example, Piers Beirne, *Inventing Criminology: Essays on the Rise of Homo Criminalis* (Albany: State University of New York Press, 1993); Beirne, ed., *The Origins and Growth of Criminology: Essays in Intellectual History, 1760–1945* (Aldershot, England: Dartmouth, 1994); Silviana Galassi, *Kriminologie im deutschen Kaiserreich. Geschichte einer gebrochenen Verwissenschaftlichung* (Stuttgart: Franz Steiner Verland, 2004); David A. Jones, *History of Criminology: A Philosophical Perspective* (New York: Greenwood Press, 1986); Hermann Mannheim, ed., *Pioneers in Criminology* (London: Stevens and Sons, 1960); Robert A. Nye, "Heredity or Milieu: The Foundations of Modern European Criminological Theory," *Isis* 67, no. 3 (September 1976): 335–55; William V. Pelfrey, *The Evolution of Criminology* (Cincinnati, OH: Anderson, 1980); Leon Radzinowicz, *Ideology and Crime* (New York: Columbia University Press, 1966); Stephen Schafer, *Theories in Criminology: Past and Present Philosophies of the Crime Problem* (New York: Random House, 1969); Alfred Soman, "Deviance and Criminal Justice in Western Europe, 1300–1800: An Essay in Structure," *Criminal Justice History* 1 (1980): 1–28; John Tierney, *Criminology: Theory and Context* (London: Prentice Hall, 1996); and Wetzell, *Inventing the Criminal*.

5. Jones, *History of Criminology*, 5–6. Beccaria and his contribution to the evolution of criminology have been widely discussed. See, for example, Coleman Phillipson, *Three Criminal Law Reformers: Beccaria, Bentham, Romilly* (London: J. M. Dent and Sons, 1923); and Mannheim, ed., *Pioneers in Criminology*; and Beirne, ed., *Origins and Growth of Criminology*, 3–97. Beccaria, *Of Crimes and Punishments*, trans. Jane Grigson, intro. Marvin Wolfgang (New York: Marsilio, 1996), is a recent translation of his most influential work.

6. Radzinowicz, *Ideology and Crime*, 7–14. Beccaria's ideas served as the basis for penal reforms in Europe during the first half of the nineteenth century. For instance, English philosopher Jeremy Bentham's ideas for prison reform and his famous Panopticon prison find their origins in Beccaria's Enlightenment thought.

7. By categorizing criminology into "schools," I do not intend to imply homogeneity among scholars. The borders and boundaries of the criminological "schools" remained porous, developing in relation and in reaction to each other and incorporating a variety of perspectives and approaches. Likewise, criminal anthropology and criminal sociology did not provide the only possible approaches to crime studies at the time.

8. Radzinowicz, *Ideology and Crime*, 30, 71–74, 83–89; Jones, *History of Criminology*, 9–10; Beirne, *Inventing Criminology*, 147; and David G. Horn, *The Criminal Body: Lombroso and the Anatomy of Deviance* (New York: Routledge, 2003), 9–10. Lombroso's theories emerged in direct connection with the political context of his time, in particular the process of Italian unification and the urge to explain differences between the northern elements (to which Lombroso belonged) and the seemingly more violent and passionate southern members of the new nation. On Tarde, Durkheim, and social theory, see Geoffrey Hawthorn, *Enlightenment and Despair: A History of Social Theory*, 2nd ed. (Cambridge: Cambridge University Press, 1987).

9. See Jones, *History of Criminology*, 4.

10. This was in contrast to the descriptive psychology advocated by Emanuel Kant. Lombroso was also influenced by Auguste Comte (1798–1853) and his ideas of positivism (see n. 31 below). See Marvin E. Wolfgang, "Pioneers in Criminology: Cesare Lombroso (1835–1909)," *Journal of Criminal Law, Criminology, and Police Science* 52, no. 4 (Nov/Dec 1961): 363. Lombroso contributed to the formation of anthropology as a modern discipline in Italy. On Lombroso, see also Wolfgang, "Cesare Lombroso," in *Pioneers in Criminology*, 168–228; Mary Gibson, *Born to Crime: Cesare Lombroso and the Origins of Biological Criminology* (Westport, CT: Praeger, 2002); David G. Horn, *The Criminal Body: Lombroso and the Anatomy of Deviance* (New York: Routledge, 2003); Daniel Pick, *Faces of Degeneration: A European Disorder, c. 1848–c. 1918* (Cambridge: Cambridge University Press, 1989), 109–52; and Ysabel Rennie, *The Search for Criminal Man: A Conceptual History of the Dangerous Offender* (Lexington, MA: Lexington Books, 1978), 67–78.

11. David G. Horn, "This Norm Which Is Not One: Reading the Female Body in Lombroso's Anthropology," in *Deviant Bodies: Critical Perspectives on Difference*

in Science and Popular Culture, ed. Jennifer Terry and Jacqueline Urla (Bloomington: Indiana University Press, 1995), 112. Despite all the commotion Lombroso's theories caused in international criminological circles, *L'Uomo deliquente. Studiato in rapporto alla antropologia, alla medicina legale, ed alle discipline carcerarie* (Milano: Hoerpli, 1876) was never translated into English during Lombroso's lifetime. An expanded revision entitled *Crime, its Causes and Remedies* (1899) was published posthumously in English in 1911. Wolfgang, "Pioneers in Criminology: Cesare Lombroso," 363–64. A new English version of *Criminal Man*, translated by Mary Gibson and Nicole Hahn Rafter, appeared in 2006 (Duke University Press). It was published in French as *L'homme criminel. Étude anthropologique et médico-légale* (Paris, F. Alcan, 1887) and in German as *Der Verbrechter, in anthropologischer, ärztlicher, und juristischer Bezeihung* (Munich: Richter, 1887–1890). As far as can be determined, Lombroso's magnum opus was not translated into Russian until after the collapse of the Soviet Union.

12. Wolfgang, "Pioneers in Criminology: Cesare Lombroso," 369–70. Lombroso's interest in explaining criminals as "primitive," or atavistic, reflected growing concern throughout Europe at this time regarding the nature of modern life. Lombroso generally sought to understand why some people did not join in modern society and to explain this in terms of a genetic defect.

13. Lombroso used the concept of degeneracy to explain malformations that prevented the normal development of the fetus, which in turn appeared as "born" anomalies in criminals. In this way, degeneracy linked environmental factors such as alcoholism and other diseases (that could affect a child's fetal development) with biological elements, making degeneracy a "hereditary" condition that could weaken future generations and make them "criminal." Gibson, *Born to Crime*, 20, 25. Many scholars have explored the concept of degeneracy and its attraction among late-nineteenth-century European elites. See, among others, Daniel Beer, *Renovating Russia: The Human Sciences and the Fate of Liberal Modernity, 1880–1930* (Ithaca, NY: Cornell University Press, 2008); J. Edward Chamberlain and Sander L. Gilman, eds., *Degeneration: The Dark Side of Progress* (New York: Columbia University Press, 1985); George Frederick Drinka, *The Birth of Neurosis: Myth, Malady, and the Victorians* (New York: Simon and Schuster, 1984); Ruth Harris, *Murders and Madness: Medicine, Law, and Society in the Fin-de-Siecle* (Oxford: Oxford University Press, 1989); and Daniel Pick, *Faces of Degeneration*.

14. Wolfgang, "Pioneers in Criminology: Cesare Lombroso," 371; Jones, *History of Criminology*, 84; and Radzinowicz, *Ideology and Crime*, 49–50. See also Mary S. Gibson, "The 'Female Offender' and the Italian School of Criminal Anthropology," *Journal of European Studies* 12, no. 3 (September 1982): 158.

15. On the development of science and scientific principles in Russia, see Loren Graham, *Science in Russia and the Soviet Union* (Cambridge: Cambridge University Press, 1993).

16. Lombroso's Russian supporters produced two journals, *Arkhiv psikhiatrii, neirologii, i sudebnoi psikhopatologii* (1883–1899), edited by Pavel Kovalevskii, and

Vestnik psikhologii, kriminal'noi antropologii, i gipnotizm (later *Vestnik psikhologii, kriminal'noi antropologii, i pedologii*, 1904–1919), edited by V. M. Bekhterev. Bekhterev, P. N. Tarnovskaia, V. M. Tarnovskii, and D. A. Dril', among others, participated in the International Congresses of Criminal Anthropology held periodically in Europe between 1885 and 1906. See Laura Engelstein, *The Keys to Happiness: Sex and the Search for Modernity in Fin-de-Siècle Russia* (Ithaca, NY: Cornell University Press, 1992), 133.

17. N. S. Lobas, *Ubiitsy. Nekotorye cherty psikhofiziki prestupnikov* (Moscow: Tip. T-va D. Sytina, 1913), 11.

18. Ibid., 12–13.

19. On the terrorism and violence of the early twentieth century, see Anna Geifman, *Thou Shalt Kill: Revolutionary Terrorism in Russia, 1894–1917* (Princeton, NJ: Princeton University Press, 1993).

20. P. N. Tarnovskaia, *Zhenshchina-ubiitsy. Antropologicheskoe issledovanie* (St. Petersburg: T-vo khudozhestvennoi pechati, 1902), 496–97.

21. Ibid., 498. Despite her enthusiasm for the work of Lombroso, Tarnovskaia diverged from his viewpoints, particularly in her unwillingness to consider female sexual desire as pathological. On Tarnovskaia's interpretation of criminal anthropology and views on prostitution, see Engelstein, *Keys to Happiness*, 137–52.

22. The most important work undertaken by Dril' was on juvenile crime. See D. A. Dril', *Maloletnye prestupniki. Etiud po voprosu o chelovecheskoi prestupnosti, ee faktorakh, i sredstvakh bor'by s nei*, 2 vols. (Moscow: Tip. A. I. Mamontova i Ko., 1884–1888). This work relied on degeneration theory to argue that both heredity and the environment contributed to children's moral and physical health. On Dril' and his role in Russia, see V. E. Eminov, ed., *Kriminologiia. Uchebnoe posobie* (Moscow: Izdatel'stvo gruppa INFRA M-NORMA, 1997), 105; S. S. Ostroumov, *Prestupnost' i ee prichiny v dorevoliutsionnoi Rossii* (Moscow: Izdatel'stvo Moskovskogo universiteta, 1960), 286; and Gernet, "D. A. Dril'," in *Entsiklopedicheskii slovar' "Granat,"* vol. 19 (St. Petersburg, 1890–1904), 86–88. Dril''s interpretation of Lombrosian theory is discussed by Daniel Beer, *Renovating Russia*, 104–8, 110, 115–21. See also Bialkowski, "The Transformation of Academic Criminal Jurisprudence," 193–245.

23. George E. Snow, "Perceptions of the Link between Alcoholism and Crime in Pre-Revolutionary Russia," *Criminal Justice History* 8 (1987): 40.

24. Dril', "Nauka ugolovnoi antropologii, ee predmet i zadachi," *Vestnik psikhologii, kriminal'noi antropologii, i gipnotizma*, no. 1 (1904): 12–13.

25. Ibid., 16.

26. Ibid., 19.

27. Lombroso's basic premise, that there is something inherent in certain persons that causes them to commit crimes, has retained its attraction even as his specific methods have been discredited as pseudoscience. For example, technological advancements in neuroscience have created the possibility that brain scans will soon be able to reveal criminal proclivities inherent in the ways suspects' brains are

constructed and function. These developments raise the possibility that individuals could be labeled as potentially dangerous and detained or monitored based solely on a scan of their brains, without their having actually committed any offense or shown any inclination toward criminal activity. David Horn mentions this trend in terms of genetic theory and gene mapping, while journalist Jeffrey Rosen discusses it in the context of neuroscience and criminal law. See Horn, *The Criminal Body*, 145–47; and Rosen, "The Brain on the Stand: How Neuroscience Is Transforming the Legal System," *The New York Times Magazine*, 11 March 2007, 82–83.

28. A. A. Gertsenzon, "Protiv biologicheskikh teorii prichin prestupnosti (Ocherk pervyi)," in *Voprosy preduprezhdeniia prestupnosti* (Moscow: Izdatel'stvo "Iuridicheskaia literatura," 1966), 14.

29. For instance, see Nye, "Heredity or Milieu: The Foundation of Modern European Criminological Theory," 342, 345. Nye notes that by the end of the nineteenth century, Lombroso's theories did not find a place in discussions of penal reform in Europe. Indeed, his theories received immediate criticism, particularly from French criminologists. See also Alfred Lindesmith and Yale Levin, "The Lombrosian Myth in Criminology," *American Journal of Sociology* 42, no. 5 (1937): 653–71, who argue that Lombroso's importance in the development of criminology has frequently been overstated and that significant work had been conducted prior to Lombroso that provided the foundations against which his theories were judged. A similar position is taken by Marie-Christine Leps, *Apprehending the Criminal: The Production of Deviance in Nineteenth-Century Discourse* (Durham, NC: Duke University Press, 1992), 32–43. In *Renovating Russia*, Daniel Beer argues that degeneration theories provided an alternative to Lombroso's atavistic determinism. In his view, Russian criminologists interpreted physical deformities as a reflection of social deformities and divisions, allowing deviants to be identified by their pathologies yet situating the causes of their deviance in the social order.

30. On Ferri, see Thorsten Sellin, "Pioneers in Criminology XV—Enrico Ferri (1856–1929)," *Journal of Criminal Law, Criminology, and Police Science* 48, no. 5 (1958): 481–92; and G. Kunov, "Enriko Ferri i ego vzgliad na prestupnost'," in *Problema prestupnosti*, ed. Ia. S. Rozanov (Kiev: Gosudarstvennoe izdatel'stvo Ukrainy, 1924), 38–42. Despite their intellectual differences, Ferri and Lombroso maintained a close personal and professional relationship.

31. Auguste Comte held that empiricism, observation, and experimentation formed the foundations of the modern science that would provide the underlying base of knowledge for ordering society. On Comte, positivism, and the positivist school, see Piers Beirne, "Adolphe Quetelet and the Origins of Positivist Criminology," *American Journal of Sociology* 92, no. 5 (1987): 1140–69; Hawthorn, *Enlightenment and Despair*, 66–89; Hermann Mannheim, "Introduction," in *Pioneers in Criminology*, 10–11; and Rennie, *The Search for Criminal Man*, 67–78. Lombroso is often considered an adherent of the positivist approach to criminology.

32. Enrico Ferri, *Criminal Sociology* (New York: D. Appleton, 1899), xvi.

33. See Sellin, "Pioneers in Criminology XV—Enrico Ferri," 490–91.

34. Ibid., 485.

35. Iu. V. Portugalov, "Nauchnye problemy kriminologii," *Vestnik psikhologii, kriminal'noi antropologii, i gipnotizma,* no. 7 (1904): 476.

36. Sellin, "Pioneers in Criminology XV—Enrico Ferri," 487. See Ferri, "Printsip legal'noi otvetstvennosti v novom russkom ugolovnom kodekse," *Pravo i zhizn'* nos. 2–3 (1928): 33–43. A Russian translation of *Criminal Sociology,* published as *Ugolovnaia sotsiologiia* and edited by S. V. Poznyshev, appeared in 1908.

37. S. V. Poznyshev, "Ob izuchenii prestupnika v nauke ugolovnogo prava," *Voprosy prava,* nos. 7 (1911): 65.

38. Ibid., 63.

39. Ibid., 68–69.

40. Poznyshev, "Ob izuchenii prestupnika v nauke ugolovnogo prava," *Voprosy prava,* nos. 6 (1911): 185–86; and A. A. Piontkovskii, *Marksizm i ugolovnoe pravo. O nekotorykh spornykh voprosakh teorii ugolovnogo prava* (Moscow: Iuridicheskoe izdatel'stvo NKIu RSFSR, 1927), 25.

41. Foinitskii also served as director of a Bureau of Criminal Law (*Kabinet ugolovnago prava*) attached to St. Petersburg University. The bureau, founded in 1890 in connection with an international penal congress held in June, maintained a penal museum that included exhibits on prison structure and organization, prison life, and penal history in Russia and abroad. It also housed a criminal law library and provided space for study and for evening courses and lectures on penology. *Kabinet ugolovnago prava pri Imperatorskom C.-Peterburgskom Universitete. Katalog museia,* izd. 3–e (St. Petersburg, Senatskaia tipografiia, 1902). This bureau can be considered a precursor to the criminological institutions that flourished after the 1917 revolutions and that are discussed in chap. 2 below. Foinitskii's involvement in this endeavor reflects an early effort by practitioners of the sociological school to promote criminology as a scientific discipline through systematic courses of study. Indeed, Foinitskii himself taught Russia's first university course in penology at St. Petersburg University in 1874. Bruce Adams, *The Politics of Punishment,* 129.

42. Ostroumov, *Prestupnost' i ee prichiny v dorevoliutsionnoi Rossii,* 244. Ostroumov noted that sometimes sociologists separated the factors of crime into only two categories, the first and third, but that this did not change the nature of the theory. See I. Ia. Foinitskii, "Faktory prestupnosti," *Severnyi vestnik,* no. 11 (1893): 79, where he discusses the importance of both environmental and social factors in understanding crime. Foinitskii's writings on crime and the law are collected in his *Na dosuge. Sbornik iuridicheskikh statei i izsledovanii c 1870 goda,* 2 vols. (St. Petersburg: Tip. M. M. Stasiulevicha, 1898–1900).

43. See Foinitskii's "Vliianie vremeni goda na raspredelenie prestuplenii," cited in L. O. Ivanov and L. V. Il'ina, *Puti i sud'by otechestvennoi kriminologii* (Moscow: Nauka, 1991), 63–64; and M. N. Gernet, *Obshchestvennye prichiny prestupnosti. Sotsialisticheskie napravleniia v nauke ugolovnogo prava* (1906), reprinted in Gernet, *Izbrannye proizvedeniia* (Moscow: Iuridicheskaia literatura, 1974), 154. Foinitskii's work is reprinted in his *Na dosuge,* vol. 1 (1898).

44. Foinitskii, "Faktory prestupnosti," 86. This understanding of "primitiveness" would emerge even more clearly in studies of female crime.

45. Ibid., 81.

46. Wetzell, *Inventing the Criminal*, 42. On the history of insanity, psychiatry, and criminality, see also Klaus Dörner, *Madmen and the Bourgeoisie: A Social History of Insanity and Psychiatry* (Oxford: Basil Blackwell, 1981); J. Edward Chamberlin and Sander L. Gilman, eds., *Degeneration: The Dark Side of Progress* (New York: Columbia University Press, 1985); Ian R. Dowbiggin, *Inheriting Madness: Professionalization and Psychiatric Knowledge in Nineteenth-Century France* (Berkeley: University of California Press, 1991); Ruth Harris, *Murders and Madness*; Robert A. Nye, *Crime, Madness, and Politics in Modern France: The Medical Concept of National Decline* (Princeton, NJ: Princeton University Press, 1984); David J. Rothman, *The Discovery of the Asylum: Social Order and Disorder in the New Republic* (Boston: Little Brown, 1971); and Vieda Skultans, *English Madness: Ideas on Insanity, 1580–1890* (London: Routledge, 1979).

47. See Miller, *Freud and the Bolsheviks*, 12–13. On psychiatry and psychology in Russia, see also R. A. Bauer, *The New Man in Soviet Psychology* (Cambridge: Harvard University Press, 1952); Elisa Marielle Becker, "Medicine, Law, and the State: The Emergence of Forensic Psychiatry in Imperial Russia" (Ph.D. diss., University of Pennsylvania, 2003); Julie Vail Brown, "Revolution and Psychosis: The Mixing of Science and Politics in Russian Psychiatric Medicine, 1905–1913," *The Russian Review* 46, no. 3 (July 1987): 283–302; and David Joravsky, *Russian Psychology: A Critical History* (Oxford: Basil Blackwell, 1989).

48. Portugalov, "Nauchnye problemy kriminologii," 471.

49. Ibid., 471–72, 475.

50. Wetzell, *Inventing the Criminal*, 64–67. Aschaffenburg's work appeared in Russia as *Prestuplenie i bor'ba s nim. Ugolovnaia psikhologiia dlia vrachei, iuristov, i sotsiologov* (Odessa: Paspopov, 1906).

51. A. L. Shcheglov, "Prestupnik, kak predmet izucheniia vrachebnoi nauki," *Vestnik psikhologii, kriminal'noi antropologii, i pedologii*, no. 1 (1913): 4.

52. Ibid., 5.

53. Ibid., 10–12.

54. On the intelligentsia, the *zemstvo*, and the "To the People" Movement, see, among others, Edith W. Clowes, Samuel D. Kassow, and James L. West, eds., *Between Tsar and People: Educated Society and the Quest for Public Identity in Late Imperial Russia* (Princeton, NJ: Princeton University Press, 1991); Terence Emmons and Wayne S. Vucinich, eds., *The Zemstvo in Russia: An Experiment in Local Self-Government* (Cambridge: Cambridge University Press, 1982); Esther Kingston-Mann, "Statistics, Social Science, and Social Justice: The Zemstvo Statisticians of Pre-Revolutionary Russia," in *Russia in the European Context, 1789–1914: A Member of the Family*, ed. Susan McCaffray and Michael Melancon (New York: Palgrave Macmillan, 2005), 113–40; Martine Mespoulet, "Statisticiens des *zemstva*. Formation d'une nouvelle profession intellectuelle en Russie dans la periode

prerevolutionnaire (1880–1917). Le case de Saratov," *Cahiers du Monde Russe* 40, no. 4 (1999): 573–624; Richard Pipes, *Russia under the Old Regime*, 2nd ed. (New York: Macmillan, 1992), 249–80; and Philip Pomper, *The Russian Revolutionary Intelligentsia*, 2nd ed. (Wheeling, IL: Harlan Davidson, 1993).

55. A. B. Sakharov, *Istoriia kriminologicheskoi nauki* (Moscow: Moskovskaia vysshaia shkola militsii MVD Rossii, 1994), 16–17.

56. E. N. Tarnovskii, "Vliianie khlebnykh tsen i urozhaev na dvizhenie prestupnosti protiv sobstvennosti v Rossii," *Zhurnal Ministerstva iustitsii*, no. 8 (1898): 103–6.

57. Gernet, *Obshchestvennye prichiny prestupnosti*, 38–201.

58. On this trip, Gernet studied in Heidelberg, Paris, and Rome, met with Franz von Liszt (see note 59 below) in Berlin, and observed prisons and criminological museums in Italy, France, Switzerland, and Germany. He also gave lectures in Paris and Brussels and collected materials on crime in Europe. See Gernet, *Izbrannye proizvedeniia*, 10, 623. Gernet's trip to visit the major European criminological centers reflects the strong influence of European criminology in Russia. Moreover, it suggests the importance of international scientific exchanges in the formulation of Russian and later Soviet scientific endeavors. On Russian international relations in science, see Loren Graham, "The Formation of Soviet Research Institutes: A Combination of Revolutionary Innovation and International Borrowing," *Social Studies of Science* 5, no. 3 (August 1975): 303–29; and Susan Gross Solomon, ed., *Doing Medicine Together: Germany and Russia between the Wars* (Toronto: University of Toronto Press, 2006).

59. Gernet, *Obshchestvennye prichiny prestupnosti*, 109, 112–15. Both Lombroso and Ferri were acquainted with Turati. Also influential for left-wing criminologists was the work of German lawyer Franz von Liszt (1851–1919), a criminal law professor who led a movement for penal reform in the late 1880s. Liszt was primarily concerned with protecting society against crime. Like Ferri, he argued that punishments should depend on the danger the criminal posed to society and should thus focus on controlling the behavior of the criminal to prevent the commission of further crimes. Believing that "crime is the product of the characteristics of the offender at the time of the crime and the external circumstances surrounding him at the time," Liszt emphasized the "economic, political and moral conditions of the working class" as central factors in causing crime. Although not a socialist, Liszt argued for easing the burden on the working class, and his view of penal reform remained influential among left-wing criminologists. See Beer, *Renovating Russia*, 124–25; Wetzell, *Inventing the Criminal*, 35; and Gernet, *Obshchestvennye prichiny prestupnosti*, 118.

60. The events and aftermath of 1905 convinced many professionals that the autocratic tsarist state was no longer the best partner for the pursuit of their professional agenda. In the case of psychiatrists, as Julie Brown suggests, state economic and political control over their activities drove many psychiatric professionals to support radical change. Julie Vail Brown, "Professionalization and

Radicalization: Psychiatrists Respond to 1905," in *Russia's Missing Middle Class*, ed. Harley D. Balzer (Armonk, NY: M. E. Sharpe, 1996), 161–62. See also Engelstein, *Keys to Happiness*; and Nancy Frieden, *Russian Physicians in an Era of Reform and Revolution, 1856–1905* (Princeton, NJ: Princeton University Press, 1981).

61. See Piontkovskii, *Marksizm i ugolovnoe pravo*, 35.

62. For instance, while he was still a student, M. N. Gernet participated in underground revolutionary circles and was briefly detained by the police for these activities, which provided him with solid revolutionary credentials. See his biographical sketch in Gernet, *Izbrannye proizvedeniia*, 9–10.

63. Gernet, *Obshchestvennye prichiny prestupnosti*, 124.

64. See Cesare Lombroso and Guglielmo Ferrero, *The Female Offender* (New York: D. Appleton and Company, 1895). The original Italian work was published as *La donna deliquente. La prostituta e la donna normale* (Torino: L. Roux, 1893) and appeared in Russian as *Zhenshchina prestupnitsa i prostitutka*, trans. Dr. G. I. Gordon (Kiev and Kharkov: F. A. Ioganson, 1897). It also appeared in French as *La femme criminelle et la prostituée* (Paris: F. Alcan, 1896) and in German as *Das Weib als Verbrecherin und Prostituirte* (Hamburg: Richter, 1894). Its rapid translation and publication in Russia (and Europe), compared to the virtual disregard of Lombroso's other seminal work, *Criminal Man*, suggests the wide influence and acceptance that Lombroso's theories on female crime had among the Russian criminological community (and indeed among the European criminologists as well), despite the general rejection of his methods. A recent English translation of the work is *Criminal Woman, the Prostitute, and the Normal Woman*, trans. Nicole Hahn Rafter and Mary Gibson (Durham, NC: Duke University Press, 2004). On Lombroso's views of female criminals, see Gibson, "The 'Female Offender' and the Italian School of Criminal Anthropology," 155–65; Horn, "This Norm Which Is Not One," 109–28; and Klein, "The Etiology of Female Crime," 265–90.

65. See M. G., "O detoubiistve," *Arkhiv sudebnoi meditsiny i obshchestvennoi gigieny*, no. 1 (1868): 21–55; Gernet, *Ukazatel' russkoi i inostrannoi literatury po statistike prestuplenii, nakazanii, i samoubiistv* (Moscow: Izdanie Tsentral'nogo statisticheskogo upravleniia, 1924), 22; S. S. Shashkov, *Istoricheskie sud'by zhenshchiny, detoubiistvo, i prostitutsiia* (St. Petersburg: Izdanie N. A. Shigina, 1871); N. Tagantsev, "O detoubiistve," *Zhurnal Ministerstva iustitsii*, no. 9 (1868): 215–50 and no. 10 (1868): 341–80; and E. N. Tarnovskii, "Prestupleniia protiv zhizni po polam, vozrastam, i semeinomu sostoianiiu," *Iuridicheskii vestnik*, no. 10 (1886): 276–97, among others.

66. Lombroso and Ferrero, *The Female Offender*, 150. See also Wolfgang, "Pioneers in Criminology: Cesare Lombroso," 373; and Wolfgang, "Cesare Lombroso," 190–91.

67. Lombroso and Ferrero, *The Female Offender*, 153.

68. See Horn, "This Norm Which Is Not One," 120.

69. Lombroso and Ferrero, *The Female Offender*, 112.

70. Ibid., 187.

71. Ibid., 109–10. Horn notes that Lombroso found the rarity of deviations between criminal and normal women to be a sign of inferiority and weakness, so that "at the precise moments that woman was identified as 'normal' and 'normalizing,' as embodying and conserving the norms of the species, she was marked as other, if not pathological, and as opposed to history and civilization." See Horn, "This Norm Which Is Not One," 117.

72. Lombroso and Ferrero, *The Female Offender*, 111.

73. Wolfgang, "Pioneers in Criminology: Cesare Lombroso," 373.

74. Lombroso and Ferrero, *The Female Offender*, 151–57.

75. Ibid., 151.

76. Ibid., 239–40.

77. Gibson, "The 'Female Offender' and the Italian School of Criminal Anthropology," 161.

78. Ibid., 163.

79. See Ferri, *Criminal Sociology*.

80. On nineteenth-century views of women, see, among others, Catherine Gallagher and Thomas Laqueur, eds., *The Making of the Modern Body: Sexuality and Society in the Nineteenth Century* (Berkeley: University of California Press, 1987); David G. Horn, *Social Bodies: Science, Reproduction, and Italian Modernity* (Princeton, NJ: Princeton University Press, 1994); Howard I. Kushner, "Suicide, Gender, and the Fear of Modernity in Nineteenth-Century Medical and Social Thought," *Journal of Social History* 26, no. 3 (Spring 1993): 461–90; James McMillan, *Housewife or Harlot: The Place of Women in French Society, 1870–1940* (New York: St. Martin's Press, 1981); Carroll Smith Rosenberg, *Disorderly Conduct: Visions of Gender in Victorian America* (New York: A. A. Knopf, 1985); Carroll Smith Rosenberg and Charles Rosenberg, "The Female Animal: Medical and Biological Views of Woman and Her Role in Nineteenth Century America," *Journal of American History* 60, no. 2 (September 1973): 332–56; Cynthia Russett, *Sexual Science: The Victorian Construction of Womanhood* (Cambridge: Harvard University Press, 1989); Elaine Showalter, *The Female Malady: Women, Madness, and English Culture, 1830–1980* (New York: Pantheon, 1985); Walkowitz, *City of Dreadful Delight*; and Lucia Zedner, *Women, Crime, and Custody in Victorian England* (Oxford: Clarendon Press, 1991).

81. Gibson, "The 'Female Offender' and the Italian School of Criminal Anthropology," 163; and Shapiro, *Breaking the Codes*, 23.

82. Horn, "This Norm Which Is Not One," 121.

83. Ibid., 117.

84. Gibson, "The 'Female Offender' and the Italian School of Criminal Anthropology," 163.

85. Foinitskii, "Zhenshchina-prestupnitsa," *Severnyi vestnik*, no. 2 (1893): 136.

86. Stephen P. Frank argues that Russian criminologists interpreted female criminality according to stereotypes of the sorts of crimes they believed women should be committing, based on their biology and their position in society, and

that these criminologists often misinterpreted the sources to fit their stereotypes. See his "Narratives within Numbers."

87. Gernet, *Prestuplenie i bor'ba s nim v sviazi s evoliutsiei obshchestva* (Moscow, 1914), reprinted in his *Izbrannye proizvedeniia*, 251–52. See also Gernet, *Moral'naia statistika (Ugolovnaia statistika i statistika samoubiistv)* (Moscow: Izdanie Tsentral'nogo statisticheskogo upravleniia, 1922), 135; Gernet, *Obshchestvennye prichiny prestupnosti*, 136–38; and A. A. Zhizhilenko, *Prestupnost' i ee faktory* (Petrograd: Mir znanii, 1922), 24–25.

88. Gernet, *Prestuplenie i bor'ba s nim v sviazi s evoliutsiei obshchestva*, 252–53.

89. Gernet, *Obshchestvennye prichiny prestupnosti*, 136–38.

90. In particular, women sought out opportunities to become doctors or midwives, professions that embodied service to society and coincided with traditional notions of women as caregivers, as well as being one of the few avenues (sometimes) open to women to pursue a professional career. On the position of women in Imperial Russia, women's involvement in society, the development of the "woman question," and the struggle for women's rights, see Stites, *The Women's Liberation Movement in Russia*.

91. Trainin, "K kharakteristike zhenskoi prestupnosti," *Vestnik prava i notariata*, no. 14 (1910): 463.

92. Frank, "Narratives within Numbers," 545.

93. Klein, "The Etiology of Female Crime," 266.

94. Shapiro, *Breaking the Codes*, 23, 66.

2—PROFESSIONALS, SOCIAL SCIENCE, AND THE STATE

1. See Stuart Finkel, "'The Brains of the Nation': The Expulsion of Intellectuals and the Politics of Culture in Soviet Russia, 1920–1924" (Ph.D. diss., Stanford University, 2001).

2. A. A. Gertsenzon, *Vvedenie v sovetskuiu kriminologiiu* (Moscow: Izd. "Iuridicheskaia literatura," 1965), 96.

3. Shelley, "Soviet Criminology: Its Birth and Demise, 1917–1936," 3, 33–38.

4. Post-Stalin criminologists were careful to point out the methodological flaws of the early criminologists, particularly their interest in the criminal individual, while at the same time they claimed this heritage as their own. Post-Soviet scholars have tried to explain why these so-called flaws led to the liquidation of the discipline under Stalin. See I. S. Noi, *Metodologicheskie problemy sovetskoi kriminologii* (Saratov: Izd. Saratovskogo universiteta, 1975), 36, 49; L. V. Il'ina and A. V. Nad'iarnyi, "Izuchenie lichnosti prestupnika v SSSR (Istoricheskii obzor)," in *Voprosy ugolovnogo prava, prokurorskogo nadzora, kriminalistiki, i kriminologii*, vol. 2 (Dushanbe: Tadzhikskii gosudarstvennyi universitet, 1968), 310; L. V. Il'ina, "Pervye kriminologicheskie uchrezhdeniia v SSSR," in *Ugolovnoe pravo v bor'be s*

prestupnost'iu (Moscow: Institut gosudarstva i prava Akademii nauk, 1981), 155; I. N. Dan'shin, "Iz istorii kriminologicheskikh uchrezhdenii v Ukrainskoi SSR v 20–30–e gody," in *Voprosy bor'be s prestupnost'iu* (Moscow: Iuridicheskaia literatura, 1980), 68–70; and Shelley, "The 1929 Dispute in Soviet Criminology," *Soviet Union* 6, no. 2 (1979): 175–85. Peter H. Solomon, Jr., in *Soviet Criminologists and Criminal Policy*, explores the role and position of the criminologists after criminology's rebirth in the late 1950s. See also his article "Soviet Criminology—Its Demise and Rebirth, 1928–1963," in *Crime, Criminology, and Public Policy*, ed. Roger Hood, 571–93 (New York: Free Press, 1974). For the post-Soviet interpretation of early Soviet criminology, see Ivanov and Il'ina, *Puti i sud'by otechestvennoi kriminologii*; N. F. Kuznetsova, "Sovetskaia kriminologiia v usloviiakh perestroiki," *Vestnik Moskovskogo universiteta*, Seriia 11, *Pravo*, no. 2 (1989): 24–31; O. L. Leibovich, "Problema prestupnosti v Sovetskoi sotsiologicheskoi literatury 20–kh godov," in *Istoriia stanovleniia Sovetskoi sotsiologicheskoi nauki v 20–30–e gody*, ed. Z. T. Golenkova and V. V. Vitiuk (Moscow: Institut sotsiologii AN SSSR, 1989), 143–55; V. V. Luneev, *Prestupnost' XX veka. Mirovye, regional'nye i rossiiskie tendentsii* (Moscow: Norma, 1997); Sakharov, *Istoriia kriminologicheskoi nauki*; and Shestakov, "K voprosu ob istorii Sovetskoi kriminologii," 74–81. A discussion of the fate of criminology under and after Stalin can be found in the epilogue of this work.

5. In her recent study of musicians during the 1920s, for example, Amy Nelson has argued that prerevolutionary specialists played an important and central role in the creation of "Soviet" music while also preserving the classical foundations of musical education. Amy Nelson, *Music for the Revolution: Musicians and Power in Early Soviet Russia* (University Park: Pennsylvania State University Press, 2006).

6. The process through which the Soviet regime created its new bureaucrats has been examined extensively, especially in relation to the technical and engineering professions on which the state placed much emphasis in its efforts to modernize and industrialize. By prioritizing technical knowledge, by providing employment opportunities for those acquiring such skills, and by fostering social mobility, the regime created new cadres of supporters who not only replaced the older specialists but who also accepted the legitimacy of the state, depended on it for their positions, and worked within its confines to promote its agenda. See, among others, Kendall E. Bailes, *Technology and Society under Lenin and Stalin: Origins of the Soviet Technical Intelligentsia, 1917–1941* (Princeton, NJ: Princeton University Press, 1978); Fitzpatrick, "Stalin and the Making of a New Elite, 1925–1939," 377–402; Fitzpatrick, *Education and Social Mobility in the Soviet Union, 1921–1934* (Cambridge: Cambridge University Press, 1979); Graham, *Science in Russia and the Soviet Union*; and Nicholas Lampert, *The Technical Intelligentsia and the Soviet State: A Study of Soviet Managers and Technicians, 1928–1935* (London: MacMillan Press, 1979).

7. Prerevolutionary professional organizations for criminology were limited to the Russian group of the International Union of Criminologists (see note 21

below). On the professions and professional groups in late Imperial Russia, see Harley Balzer, ed., *Russia's Missing Middle Class: The Professions in Russian History* (Armonk, NY: M. E. Sharpe, 1996); Brown, "Revolution and Psychosis," 283–302; Engelstein, *Keys to Happiness*; Frieden, *Russian Physicians in an Era of Reform and Revolution*; and Christine Ruane, *Gender, Class, and the Professionalization of Russian City Teachers, 1860–1914* (Pittsburgh: Pittsburgh University Press, 1994). See also Bialkowski, "Transformation of Academic Criminal Jurisprudence."

8. Elizabeth A. Hachten notes, for instance, that "many scientists developed an ethos of service that linked professional values with the moral world of *obshchestvennost'* [public duty], thus encouraging them to find ways to link their enterprises to the needs of society." Furthermore, she adds that "service to society provided a public identity removed from that of a servant of the state, a mere *chinovnik* (state bureaucrat). That was a priority for educated Russians in most professions, even as they remained dependent on the state in a myriad of ways." See her "In Service to Science and Society: Scientists and the Public in Late-Nineteenth-Century Russia," *Osiris* 17 (2002): 194–95. For a discussion of the meaning of *obshchestvennost'*, see pp. 175–79.

9. Hachten, "In Service to Science and Society," 195.

10. Joseph Bradley, "Subjects into Citizens: Societies, Civil Society, and Autocracy in Tsarist Russia," *American Historical Review* 107, no. 4 (October 2002): 1121. See also Harley Balzer, "The Problem of Professions in Imperial Russia," in *Between Tsar and People: Educated Society and the Quest for Public Identity in Late Imperial Russia*, ed. Edith Clowes, Samuel Kassow, and James West (Princeton, NJ: Princeton University Press, 1991), 187. The question of the existence of a civil society in Russia remains a much debated topic, relating as it does to traditions of public engagement and autonomous activity that might be interpreted as a "usable past" or native alternatives to authoritarian rule in Russia. Recent studies addressing civil society in late Imperial Russia include Joseph Bradley, "Voluntary Organizations, Civic Culture, and *Obshchestvennost'* in Moscow," in *Between Tsar and People*, ed. Clowes, Kassow, and West, 131–48; James Downey, "Civil Society and the Campaign against Corporal Punishment in Late Imperial Russia, 1863–1904" (Ph.D. diss., Indiana University, 1993); Frieden, *Russian Physicians in an Era of Reform and Revolution*; John F. Hutchinson, *Politics and Public Health in Revolutionary Russia, 1890–1918* (Baltimore, MD: Johns Hopkins University Press, 1990); Samuel Kassow, "Russia's Unrealized Civil Society," in *Between Tsar and People*, ed. Clowes, Kassow, and West, 367–71; Adele Lindenmeyr, *Poverty Is Not a Vice: Charity, Society, and the State in Imperial Russia* (Princeton, NJ: Princeton University Press, 1996); Louise McReynolds, *The News under Russia's Old Regime: The Development of a Mass Circulation Press* (Princeton, NJ: Princeton University Press, 1991); Benjamin Nathans, *Beyond the Pale: The Jewish Encounter with Late Imperial Russia* (Berkeley: University of California Press, 2004); Ruane, *Gender, Class, and the Professionalization of Russian City Teachers*; and David Wartenweiler, *Civil Society and Academic Debate in Russia, 1905–1914* (Oxford: Clarendon Press, 1999). Civil

organizations posed a challenge to the tsarist state but often filled a crucial need for social services that the government could not meet. This became particularly true during World War I and may have contributed to the loss of confidence in the tsarist regime. See Peter Gatrell, *A Whole Empire Walking: Refugees in Russia during World War I* (Bloomington: Indiana University Press, 1999).

11. See Brown, "Revolution and Psychosis."

12. Studies of the nonparty professionals include James T. Andrews, *Science for the Masses: The Bolshevik State, Public Science, and the Popular Imagination in Soviet Russia, 1917–1934* (College Statton: Texas A&M University Press, 2003); James W. Heinzen, "Professional Identity and the Vision of the Modern Soviet Countryside: Local Agricultural Specialists at the End of the NEP, 1928–1929," *Cahiers du Monde Russe* 39, nos. 1–2 (January–June 1998): 9–25; Heinzen, *Inventing a Soviet Countryside*; Eugene Huskey, *Russian Lawyers and the Soviet State: The Origins and Development of the Soviet Bar, 1917–1939* (Princeton, NJ: Princeton University Press, 1986); Joravsky, *Russian Psychology*; Martine Mespoulet, *Statistique et révolution en Russie*; Miller, *Freud and the Bolsheviks*; Julie Kay Mueller, "Staffing Newspapers and Training Journalists in Early Soviet Russia," *Journal of Social History* 31, no. 4 (Summer 1998): 851–73; and Amy Nelson, *Music for the Revolution*.

13. In the Bolshevik conception, the intelligentsia became a social group serving the vanguard of the proletariat but not posing any intellectual threat or alternative to the new regime. This contributed to the reconceptualization of the concept of civil society and the creation of a Soviet *obshchestvennost'* in which the state attempted to define the limits of public organization and engagement. Finkel, "Purging the Public Intellectual," 589–613; and Finkel, "'The Brains of the Nation,'" 20–21. See also Jane Burbank, *Intelligentsia and Revolution: Russian Views of Bolshevism, 1917–1922* (Oxford: Oxford University Press, 1986); Michael David-Fox, *Revolution of the Mind: Higher Learning among the Bolsheviks, 1918–1929* (Ithaca, NY: Cornell University Press, 1997); I. N. Il'ina, *Obshchestvennye organizatsii Rossii v 1920-e gody* (Moscow: Institut Rossiiskoi istorii RAN, 2000); and Vera Tolz, *Russian Academicians and the Revolution: Combining Professionalism and Politics* (New York: St. Martin's Press, 1997).

14. Solomon argues that, in the end, the People's Commissariat of Health, after its reorganization and the replacement of N. Semashko as commissar, was not powerful enough to protect the field of social hygiene. Susan Gross Solomon, "The Limits of Government Patronage of Science: Social Hygiene and the Soviet State, 1920–1930," *Social History of Medicine* 3, no. 3 (December 1990): 405–35; and her article "Social Hygiene and Soviet Public Health, 1921–1930," in *Health and Society in Revolutionary Russia*, ed. Susan Gross Solomon and John F. Hutchinson (Bloomington: Indiana University Press, 1990), 175–99. See also the discussion of social hygiene and eugenics in Mark B. Adams, "Eugenics as Social Medicine in Revolutionary Russia: Prophets, Patrons, and the Dialectics of Discipline-Building," in *Health and Society in Revolutionary Russia*, ed. Gross and Solomon, 200–23; and Bernstein, *Dictatorship of Sex*.

15. David Horn makes a similar observation in his study of Lombroso and the criminal body, writing: "criminology's claims to the status of science were dependent on access to bodies that lent themselves to a discriminating quantification." Horn, *The Criminal Body: Lombroso and the Anatomy of Deviance* (New York: Routledge, 2003), 61.

16. On the creation of scientific institutions in the early Soviet period, see Graham, "The Formation of Soviet Research Institutes," 303–29; Zhores Medvedev, *Soviet Science* (New York: W. W. Norton, 1978), 13–21; Alexander Vucinich, *Empire of Knowledge: The Academy of Sciences of the USSR (1917–1970)* (Berkeley: University of California Press, 1984), 72–122; and *Organizatsiia nauki v pervye gody Sovetskoi vlasti (1917–1925). Sbornik dokumentov* (Leningrad: Izdatel'stvo "Nauka," 1968).

17. It is notoriously difficult to discern crime rates for the immediate post-revolutionary years, primarily due to a lack of systematic compilation at the time. Publication of Imperial crime statistics ended in 1913. Statistics were not collected for 1914, were gathered only sporadically in 1915–1917, and stopped altogether after the Bolshevik Revolution. Publication of crime statistics did not begin again until 1922 with the founding of the Central Statistical Administration's Department of Moral Statistics. Gernet provides some rough figures. He notes that in the first half of 1919, there were 167,722 criminal cases, and 170,036 in the second half. In 1920, people's courts heard 1,248,862 cases; revolutionary tribunals heard 36,903 cases; and military revolutionary tribunals judged 89,466 people. As of November 1921, prisons were overcrowded with some 73,194 prisoners, while having places for only 60,468. Gernet does note a significant increase in crime in this period: in Moscow, complaints about crimes increased from 4,191 in 1914 to 10,676 in 1921. Gernet, *Moral'naia statistika*, 96–97. On statistics, see also D. P. Rodin, "O moral'noi statistiki," *Vestnik statistiki*, nos. 9–12 (1922): 105–6; and Kenneth Pinnow, "Making Suicide Soviet." One must also consider that the revolutionary period brought changes to definitions of crimes and thus to the focus of police repression. On efforts to fight crime during the Civil War, see Musaev, *Prestupnost' v Petrograde v 1917–1921 gg.*

18. A. G., "Moskovskaia obshcheugolovnaia prestupnost' v period voennogo kommunizma," *Prestupnik i prestupnost'*, no. 2 (1927): 369, 371.

19. *Izvestiia* (Moscow), 25 January 1918, quoted in Ivanov and Il'ina, *Puti i sud'by otechestvennoi kriminologii*, 96.

20. S. T., "V iuridicheskoi klinike Kievskogo INKh'oza," *Sovetskoe gosudarstvo i pravo*, no. 3 (1927): 105.

21. The Russian group of the International Union of Criminologists could be considered an early professional criminological organization. It published a journal, *Zhurnal ugolovnogo prava i protsessa* (*Journal of Criminal Law and Process*) in 1912 and 1913. Contributors included M. N. Gernet, A. A. Zhizhilenko, and P. I. Liublinskii, among others, all of whom figure prominently in this study. The Russian group sent representatives to union meetings in Europe and even hosted an annual meeting in St. Petersburg in September 1902, where the eminent

German criminologist Franz von Liszt spoke about the social causes of crime. See his "Obshchestvennye faktory prestupnosti," *Zhurnal Ministerstva iustitsii*, no. 2 (1903): 38–54.

22. See *Svod statisticheskikh svedenii po delam ugolovnym* (St. Petersburg, 1873–1915).

23. During the Civil War, the Petrograd Soviet sponsored studies of crime and criminals, opening a small bureau in 1918. Iu. Iu. Bekhterev, *Izuchenie lichnosti zakliuchennogo (Istoriia, zadachi, metodiki, i tekhnika)* (Moscow: Izdat. NKVD RSFSR, 1928), 4, 14; and Il'ina, "Pervye kriminologicheskie uchrezhdeniia v SSSR," 151.

24. The Diagnostic Institute of Criminal Neurology and Psychiatry (Diagnosticheskii institut sudebnoi nevrologii i psikhiatrii) was founded in November 1918 on the initiative of L. G. Orshanskii as a way to evaluate the "etiological role of the psychopathological moment in the growth and distinctiveness of manifestations of Russian criminality in our current conditions." Indeed, Orshanskii argued that psychological evaluation of prisoners was necessary to determine "those who are on the border between health and illness, who easily fall into crime and become antisocial." The Diagnostic Institute had a clinical laboratory, an anthropological bureau, a psychological laboratory, a photography bureau, a library, an archive, a pharmacy, and a department for organizing courses and lectures. In its first year of existence, it conducted work in various prisons, including the Women's Correctional Prison. Gosudarstvennyi arkhiv Rossiiskoi Federatsii (GARF), f. A-482, op. 3, d. 64, ll. 27–27ob, 29–31ob, 32–33, 35–35ob. On the formation of psychiatric surveillance in prisons, see the resolution of 16 April 1920 in GARF, f. A-482, op. 1, d. 164, ll. 3–3ob.

25. GARF, f. A-2307, op. 2, d. 234, ll. 19–20.

26. GARF, f. A-2307, op. 2, d. 234, ll. 17–18 (quote from l. 18), 19–20. The Institute of Soviet Law, of the Commissariat of Enlightenment (Narkompros), petitioned on behalf of the criminological department for funds to support its work on 27 June 1921. GARF, f. A-2307, op. 2, d. 234, l. 16. On the Institute of Soviet Law, see note 57 below.

27. G. Ivanov, "Iz praktiki Saratovskogo gubernskogo kabineta kriminal'noi antropologii i sudebno-psikhiatricheskoi ekspertizy," *Sovetskoe pravo*, no. 1 (1925): 84–85. Few published works illustrate the Saratov Bureau's research. One article, by S. M. Zhelikhovskii and M. V. Solov'eva, "K kazuistike detskikh ubiitsv," *Zhurnal nevropatologii i psikhiatrii im. S. S. Korsakova*, nos. 5–6 (1928): 673–81, reflects the psychiatric orientation of the Saratov Bureau's work, even after it was co-opted by the State Institute (see discussion below). B. N. Khatuntsev, "O sotsial'no-psikhologicheskom issledovanii lichnosti obviniaemogo na predvaritel'nom sledstvii i na sude," *Pravo i sud*, nos. 2 (1924): 51–56, also discusses the psychological research of the Saratov Bureau. Moreover, Shtess incorporated Freudian psychoanalysis into his evaluations of criminals and sexual deviants. See Healey, *Homosexual Desire*, 66–68, 142.

28. M. P. Kutanin, "Saratovskii kabinet po izucheniiu prestupnosti i pre-

stupnika," in *Puti Sovetskoi psikho-nevrologii* (Samara: Srednevolzhskii kraizdrav, 1931), 61–62. The Saratov Bureau began its work on 22 October 1922. Kutanin also notes the establishment in 1923 of a neuropsychological department within the Saratov Bureau.

29. The Presidium of the Mossovet, led by member V. L. Orleanskii, took the decision to form the Moscow Bureau on 11 June 1923. Tsentral'nyi gosudarstvennyi arkhiv Moskovskoi oblasti (TsGAMO), f. 66, op. 13, d. 203, l. 218(ob); Iu. Iu. Bekhterev, "Eksperimental'nyi penitentsiarnyi institut," *Sovetskoe pravo*, no. 6 (1926): 121; Gernet, "Predislovie," in *Prestupnyi mir Moskvy*, vii; and Gernet, "Pervaia russkaia laboratoriia po izucheniiu prestupnosti," *Pravo i zhizn'*, no. 2 (1924): 31. The Moscow Bureau brought together psychiatrists, anthropologists, criminologists, and statisticians to perform its work. These specialists believed university students were best suited for gathering information from prisoners because convicts would be more willing to talk to eager students than to police officers. Indeed, after 1925, internships in the Moscow Bureau became a required element of the curriculum for students studying forensic medicine in the Faculty of Soviet Law at Moscow State University. See Tsentral'nyi Munitsipal'nyi arkhiv g. Moskvy (TsMAM), f. 1609, op. 1, d. 1056, l. 87. A budget for the Moscow Bureau, originally called the Bureau for Research on the Criminal Personality and Crime (Kabinet po issledovaniiu lichnosti prestupnika i prestupnosti), submitted on 9 July 1923 to the Moscow Financial Department (Mosfinotdel), requested funds for the establishment of a psychological laboratory, a biological laboratory, a library and subscriptions to periodical literature, and the printing of questionnaires (*ankety*) and payment of salaries. The bureau was also authorized by the Mossovet presidium to hire a *zaved* (head), a doctor-psychiatrist, a sociologist-criminologist, a technician, and a statistician to conduct this work. See TsMAM, f. 1215, op. 2, d. 195, ll. 2, 5. Reports of the work of the Moscow Bureau can be found in *Ezhenedel'nik Sovetskoi iustitsii*, no. 1 (1925): 17; and no. 38 (1925): 879.

30. Gernet, ed., *Prestupnyi mir Moskvy*. See also Gernet, "Pervaia russkaia laboratoriia po izucheniiu prestupnosti," 29.

31. "Khronika. Klinika po izucheniiu prestupnosti v Moskve," *Ezhenedel'nik Sovetskoi iustitsii*, no. 31 (1923): 711–12; V. O. Akkerman, "Kriminologicheskaia klinika," *Prestupnik i prestupnost'*, no. 2 (1927): 207–10; and E. K. Krasnushkin, "Moskovskii kabinet po izucheniiu lichnosti prestupnika i prestupnosti i obshchaia kharakteristika Moskovskikh pravonarushitelei," in *Sudebno-meditsinskaia ekspertiza. Trudy II Vserossiiskogo s''ezda sudebno-meditsinskikh ekspertov*, ed. Ia. L. Leibovich (Ul'ianovsk: Ul'ianovsk kombinat PPP, 1926), 157. Krasnushkin noted that in 1924 the Moscow Bureau and MUUR began a new project focusing on female murderers and brothel-keepers incarcerated in Novinskii Women's Prison.

32. Gernet, "Pervaia russkaia laboratoriia po izucheniiu prestupnosti," 30.

33. See *Prestupnik i prestupnost'*, no. 1 (1926) and no. 2 (1927); and the following works all edited by E. K. Krasnushkin, G. M. Segal, and Ts. M. Feinberg and published in Moscow by Moszdravotdela: *Khuliganstvo i ponozhovshchina* (1927);

Pravonarusheniia v oblasti seksual'nykh otnoshenii (1927); *Ubiistva i ubiitsy* (1928); and *Nishestvo i besprizornost'* (1929).

34. A. A. Gertsenzon, "Izuchenie Moskovskoi prestupnosti (Otchet za 1926 god)," *Proletarskii sud*, nos. 17–18 (1927): 11. See also Akkerman, "Kriminologicheskaia klinika," 211.

35. A. M. Rapoport, "K praktike izucheniia lichnosti prestupnika," *Prestupnik i prestupnost'*, no. 1 (1926): 34–35.

36. Il'ina, "Pervye kriminologicheskie uchrezhdeniia v SSSR," 152–53.

37. E. G. Shirvindt, "K istorii voprosa ob izuchenii prestupnosti i mer bor'by s nei," *Sovetskoe gosudarstvo i pravo*, no. 5 (1958): 139.

38. See I. Varshavskii, "Vserossiiskii s"ezd po pedologii, eksperimental'noi pedagogike i psikhonevrologii v Leningrade," *Rabochii sud*, nos. 1–2 (1924): 53–62; and nos. 3–5 (1924): 29–36 [quote from nos. 1–2 (1924): 56]. Participants in the conference's forum on criminal reflexology and criminal psychology included P. I. Liublinskii, A. K. Lents, A. S. Zvonitskaia, L. G. Orshanskii, S. V. Poznyshev, and A. A. Zhizhilenko, among others.

39. K. K., "Nash kriminologicheskii kabinet," *Rabochii sud*, no. 21 (1927): 1705–6. The Leningrad Bureau officially began its work on 7 May 1925. Leningrad Gubsud director F. M. Nakhimson petitioned the Leningrad Regional Executive Committee (Gubispolkom) to create the Leningrad Criminological Bureau. See O. D., "Novoe uchrezhdenie," *Rabochii sud*, nos. 9–10 (1925): 412. Reports of the activities of the Leningrad Bureau can be found in the journal *Rabochii sud* (*Worker's Court*), 1927–1929. Beyond activity reports, however, little of the Leningrad Bureau's research remains extant.

40. O. D., "Novoe uchrezhdenie," 413.

41. See reports on the activities of the Leningrad Criminological Bureau in *Rabochii sud*, no. 6 (1927): 527–29; no. 7 (1927): 623–24; no. 8 (1927): 731–32; and no. 19 (1928): 1469–76.

42. Criminological bureaus were also established in Odessa in 1925, in Rostov-na-Donu and Minsk in 1926, and in Khar'kov in 1927. Il'ina, "Pervye kriminologicheskie uchrezhdeniia v SSSR," 153.

43. See Wetzell, *Inventing the Criminal*. On psychiatry in the Soviet Union, see Joravsky, *Russian Psychology*; Miller, *Freud and the Bolsheviks*; and T. I. Iudin, *Ocherki istorii otechestvennoi psikhiatrii* (Moscow: Gosudarstvennoe izdatel'stvo meditsinskoi literatury, 1951).

44. The promotion of forensic expertise was furthered by the establishment of a Central Forensic-Medical Laboratory (Tsentral'naia sudebno-meditsinskaia laboratoriia) under Narkomzdrav in 1924, as well as an Institute of Forensic-Medical Expertise. GARF, f. A-482, op. 1, d. 635, ll. 259–259ob. On forensic expertise in the early Soviet period, see I. F. Krylov, *Ocherky istorii kriminalistiki i kriminalisticheskoi ekspertizy* (Leningrad: Izdatel'stvo Leningradskgo universiteta, 1975); Krylov, "Stranitsy istorii Sovetskoi kriminalistiki za 50 let," *Izvestiia vysshchikh uchebnykh zavedenii. Pravovedenie*, no. 5 (1967): 113–21; Ia. L. Leibovich,

"Tri goda sudebnoi meditsiny," *Ezhenedel'nik Sovetskoi iustitsii*, no. 7 (1922): 7–8; Leibovich, "Sudebno-meditsinskaia ekspertiza pri NEPe," *Ezhenedel'nik Sovetskoi iustitsii*, no. 2 (1923): 36–38; Leibovich, "Itogi deiatel'nosti sudebno-meditsinskoi ekspertisy za 7 let i ee zadachi," *Administrativnyi vestnik*, no. 5 (1926): 20–26; and V. I. Prozorovskii and O. A. Panfilenko, "Razvitie sudebno-meditsinskoi nauki i ekspertizy za gody Sovetskoi vlasti," *Sudebno-meditsinskaia ekspertiza*, no. 3 (1967): 3–10. See also Pinnow, "Making Suicide Soviet," 80–135.

45. Some studies of the efforts to transform life during the NEP include Frances Bernstein, *Dictatorship of Sex*; Katerina Clark, *Petersburg: Crucible of Cultural Revolution* (Cambridge: Harvard University Press, 1995); Lynn Mally, *Culture of the Future*; and Amy Nelson, *Music for the Revolution*.

46. "Predislovie," in *Izuchenie lichnosti prestupnika v SSSR i za granitsei* (Moscow: Izd. Moszdravotdela, 1925), 3.

47. A. S. Zvonitskaia, "K voprosu ob izuchenii prestupnika i prestupnosti," *Tekhnika, ekonomika i pravo*, no. 3 (1924): 82–83.

48. Ibid., 91–92, 77.

49. Evgenii Konstantinovich Krasnushkin (1885–1951), the son of a Don Cossack, actively participated in student protests during the 1905 Revolution and served as an army psychiatrist during World War I, but does not appear to have engaged in any specific Soviet or Bolshevik revolutionary activities. He co-edited, together with jurist G. M. Segal and psychiatrist Ts. M. Feinberg, volumes on hooliganism (1927), sexual crimes (1927), murder and murderers (1928), and poverty and homelessness (1929) for the Moscow Bureau, in addition to contributing articles on forensic psychiatry and psychopathology to various Soviet legal journals. In the late 1930s he organized a psychiatric clinic as part of the Moscow Region Clinical Scientific-Research Institute and from 1943 until his death served as director of the Moscow Region Psychoneurological Clinic. He also participated in the Nuremberg Trials following World War II. After 1930, however, Krasnushkin turned his attention away from crime to focus on his core discipline, specifically clinical psychiatry, neuroses, and recovery from psychiatric illnesses. Indeed, Krasnushkin's views of the relationship between the criminal personality and crime and the work of the Moscow Bureau came under criticism in 1929 and may have prompted his shift in research to subjects more acceptable to the regime. See *Bol'shaia meditsinskaia entsiklopediia*, vol. 11 (Moscow, 1979), 51; and E. K. Krasnushkin, *Izbrannye trudy* (Moscow: Medgiz, 1960).

50. Krasnushkin, "Chto takoe prestupnik?" 32–33. On degeneracy theory in the Soviet period, see Daniel Beer, *Renovating Russia*, 165–204; and Frances Bernstein, *Dictatorship of Sex*.

51. Shirvindt, "K istorii voprosa ob izuchenii prestupnosti i mer bor'by s nei," 140.

52. Evsei Gustavovich Shirvindt (1891–1958) served as head of GUMZ throughout the 1920s and wrote extensively about prisons, Soviet penal politics, and penal affairs, as well as co-editing the State Institute's annual journal, *Problemy prestupnosti*

(*Problems of Criminality*). Born in Kiev to an intelligentsia family, Shirvindt received a law degree in 1914 from Odessa University and had begun medical school in Moscow when the revolution occurred. He joined the Communist Party in 1918. Shirvindt began his administrative service in the judicial department of the Moscow Soviet in 1917 and later became deputy minister of justice in Ukraine and a member of the Ukrainian NKIu and Cheka. With the reorganization of the NKVD in 1930, Shirvindt lost the position as head of GUMZ that he had held since its creation in 1922. He went to work at the Commissariat of Water Transportation but in 1933 returned to penal affairs when appointed senior supervisor of prisons for the USSR Procuracy. A victim of the purges, he was arrested in 1937 and released in 1955, after which he helped revive penology in the Ministry of Internal Affairs. Shirvindt died on 22 September 1958. See Solomon, *Soviet Criminologists and Criminal Policy*, 180–81; Michael Jakobson, *Origins of the Gulag: The Soviet Prison Camp System, 1917–1934* (Lexington: University Press of Kentucky, 1993), 71; and Wimberg, "'Replacing the Shackles,'" 37–38. No biographical information has been found for N. N. Spasokukotskii.

    53. Letter No. 15297 from the RSFSR Narodnyi Komissariat Zdravookhraneniia, dated 11 February 1925, to Glavumzak, Narodnyi Komissariat Vnutrennykh Del. GARF, f. R-4042, op. 10, d. 7, ll. 10–10ob.

    54. E. G. Shirvindt, "Izucheniiu problem prestupnosti (K otkrytiiu Gosudarstvennogo Instituta po izucheniiu prestupnosti)," *Rabochii sud*, nos. 47–48 (1925): 1791–94.

    55. Aleksandr Georgievich Beloborodov (1891–1938) was the quintessential old Bolshevik. The son of a worker, Beloborodov was born in 1891 in the Perm region. He became involved in revolutionary work as a factory apprentice and joined the local Bolshevik party in 1907. He spent several years in prison for revolutionary activities. During the Civil War, he fought with the Red Army in the Urals and in 1920 became a candidate member of the Central Committee, later serving as People's Commissar of the NKVD RSFSR (1923–1927), in which capacity he participated in the work of the State Institute and edited a 1927 volume based on material gathered during the 1926 prison census [See *Sovremennaia prestupnost' (Prestuplenie, pol, repressiia, retsidiv)* (Moscow: Izdatel'stvo NKVD, 1927)]. The VTsIK relieved Beloborodov of his responsibilities at the NKVD on 18 November 1927 and replaced him with V. N. Egorov. Beloborodov's biography is silent about activities after 1930 (and Beloborodov does not appear as editor of a second volume of *Sovremennaia prestupnost'* published in 1930). No indication is given on the cause of his death in 1938. GARF, f. A-259, op. 11b, d. 414, l. 1; *Bol'shaia Sovetskaia Entsiklopediia*, vol. 3 (Moscow, 1970), 118; and *Deiateli Soiuza Sovetskikh Sotsialisticheskikh Respublik i Oktiabr'skoi Revoliutsii (Avtobiografii i biografii)* (Moscow: Izdatel'stvo "Kniga," 1989), 26–28. On Nikolai Aleksandrovich Semashko (1874–1949), the well-known first People's Commissar of Health, see B. M. Potulov, *N. A. Semashko—vrach i revoliutsioner* (Moscow: Meditsina, 1986); and Z. Tikhonova, *Narodnyi komissar zdorov'ie (o N.*

A. Semashko) (Moscow: Gos. izd. politicheskoi literatury, 1960).

56. Glavnauka is an acronym for Glavnoe upravlenie nauchnymi, nauchno-khudozhestvennymi i muzeinymi uchrezhdeniiami (Main Administration of Scientific, Scientific-Artistic, and Museum Organizations), a division of the People's Commissariat of Enlightenment (Narkompros). On Narkompros, see Sheila Fitzpatrick, *The Commissariat of Enlightenment: Soviet Organization of Education and the Arts under Lunacharsky, October 1917–1921* (Cambridge: Cambridge University Press, 1970).

57. GARF, f. R-4042, op. 10, d. 7, l. 12. The Institute of Soviet Law (Institut Sovetskogo prava), founded in 1920, was incorporated into Moscow State University in April 1925 as part of an effort to create more specialized departments within the Faculty of Social Sciences. Nearly all the major Soviet legal scholars, including E. K. Krasnushkin, N. V. Krylenko, S. G. Strumilin, A. N. Trainin, A. I. Trakhtenberg, G. M. Segal, M. N. Gernet, Ia. A. Berman, M. M. Isaev, E. B. Pashukanis, A. A. Piontkovskii, and Z. R. Tettenborn, taught in the Institute of Soviet Law at some point during the 1920s. See N. Cheliapov, "Fakul'tet Sovetskogo prava i Moskovskogo Gos. universiteta," *Revoliutsiia prava*, no. 3 (1928): 96–98; TsMAM, f. 1609, op. 5, d. 135, ll. 2, 8; and GARF, f. A-259, op. 9b, d. 565, l. 10.

58. See, for example, Terry Martin, "Interpreting the New Archival Signals: Nationalities Policy and the Nature of the Soviet Bureaucracy," *Cahiers du Monde Russe* 40, nos. 1–2 (1999): 113–24, who argues that "hard" commissariats like the NKVD and "soft" commissariats like Narkompros had overlapping areas of responsibility, a result of needing to apply both repression and incentives in the building of socialism.

59. GARF, f. R-4042, op. 10, d. 7, ll. 9–9ob. Sovnarkom approved the creation of the State Institute on 25 March 1925. That the State Institute became the client of four different bureaucracies suggests that its foundation in this manner was a compromise designed to satisfy all commissariats perceived to have an interest in its work.

60. NKVD Order No. 98 established the representatives of the State Institute's soviet. See GARF, f. R-4042, op. 10, d. 7, l. 65. For changes to the soviet's membership, see Protocol No. 1 of the meeting of the soviet of the State Institute dated 15 July 1925, GARF, f. R-4042, op. 10, d. 7, l. 99 and Protocol No. 2 dated 23 September 1925, GARF, f. R-4042, op. 10, d. 7, l. 105. Initially, the State Institute had 44 members, including A. A. Piontkovskii, M. M. Isaev, P. B. Gannushkin, N. N. Vvedenskii, and Ia. L. Leibovich. The State Institute officially began its work on 1 October 1925. On its organization and activities, see "Khronika. Gosudarstvennyi institut po izucheniiu prestupnosti i prestupnika," *Ezhenedel'nik Sovetskoi iustitsii*, no. 32 (1925): 1091; Gernet, "Gosudarstvennyi institut po izucheniiu prestupnosti," *Administrativnyi vestnik*, no. 11 (1925): 32; N. N. Spasokukotskii, "Organizatsiia i pervye shagi deiatel'nosti Gosudarstvennogo Instituta po izucheniiu prestupnosti i prestupnika pro NKVD," *Problemy prestupnosti*, no. 1 (1926): 270–71; Spasokukotskii, "Deiatel'nost' Gosudarstvennogo instituta po izucheniiu prestupnosti i

prestupnika," *Problemy prestupnosti*, no. 2 (1927): 233–47; Spasokukotskii, "Gosu-darstvennyi institut po izucheniiu prestupnosti i prestupnika pri NKVD i ego deiatel'nosti," 113–14; and B. S. Utevskii, "Gosudarstvennyi Institut po izucheniiu prestupnosti i prestupnika pri NKVD," *Administrativnyi vestnik*, no. 4 (1926): 7–8.

61. NKVD Order No. 97. GARF, f. R-4042, op. 10, d. 7, l. 55. Most likely a gesture to secure the support of Glavnauka for the creation of the State Institute, Order No. 97 indicated Narkompros would supervise the institute's scientific work. The NKVD applied to the Sovnarkom for 91,102 rubles to fund the institute for 1925–1926. Sovnarkom approved the incorporation of the institute into the state budget and authorized the release of funds from its own reserves to finance the institute in 1925–1926, based on the NKVD's estimates. GARF f. A-259, op. 95, d. 779, l. 3–4; GARF, f. R-4042, op. 10, d. 7, l. 126.

62. NKVD Order No. 97. GARF, f. R-4042, op. 10, d. 7, l. 54.

63. Ibid., l. 107.

64. *Problemy prestupnosti* (*Problems of Criminality*), an annual journal edited by M. N. Gernet, E. G. Shirvindt, and F. Traskovich, was published directly by the State Institute in 1926 and 1927 and by the NKVD in 1928 and 1929. Reports of the activities of the State Institute appeared regularly in *Ezhenedel'nik Sovetskoi iustitsii* (NKIu) and *Administrativnyi vestnik* (NKVD). The State Institute also sponsored a series of volumes on crime "hot topics," including: *Rastraty i rastrat-chiki. Sbornik statei* (Moscow: Izdatel'stvo NKVD, 1926); *Khuliganstvo i khuligany* (Moscow: Izdatel'stvo NKVD RSFSR, 1929); and *Sovremennaia prestupnost'*, vols. 1 and 2 (Izdatel'stvo NKVD, 1927 and 1930); among others. Its members regularly published monographs and articles supported by its patrons, particularly the NKVD and the NKIu.

65. M. M. Grodzinskii, "Gosudarstvennyi institut po izucheniiu prestupno-sti i prestupnika," *Vestnik Sovetskoi iustitsii*, no. 19 (1926): 775.

66. GARF, f. R-4042, op. 10, d. 7, l. 108.

67. Ivanov and Il'ina, *Puti i sud'by otechestvennoi kriminologii*, 182; and Spasokukotskii, "Deiatel'nost' Gosudarstvennogo Instituta po izucheniiu prestup-nosti i prestupnika pri NKVD," *Problemy prestupnosti*, no. 4 (1929): 136–45. See also Bekhterev, *Izuchenie lichnosti zakliuchennogo*, 4.

68. Gernet, "Gosudarstvennyi institut po izucheniiu prestupnosti," 33.

69. Kutanin, "Saratovskii kabinet po izucheniiu prestupnosti i prestupnika," 62–63.

70. Louise Shelley emphasizes that despite their affiliation with the State Institute, the local bureaus retained their independence and did not always con-form to the central institute's theoretical position. See her "Soviet Criminology: Its Birth and Demise, 1917–1936," 89–90.

71. V. V. Brailovskii, "Sotsiologicheskii ili biologicheskii uklon v izuchenii prestupnosti?" *Voprosy izucheniia prestupnosti v Severnom Kavkaze*, no. 1 (1926): 9. Post-Stalin criminologists Il'ina and Nad'iarnyi later criticized the narrow approach of the Rostov Bureau, arguing that "such studies of the criminal personality, where

the causes of crime boil down to the inborn psychological and biological qualities of the offender, could hardly have been of any use to prison employees in
their practical efforts to correct and reeducate criminals." Il'ina and Nad'iarnyi,
"Izuchenie lichnosti prestupnika v SSSR (Istoricheskii obzor)," 306.

72. Shirvindt, "K istorii voprosa ob izuchenii prestupnosti i mer bor'by s
nei," 139.

73. B. S. Utevskii, "Gosudarstvennyi institut po izucheniiu prestupnosti i
prestupnika," *Ezhenedel'nik Sovetskoi iustitsii*, no. 18 (1926): 569.

74. Gernet, "Gosudarstvennyi institut po izucheniiu prestupnosti," 30–32.
Utevskii also noted that the State Institute's tasks and approach separated it from
similar criminological organizations abroad, such as those in Buenos Aries and
Brussels. See Utevskii, "Gosudarstvennyi institut po izucheniiu prestupnosti i
prestupnika," 570.

75. Utevskii, "Gosudarstvennyi institut po izucheniiu prestupnosti i prestupnika," 570.

76. Gernet, "Gosudarstvennyi institut po izucheniiu prestupnosti," 33.

77. These included, among others, A. Ia. Estrin, P. B. Gannushkin, N. Gedeonov,
M. N. Gernet, V. R. Iakubson, M. M. Isaev, E. K. Krasnushkin, V. I. Kufaev, P. I. Liublinskii,
L. G. Orshanskii, A. E. Petrova, A. A. Piontkovskii, D. P. Rodin, T. E. Segalov, A. N.
Trainin, and S. Ukshe. GARF, f. R-4042, op. 10, d. 7, l. 100.

78. These institutes and organs included the Supreme Court of the RSFSR
and SSSR, the Supreme Court Procuracy of the RSFSR and SSSR, the Central Procuracy, the Moscow Regional Procuracy, the Moscow Regional Court (Mosgubsud),
the Moscow Department of Criminal Investigation (MUUR), the Moscow Militsiia
(Police), the Moscow College of Advocates, the Moscow Soviet (Mossovet) Admin-
istrative Department, the Central Prison Administration, representatives from
Moscow's Taganskii, Sokol'niki, and Lefortovo prisons, the Serbskii Institute of
Forensic Psychiatry, the Lenin Institute of Forensic Psychiatry and Neurology in
Leningrad, the Moscow Bureau for the Study of Criminality and the Criminal,
the Biochemical Institute, the Neuropsychiatric Dispenser, the Anthropological
Institute, the State Psychiatric Institute, the Leningrad Pathological-Reflexological
Institute, the Moscow Institute of Pedagogy and Defectology, and the Moscow State
University Department of Psychiatry. GARF, f. R-4042, op. 10, d. 7, ll. 100–101.
See also Spasokukotskii, "Gosudarstvennyi Institut po izucheniiu prestupnosti i
prestupnika pri NKVD i ego deiatel'nosti," 114; and Grodzinskii, "Gosudarstven-
nyi Institut po izucheniiu prestupnosti i prestupnika," 773–74.

79. Letter No. 7874 of 9 July 1926 from the TsIK of the Tatar SSR to SNK
RSFSR. GARF, f. R-4042, op. 10, d. 7, ll. 80–81.

80. Letter dated 20 July 1926 signed by Beloborodov (People's Commissar
of Internal Affairs) and Shirvindt (head of GUMZ). GARF, f. R-4042, op. 10, d.
7, l. 78.

81. B. N. Zmiev taught law courses in Kazan and published several studies of
crime in the Tatar Republic, highlighting in particular the nature of crime in rela-

tion to ethnicity, in Tatar and Moscow journals. See, for example, his "Prestupnost' v Tatrespublike," *Problemy prestupnosti*, no. 4 (1929): 39–57; his "Prestupleniia v oblasti polovykh otnoshenii v gorode i v derevne," *Problemy prestupnosti*, no. 2 (1927): 41–50; and his "Pokhishchenie zhenshchin," *Vestnik Sovetskoi iustitsii Avtonomnoi Tatarskoi Sotsialisticheskoi Sovetskoi Respubliki*, nos. 8–9 (1923): 3–5. If the Kazan organization conducted criminological research, it does not appear to have had a psychiatric orientation.

82. Shelley, "Soviet Criminology: Its Birth and Demise," 91. Shelley writes that "the massive research conducted by the locally based institutions testified to the activity and organization of the criminological scholars of the 1920s. The diversity of approach and purpose that existed indicated the liberality of the intellectual environment. The scholars' desire to contribute to the policies of the new society and the belief that they could help shape decision making contributed to the creative outburst seen in the criminological institutions scattered throughout the country" [p. 117]. On the criminological bureaus in the republics, see S. N. Slupskii, "Belorusskii kabinet po izucheniiu prestupnosti," *Problemy prestupnosti*, no. 4 (1929): 149–51; V. Zivert, "Kievskii institut nauchno-sudebnoi ekspertizy i ego rabota v oblasti izucheniia prestupnika i prestupnosti," *Sovetskoe gosudarstvo i pravo*, no. 24 (1927): 838–39; V. Trakhterov, "Vseukrainskii kabinet po izucheniiu lichnosti prestupnika," *Vestnik Sovetskoi iustitsii*, no. 4 (1927): 126–28; I. N. Dal'shin, "Iz istorii kriminologicheskikh uchrezhdenii v Ukrainskoi SSR v 20–30-e gody"; and Il'ina, "Pervye kriminologicheskie uchrezhdeniia v SSSR," 155.

83. See Finkel, "Purging the Public Intellectual."

84. See Bradley, "Voluntary Organizations Civic Culture, and *Obshchestvennost'* in Moscow."

85. See Michael David-Fox's review of I. N. Il'ina, *Obshchestvennye organizatsii Rossii v 1920–e gody* (Moscow, 2000), in *Kritika* 3, no. 1 (Winter 2002): 173–81.

3—THE WOMAN'S SPHERE

1. The term "struggle for existence" was used by criminologists in both the late Imperial and Soviet periods. It has its origins in the theories of Charles Darwin (1809–1882) [expounded in his *On the Origin of Species* (1859)], Herbert Spencer (1820–1903), and Thomas Robert Malthus (1766–1834), referring to competition, among and within species for scarce resources, that resulted in survival and reproduction or death and dying out. Russian philosophers, scientists, and naturalists found Darwin's ideas, particularly their Malthusian elements, unsatisfactory in light of Russian conditions (specifically the vastness of Siberian geographical space compared to the density of the tropical regions Darwin observed). In their efforts to adapt Darwin to suit the Russian perspective, these thinkers placed more emphasis on the individual struggle to survive, often in harsh conditions, rather than on interspecies competition for resources. This focus on individual ingenuity rather than on evolutionary superiority gave the term a more sociological orientation in

the Russian context, and it is from this perspective that criminologists employed the term. On Darwin's "struggle" in Russia, see Daniel P. Todes, *Darwin Without Malthus: The Struggle for Existence in Russian Evolutionary Thought* (Oxford: Oxford University Press, 1989); and Graham, *Science in Russia and the Soviet Union*, 56–75.

2. Klein, "The Etiology of Female Crime," 267.

3. Growing interest in science and medicine, and the scientific exploration and analysis of women's bodies, provided "scientific" evidence to support the myths of women's essential nature and perceptions of women's proper social position. See Liudmilla Jordanova, *Sexual Visions: Images of Gender in Science and Medicine between the Eighteenth and Twentieth Centuries* (Madison: University of Wisconsin Press, 1989); Orvilla Moscucci, *The Science of Woman: Gynecology and Gender in England, 1800–1929* (Cambridge: Cambridge University Press, 1990); and Carol Groneman, "Nymphomania: The Historical Construction of Female Sexuality," in *Deviant Bodies: Critical Perspectives on Difference in Science and Popular Culture*, ed. Jennifer Terry and Jacqueline Urla (Bloomington: Indiana University Press, 1995), 219–49.

4. Rosenberg and Rosenberg, "The Female Animal" 334.

5. The medical profession saw hysteria, together with mental degeneration, as the manifestation of female sexuality's influence on women that could lead them to criminal activity. As Elaine Abelson notes in explaining kleptomania, "female sexuality became an active force, blindly pursuing its own ends, outside of the normal rhythms of the female body." Elaine A. Abelson, *When Ladies Go A-Thieving: Middle-Class Shoplifters in the Victorian Department Store* (New York: Oxford University Press, 1989), 199. On hysteria and crime, see also Ruth Harris, "Melodrama, Hysteria, and Feminine Crimes of Passion in the Fin-de-Siècle," *History Workshop Journal* 25 (1988): 31–63; and Jann Matlock, *Scenes of Seduction: Prostitution, Hysteria, and Reading Difference in Nineteenth-Century France* (New York: Columbia University Press, 1994).

6. Rosenberg and Rosenberg, "The Female Animal," 335–36.

7. I. Ia. Foinitskii, "Zhenshchina-prestupnitsa," *Severnyi vestnik*, no. 2, 123.

8. See, among others, Barbara Engel, *Between the Fields and the City: Women, Work, and Family in Russia, 1861–1914* (Cambridge: Cambridge University Press, 1995); Engel, *Women in Russia, 1700–2000*; Engelstein, *Keys to Happiness*; Marcelline J. Hutton, *Russian and West European Women, 1860–1939: Dreams, Struggles, Nightmares* (Lanham, MD: Rowman and Littlefield, 2001); and Christine Worobec, *Peasant Russia: Family and Community in the Post-Emancipation Period* (Princeton, NJ: Princeton University Press, 1991).

9. *Itogi Russkoi ugolovnoi statistiki za 20 let (1874–1894 gg)* (St. Petersburg: Tip. Pravitel'stvuiushchogo Senata, 1899), 144.

10. Russian sexologists were concerned with masturbation and the detrimental effect it had on sexual hygiene and health, especially among children. This concern continued into the Soviet period. See I. K. Shmukler, *Onanizm u detei. Ego prichiny, simptomy, posledstviia i lechenie*, 2nd ed. (Kiev: Tip. L. I. Shliter, 1897);

L. Ia. Iakobzon, *Onanizm i bor'ba s nim,* 2nd ed. (Moscow: Izdatel'stvo "Okhrana materinstva i mladenchestva NKZ," 1928); N. I. Ozeretskii, "Polovye pravonarusheniia nesovershennoletnikh," in *Pravonarusheniia v oblasti seksual'nykh otnoshenii,* ed. Krashnushkin, Segal, and Feinberg, 128–57; and Bernstein, *Dictatorship of Sex,* 138–45.

11. Julie Vail Brown, "Female Sexuality and Madness in Russian Culture: Traditional Values and Psychiatric Theory," *Social Research* 53, no. 2 (Summer 1986): 377–78.

12. P. N. Tarnovskaia, "Zhenskaia prestupnost' v sviazi s rannimi brakami," *Severnyi vestnik,* no. 5 (1898): 133–49.

13. Ibid., 133–37. Soviet medical professionals continued to view early marriage as a form of deviant sexual behavior. See Bernstein, *Dictatorship of Sex,* 145–47.

14. Tarnovskaia, "Zhenskaia prestupnost' v sviazi s rannimi brakami," 147–49.

15. Ibid., 147.

16. Ibid., 133. This interest in zoology and comparing the animal world to the human world continued after the revolution. See the discussions of endocrinology and eugenics in Bernstein, *Dictatorship of Sex,* 43–59, 171–75.

17. Tarnovskaia, "Zhenskaia prestupnost' v sviazi s rannimi brakami," 134. Tarnovskaia noted that an average of 27 percent of infants in Russia died before the age of one; the figure reached 70–90 percent in foundling homes.

18. Ibid.

19. The emphasis on the health and strength of the peasantry may derive from the belief among some nineteenth-century Russian intellectuals, and populists in particular, in the purity of the peasantry and the importance of the peasants for the future of the Russian nation. While the earlier sexual development of workers might suggest progressiveness and modernity, concerns about the degeneration of the urban working classes undermined any positive interpretation of the phenomenon and reflected a sense that attention should be focused on preserving the health of the peasantry.

20. I. Ozerov, "Sravnitel'naia prestupnost' polov v zavisimosti ot nekotorykh faktorov," *Zhurnal Iuridicheskogo Obshchestva pri Imperatorskom S-Peterburgskom Universitete,* no. 4 (1896): 59–60. Natal'ia Pushkareva notes that to improve their social and economic status, young women were often pressed into unhappy marriages. See N. Pushkareva, *Women in Russian History,* 235.

21. Ozerov, "Sravnitel'naia prestupnost' polov," 60.

22. Ibid., 65–66.

23. Klein, "The Etiology of Female Crime," 267.

24. See Engel, *Between the Fields and the City;* Engelstein, *Keys to Happiness;* Frieden, *Russian Physicians in an Era of Reform and Revolution;* Christine Ruane, "The Vestal Virgins of St. Petersburg: Schoolteachers and the 1897 Marriage Ban," *The Russian Review* 50, no. 2 (April 1991): 163–82; and Stites, *The Women's Lib-*

eration Movement in Russia. Approximately 32 percent of workers were women in 1914, a proportion that would continue to grow during the war years. By 1920, women made up 46 percent of large-scale industrial workers. See Wood, *The Baba and the Comrade*, 27, 44.

25. On reactions to this perceived increase in women's involvement in public life and worries over women's participation in crime, see Frank, "Narratives within Numbers," 541–66. These concerns were not limited to Russia. In the European context, see Eric Johnson, "Women as Victims and Criminals: Female Homicide and Criminality in Imperial Germany, 1873–1914," *Criminal Justice History* 6 (1985):151–75; Shapiro, *Breaking the Codes*; and Walkowitz, *City of Dreadful Delight*.

26. Ozerov, "Sravnitel'naia prestupnost' polov," 59.

27. *Itogi Russkoi ugolovnoi statistiki za 20 let*, 143. Foinitskii also noticed that the more domestic and sedentary life of women led to lower levels of female crime. See Foinitskii, "Zhenshchina-prestupnitsa," no. 2, 130.

28. E. N. Tarnovskii, "Prestupleniia protiv zhizn po polam, vozrastam i semeinomu sostioaniiu," quoted in Foinitskii, "Zhenshchina prestupnitsa," no. 2, 134.

29. Ozerov, "Sravnitel'naia prestupnost' polov," 51.

30. Ibid., 83.

31. Ibid., 81.

32. I. Ia. Foinitskii, "Zhenshchina-prestupnitsa," *Severnyi vestnik*, no. 3 (1893): 111.

33. Gernet, *Prestuplenie i bor'ba s nim v sviazi s evoliutsiei obshchestva*, 253.

34. Ozerov, "Sravnitel'naia prestupnost' polov," 82.

35. Ibid., 51.

36. Russian and Soviet specialists were concerned not only with increased rates of female criminality as women entered the public sphere, but feared that women's participation in a range of deviant behaviors, for example lesbianism, onanism, and suicide, would increase under the pressures of public engagement, seeing this as an unfortunate consequence of "progress." See Healey, *Homosexual Desire*, 143–44; and Pinnow, "Making Suicide Soviet," 178–95. On the history of suicide in Russia, see Susan K. Morrissey, *Suicide and the Body Politic in Imperial Russia* (Cambridge: Cambridge University Press, 2007); and Irina Paperno, *Suicide as a Cultural Institution in Dostoevsky's Russia* (Ithaca, NY: Cornell University Press, 1997).

37. This theory has proved extremely persistent in criminology well into the twentieth century. Studies of female offenders in the 1970s in the United States, for instance, linked changes in female crime rates to the women's liberation movement. See Meda Chesney-Lind, "Women and Crime: The Female Offender," *Signs* 12, no. 1 (Autumn 1986): 79. See also Timothy Hartnagel, "Modernization, Female Social Roles, and Female Crime: A Cross-National Investigation," *Sociological Quarterly* 23, no. 4 (Autumn 1982): 477–90, who correlates modernization with

female crime rates and finds, contrary to expectation, that modernization is not an adequate predictor of women's criminality.

38. Nineteenth-century criminologists made these connections, seeing a threat to social order in the growing working-class populations of industrializing cities. Some scholars have identified a correlation between this modernization and crime rates, although such theories have been criticized. See Howard Zehr, *Crime and the Development of Modern Society* (London: Croom Helm, 1976); and Eric Johnson, *Urbanization and Crime*.

39. Johnson, "Women as Victims and Criminals," 171.

40. Helen Boritch and John Hagan, "A Century of Crime in Toronto: Gender, Class, and Patterns of Social Control, 1859 to 1955," *Criminology* 28, no. 4 (November 1990): 595. Boritch and Hagan also note that increases in female property crime rates reflected the economic marginalization of women more than the expansion of their economic opportunities [p. 569].

41. Frank, "Narratives within Numbers," 542. On the relationship between female crime and modernity in the late Imperial period, see also Engelstein, *Keys to Happiness*, 96–114.

42. *Itogi Russkoi ugolovnoi statistiki za 20 let*, 136. According to Ozerov, between 1879 and 1885, women made up 12.9 percent of all criminals, 7.7 times fewer than among men. Trainin's figures for 1897–1904 indicated that 12.7 percent of criminals were women. Gernet noted that between 1903 and 1906, only 9.3 percent of offenders were women, although 13.6 percent of those convicted in local courts were women. Ozerov, "Sravnitel'naia prestupnost' polov," 48; A. N. Trainin, "Prestupnost' gorod i derevni v Rossii," *Russkaia mysl'*, no. 7 (1909): 10; Trainin, "K kharakteristike zhenskoi prestupnosti," 464; and Gernet, *Prestuplenie i bor'ba s nim v sviaizi s evoliutsiei obshchestva*, 250.

43. Ozerov, "Sravnitel'naia prestupnost' polov," 57–58; Foinitskii, "Zhenshchina-prestupnitsa," no. 2, 132. Gernet, *Moral'naia statistika*, 137, indicated that in 1911 women made up 98.9 percent of cases for child abandonment. Furthermore, while women committed only 3.4 percent of murders in general, they were guilty of 27.9 percent of the murder of relatives. Men, in contrast, were responsible for nearly all crimes involving the misuse of natural resources, the violation of female honor, horse and cattle theft, theft of weapons, deadly injury, counterfeiting, forgery, and property violation, among others. Gernet noted that men, in addition to committing more crimes that required physical strength than women, also engaged more frequently in crimes that required contact with the social and political worlds, while women's crimes remained isolated in the domestic sphere.

44. Stephen Frank provides statistics for felony growth rates between 1874 and 1913. In almost all cases, the growth rates were greater for women than men, including for robbery (9.1 for women compared to 3.9 for men), dealing in stolen goods (18.9 compared to 12.0), liquor and customs violations (29.8 compared to 12.4), and sacrilege (66.2 compared to 5.3). These figures suggest significant shifts in female criminality in rural areas as a result of social and economic changes that

are not reflected in criminologists' discussions. Frank, *Crime, Cultural Conflict, and Justice in Rural Russia*, 74.

45. Foinitskii, "Zhenshchina-prestupnitsa," no. 2, 142.

46. On the idea that worker solidarity, mutual support, independence, and financial stability served as a counterbalance to female deviance, see Laurie Bernstein, *Sonia's Daughters: Prostitutes and their Regulation in Imperial Russia* (Berkeley: University of California Press, 1995), 116–17. Barbara Engel, in *Between the Fields and the City*, makes a similar observation.

47. In 1897, approximately 28.4 percent of the Russian population could read, with male literacy at 40.3 percent and female literacy at 16.6 percent. Rates diverged according to urban or rural residency, with higher literacy rates in urban centers (57 percent compared to 23.8 percent in the countryside). Boris N. Mironov, "The Development of Literacy in Russia and the USSR from the Tenth to the Twentieth Centuries," *History of Education Quarterly* 31, no. 2 (Summer 1991): 243. On literacy in Imperial Russia, see Jeffrey Brooks, *When Russia Learned to Read: Literacy and Popular Culture, 1861–1917* (Princeton, NJ: Princeton University Press, 1985); and Ben Eklof, *Russian Peasant Schools: Officialdom, Village Culture, and Popular Pedagogy, 1861–1914* (Berkeley: University of California Press, 1987).

48. Foinitskii, "Zhenshchina-prestupnitsa," no. 3, 125–26.

49. Ibid., 128.

50. Frank, "Narratives within Numbers," 565.

51. According to Gernet, *Moral'naia statistika*, 37, criminal statistics were not collected for 1914 and were only partially gathered and published for 1915–1917, stopping altogether after the October Revolution. The collection of criminal statistics remained scattered until the foundation of the Central Statistical Administration and its Department of Moral Statistics in 1922. On statistics in early Soviet Russia, see D. P. Rodin, "O moral'noi statistiki," 105–6; and Kenneth Pinnow, "Making Suicide Soviet."

52. Bernstein, *Dictatorship of Sex*, 132; and Sheila Fitzpatrick, "Sex and Revolution: An Examination of Literary and Statistical Data on the Mores of Soviet Students in the 1920s," *Journal of Modern History* 50 (1978): 252–79. Recently, historical studies have focused on this sense of anxiety in the NEP, particularly regarding sexuality and sexual behavior. See, among others, Frances Bernstein, "Panic, Potency, and the Crisis of Nervousness in the 1920s," in *Everyday Life in Early Soviet Russia: Taking the Revolution Inside*, ed. Christina Kiaer and Eric Naiman, 153–82 (Bloomington: Indiana University Press, 2006); Gregory Carleton, *Sexual Revolution in Bolshevik Russia*; Anne Gorsuch, *Youth in Revolutionary Russia: Enthusiasts, Bohemians, Delinquents* (Bloomington: Indiana University Press, 2000); and Eric Naiman, *Sex in Public*.

53. See Naiman, *Sex in Public*, 182.

54. L. M. Vasilevskii, *Prostitutsiia i molodezh'. Sotsialno-gigienicheskii ocherk* (Moscow: Novaia Moskva, 1926), 19–20.

55. The criminologists devoted many books and articles to the influence of

the war and revolution on crime rates. Emphasis on the war period as a significant factor shaping criminality continued until the late 1920s, when the time lapse since the war seemed to undermine such arguments. See, among others, M. N. Gernet, *Prestupnost' i samoubiistva vo vremia voiny i posle nee. Vtoroi [2nd] vypusk 'Moral'noi statistiki'* (Moscow: Izdatel'stvo TsSU SSSR, 1927); A. A. Gertsenzon, "Prestupnost' epokhi pervoi russkoi revoliutsii," *Sovetskoe pravo*, no. 3 (1926): 95–103 and no. 4 (1926): 96–107; E. N. Tarnovskii, "Voina i dvizhenie prestupnosti v 1911–1916 gg.," *Sbornik statei po proletarskoi revoliutsii i pravu*, nos. 1–4 (1918): 100–22; and D. P. Rodin, "Statistika prestupnosti vo vremia i posle Evropeiskoi voiny v raznykh stranakh," *Problemy prestupnosti*, no. 1 (1926): 173–91.

56. M. N. Gernet, "Zhenshchiny-ubiitsy," *Pravo i zhizn'*, nos. 6–7 (1926): 85. The significant drop in male crime was specifically for crimes against the person. N. Visherskii noted that levels of female crime rose from 17 percent in 1912 to 24 percent in 1916. This discrepancy may be explained by the different statistical sources used by the authors. Nevertheless, the general picture remains the same. See N. Visherskii, "Raspredelenie zakliuchennykh po polu i prestupleniem," in *Sovremennaia prestupnost' (Prestuplenie, pol, repressiia, retsidiv)*, ed. A. G. Beloborodov (Moscow: Izdatel'stvo NKVD RSFSR, 1927), 16.

57. Rodin, "Statistika prestupnosti," 176. Rodin noted that these were mostly petty crimes resulting from wartime conditions. A. G., "Moskovskaia obshcheugolovnaia prestupnost' v period voennogo kommunizma," *Prestupnik i prestupnost'*, no. 2 (1927): 369, 371, determined that crime was four times greater in 1917 than it had been at the beginning of the century.

58. Gernet, *Prestuplenie i bor'ba s nim v sviazi s evoliutsiei obshchestva*, 309. See also Rodin, "Statistika prestupnosti," 176.

59. Gernet, *Prestupnost' i samoubiistva vo vremia voiny i posle nee*, 120. See also Rodin, "Statistika prestupnosti," 186–87, who provides a list of the various crimes committed by women during the war.

60. V. D. Men'shagin, "Ubiistva," in *Ubiistva i ubiitsy*, ed. Krasnushkin, Segal, and Feinberg, 60.

61. Iu. Khodakov, "Sovremennaia prestupnost' zhenshchin," *Vlast' sovetov*, nos. 11–12 (1923): 87.

62. Gernet, *Prestupnost' i samoubiistva vo vremia voiny*, 134.

63. Ibid., 136–37; See also his *Prestupnosti za granitsei i v SSSR* (Moscow: Sovetskoe zakonodatel'stvo, 1931), 142.

64. Gernet, *Obshchestvennye prichiny prestupnosti*, 142.

65. Shelley, "Female Criminality in the 1920s," 266.

66. Ibid., 284.

67. On the "woman question" and the Bolsheviks, see Stites, *The Women's Liberation Movement in Russia*; and Wood, *The Baba and the Comrade*.

68. Gernet, *Prestupnost' i samoubiistva vo vremia voiny*, 127. Gernet's statistics indicated that women made up 15.4 percent of violent criminals in 1922 and 16.6 percent in 1924.

69. Ibid., 129. Although abortion was legalized in 1920, this status applied only to abortions approved by a commission and performed by doctors in hospitals. All other instances of artificially induced pregnancy termination remained subject to criminal prosecution. On abortion and infanticide, see the discussion in chap. 5.

70. Gernet, *Moral'naia statistika*, 136.

71. V. R. Iakubson, "Repressiia lisheniem svobody," in *Sovremennaia prestupnost' (Prestuplenie, pol, repressiia, retsidiv)*, ed. A. G. Beloborodov, 33 (Moscow: Izdatel'stvo Narodnogo Komissariata Vnutrennikh Del RSFSR, 1927).

72. A. V. Nemilov, *Biologicheskaia tragediia zhenshchiny* (Leningrad: Knigoizdatel'stvo "Seiatel'," 1927), 47. Nemilov's "biological tragedy" of women was a result of her physiological responsibilities that, according to Frances Bernstein, provided "an elaborate scientific justification of women's inequality and intellectual inferiority." Bernstein, *Dictatorship of Sex*, 55. Eric Naiman argues that Nemilov linked women's sexuality with the idea of an intransigent body inherited from the past that resisted Bolshevik efforts for universal transformation. Naiman, *Sex in Public*, 192–94.

73. Zhizhilenko, *Prestupnost' i ee faktory*, 26.

74. V. L. Sanchov, "Toska po domu, kak faktor prestupnosti," *Rabochii sud*, nos. 11–12 (1924): 34.

75. Nemilov, *Biologicheskaia tragediia zhenshchiny*, 90.

76. T. E. Segalov, "Psikhologiia polovykh prestuplenii," *Vestnik prava i notariata*, no. 25 (1910): 808–9.

77. Naiman, *Sex in Public*, 181–207, focuses on the position of women in NEP ideology.

78. A. S. Zvonitskaia, "K voprosu ob izuchenii prestupnika i prestupnosti," *Tekhnika, ekonomika i pravo*, no. 3 (1924): 92.

79. Zhizhilenko, *Prestupnost' i ee faktory*, 27.

80. S. Ukshe, "Ubiitsy," in *Prestupnyi mir Moskvy*, ed. M. N. Gernet (Moscow: Izdatel'stvo "Pravo i zhizn'," 1924), 44. These statistics were based on a small sample of 22 men and 8 women murderers.

81. S. Ukshe, "Muzheubiitsy," *Pravo i zhizn'*, nos. 2–3 (1926): 101.

82. S. Ukshe, "Muzheubiitsy," *Pravo i zhizn'*, nos. 4–5 (1926): 103–5. D. received an eight-year sentence for premeditated murder, commuted to three years.

83. Ibid., 105.

84. Ibid., 106.

85. A. A. Gertsenzon, "Osnovnye tendentsii dinamiki prestupnosti za desiat' let," *Sovetskoe pravo*, no. 1 (1928): 79.

86. Gernet, *Prestupnost' i samoubiistva vo vremia voiny*, 135.

87. A. A. Gertsenzon, "Bor'ba s prestupnost'iu v RSFSR," *Sovetskoe pravo. Zapiski Instituta Sovetskogo prava*, no. 3 (1929): 26. In 1926 the State Institute for the Study of Crime and the Criminal published a volume of essays analyzing

embezzlement and embezzlers. See *Rastraty i rastratchiki. Sbornik statei* (Moscow: Izdatel'stvo NKVD, 1926). Other discussions of embezzlers and the fight against embezzlement include M. Chalisov, "Opyt bio-sotsial'nogo obsledovaniia rastratchikov v Rostove-na-Donu," *Voprosy izucheniia prestupnosti v Severnom Kavkaze*, no. 2 (1927): 45–75; N. Polianskii, *Dolzhnostnye rastraty. Ikh ugolovnoe presledovanie* (Moscow: Pravovaia zashchita, 1926); and A. Stel'makhovich, *Bor'ba s rastratami* (Moscow: Novaia Moskva, 1925). *Proletarskii sud* also published a number of articles on embezzlement in 1925 and 1926. Part of the rise in embezzlement rates may have been the result of increased repression targeted against the crime in connection with efforts to patrol and control the burgeoning Soviet bureaucratic apparatus, as changing definitions of the offense broadened its scope and as the state concentrated economic resources in its hands. On economic crimes during the NEP, see L. V. Borisova, "'Tretii vrag revoliutsii.' Bor'ba so vziatochnichestvom i khoziaistvennymi prestupleniami v nachale NEPa," *Soviet and Post-Soviet Review* 30, no. 3 (2003): 245–77; and her "NEP v zerkale pokazatel'nykh protsessov po vziatochnichestvu i khoziaistvennym prestupleniiam," *Otechestvennaia istoriia* no. 1 (2006): 84–97.

88. A. N. Terent'eva, "Dva sluchaia zhenshchin-rastratchits," *Prestupnik i prestupnost'*, no. 2 (1927): 290–95.

89. L. Kandinskii, "Zhenshchina-rastratchik," *Proletarskii sud*, nos. 23–24 (1926): 12. Kandinskii noted that S. turned herself in after six months and was sentenced to six years' isolation with deprivation of rights, commuted to a one-year suspended sentence. The actual sentencing in this case cannot be verified.

90. On the Soviet penal theory and the penal system, see Adams, *The Politics of Punishment*; Solomon, "Soviet Penal Policy," 195–217; and Wimberg, "'Replacing the Shackles.'" Solomon notes that the Soviet progressivist approach to penal policy "stressed leniency and differentiation. Leniency was reflected in reliance to the extent possible upon noncustodial sanctions in place of imprisonment . . . use of shorter terms of imprisonment . . . and design of prison regimes to rehabilitate rather than to punish or deter. Differentiation meant a commitment to distinguishing among categories of offenders." Solomon, "Soviet Penal Policy," 196.

91. E. N. Tarnovskii, "Osnovnye cherty sovremennoi prestupnosti," *Administrativnyi vestnik*, no. 11 (1925): 53. Tarnovskii found that approximately 10 percent of rural offenders and closer to 20 percent of urban offenders were recidivists, according to statistics for 1924. By the end of 1924, overall recidivism rates were at 9.9 percent, with 9.3 percent for men and 13.1 percent for women. *Statisticheskii obzor deiatel'nosti mestnykh administrativnykh organov NKVD RSFSR*, vol. 3 (Moscow: Izdatel'stvo NKVD, 1925), 55.

92. B. S. Utevskii, "Sovremennaia prestupnost' po dannym perepisi mest zakliucheniia," *Administrativnyi vestnik*, no. 1 (1928): 42; and Utevskii, "Prestupnost' v RSFSR po dannym vsesoiuznoi perepisi," *Ezhenedelnik Sovetskoi iustitsii*, no. 41 (1927), 1281.

93. See Solomon, "Soviet Penal Policy," 195–217; and Wimberg, "'Replac-

ing the Shackles'.'" Another impetus for the shift to administrative sanctions was the tremendous overcrowding endemic to the Soviet prison system, a result of outdated facilities and periodic "campaigns" against certain offenses (for instance against the illicit production of vodka) that served to raise the prison population levels.

94. B. S. Utevskii, "Vozrast i gramotnost' retsidivistov," in *Sovremennaia prestupnost'*, vol. 2, *Sotsial'nyi sostav, professii, vozrast, gramotnost'* (Moscow: Izdatel'stvo Narodnogo Komissariata Vnutrennikh Del RSFSR, 1930), 85–86.

95. Tarnovskii, "Osnovnye cherty sovremennoi prestupnosti," 53; B. S. Utevskii, "Prestupnost' i retsidiv," in *Sovremennaia prestupnost' (Prestuplenie, pol, repressiia, retsidiv)*, ed. A. G. Beloborodov (Moscow: Izdatel'stvo Narodnogo Komissariata Vnutrennikh Del RSFSR, 1927).

96. Utevskii, "Prestupnost' i retsidiv," 42. In 1926, women made up 5.9 percent of the overall prison population.

97. Ibid., 42.

98. Utevskii, "Sovremennaia prestupnost' po dannym perepisi mest zaklicheniia," 41.

99. M. Kessler, "Imushchestvennye prestupleniia po dannym perepisi 1926 g.," in *Sovremennaia prestupnost' (Prestuplenie, pol, repressiia, retsidiv)*, ed. A. G. Beloborodov (Moscow: Izdatel'stvo Narodnogo Komissariata Vnutrennikh Del RSFSR, 1927), 53.

100. Utevskii, "Prestupnost' i retsidiv," 42. The effectiveness of the Soviet prison system to rehabilitate both first-time and repeat offenders remains to be studied.

101. S. B., "Sovremennaia prestupnost' i sudebnaia praktika," *Revoliutsiia prava*, no. 3 (1928): 114.

102. Utevskii, "Prestupnost' i retsidiv," 47.

103. Ibid., 41.

104. The Imperial regulation system was established in 1843 and patterned on those used in western Europe. Historian Laurie Bernstein argues that regulation in Russia developed as a way to preserve the patriarchal structure of society by instituting supervision over those women who fell through the cracks. Women identified as prostitutes received a "yellow ticket" (*zheltyi bilet*) and became subject to police surveillance and regular health inspections. Bernstein suggests that the yellow ticket in effect created a new social category, that of "public woman." Although it freed prostitutes from police harassment, it brought them fully under police control. The yellow ticket also made it extremely difficult for a woman to leave the profession and seek alternative employment. After 1861, the yellow ticket and the regulation system became a means of surveillance over all working-class women. The police often rounded up women in public places and registered them as prostitutes, in effect forcing women into prostitution. See Bernstein, *Sonia's Daughters*, 17–18, 22, 28–29, 33–38, 40. On prostitution in the late Imperial period, see also Barbara Alpern Engel, "St. Petersburg Prostitutes in

the Late Nineteenth Century: A Personal and Social Profile," *Russian Review* 48, no. 1 (1989): 21–44; Laura Engelstein, "Gender and the Juridical Subject: Prostitution and Rape in Nineteenth-Century Russian Criminal Codes," *Journal of Modern History* 60, no. 3 (1988): 458–95; N. B. Lebina and M. V. Shkarovskii, *Prostitutsiia v Peterburge, 40–e gg XIX – 40–e gg XX v.* (Moscow: Progress-Akademiia, 1994); and Richard Stites, "Prostitute and Society in Pre-Revolutionary Russia," *Jahrbücher für Geschichte Osteuropas* 31, no. 3 (1983): 348–64.

105. Maria I. Pokrovskaia, "Prostitutsiia i alkogolizm," in *Russian Women, 1698–1917: Experience and Expression*, ed. Robin Bisha et al. (Bloomington: Indiana University Press, 2002), 361.

106. See Bernstein, *Sonia's Daughters*, 267–73.

107. Wood, *The Baba and the Comrade*, 112–14. On the Interdepartmental Commission, see also Lebina and Shkarovskii, *Prostitutsiia v Peterburge*, 142–43.

108. N. B. Lebina, *Povsednevnaia zhizn' Sovetskogo goroda. Normy i anomalii 1920–1930 gody* (St. Petersburg: Zhurnal "Neva", 1999), 84.

109. See, for example, Stephen Frank, "Narratives within Numbers," 541–66; David Forgacs, "Imagined Bodies: Rhetorics of Social Investigation in Nineteenth-Century Italy and France," *Journal of the Institute of Romantic Studies* 1 (1992): 375–94; Jann Matlock, *Scenes of Seduction*; Shapiro, *Breaking the Codes*; and Judith Walkowitz, *Prostitution and Victorian Society: Women, Class, and the Stage* (Cambridge: Cambridge University Press, 1980).

110. Lombroso noted, "Primitive woman was rarely a murderess; but she was always a prostitute." Cesare Lombroso and Guglielmo Ferrero, *The Female Offender* (New York and London: D. Appleton and Company, 1895), 111. On nineteenth-century Russian attitudes toward prostitutes and female sexual deviance, see Engelstein, *Keys to Happiness*, 128–144.

111. Elizabeth Waters, "Victim or Villain? Prostitution in Post-Revolutionary Russia," in *Women and Society in Russia and the Soviet Union*, ed. Linda Edmondson (Cambridge: Cambridge University Press, 1992), 161. Waters notes that the high levels of unemployment during the NEP made it difficult to reinforce the claim that prostitutes were shirking work.

112. Lebina, *Povsednevnaia zhizn' Sovetskogo goroda*, 82.

113. D. M. Levin, "Bor'ba s prostitutsiei," *Administrativnyi vestnik*, no. 1 (1926): 29.

114. A. Uchevatov, "Iz byta prostitutsii nashikh dnei," *Pravo i zhizn'*, no. 1 (1928): 51. See also Wendy Goldman, *Women, the State, and Revolution*, 118–20.

115. P. I. Liublinskii, *Prestupleniia v oblasti polovykh otnoshenii* (Moscow and Leningrad: Izdatel'stvo L. D. Frenkel', 1925), 178.

116. L. Eratov, "Nakazuema li prostitutsiia?" *Ezhenedel'nik Sovetskoi iustitsii*, no. 4 (1922): 5.

117. Zhizhilenko, *Prestupnost' i ee faktory*, 24–25.

118. Vasilevskii, *Prostitutsiia i molodezh'*, 76.

119. M. Strogovich, "Bor'ba s prostitutsiei putem ugolovnoi repressii,"

Ezhenedel'nik Sovetskoi iustitsii, no. 37 (1925): 1214.

120. Accordingly, the "social dangerousness" of the brothel keeper necessitated severe measures of repression. In one sample of 155 brothel keepers, 80 percent received prison sentences for three years, and 58 were subject to deportation to areas where they would not be able to engage in this activity again. See V. D. Men'shagin, "Pritonoderzhatel'stvo (Sotsiologicheskii ocherk)," in *Pravonarusheniia v oblasti seksual'nykh otnoshenii*, ed. Krasnushkin, Segal, and Feinberg, 178. Men'shagin gives the following figures for length of sentences for brothel keepers: up to 6 months, 4 people; 6 months to one year, 4; 1–2 years, 4; 2–3 years, 125; 3–4 years, 8; 4–5 years, 10. See also Julie A. Cassidy and Leyla Rouhi, "From Nevskii Prospekt to Zoia's Apartment: Trials of the Russian Procuress," *Russian Review* 58, no. 3 (1999): 413–31. Brothel keepers were also targeted as a means of prosecuting homosexual behavior in the 1920s. See Healey, *Homosexual Desire*, 128–29.

121. Vasilevskii, *Prostitutsiia i molodezh'*, 76.

122. Zhizhilenko, *Prestupnost' i ee faktory*, 24–25, 46. See also N. N. Gedeonov, "Grabiteli i bandity," in *Prestupnyi mir Moskvy*, ed. M. N. Gernet (Moscow: Izdatel'stvo "Pravo i zhizn'," 1924), 28.

123. Gedeonov, "Grabiteli i bandity," 28.

124. On the Chubarov Alley case, see Naiman, "The Case of Chubarov Alley" 1–30. On hooliganism in Russia, see Neuberger, *Hooliganism: Crime, Culture, and Power in St. Petersburg*; and Neil B. Weissman, "Rural Crime in Tsarist Russia: The Question of Hooliganism, 1905–1914," *Slavic Review* 37, no. 2 (1978): 228–40. Evidence for the concern regarding hooliganism can be seen in a report on hooliganism and the struggle against it presented to Sovnarkom on 22 September 1926 by Beloborodov and Sergievskii of the NKVD. See GARF, f. A-259, op. 11b, d. 823, ll. 89–94ob. Hooliganism remains understudied as a phenomenon in the early Soviet period.

125. L. G. Orshanskii, "Analiz psikhologicheskii i psikhopatologicheskii," in Zhizhilenko and Orshanskii, *Polovye prestupleniia* (Leningrad: Izd. "Rabochii sud," 1927), 60.

126. A. M. Rapoport and A. G. Kharlamova, "O zhenskom khuliganstve," in *Khuliganstvo i ponozhovshchina*, ed. Krasnushkin, Segal and Feinberg, 143. This study used a sample of 75 female hooligans in Moscow in 1925–1926. Of the other professions indicated, 12 (16%) were traders, 11 (14.7%) had no particular occupation, 8 (10.7%) were unemployed laborers, 6 (8%) were artisans, 5 (6.7%) were domestic servants, 4 (5.3%) were unemployed white-collar workers, 4 (5.3%) were criminals (thieves), 2 (2.7%) were laborers, 2 (2.7%) were white-collar workers, and 1 (1.3%) was unknown. S. Ukshe, "Zhenshchiny, osuzhdennye za khuliganstvo," in *Khuliganstvo i khuligany* (Moscow: Izdatel'stvo NKVD RSFSR, 1929), 147–49, notes that in a sample of 46 female hooligans, 15 (32.6 percent) were prostitutes. Of the 15, 6 had former convictions for hooliganism and 11 had committed their offenses under the influence of alcohol.

127. Rapoport and Kharlamova, "O zhenskom khuliganstve," 145.

128. Ibid., 145. They noted that 62 percent of male hooligans had no pre-vious arrests. Other studies confirmed this disparity. B. S. Utevskii found in his sample of recidivist criminals that 35.3 percent of female hooligans had multiple convictions, compared to only 17 percent among men. See Utevskii, "Prestupnost' i retsidiv," 47. D. P. Rodin also noted that in a survey of 121 prostitutes conducted in 1927, 13 had been charged with hooliganism and 11 with theft. See Rodin, "Iz dannykh o sovremennoi prostitutsii," *Pravo i zhizn'*, no. 5 (1927): 64–65. The Criminal Code reflected the sense of hooliganism as both a behavioral problem and a criminal activity. Article 74 of the Criminal Code (1926 version) dealt with the offense and set out prison terms of up to three months for a first offense. However, for repeat offenses and if the hooligan was disruptive to social order, penalties increased to two years' imprisonment. See *Ugolovnyi kodeks RSFSR redaktsii 1926 g.* (Moscow: Iuridicheskoe izdatel'stvo NKIu RSFSR, 1926).

129. Rapoport and Kharlamova, "O zhenskom khuliganstve," 149.

130. Mary Louise Roberts, *Civilization without Sexes: Reconstructing Gender in Postwar France, 1917–1927* (Chicago, IL: University of Chicago Press, 1994).

131. Klein, "The Etiology of Female Crime," 287.

4—THE GEOGRAPHY OF CRIME

1. Gernet, "Predislovie," in *Prestupnyi mir Moskvy*, i, v-vi. See also Gernet, *Moral'naia statistika*, 190–91.

2. G. Manns, "Derevenskie ubiistva i ubiitsy," *Problemy prestupnosti*, no. 2 (1927): 25.

3. See David Herbert, *The Geography of Urban Crime* (London: Longman, 1982); David J. Evans and David T. Herbert, eds., *The Geography of Crime* (London: Routledge, 1989); Keith D. Harries, *The Geography of Crime and Justice* (New York: McGraw Hill, 1974); and Victor Goldsmith et al., eds., *Analyzing Crime Patterns: Frontiers of Practice* (Thousand Oaks, CA: Sage Publications, 2000).

4. Louise Shelley, "The Geography of Soviet Criminality," *American Sociological Review* 45, no. 1 (February 1980): 111–22. Criminality could also be determined by geography, as was the case with the creation of closed cities in the 1930s, which further curtailed and even criminalized population movement. As Kate Brown, "Out of Solitary Confinement: The History of the Gulag," *Kritika* 8, no. 1 (Winter 2007): 67–103, writes, "zoned space criminalized desire and the mobility necessary to satisfy it" (97). Furthermore, the widespread use of prison and exile as devices to control the population added to the geographical nature of Soviet crime. Brown sees the Stalinist gulag "as located along a continuum of incarcerated space" (78) that defined and shaped Stalinist society and argues for the importance of under-standing spatial practices, particularly regarding incarceration.

5. Recent scholarship that focuses on issues of identity, citizenship, and class consciousness in Soviet Russia includes Golfo Alexopoulos, *Stalin's Outcasts*; Igal Halfin, *From Darkness to Light*; Anna Krylova, "Beyond the Spontaneity-

Consciousness Paradigm: 'Class Instinct' as a Promising Category of Historical Analysis," *Slavic Review* 62, no. 1 (Spring 2003): 1–23; and the issue of *Kritika*, vol. 7, no. 3 (Summer 2006), devoted to "Subjecthood and Citizenship, part 2, From Alexander II to Brezhnev."

6. See Cathy A. Frierson, *Peasant Icons: Representations of Rural People in Late Nineteenth-Century Russia* (Oxford: Oxford University Press, 1993). Corinne Gaudin, *Ruling Peasants: Village and State in Late Imperial Russia* (DeKalb: Northern Illinois University Press, 2007), notes that the view of the peasantry as backward was particularly persistent among the late-nineteenth-century intelligentsia. See also A. N. Engelgardt, *Letters from the Country, 1872–1887*, trans. and ed. Cathy A. Frierson (Oxford: Oxford University Press, 1993).

7. See E. N. Tarnovskii, "Statistika prestuplenii za 1924–1925 gg.," *Ezhenedel'nik Sovetskoi iustitsii*, no. 22 (1926): 675. On Soviet population trends, see Frank Lorimer, *The Population of the Soviet Union: History and Prospects* (Geneva: League of Nations, 1946).

8. *Statistika osuzhdennykh v SSSR 1923–1924* (Moscow: Izdanie TsSU SSSR, 1927), 88–95.

9. Tarnovskii, "Osnovnye cherty sovremennoi prestupnosti," 28. See also Tarnovskii, "Statistika prestuplenii za 1924–1925 gg.," 675; and Iu. B., "Prestupnost' goroda i derevni v 1924 g. (Po dannym statisticheskogo biuro NKVD)," *Administrativnyi vestnik*, no. 6 (1925): 24.

10. Gernet, *Prestupnost' i samoubiistva vo vremia voiny i posle nee*, 160. For 1 percent of female crimes, the location of the offense was unknown.

11. Gernet, *Moral'naia statistika*, 191.

12. *Statisticheskii obzor deiatel'nosti mestnykh administrativnykh organov NKVD RSFSR*, no. 2 (Moscow: Izdatel'stvo NKVD, 1925), 27.

13. Gernet, *Moral'naia statistika*, 191.

14. Manns, "Derevenskie ubiistva i ubiitsy," 26. See also D. P. Rodin, "Gorodskaia i sel'skaia prestupnost'," *Pravo i zhizn'*, nos. 2–3 (1926): 95.

15. Gernet, *Prestupnost' i samoubiistva vo vremia voiny*, 163; and Gernet, "Statistika gorodskoi i sel'skoi prestupnosti," *Problemy prestupnosti*, no. 2 (1927): 19.

16. Tarnovskii, "Statistika prestuplenii za 1924–1925 gg.," 675. In "Statistika gorodskoi i sel'skoi prestupnosti," 18, Gernet indicated that in 1924, 34.8 percent of military offenses were committed in the countryside, 52.4 percent of property crimes, 54.6 percent of abuse of authority, 67.3 percent of crimes against the state, 79.2 percent of crimes against the person, and 84.4 percent of crimes against state authority.

17. N. Ezerskii, "Gorodskaia i sel'skaia prestupnost' v byvsh. Leningradskoi gub. (Po dannym statistiki osuzhdennykh za 1925/26 g.)," *Vestnik statistiki*, no. 2 (1928): 222.

18. *Statistika osuzhdennykh v RSFSR za 1926 god* (Moscow: Izdanie TsSU RSFSR, 1928), xiv.

19. Gernet, "Statistika gorodskoi i sel'skoi prestupnosti," 15–16; and Gernet, *Prestupnost' i samoubiistva vo vremia voiny*, 158–59.

20. Rodin, "Gorodskaia i sel'skaia prestupnost'," 95. For criminologists, "rural" generally meant everything outside major urban centers and provincial cities, including district or *uezd* towns and villages.

21. Gernet, "Predislovie," xxiii.

22. L. G. Orshanskii, "Ubiitsy (Psikhologicheskii ocherk), in *Ubiitsy, s 75 tablitsami i fotograficheskimi snimkami* (Leningrad: Izdatel'stvo "Rabochii sud," 1928), 126–29.

23. Manns, "Derevenskie ubiistva i ubiitsy," 38.

24. See, for instance, Walkowitz, *City of Dreadful Delight*. See also Barrie Ratcliffe, "Perceptions and Realities of the Urban Margin: The Rag Pickers of Paris in the First Half of the Nineteenth Century," *Canadian Journal of History* 27, no. 2 (August 1992): 197–233.

25. David Cohen and Eric A. Johnson, "French Criminality: Urban-Rural Differences in the Nineteenth Century," *Journal of Interdisciplinary History* 12, no. 3 (Winter 1982): 494. Johnson, who primarily studies urbanization and crime in turn-of-the-century Germany, argues against "modernization" theories of crime that posit an increase in property crimes and corresponding decrease in violent crimes accompanying the rise of modern societies. See also Eric A. Johnson, "The Roots of Crime in Imperial Germany," *Central European History* 15, no. 4 (December 1982): 351–76; Johnson, "Cities Don't Cause Crime: Urban-Rural Differences in Late Nineteenth- and Early Twentieth-Century German Criminality," *Social Science History* 16, no. 1 (Spring 1992): 129–76; Johnson, *Urbanization and Crime*; Johnson and Eric H. Monkkonen, eds., *The Civilization of Crime: Violence in Town and Country since the Middle Ages* (Urbana: University of Illinois Press, 1996); Frank, *Crime, Cultural Conflict, and Justice in Rural Russia*, 58–66; O. H. Hufton, "The Urban Criminal in Eighteenth-Century France," *Bulletin of the John Rylands University Library of Manchester* 67, no. 1 (Autumn 1984): 474–99; Abdul Quaiyum Lodhi and Charles Tilly, "Urbanization, Crime, and Collective Violence in Nineteenth-Century France," *American Journal of Sociology* 79, no. 2 (September 1973): 296–318; Louise Shelley, *Crime and Modernization: The Impact of Industrialization and Urbanization on Crime* (Carbondale: Southern Illinois University Press, 1981); and Howard Zehr, "The Modernization of Crime in Germany and France," *Journal of Social History* 8, no. 4 (Summer 1975): 117–41.

26. See Joseph Bradley, *Muzhik and Muscovite: Urbanization in Late Imperial Russia* (Berkeley: University of California Press, 1985); Barbara Engel, *Between the Fields and the City*; David Hoffman, *Peasant Metropolis: Social Identities in Moscow, 1929–1941* (Ithaca, NY: Cornell University Press, 1994); and Robert Johnson, *Peasant and Proletariat: The Working Class of Moscow in the Late Nineteenth Century* (New Brunswick, NJ: Rutgers University Press, 1979).

27. On the liquidation of crime with the achievement of socialism, see, for example, Robert Sharlet, "Pashukanis and the Withering Away of Law in the

USSR," in *Cultural Revolution in Russia, 1928–1931*, ed. Sheila Fitzpatrick (Bloomington: Indiana University Press, 1978), 168–88.

28. M. Zamengof, "Gorod i derevnia v prestupnosti," *Zhurnal ugolovnogo prava i protsessa*, no. 1 (1913): 64.

29. Manns, "Derevenskie ubiistva i ubiitsy," 25.

30. B., "Prestupnost' goroda i derevni v 1924 g.," 24.

31. Gernet, *Prestupnost' i samoubiistva vo vremia voiny*, 120.

32. Gernet, *Moral'naia statistika*, 137. Statistics are from 1911.

33. V. D. Men'shagin, "Ubiistva," 60. Men'shagin noted that this ideology tended to turn women into the murdered victims of their jealous husbands. See also Engelstein, *Keys to Happiness*, 72–74. In "Narratives within Numbers: Women, Crime, and Juridical Statistics in Imperial Russia, 1834–1913," *The Russian Review* 55, no. 4 (October 1996): 545, Stephen Frank argues that in the nineteenth century criminologists understood that lower female crime rates related to the social constraints and restrictions placed on women, which once removed, led to increased participation in urban crime.

34. B., "Prestupnost' goroda i derevni v 1924 g.," 24; Tarnovskii, "Osnovnye cherty sovremennoi prestupnosti," 28; and Gernet, *Prestupnost' i samoubiistva vo vremia voiny*, 160.

35. Overall, female crime rose from 6.5 percent in 1912 to 15.5 percent in 1916, decreasing again to 12.7 percent by 1922. Murder rates for women provide a more telling swing, rising from 5.5 percent in 1913 to peak at 33.4 percent in 1916 before declining to 14.8 percent by 1924. Gernet, *Prestupnost' i samoubiistva vo vremia voiny*, 125; Gernet, "Zhenshchiny-ubiitsy," 84–85; and A. A. Gertsenzon and N. S. Lapshina, "Ubiistva v RSFSR i za granitsei," in *Ubiistva i ubiitsy*, ed. Krasnushkin, Segal, and Feinberg, 358.

36. Gernet, *Prestupnost' i samoubiistva vo vremia voiny*, 120. See also Ukshe, "Ubiitsy," 42–43.

37. Rodin, "Gorodskaia i sel'skaia prestupnost'," 99.

38. Manns, "Derevenskie ubiistva i ubiitsy," 27; and M. N. Gernet and D. P. Rodin, "Statistika osuzhdennykh v 1922 g. i statistika samoubiistv v 1922–23 gg.," *Biulleten' Tsentral'nogo Statisticheskogo Upravleniia*, no. 84 (1924): 117.

39. B., "Prestupnost' goroda i derevni v 1924 g.," 27–28.

40. Utevskii, "Sovremennaia prestupnost' po dannym perepisi mest zakliucheniia," 39.

41. Sheila Fitzpatrick, "Ascribing Class: The Construction of Social Identity in Soviet Russia," *Journal of Modern History* 65, no. 4 (December 1993): 745–70.

42. See *Ugolovnyi kodeks RSFSR* (Moscow, 1922) and its 1926 revision *Ugolovnyi kodeks RSFSR redaktsii 1926 g.* (Moscow, 1926). The 1926 version of the criminal code separated counterrevolutionary crimes (punishable by death) from crimes against state authority.

43. Historians have shown that peasant women often instigated or were promiantly involved in anti-government protests. Because officials did not expect

women to take leading roles, these *babi* were able to challenge authority in ways men could not. See Lynn Viola, *Peasant Rebels under Stalin: Collectivization and the Culture of Peasant Resistance* (Oxford: Oxford University Press, 1996).

44. *Statistika osuzhdennykh v SSSR 1923–1924*, 58–61, 74–77. The statistics include large numbers of women lumped together in "other" or "unknown" categories for their social status, which makes it more difficult to determine accurate levels of criminality according to social background.

45. Ibid., 15, 95. The place was unknown for 1.4 percent of crimes in 1923 and 1 percent in 1924.

46. Ibid., 32–33, 122–23. Figures indicated that 17.7 percent of women sentenced in 1922 spent time in prison (and 22.2 percent of men—making up 21.7 percent of offenders overall). See *Statisticheskii ezhegodnik*, part 2 (Moscow: Tsentral'noe Statisticheskoe Upravleniia, 1925), 74.

47. *Statistika osuzhdennykh v SSSR 1923–1924*, 32–33, 122–23.

48. D. P. Rodin, "Obshchii obzor dannykh perepisi zakliuchennykh," in *Sovremennaia prestupnost' (Prestuplenie, pol, repressiia, retsidiv)*, ed. A. G. Beloborodov (Moscow: Izdatel'stvo NKVD RSFSR, 1927), 12.

49. For example, according to statistics on property crimes from 1922, 38.3 percent of men were detained for less than fifteen days, compared to 52.2 percent of women. In contrast, 0.4 percent of men, and only 0.2 percent of women, received sentences of over one year for these crimes. See *Statisticheskii ezhegodnik* (1925), 74.

50. Iakubson, "Repressiia lisheniem svobody," 33.

51. *Statistika osuzhdennykh v SSSR v 1925, 1926, i 1927 gg.* (Moscow: Izdanie TsSU SSSR, 1930), 43 [quote], 57.

52. *Statistika osuzhdennykh v SSSR 1923–1924*, 32–33, 122–23.

53. On Soviet penal theory and practice, see Wimberg, "'Replacing the Shackles'"; and Solomon, "Soviet Penal Policy," 195–217.

54. In the mid-1920s an Experimental Penitentiary Institute (Eksperimental'nyi Penitentsiarnyi Institut) was established as part of the State Institute for the Study of Crime and the Criminal, the central criminological organization of the 1920s, to explore new methods of reeducation within the prison system. Although the experimental prison met with some successes, it could accommodate few prisoners, and the state lacked the resources to implement the methods it developed on a wider scale. See Iu. Bekhterev, "Eksperimental'nyi Penitentsiarnyi Institut," *Sovetskoe pravo*, no. 6 (1926): 119–24; and B. S. Utevskii, "Ob Eksperimental'nom Penitentsiarnom otdelenii Gosudarstvennogo Instituta po izucheniiu prestupnosti i prestupnika," *Administrativnyi vestnik*, no. 12 (1926), 31–36. On the role of cultural enlightenment and education in Soviet penal policy, see Wimberg, "'Replacing the Shackles,'" 113–58.

55. This dynamic of incentives combined with repression existed throughout the Soviet state structure. See Terry Martin, "Interpreting the New Archival Signals," 113–24, who discusses these trends in terms of "hard" and "soft" commissariats.

56. Gernet, *Prestupnost' i samoubiistva vo vremia voiny*, 163; and Gernet, "Statistika gorodskoi i sel'skoi prestupnosti," 19.

57. Gernet, "Statistika gorodskoi i sel'skoi prestupnosti," 15–16; and Gernet, *Prestupnost' i samoubiistva vo vremia voiny*, 158–59.

58. Mironov, "The Development of Literacy in Russia and the USSR," 243, gives the literacy level as 44.1 percent for 1920, up from 28.4 percent in 1897. A majority of those considered literate in 1920, however, possessed only the most rudimentary reading, writing, and counting skills.

59. Gregory Guroff and S. Frederick Starr, "A Note on Urban Literacy in Russia, 1890–1914," *Jahrbücher für Geschichte Osteuropas* 19, no. 4 (1971): 531. Historians remain interested in literacy and efforts to increase literacy in Russia as a means to assess the attitudes of the population toward revolution and reform. See, for example, Jeffrey Brooks, *When Russia Learned to Read*; Joseph Bradley, "Patterns of Peasant Migration to Late Nineteenth-Century Moscow: How Much Should We Read into Literacy Rates?" *Russian History* 6, pt. 1 (1979): 22–38; and Ben Eklof, "Peasant Sloth Reconsidered: Strategies of Education and Learning in Rural Russia before the Revolution," *Journal of Social History* 14, no. 3 (Spring 1981): 355–85.

60. Charles E. Clark, *Uprooting Otherness: The Literacy Campaign in NEP-Era Russia* (London: Associated University Presses, 2000), 17.

61. On the Soviet campaigns against illiteracy see Michael S. Gorham, "Tongue-tied Writers: The Rabsel'kor Movement and the Voice of the 'New Intelligentsia' in Early Soviet Russia," *The Russian Review* 55, no. 3 (July 1996): 412–29; Peter Kenez, "Liquidating Illiteracy in Revolutionary Russia," *Russian History* 9, pts. 2–3 (1982): 173–86; and V. A. Kumanev, "Opyt likvidatsii negramotnosti v SSSR," *Vestnik istorii mirovoi kul'tury*, no. 25 (1961): 14–29.

62. Iu. Iu. Bekhterev, "Gramotnost' zakliuchennykh v sviazi s polom, vozrastom, i retsidivom," in *Sovremennaia prestupnost'*, vol. 2, *Sotsial'nyi sostav, professii, vozrast, gramotnost'* (Moscow: Izdatel'stvo NKVD RSFSR, 1930), 52–53.

63. Mironov, "Development of Literacy in Russia and the USSR," 243. Statistics from 1920 give levels of literacy at 52.4 percent for rural men, 25.2 percent for rural women, 80.7 percent for urban men, and 66.7 percent for urban women.

64. B., "Prestupnost' goroda i derevni v 1924 g.," 27. See also Tarnovskii, "Osnovnye cherty sovremennoi prestupnosti," 48. Percentage totals are broken down according to sex and place of residence. B. indicated that the literacy level was unknown for about 4–5 percent in each category.

65. P. V. Verkhovskii, "Bor'ba s prestupnost'iu v derevne," *Vlast' sovetov*, no. 43 (1925): 3.

66. L. Artimenkov, "O revoliutsionnoi zakonnosti v derevne," *Ezhenedel'nik Sovetskoi iustitsii*, no. 10 (1925): 241.

67. A. Shestakova, "Prestupleniia protiv lichnosti v derevne," *Problemy prestupnosti*, no. 1 (1926): 223.

68. B., "Prestupnost' goroda i derevni v 1924 g.," 26.

69. Ibid., 28.

70. I. Ia. Bychkov, *Detoubiistvo v sovremennykh usloviiakh* (Moscow: Gosudarstvennoe meditsinskoe izdatel'stvo, 1929), 14–15.

71. Bekhterev, "Gramotnost' zakliuchennykh v sviazi s polom, vozrastom i retsidivom," 58.

72. Ibid., 70.

73. See Clark, *Uprooting Otherness*, who argues that the literacy campaigns of the NEP years provided lessons on the benefits and potential of peaceful and incremental methods of change and modernization that went unheeded as the Bolsheviks embarked on the Five-Year Plans. See also Wimberg, "'Replacing the Shackles.'"

74. For a more detailed analysis of the campaign against illegal spirits and the temperance movement in early Soviet Russia, see Laura L. Phillips, *Bolsheviks and the Bottle: Drink and Worker Culture in St. Petersburg, 1900–1929* (De Kalb: Northern Illinois University Press, 2000); Kate Transchel, *Under the Influence*; and Neil Weissman, "Prohibition and Alcohol Control in the USSR: The 1920s Campaign against Illegal Spirits," *Soviet Studies* 38, no. 3 (July 1986): 349–68.

75. See A. Aronovich, "Samogonshchiki," in *Prestupnyi mir Moskvy*, 174–91.

76. K. B. Litvak, "Samogonovarenie i potreblenie alkogolia v Rossiiskoi derevne 1920–x godov," *Otechestvennaia istoriia*, no. 4 (1992): 76.

77. Tsirkuliar No. 77 dated 8 September 1922, "Ob usilenii repressii za nezakonnoe prigotovlenie i khranenie spirtnykh napitkov," *Ezhenedel'nik Sovetskoi iustitsii*, no. 33 (1922): I–II (Ofitsial'noe prilozhenie).

78. *Ugolovnyi kodeks RSFSR* (1922), 24.

79. Tsirkuliar No. 77.

80. "140a. Persons engaging in the illegal production and storage of alcoholic beverages for trade (recidivists), are punished by imprisonment for a period of not less than three years with confiscation of all property. 140b. Preparation of alcoholic beverages and alcoholic products without intention of sale, and also the storage of such beverages and products on which the excise tax has not been paid, are punishable by fines of up to 500 gold rubles or forced labor for up to six months." Quoted in Litvak, "Samogonovarenie," 76. See also Aronovich, "Samogonshchiki," 175–76.

81. See Susan Gross Solomon, "David and Goliath in Soviet Public Health: The Rivalry of Social Hygienists and Psychiatrists for Authority over the Bytovoi Alcoholic," *Soviet Studies* 41, no. 2 (April 1989): 254–75.

82. Tsirkuliar No. 113 dated 2 June 1923, "O meropriiatiiakh po bor'be s samogonom," *Ezhenedel'nik Sovetskoi iustitsii*, no. 23 (1923): 548.

83. D. Kniazev, "Dva mesiatsa raboty osobykh kamer narodnogo suda po delam o samogonkakh v Moskve (s 25–IX po 25–XI 1922 goda)," *Proletarskii sud*, nos. 2–3 (1922): 48.

84. Aronovich, "Samogonshchiki," 175; and L. Skliar, "Prestupnost' v RSFSR v pervykh chertvertiakh 1921–1923 g. (Po dannym upravleniia ugolovnogo rozyska respubliki)," *Vlast' sovetov*, nos. 6–7 (1923): 125. Skliar attributed this increase to

the end of the famine and the availability of grain for alcohol production.

85. Gernet, *Moral'naia statistika*, 97; and I. A. Smirnov, "Rabota suda Moskovskoi gubernii v 1923 godu. Doklad predsedatelia gubsuda I. A. Smirnova plenumu Ispolkoma Moskovskogo Soveta 6 iunia 1924 g.," *Proletarskii sud*, nos. 1–2 (1924): 5.

86. A. Uchevatov, "Itogi za piat' let (Iz materialov registr.-daktiloskopicheskogo biuro MUURa)," *Proletarskii sud*, nos. 8–9 (1925): 21. He noted rates of 17.2 percent for 1922 and a decrease to 12.5 percent in 1924.

87. V. Khal'fin, "Razmery prestupnosti v SSSR po dannym ugolovnogo-administrativnykh organov na 1923 g. (Po materialam statisticheskogo biuro NKVD)," *Proletarskii sud*, nos. 1–2 (1924): 24. Here, crimes against the administrative order (*protiv poriadka upravleniia*) encompassed eight different categories of offense, including economic crimes (under which samogon offenses fell).

88. A. Semenov, "Samogon i russkaia gor'kaia," *Administrativnyi vestnik*, nos. 9–10 (1925): 38.

89. *Statistika osuzhdennykh v SSSR 1923–1924*, 88–95. Ger van der Berg, *The Soviet System of Justice: Figures and Policy* (Dordrecht, Netherlands: Martinus Nijhoff, 1985), 44, indicates that samogon offenses made up 30 percent of sentenced crimes in 1922, but only 3.3 percent by 1926, due to decriminalization of the activity.

90. E. N. Tarnovskii, "Dvizhenie prestupnosti v RSFSR za 1920–23 gg.," *Vlast' sovetov*, no. 10 (1923): 114. See also D. P. Rodin, "Prestupnost' muzhchin, zhenshchin i nesovershennoletnikh v 1922 godu," *Biulleten' Tsentral'nogo Statisticheskogo Upravleniia*, no. 79 (1923): 68.

91. Aronovich, "Samogonshchiki," 191.

92. Litvak, "Samogonovarenie," 77. See also van der Berg, *The Soviet System of Justice*, 33. A shift in focus to the fight against hooliganism, to prosecuting the behaviors that occurred as a result of drunkenness rather than the suppliers of drink, might have also contributed to halting the anti-samogon campaign in late 1926. The campaign was reinitiated in 1928, however, in connection with industrialization during the First Five-Year Plan. Industrialization necessitated securing an adequate food supply for the growing cities and their workers, which led to agricultural collectivization and greater controls over the countryside. Samogon production, when it was not prosecuted (1927), increased tremendously. The state may have restarted the anti-samogon campaign both as a way to ensure an adequate food supply for the cities and to place more controls on the peasantry as they were collectivized, for the selling of samogon could be interpreted as an act of speculation committed by a kulak.

93. *Statisticheskii obzor deiatel'nosti mestnykh administrativnykh organov NKVD RSFSR*, no. 2 (1925): 26.

94. *Statistika osuzhdennykh v SSSR 1923–1924*, 90–91.

95. "Kharakter dvizhenii prestupnosti za 1924–1928 gody," *Administrativnyi vestnik*, no. 2 (1930): 54.

96. S. Krylov, "Bor'ba s samogonom (Ivanovo-Voznesenskaia guberniia)," *Administrativnyi vestnik*, no. 4 (1925): 61–62.

97. V. Mokeev, "Prestupnost' v derevne," *Ezhenedel'nik Sovetskoi iustitsii*, no. 16 (1925): 419–20.

98. A. Uchevatov, "Tainoe vinokurenie v gorode i derevne," *Problemy prestupnosti*, no. 2 (1927): 120.

99. Iu. Khodakov, "Sovremennaia prestupnost' zhenshchin," *Vlast' sovetov*, nos. 11–12 (1923): 89; and V. I. Kufaev, "Retsidivitsy (povtorno-obviniaemye)," in *Prestupnyi mir Moskvy*, 106. Kufaev noted that among thieves, 48.7 percent of women were recidivists and 41.3 percent of men; for murder, recidivist rates were 9 percent for women and 25.9 percent for men. Figures were for Moscow only.

100. A. Uchevatov, "Ugolovnye prestupniki," *Proletarskii sud*, nos. 4–5 (1924): 55; Ukshe, "Ubiitsy," 41; and D. P. Rodin, "Sotsial'nyi sostav osuzhdennykh v 1923 g.," *Biulleten' Tsentral'nogo Statisticheskogo Upravleniia*, no. 93 (1924): 130. See also "Khronika. Iz itogov bor'by s samogonom v Moskve i Moskovskoi guberni," *Ezhenedel'nik Sovetskoi iustitsii*, no. 30 (1923): 687.

101. E. G. Shirvindt, "Udarnye kampanii v svete vsesoiuznoi perepisi po mestam zakliucheniia," in *Sovremennaia prestupnost'*, 7. Shirvindt noted that 13 percent of men in prison were sentenced for samogon crimes in 1923 (the percentage of women was not recorded), 9 percent of men and 21 percent of women in 1925, 3 percent of men and 18 percent of women in the first half of 1926, and 2 percent of men and 20 percent of women as of the date of the 1926 (December) prison census.

102. *Statistika osuzhdennykh v SSSR v 1925, 1926 i 1927*, 18; and Utevskii, "Sovremennaia prestupnost' po dannym perepisi mest zakliucheniia," 40. See also Utevskii, "Prestupnost' v RSFSR po dannym vsesoiuznoi perepisi," 1280. Women made up 46.6 percent of those sentenced for theft, 38 percent for crimes against property, 33.7 percent for crimes against state authority, 24.1 percent for crimes against the person, and 12.7 percent for abuse of power. N. Visherskii, "Professiia i prestupnost'," in *Sovremennaia prestupnost'*, vol. 2: 48, noted that women committed samogon offenses 8–10 times more often than men.

103. *Statisticheskii obzor deiatel'nosti mestnykh administrativnykh organov NKVD RSFSR*, no. 2 (1925), 26.

104. Tarnovskii, "Statistika prestupleniia za 1924–1925," 677. Tarnovskii noted that only among unemployed women did rates of property crime exceed rates of samogon offenses.

105. A. Uchevatov, "Bezrabotnye i prestupnost'," *Proletarskii sud*, nos. 1–2 (1925): 50. Rodin, "Sotsial'nyi sostav osuzhdennykh v 1923 g.," 130, noted that 56 percent of unemployed women committed samogon crimes, compared to 25.3 percent of unemployed men. Uchevatov, "Tainoe vinokurenie v gorode i derevne," 123, noted that 18.1 percent of all samogon offenders were unemployed.

106. See Aronovich, "Samogonshchiki," 186–87; M. N. Gernet, "Prestupnosti' v sviazi s klassovo-sotsial'nym sostavom osuzhdennykh v 1922 g.," *Vestnik*

statistiki, nos. 1–3 (1924): 150–51; R. Novitskii, "Semeinoe polozhenie zakliuchennykh," in *Sovremennaia prestupnost'*, vol. 2 (1930), 31; and B. Zmiev, "Prestupnost' v Tatrespublike," 50. Novitskii's analysis of 1926 prison census data showed that 48.7 percent of those convicted of samogon crimes were widowed, 37.2 percent were married, and only 11.9 were single or divorced.

107. Utevskii, "Prestupnost' i retsidiv," 46–47. The vast majority of those arrested for samogon crimes, however, were first-time offenders. According to Aronovich, "Samogonshchiki," 178–79, 78.5 percent of samogon offenders had nos prior criminal record, and only 6.4 percent had two or more previous convictions. He compared these rates to those for thieves and robbers, noting that 58.5 percent of thieves and 67.8 percent of robbers were first-time offenders, and 17 percent of thieves and 13.7 percent of robbers had two or more offenses.

108. Rodin, "Prestupnost' muzhchin, zhenshchin, i nesovershennoletnikh v 1922 godu," 68.

109. V. D. Men'shagin, "Pritonoderzhatel'stvo (Sotsiologicheskii ocherki)," in *Pravonarusheniia v oblasti seksual'nykh otnoshenii*, ed. Krasnushkin, Segal, and Feinberg, 169.

110. *Statistika osuzhdennykh v RSFSR za 1926 god* (Moscow: Izdanie TsSU RSFSR, 1928), xii.

111. B., "Prestupnost' goroda i derevni v 1924 g.," 25. See also Tarnovskii, "Osnoynye cherti sovremennoi prestupnosti," 28. Samogon offenses were the most common crime that women committed, according to the statistics. The next most common crime for women was theft, with rates of 25.5 percent for urban and 21.2 percent for rural women. Official statistics indicated that 30 percent of women committed samogon crimes in the cities and 69.5 percent in the countryside (compared to 15 percent and 84 percent, respectively, for men). These rates did not reflect the population differences between the countryside and the city. See *Statistika osuzhdennykh v SSSR 1923–1924*, 90–91.

112. Uchevatov, "Tainoe vinokurenie v gorode i derevne," 120. In the 1926 revision of the criminal code, the articles on samogon were placed under the general category of crimes against state authority (*protiv poriadka upravleniia*) and the category of economic crimes was eliminated.

113. Aronovich, "Samogonshchiki," 181–82. See also Gernet, *Prestupnost' i samoubiistva vo vremia voiny*, 158.

114. Aronovich, "Samogonshchiki," 182.

115. Ibid., 189–90.

116. I. Smirnov, "Doklad predsedatelia Moskovskogo Gubsuda tov. I. Smirnova na plenume Mossoveta 3 fevralia 1925 goda," *Proletarskii sud*, no. 3 (1925): 4. See also *Statistika osuzhdennykh v RSFSR za 1926 god*, xii–xiii; and *Statisticheskii obzor deiatel'nosti mestnykh administrativnykh organov NKVD RSFSR*, no. 2 (1925): 78.

117. M. Solov'ev, "O klassovoi prirode st. 140 Ug. Kod. v novoi redaktsii," *Ezhenedel'nik Sovetskoi iustitsii*, no. 18 (1924): 424–25.

118. Gernet, "Prestupnost' v sviazi s klassovo-sotsial'nym sostavom osuzh-dennykh v 1922 g.," 151.

119. Aronovich, "Samogonshchiki," 189–90.

120. Gernet, "Predislovie," xx.

121. Ibid., xxiii–xxiv.

122. A. A. Gertsenzon, *Bor'ba s prestupnost'iu v RSFSR po materialam obsle-dovaniia NK RKI SSSR* (Moscow: Iuridicheskoe izdatel'stvo NKIu RSFSR, 1928), 137–38.

5—A REMNANT OF THE OLD WAY OF LIFE

1. E. K. Krasnushkin, G. M. Segal, and Ts. M. Feinberg, eds., *Ubiistva i ubiitsy* (Moscow: Izdatel'stvo Moszdravotdela, 1928).

2. Gernet, "Zhenshchiny-ubiitsy," 85. Typically, women made up the vast majority of infanticide offenders. According to Gernet, 100 percent of those charged for infanticide in late Imperial Russia were women, 100 percent in Germany, 95.6 percent in France, and 91.95 percent in Italy. Comparatively, women made up approximately 10 percent of the overall criminal population in Europe (ranging from a low of 2 percent in Greece to a high of 21.3 percent in England, with France at 13 percent and Imperial Russia at 13.6 percent). See M. N. Gernet, *Detoubiistvo. Sotsiologicheskoe i sravnitel'no-iuridicheskoe issledovanie* (Moscow: Tip. Imperatorskogo Moskovskogo Universiteta, 1911), 104–6, 109, 111.

3. The publication of *Svod statisticheskikh svedenii po delam ugolovnym*, beginning in 1873, made the systematic scholarly study of crime, based on empirical data, possible (see chap. 1). Some early discussions of infanticide include N. Tagantsev, "O detoubiistve," *Zhurnal Ministerstva iustitsii*, no. 9 (1868): 215–50 and no. 10 (1868): 341–80; M. G., "O detoubiistve," *Arkhiv sudebnoi meditsiny*, no. 1 (1868): 21–55; A. Zhukovskii, "Detoubiistvo v poltavskoi gubernii i pre-dovrashchenie ego," *Arkhiv sudebnoi meditsiny*, no. 3 (1870): 1–13; and Shashkov, *Istoricheskie sud'by zhenshchiny*.

4. Ann R. Higginbotham, "'Sin of the Age': Infanticide and Illegitimacy in Victorian London," *Victorian Studies* 32, no. 3 (Spring 1989): 319–37. See also William Langer, "Infanticide: A Historical Survey," *History of Childhood Quarterly* 1, no. 3 (1974): 353–66; and Kristin Ruggiero, "Honor, Maternity, and the Disciplining of Women: Infanticide in Late Nineteenth-Century Buenos Aires," *Hispanic American Historical Review* 72, no. 3 (August 1992): 353–73. Historical studies of infanticide in Europe include, among others, James M. Donovan, "Infanticide and the Juries in France, 1825–1913," *Journal of Family History* 16, no. 2 (April 1991): 157–76; Karen Huber, "Sex and its Consequences: Abortion, Infanticide, and Women's Reproductive Decision-Making in France, 1901–1940" (Ph.D. diss., Ohio State University, 2007); Mark Jackson, ed., *Infanticide: Historical Perspectives on Child Murder and Concealment, 1550–2000* (Aldershot, England: Ashgate, 2000); Ren Leboutte, "Offense against Family Order: Infanticide in Belgium from the

Fifteenth to the Early Twentieth Centuries," *Journal of the History of Sexuality* 2, no. 2 (April 1991): 159–85; Stephen Wilson, "Infanticide, Child Abandonment, and Female Honour in Nineteenth-Century Corsica," *Comparative Studies in Society and History* 30, no. 4 (1988): 762–83; and Keith Wrightson, "Infanticide in European History," *Criminal Justice History* 3 (1982): 1–20. See also Brigitte H. Bechtold and Donna Cooper Graves, eds., *Killing Infants: Studies in the Worldwide Practice of Infanticide* (Lewiston, NY: The Edwin Mellen Press, 2006).

5. Shashkov, *Istoricheskie sud'by zhenshchiny, detoubiistvo, i prostitutsiia.*

6. Gernet, *Detoubiistvo*, 90, 244.

7. As historian Keith Wrightson observes, "if Christian social morality had done so much to overcome the practice of infanticide motivated by considerations of communal or familial interest, it may have exacerbated resort to it to avoid the stigma of illegitimacy." Wrightson, "Infanticide in European History," 5. See also Langer, "Infanticide: A Historical Survey," 354–55; and Clarice Feinman, *Women in the Criminal Justice System* (New York: Praeger, 1986), 5.

8. Eve Levin, "Infanticide in Pre-Petrine Russia," *Jahrbücher für Geschichte Osteuropas* 34, no. 2 (1996): 221–23; and David L. Ransel, *Mothers of Misery: Child Abandonment in Russia* (Princeton, NJ: Princeton University Press, 1988), 10–12. See also Gernet, *Detoubiistvo*, 50; and Bychkov, *Detoubiistvo v sovremennykh usloviiakh*, 52. Punishments set out in the Ulozhenie for other types of murder committed by women were much more substantial than those for child murder. For example, wives who killed their husbands were to be buried alive (punishments for husbands who murdered their wives varied according to the circumstances). David Ransel emphasizes that the severe punishments for the murder of illegitimate children do not suggest a high value was placed on children but rather that the law sought to set an example to deter illicit sexual relationships. Ransel, *Mothers of Misery*, 16–17.

9. David Ransel argues that Peter I created the foundling homes as part of his military reforms in 1714 and 1715. Motivated in this action by a desire to increase his labor supply, Peter saw these illegitimate children as future workers and soldiers and emphasized the importance of preserving as many lives as possible. Ransel also suggests that Peter's policies of assigning peasants to work for manufacturing enterprises, and his military conscription policies, contributed to increasing the visibility of illegitimacy and infanticide and made them of greater social concern than previously in Russia. Ransel, *Mothers of Misery*, 20–22, 26. Gernet, in *Detoubiistvo*, 55–56, noted that Peter I understood that the reason women killed their illegitimate infants was out of shame and fear before their community and that this motivated his creation of the foundling homes. At the same time, he retained the harsh punishments for women who committed infanticide.

10. Ransel, *Mothers of Misery*, 31. See also Valery Chalidze, *Criminal Russia: Essays on Crime in the Soviet Union*, trans. P. S. Falla (New York: Random House, 1977), 124–25.

11. Zmiev, "Detoubiistvo," 2. This trend in Russia reflected larger intellectual

developments in Europe. See Wrightson, "Infanticide in European History," 11.

12. Schrader, *Languages of the Lash*, 132–33.

13. According to the law code, infanticides received prison sentences from four to six years, in addition to a loss of rights. For all other cases in which women committed murder, the punishment was a loss of rights and forced labor for life. The reduced sentence for infanticide applied only to first-time offenders. See article 1451 of the Ulozhenie o nakazaniiakh ugolovnykh i ispravitel'nykh in *Svod zakonov Rossiiskoi Imperii*, vol. 15 (Petrograd: I. I. Zubkova, 1916), 325. The 1845 criminal code remained in effect until the Bolshevik Revolution, although a new draft code was prepared in 1903.

14. M. M. Borovitinov, *Detoubiistvo v ugolovnom prave* (St. Petersburg: Tipolit. St. Petersb. tiur'my, 1905), 14–15; and Bychkov, *Detoubiistvo v sovremennykh usloviiakh*, 52. See also Gernet, *Detoubiistvo*, 50–62. According to V. Lindenberg, the courts often found that an infant's death was not the mother's fault and thus sentenced such women for concealing the infant's body, a lesser charge than infanticide. See his *Materialy k voprosu o detoubiistve i plodoizgnanii v Vitebskoi gubernii* (Iuriev: Tip. K. Mattisena, 1910), 54. Courts had high conviction rates for the concealment of a newborn's body, seeing this as a crime "symbolic of moral decline and sexual danger," but also one that was less difficult to prove than infanticide. Frank, "Narratives within Numbers," 556. See also Zmiev, "Detoubiistvo (po dannym sudebnoi statistiki)," 89.

15. Ransel, *Mothers of Misery*, 19.

16. A more compassionate outlook toward illegitimacy in the seventeenth and eighteenth centuries led to the spread throughout Europe of foundling homes where unwanted children could be deposited anonymously, as an alternative to infanticide. See Ransel, *Mothers of Misery*; and Otto Ulbricht, "The Debate about Foundling Hospitals in Enlightenment Germany: Infanticide, Illegitimacy, and Infant Mortality Rates," *Central European History* 18, nos. 3–4 (Sept.–Dec. 1985): 211–56. Engelstein, *Keys to Happiness*, 145, discusses late-nineteenth-century medical discourses that linked sexual deviance and "mental imbalance" to irregularities in the menstrual cycle.

17. Gernet, *Detoubiistvo*, 186–87, 189, 203, 208.

18. Within the patriarchal Russian family structure, women were expected to remain virgins until marriage. Fathers and husbands were responsible for safeguarding women's honor, which demonstrated their ability to control women and secured their status in the community. See Christine D. Worobec, "Temptress or Virgin? The Precarious Sexual Position of Women in Postemancipation Ukrainian Peasant Society," in *Russian Peasant Women*, ed. Beatrice Farnsworth and Lynn Viola (Oxford: Oxford University Press, 1992), 44; and Stephen P. Frank, "Cultural Conflict and Criminality in Rural Russia, 1861–1900" (Ph.D. diss., Brown University, 1987), 163–64. See also Eve Levin, *Sex and Society in the World of the Orthodox Slavs, 900–1700* (Ithaca, NY: Cornell University Press, 1989); Engelstein, *Keys to Happiness*; and Engel, *Between the Fields and the City*, 7–33.

19. Olga Semenova Tian-Shanskaia, *Village Life in Late Tsarist Russia*, trans. David Ransel (Bloomington: Indiana University Press, 1993), 7–8, 57–59, 98–99. "Overlaying" or rolling over and smothering an infant in its sleep was a common means of infanticide in early modern Europe. Feinman, *Women in the Criminal Justice System*, 5. Child abandonment and infanticide rates in Russia also may have been affected by the restrictions placed on admissions to foundling homes for illegitimate children, which after 1891 sought to reinforce parental responsibility over guardianship by the state of unwanted children. See Ransel, *Mothers of Misery*, 106–29.

20. Bychkov, *Detoubiistvo v sovremennykh usloviiakh*, 53. See also *Ugolovnyi kodeks RSFSR* (1922), 36. Infanticide was sentenced under article 142, parts d and e, for premeditated murder in cases where the perpetrator bears responsibility for the care of the victim. Punishments were to be prison sentences of not less than eight years. The 1926 revision of the criminal code altered only the numbering of the articles (article 142 became article 136) and increased the punishment for murder to a maximum of ten years. See *Ugolovnyi kodeks RSFSR redaktsii 1926 g.*, 37.

21. A. Shestakova, "Ubiistvo mater'iu novorozhdennogo rebenka," *Problemy prestupnosti*, no. 3 (1928): 154–63, discussed mitigating factors in cases of infanticide. She noted that the Supreme Court's instructions left sentencing to the discretion of the local courts.

22. As an example of the leniency, Bychkov indicated that the Moscow Regional Court sentenced 60 percent of infanticide offenders to suspended sentences in 1926 and 46 percent to such sentences in 1927. See Bychkov, *Detoubiistvo v sovremennykh usloviiakh,* 55. Shmidt provided very different figures, indicating that suspended sentences for infanticide reached 70 percent in 1927. See Shmidt, "Detoubiistvo," *Proletarskii sud*, no. 5 (1928): 8. The discrepancies in these figures must be explained by the sources each scholar used to derive his statistics.

23. Gernet, "Statistika detoubiistv," *Statisticheskoe obozrenie*, no. 2 (1928): 102, 106. Most received sentences of up to two years in prison.

24. B. S. Man'kovskii, "Detoubiistvo," in *Ubiistva i ubiitsy*, ed. Krasnushkin, Segal, and Feinberg, 272. See also Bychkov, *Detoubiistvo v sovremennykh usloviiakh,* 57–58.

25. B. N. Zmiev, "Detoubiistvo," 6–7. Article 144 of the 1922 Criminal Code addressed murder committed under the condition of mental illness. See also Gernet, *Detoubiistvo*, 186, who noted that the psychological condition of a woman at birth was a deciding factor in Russian laws on infanticide.

26. Bychkov, *Detoubiistvo v sovremennykh usloviiakh,* 53–54. The draft article was not adopted.

27. Man'kovskii, "Detoubiistvo," 271–72.

28. "Instruktivnoe pis'mo UKK Verkhsuda RSFSR no. 2, 1926 g.," *Ezhenedel'nik Sovetskoi iustitsii*, no. 50 (1926): 1415.

29. Ibid.

30. According to article 36 of the criminal code, suspended sentences could

be handed down instead of prison terms for first offenses, in light of the difficult circumstances facing the offender, and when the offender's "social dangerousness" did not demand isolation or corrective labor. See *Ugolovnyi kodeks RSFSR* (1922), 7.

31. "Instruktivnoe pis'mo no. 2," 1415.

32. Shmidt, "Detoubiistva," 8. The percentage of those sentenced to less than one year fell from 17 percent in 1926 to 12.5 percent in 1927; likewise those sentenced to 1–2 years dropped from 8.9 percent to 7 percent. The proportion of those sentenced to more than 2 years remained constant at 7 percent.

33. M. Andreev, "Detoubiistvo," *Rabochii sud*, no. 2 (1928): 144. See also Bezpal'ko, "Detoubiistvo," *Ezhenedel'nik Sovetskoi iustitsii*, no. 20 (1927): 603; and I. Nemchenkov, "Detoubiistvo," *Ezhenedel'nik Sovetskoi iustitsii*, no. 30 (1927): 924.

34. Man'kovskii, "Detoubiistvo," 270.

35. Shestakova, "Ubiistvo mater'iu novorozhdennogo rebenka," 161. Married women's circumstances did not fit the Supreme Court's understanding of infanticide, so when such women did commit the crime the court believed they did so out of selfishness or because of male influence. Semenova Tian-Shanskaia's observations about infanticide practiced as a contraceptive measure, discussed above, are not reflected in the court's interpretations. Between 1897 and 1906, married women made up 16.8 percent of infanticide offenders. In 1924–1925 they were 21 percent of infanticides, but only 7 percent in 1926–1927. Gernet, *Moral'naia statistika*, 194; Gernet, "Statistika detoubiistv," 105; and Bychkov, *Detoubiistvo v sovremennykh usloviiakh*, 11. These statistics indicated that in court practice infanticide remained a crime committed primarily by single women.

36. "D. No. 216432," *Sudebnaia praktika RSFSR*, no. 4 (1929): 176–80. Both Gugina and Kiselev were sentenced to two years in prison; Gugina was released on appeal. On this case and criminal responsibility, see Sharon A. Kowalsky, "Who's Responsible for Female Crime? Gender, Deviance, and the Development of Soviet Social Norms in Revolutionary Russia," *The Russian Review* 62, no. 3 (July 2003): 366–86.

37. Andreev, "Detoubiistvo," 142. See also P. A. Aliavdin, "Ugolovnye prestupleniia v sviazi s alimentami v Ivanovo-Voznesenskoi gubernii," *Sudebno-meditsinskaia ekspertiza*, no. 11 (1929): 113–15. Bychkov, *Detoubiistvo v sovremennykh usloviiakh*, 33, noted that in 1926–1927, men made up 11 percent of those found guilty of physically committing infanticide by the Moscow Regional Court. He also indicated that a number of cases involved men who encouraged their pregnant lovers to commit the crime.

38. V. V. Brailovskii, *Opyt bio-sotsial'nogo issledovaniia ubiits: Po materialam mest zakliucheniia Severnogo Kavkaza* (Rostov-na-Donu, 1929), 74. Brailovskii did not indicate the sentencing in this case.

39. On the Soviet family code and the debates over its provisions, see Goldman, *Women, the State and Revolution*. The strengthening of the family did

not necessarily reflect a return to its prerevolutionary conception but rather an emphasis on the needs and priorities of the Soviet state. See Hoffmann, *Stalinist Values*, 88–117.

40. "Instruktivnoe pis'mo UKK Verkhovnogo Suda RSFSR no. 1," *Sudebnaia praktika RSFSR*, no. 3 (1928): 5. Such cases were sentenced under article 158, part 2, which provided for prison terms of up to six months or fines up to 300 rubles for parents who abandoned their young children without any means of support.

41. Man'kovskii, "Detoubiistvo," 267. Only 2.2 percent of women received prison terms of over two years for infanticide.

42. Bychkov, *Detoubiistvo v sovremennykh usloviiakh*, 27–28. The father was sent to prison for three years.

43. Man'kovskii, "Detoubiistvo," 267.

44. Bychkov, *Detoubiistvo v sovremennykh usloviiakh*, 34–35.

45. Zmiev, "Detoubiistvo (po dannym sudebnoi statistiki)," 93.

46. Bychkov, *Detoubiistvo v sovremennykh usloviiakh*, 20. V. was punished with a two-year suspended sentence.

47. Ibid., 25. K. claimed that her pregnancy was the result of a rape she had hidden out of shame, and that she had acted unconsciously during the birth. She received a three-year suspended sentence.

48. Ibid., 26. M. was sentenced to two years in prison for her action.

49. Ibid., 23–24.

50. Shmidt, "Detoubiistva," 8, indicated that 78.4 percent of infanticides suffocated their children, 13 percent drowned them, 4 percent poisoned them, and 4.6 percent starved them. Man'kovskii, "Detoubiistvo," 254, noted a similar breakdown of infanticide methods. See also Bychkov, *Detoubiistvo v sovremennykh usloviiakh*, 23. Statistics from 1924 indicated that in the Moscow region 22.4 percent of infanticides employed strangulation by hand, but only 2.6 percent did so in Moscow city. Other (unspecified) forms of asphyxiation were more common in the city. A. Uchevatov, "Ugolovnye prestupniki," *Proletarskii sud*, nos. 4–5 (1924): 58.

51. P. A. Aliavdin, "Detoubiistvo v Ivanovo-Voznesenskoi gubernii za 1925 i 1926 g.," *Sudebno-meditsinskaia ekspertiza*, no. 7 (1927): 98.

52. I. Ia. Bychkov, "Sposoby detoubiistva," *Sudebno-meditsinskaia ekspertiza*, no. 8 (1928): 75.

53. See Semenova Tian-Shanskaia, *Village Life in Tsarist Russia*.

54. Bychkov, *Detoubiistvo v sovremennykh usloviiakh,* 14. Anna received a one-year prison term for her actions; her husband went to prison for two years. I cannot speculate on the motives of the witnesses in this case.

55. See Aliavdin, "Detoubiistvo v Ivanovo-Voznesenskoi gubernii za 1925 i 1926 g.," 98. The role of the forensic investigator in infanticide has been discussed by Mark Jackson, "Suspicious Infant Deaths: The Statute of 1624 and Medical Evidence at Coroners' Inquests," and Mary Nagle Wessling, "Infanticide Trials and Forensic Medicine: Württemberg 1757–93," both in *Legal Medicine in History*, ed.

Michael Clark and Catherine Crawford (Cambridge: Cambridge University Press, 1994), 64–86, 117–44. On forensic investigation in Soviet Russia, see also Becker, "Medicine, Law, and the State"; R. S. Belkin and A. I. Vinberg, *Istoriia sovetskoi kriminalistiki. Etap vozniknoveniia i stanovleniia nauki (1917–1930–e gody)* (Moscow: Akademiia MVD SSSR, 1982); Dan Healey, "Early Soviet Forensic Psychiatric Approches to Sex Crime, 1917–1934," in *Madness and the Mad in Russian Culture*, ed. Angela Britlinger and Ilya Vinitsky (Toronto: University of Toronto Press, 2007), 150–72; Krylov, *Ocherki istorii kriminalistiki i kriminalisticheskoi ekspertizy*; Leibovich, "Sudebno-meditsinskaia ekspertiza pri NEPe," 36–38; and Pinnow, "Making Suicide Soviet."

56. A. E., "Sud i byt. Mat'-detoubiitsa," *Rabotnitsa*, no. 1 (1926): 22.

57. Bychkov, *Detoubiistvo v sovremennykh usloviiakh*, 36–37.

58. Zmiev, "Detoubiistvo (po dannym sudebnoi statistiki)," 95–96; Man'kovskii, "Detoubiistvo," 250; and Gernet, "Statistika detoubiistv," 102. These statistical trends may result from improved forensic investigation methods that allowed a greater number of infant deaths to be classified as infanticide.

59. Zmiev, "Detoubiistvo (po dannym sudebnoi statistiki)," 90; Gernet, "Statistika detoubiistv," 104. For comparison, 82 percent of all crimes against the person were committed in rural areas. At this time, over 80 percent of Russia's population resided in the countryside. Zmiev did acknowledge that the autonomy of the city made it easier to conceal births and hide infant bodies, which may have contributed to the lower incidence of urban infanticide [p. 91].

60. A. O. Edel'shtein, "K psikhopatologii detoubiistv," in *Ubiistva i ubiitsy*, ed. Krasnushkin, Segal, and Feinberg, 281. See also Bychkov, *Detoubiistvo v sovremennykh usloviiakh*, 37.

61. Zmiev, "Detoubiistvo (po dannym sudebnoi statistiki)," 96.

62. Man'kovskii, "Detoubiistvo," 257. See also Gernet, "Statistika detoubiistv," 105.

63. Zmiev, "Detoubiistvo (po dannym sudebnoi statistiki)," 89–91. Zmiev added that these unmarried mothers knew that life would be difficult for their children, who would carry the shame of their illegitimacy with them.

64. Shestakova, "Ubiistvo mater'iu novorozhdennogo rebenka," 159–60. The court sentenced Cherina to two years in prison, mitigating her punishment because it did not consider her "socially dangerous." Peasant women "hid" their pregnancies by wearing loose clothing and not discussing their condition. Most likely, other village residents knew when a woman was pregnant.

65. Gernet, *Moral'naia statistika*, 192–93.

66. Andreev, "Detoubiistvo," 138, 143–44.

67. V. Khonin, "O detoubiistve," *Rabochii sud*, no. 9 (1926): 622. See also Man'kovskii, "Detoubiistvo," 263.

68. Man'kovskii, "Detoubiistvo," 263.

69. S. V. Poznyshev, *Prestupniki iz-za alimentov. Tipy ikh i mery bor'by s nimi* (Moscow and Leningrad: Gosudarstvennoe izdatel'stvo, 1928), 161.

70. Gernet, "Abort v zakone i statistika abortov," in *Aborty v 1925 godu* (Moscow: Izdanie TsSU SSSR, 1927), 19.

71. Gernet, *Moral'naia statistika*, 193; Andreev, "Detoubiistvo," 137. See also Man'kovskii, "Detoubiistvo," 261–62.

72. E. K. Krasnushkin, "Kriminal'nye psikhopaty sovremennosti i bor'ba s nimi," in *Prestupnyi mir Moskvy*, ed. M. N. Gernet, 205.

73. Shashkov, *Istoricheskie sud'by zhenshchiny, detoubiistvo, i prostitutsiia*, 438.

74. See Gernet, *Detoubiistvo*, 186, who noted that the psychological condition of a woman at birth was the deciding factor in Russian laws on infanticide.

75. Edel'shtein, "K psikhopatologii detoubiistv," 273.

76. Zhizhilenko, *Prestupnost' i ee faktory*, 26 (italics mine). See also Shashkov, *Istoricheskie sud'by zhenshchiny, detoubiistvo, i prostitutsiia*, 438; and Gernet, *Detoubiistvo*, 186. Writing about infanticide in 1920s America, J. Stanley Hopwood emphasized that insanity accompanying the strain of lactation in women led to the crime. See his "Child Murder and Insanity," *Journal of Mental Science* 73, no. 300 (1927): 96–97. This phenomenon was not unique to infanticide. S. Ukshe, "Muzheubiitsy," *Pravo i zhizn'*, nos. 4–5 (1926): 105, noted that women often killed their husbands under the influence of temporary insanity [*affekt*] that emerged in connection with pregnancy.

77. Edel'shtein, "K psikhopatologii detoubiistv," 281.

78. V. A. Vnukov, "Zhenshchiny-ubiitsy," in *Ubiistva i ubiitsy*, ed. Krasnushkin, Segal, and Feinberg, 247. See also A. V. Nemilov, *Biologicheskaia tragediia zhenshchiny* (Leningrad: Knigoizdatel'stvo "Seiatel'," 1927), 47.

79. Vnukov, "Zhenshchiny-ubiitsy," 194–95.

80. Stites, *The Women's Liberation Movement in Russia*, 355; and Hoffmann, *Stalinist Values*, 97–105. The pro-natalist tendencies in Soviet policy increased in the 1930s and after World War II, with special privileges and benefits awarded to women who raised ten or more children.

81. Man'kovskii, "Detoubiistvo," 264–65. See also Andreev, "Detoubiistvo," 140; and Manns, "Derevenskie ubiistva i ubiitsy," 36. Despite high ideals and promises, these new services had a limited impact. They were not available or readily accessible to all women, nor were they adequate to cover the demand, and made little real difference in the lives of most ordinary women.

82. According to Man'kovskii's statistics about infanticides, 29.5 percent were illiterate, 64.7 percent had an elementary education, and none had a higher education. Infanticide compared unfavorably with other types of murders, where 12.3 percent were illiterate, 77.9 percent had an elementary education, 9.5 percent had a secondary education, and 0.3 percent had a higher education. Man'kovskii, "Detoubiistvo," 253. See Bychkov, *Detoubiistvo v sovremennykh usloviiakh*, 14–15; and Shmidt, "Detoubiistva," 8, who give similar figures; and A. L. "Detoubiistvo (po dannym Kostromskogo Gubsuda)," *Rabochii sud*, no. 1 (1928): 71.

83. Bezpal'ko, "Detoubiistvo," 603.

84. B. Ia. Arsen'ev, "Ubiistva i sudebnaia bor'by s nimi," in *Ubiistva i ubiitsy*, ed. Krasnushkin, Segal, and Feinberg, 370. See also M. Chelyshev, "Detoubiistvo," *Rabochii sud*, no. 1 (1927): 13. This need for socialist education reflects a larger effort by the state to instill socialist ideals among peasants and workers and create a new "Soviet" man and woman. See, among others, Barbara Evans Clements, "The Birth of the New Soviet Woman," 220–37; Kotkin, *Magnetic Mountain*; and Kathy S. Transchel, "Under the Influence: Drinking, Temperance, and Cultural Revolution in Russia, 1900–1932" (Ph.D. diss., University of North Carolina at Chapel Hill, 1996), 223–84.

85. Shmidt, "Detoubiistva," 9.

86. Bychkov, *Detoubiistvo v sovremennykh usloviiakh*, 37–38.

87. On the role of *Rabotnitsa* and other women's magazines in early Soviet society, see also Lynne Attwood, *Creating the New Soviet Woman: Women's Magazines as Engineers of Female Identity, 1922–1953* (New York: St. Martin's Press, 1999); and Heather DeHaan, "Engendering a People: Soviet Women and Socialist Rebirth in Russia," *Canadian Slavonic Papers* 41, nos. 3–4 (1999): 431–55.

88. A. E., "Sud i byt. Mat'-detoubiitsa," 22. There is no indication in this report that the offender's father's social background affected the outcome of the case.

89. A. E., "Sud i byt. Mat'-ubiitsa," *Rabotnitsa*, no. 24 (1926): 24.

90. "Sud i byt. Styd pogubil," *Rabotnitsa*, no. 19 (1925): 23.

91. There may have been a practical element to the sentence reductions as well—at this time prisons were severely overcrowded and there was considerable interest in the application of administrative (fines, forced labor, etc.) rather than penal sanctions for less "socially dangerous" criminals. On Soviet penal policy, see Solomon, "Soviet Penal Policy," 195–217; and Wimberg, "'Replacing the Shackles.'"

92. "Sud i byt. Na detei plati," *Rabotnitsa*, no. 22 (1925): 24.

93. S. Bonnar, "Sud i byt. Otets ne mozhet, pust' platit ded," *Rabotnitsa i krest'ianka*, nos. 23 (1926): 33.

94. See articles 140–144, 162–169 of *The Marriage Laws of Soviet Russia*, 56–57, 61–62.

95. V. Luchaninov, "Stat'ia 38–a ugolovnogo kodeksa i alimenty," *Proletarskii sud*, no. 1–2 (1925): 24.

96. Goldman, *Women, the State, and Revolution*, 51–57, 248–49.

97. Poznyshev, *Prestupniki iz-za alimentov*, 137.

98. Ibid., 48.

99. Ibid., 86.

100. Ibid., 151. Vasilii was sentenced to eight years in prison, but his sentence was reduced due to mental illness and he was sent to a psychiatric hospital. Poznyshev emphasized the role that alcoholism as a mitigating factor played in the crime.

101. Ibid., 41–42.

102. Man'kovskii, "Detoubiistvo," 267.

103. Poznyshev, *Prestupniki iz-za alimentov*, 108–12 (quote on p. 112).

104. Ibid., 136.

105. Ibid., 35–36.

106. Historians have shown that before the revolution, peasant women had turned to the courts to secure their rights, particularly in terms of property claims. Their willingness to use the courts for alimony requests thus built on a previously established pattern. See Beatrice Farnsworth, "The Litigious Daughter-in-Law: Family Relations in Rural Russia in the Second Half of the Nineteenth Century," in *Russian Peasant Women*, ed. Beatrice Farnsworth and Lynn Viola (New York: Oxford University Press, 1992), 89–106. On peasant use of courts, see also Jane Burbank, *Russian Peasants Go to Court: Legal Culture in the Countryside, 1905–1917* (Bloomington: Indiana University Press, 2004); and Corinne Gaudin, *Ruling Peasants: Village and State in Late Imperial Russia* (DeKalb: Northern Illinois University Press, 2007).

107. Poznyshev, *Prestupniki iz-za alimentov*, 49. Poznyshev notes Maxim as having expressed frustration with the notion that he was sent to jail because of a woman.

108. Smirnov, "Doklad predsedatelia Moskovskogo Gubsuda tov. I. Smirnova," 5.

109. See Goldman, *Women, the State, and Revolution*, 237–46.

110. Gernet, "Abort v zakone i statistika abortov," 13. In St. Petersburg, 4,374 out of 5,874 hospitalized persons were made ill from abortions.

111. On the debates over abortion in the late nineteenth century, see Engelstein, *Keys to Happiness*, 334–58.

112. I. B. Fuks, *Problema prestupnosti plodoizgnaniia* (Khar'kov: Tipo-litografiia M. Sergeeva i K. Gal'chenka, 1910), 21–22.

113. Ibid., 20.

114. A. Gens, "K probleme legalizatsii i statistiki abortov v RSFSR," in *Aborty v 1925 godu* (Moscow: Izdanie TsSU SSSR, 1927), 21–22; and Gernet, "Abort v zakone i statistika abortov," 3. Gernet noted that the RSFSR adopted this decree on 18 November 1920, Ukraine on 5 July 1921. Abortion was advocated by its supporters as a temporary measure to eliminate the hazardous conditions of illegal abortions and to allow for the scientific, statistical study of the procedure. Medical personnel were supposed to encourage women to have legal abortions and to dissuade them from having abortions altogether by advocating alternatives and by setting up nurseries and shelters linked to factories. A. Gens, "Abort—sotsial'noe zlo," *Meditsina*, no. 7 (1926): 11. On Soviet abortion policy, see also L. A. Vasilevskii and L. M. Vasilevskii, *Abort kak sotsial'noe iavlenie. Sotsial'no-gigienicheskii ocherk* (Moscow and Leningrad: Izdatel'stvo L. D. Frenkel', 1924); Goldman, *Women, the State, and Revolution*, 261–64; and Wood, *The Baba and the Comrade*, 106–11.

115. Gens, "K probleme legalizatsii i statistiki abortov v RSFSR," 22–23. V. Khalfin, "Istreblenie ploda (abort) v Moskve i Moskovskoi gubernii," *Problemy*

prestupnosti, no. 2 (1927): 210, provided figures for abortions in the Moscow region in 1925 that indicated the vast majority of women having abortions were workers' wives or workers (including domestic servants). Those denied free state abortions could terminate their pregnancies in private clinics for a fee. In 1925 the commission granted doctors more latitude in making decisions to perform abortions in emergency situations when the mother's health was in danger. By 1926 abortions performed after the first trimester had been outlawed.

116. A. F., "Aborty v gubernskikh gorodakh, prochikh gorodakh, i sel'skikh mestnostakh," in *Aborty v 1925 godu* (Moscow: Izdanie TsSU SSSR, 1927), 61–62. In the same work, see also V. Paevskii, "Aborty v Moskve i Leningrade," 35. Comparatively, among those convicted for infanticide, 71.2 percent were single, 12.8 percent married, and 16 percent widowed or divorced. Man'kovskii, "Detoubiistvo," 254.

117. At the same time that legal abortions were permitted, little or no effort was taken to make other methods of contraception available. This had the result of severely limiting women's birth control options and making abortion a primary method for controlling family size. See Goldman, *Women, the State, and Revolution,* 257–61.

118. A. A. Piontkovskii, "Sistema osobennoi chasti ugolovnogo prava," *Sovetskoe pravo,* no. 2 (1926): 62. Abortion was covered in article 146 of the 1922 criminal code.

119. See by Gernet: *Moral'naia statistika,* 181–82; *Detoubiistvo,* 127; and "Istreblenie ploda s ugolovno-sotsiologicheskoi tochki zreniia," *Vestnik prava,* no. 8 (1914): 237. See also Shashkov, *Istoricheskie sud'by zhenshchiny, detoubiistvo i prostitutsiia,* 498.

120. Engelstein, *Keys to Happiness,* 355.

121. Vasilevskii and Vasilevskii, *Abort kak sotsial'noe iavlenie,* 64. See also Gernet, *Prestuplenie i bor'ba s nim v sviazi s evoliutsiei obshchestva* (1914), reprinted in his *Izbrannye proizvedeniia,* 242–43.

122. F., "Aborty v gubernskikh gorodakh i sel'skikh mestnostakh," 55, 60. See also M. N. Gernet, "K statistike abortov," *Statisticheskoe obozrenie,* no. 3 (1927): 68. The abortion commission tended to approve abortions for material need more often than for any other reason. See Paevskii, "Aborty v Moskve i Leningrade," 46. Of course, women who wanted to conceal their pregnancies would be less likely to request an abortion from the commission.

123. Vasilevskii and Vasilevskii, *Abort kak sotsial'noe iavlenie,* 65; Zmiev, "Detoubiistvo (po dannym sudebnoi statistiki): 89–96; and Aliavdin, "Detoubiistva v Ivanovo-Voznesenskoi gubernii za 1925 i 1926," 96–97. V. Khonin, "O detoubiistve," 621–22, noted that to end the necessity of abortion and to eliminate infanticide there needed to be an equality of rights for both common-law and registered marriages and a decisive increase in and expansion of the struggle against the *besprizornye,* as homeless children at the time were called.

124. Gernet, *Moral'naia statistika*, 193. In response to falling birth rates, abortion was recriminalized on 27 July 1936. Birth rates were not affected significantly by the ban, however, and on 23 November 1955 abortion was once again decriminalized. This led to an almost immediate doubling of abortion rates. By the 1970s, abortion had become a primary method of birth control for Soviet women. Jeff Chinn, *Manipulating Soviet Population Resources* (New York: Holmes & Meier, 1977), 109–10.

125. Shmidt, "Detoubiistva," 8. Gernet noted a 106.8 percent rise in infanticide cases between 1924 and 1925, compared to an increase of only 17.7 percent for crimes against the person overall. See Gernet, "Statistika detoubiistv," 102; and Gernet, *Prestupnost' i samoubiistva vo vremia voiny*, 129.

126. Brailovskii, *Opyt bio-sotsial'nogo issledovaniia ubiits*, 70.

127. Zmiev, "Detoubiistvo (po dannym sudebnoi statistiki)," 90–91; and Gernet, *Detoubiistvo*, 143. Gernet gave the figures for urban and rural infanticides as 88.5 percent and 11.5 percent for the years 1897–1906, while Zmiev's were 86.5 percent and 13.5 percent, respectively. Zmiev also noted that in the countryside it was more difficult to conceal an unwanted birth than in the city, where greater autonomy often prevented the identification of a murdered infant's mother.

128. Man'kovskii, "Detoubiistvo," 250–51. These changes may be explained in part by urban migration. See Fitzpatrick, Rabinowitch, and Stites, eds., *Russia in the Era of NEP*, for more on Russian society during the NEP years.

129. Rapid urbanization in the early Soviet period resulted in a "ruralization" of the cities, as large numbers of peasants migrated to the urban centers, bringing their rural traditions with them. On urbanization and peasant migration in early-twentieth-century Russia, see Bradley, *Muzhik and Muscovite*; Engel, *Between the Fields and the City*; and David Hoffmann, *Peasant Metropolis: Social Identities in Moscow, 1929–1941* (Ithaca: Cornell University Press, 1994). On urbanization and crime, see Eric Johnson, *Urbanization and Crime*.

130. Man'kovskii, "Detoubiistvo," 252. Criminologists equated peasant women with domestic servants, identifying 62.3 percent of infanticide perpetrators in 1925 as peasants, 76.2 percent in 1926, and 50 percent in 1927. Workers consistently made up approximately 10 percent of offenders. Man'kovskii also noted that over 70 percent of those convicted of infanticide were under twenty-five years of age. On early Soviet domestic servants, see Rebecca Spagnolo, "When Private Home Meets Public Workplace: Service, Space, and the Urban Domestic in 1920s Russia," in *Everyday Life in Early Soviet Russia: Taking the Revolution Inside*, ed. Christina Kiaer and Eric Naiman, 230–55 (Bloomington: Indiana University Press, 2006), who discusses the efforts of domestic workers' unions to alleviate the conditions of domestic service and regulate the profession. On domestic service in the prerevolutionary period, see Engel, *Between the Fields and the City*, 140–49, who suggests that pregnancy jeopardized a woman's position as a domestic worker, but does not mention infanticide as a solution to this problem.

131. Man'kovskii, "Detoubiistvo," 250–51. See also Shestakova, "Ubiistvo

mater'iu novorozhdennogo rebenka," 158; and Frank, "Cultural Conflict and Criminality in Rural Russia," 161.

132. Bychkov, *Detoubiistvo v sovremennykh usloviiakh,* 25. P. was sentenced to three years in prison.

133. Man'kovskii, "Detoubiistvo," 257–58. Man'kovskii noted that 50 percent of workers, 82.8 percent of peasants, and 55.5 percent of other social groups committed infanticide out of shame.

134. Andreev, "Detoubiistvo," 137–38.

135. Man'kovskii, "Detoubiistvo," 252. Criminologists rarely mentioned working women in their discussions of infanticide. Bychkov indicated that in 1926–1927, 63 percent of women guilty of infanticide in Moscow were peasants, 11 percent were domestic servants, and 12 percent were workers. Bychkov, *Detoubiistvo v sovremennykh usloviiakh,* 18. A. A. Gertsenzon's statistics for 1913 indicated that over 60 percent of infanticides were committed by peasants and 3 percent by workers. See Gertsenzon and Lapshina, "Ubiistva v RSFSR i za granitsei," 350.

136. Some historians have suggested that greater economic stability, solidarity, independence, and mutual support experienced by female industrial workers may have contributed to their lower rates of criminality. See Laurie Bernstein, *Sonia's Daughters,*116–17; and Engel, *Between the Fields and the City.*

137. Andreev, "Detoubiistvo," 143–44.

138. On the position of women in early Soviet society, see Goldman, *Women, the State, and Revolution*; Hutton, *Russian and West European Women, 1860–1939*; and Wood, *The Baba and the Comrade,* among others.

CONCLUSION

1. See Klein, "The Etiology of Female Crime," 265–90.

2. Goldman, *Women, the State, and Revolution,* 341–43; and Hoffmann, *Stalinist Values,* 97–99. On the Soviet state and women, see also Mary Buckley, *Women and Ideology in the Soviet Union* (Ann Arbor: University of Michigan Press, 1989); Stites, *The Women's Liberation Movement in Russia*; and Wood, *The Baba and the Comrade.*

3. Victoria Bonnell, "The Peasant Woman in Stalinist Political Art of the 1930s," *American Historical Review* 98, no. 1 (February 1993): 79. See also her *Iconography of Power: Soviet Political Posters under Lenin and Stalin* (Berkeley: University of California Press, 1997), 82–85.

4. See Michael David-Fox, "What is Cultural Revolution?" 181–201.

EPILOGUE

1. See Susan Gross Solomon, "The Limits of Government Patronage of Science," 405–35.

2. On the new "Soviet" intelligentsia, see Fitzpatrick, "Stalin and the Making of a New Elite, 1925–1939," 377–402.

3. Similar criticisms were leveled at a variety of the more revolutionary efforts at social change conducted during the 1920s. See, for example, Mally, *Culture of the Future*; and Wood, *The Baba and the Comrade*.

4. The Communist Academy's Department of State and Law (Sektsiia gosudarstva i prava) was established in 1923 and by 1925 had become the center for Marxist legal study in the Soviet Union. Its scholars focused their research on formulating theoretical positions on questions of the state and the law. They contributed to the *Bol'shaia Sovetskaia Entsiklopediia* (*Great Soviet Encyclopedia*) and published a journal called *Revoliutsiia prava* (*Revolution of Law*) from 1927 to 1929. (The journal was renamed *Sovetskoe gosudarstvo i revoliutsiia prava* in 1930, changing its name again to *Sovetskoe gosudarstvo* in 1932 and *Sovetskoe gosudarstvo i prava* in 1939. It continues to be published in post-Soviet Russia as *Gosudarstvo i prava* [beginning in 1992].) Members of the Department of State and Law included A. Ia. Vyshinskii, E. B. Pashukanis, P. I. Stuchka, A. Ia. Estrin, N. V. Krylenko, D. I. Kurskii, and A. G. Beloborodov, among others. See I. Razumovskii, "Sektsiia prava Kommunisticheskoi Akademii pri TsIK SSSR," *Ezhenedel'nik Sovetskoi iustitsii*, no. 16 (1926): 502–3.

5. Sergei Iakovlevich Bulatov (born 1898) was a graduate student in the criminal law department of the Institute of Soviet Law, together with A. A. Gertsenzon and B. S. Man'kovskii. He had finished his studies by 1928 (A. N. Trainin, a law professor at the institute, criticized his diploma work as being too political). GARF, f. A-4655, op. 1, d. 224, l. 6; and d. 227. The Institute of Soviet Law (Institut Sovetskogo prava) was founded in 1920 as a department of Moscow State University to study problems of Soviet law and socialist construction, to provide advice to the courts and prosecutors, to examine contemporary bourgeois law, and to prepare graduate students and other trained professionals in the legal disciplines. It had three sections: state and administrative law, economic labor law, and criminal law; it also published a journal, *Sovetskoe pravo* (*Soviet Law*), from 1922 to 1928. The institute's faculty included A. Ia. Vyshinskii, M. M. Isaev, N. V. Krylenko, D. I. Kurskii, A. A. Piontkovskii, A. N. Trainin, E. G. Shirvindt, and A. Ia. Estrin. In 1929 the decision was taken to liquidate the Institute of Soviet Law and transfer its functions to the Communist Academy's Department of State and Law. This was also a way to remove the more non-Marxist professors from their positions at the institute and the university. GARF, f. A-4655, op. 1, d. 212, ll. 1–2; d. 224, l. 6; d. 250, ll. 11–12. See also "Khronika. Institut Sovetskogo prava," *Ezhenedel'nik Sovetskoi iustitsii*, no. 18 (1922): 12–13; "Otchet Instituta Sovetskogo prava RANION za 1925/26 g.," *Sovetskoe pravo*, no. 2 (1927): 162–70; and *Pervyi Moskovskii Gosudarstvennyi Universitet za pervoe Sovetskoe desiatiletie (1917–1927 gg.)* (Moscow: Izdatel'stvo I-go [Pervogo] Moskovskogo Gosudarstvennogo Universiteta, 1928), 60–67.

6. S. Ia. Bulatov, "Vozrozhdenie Lombrozo v Sovetskoi kriminologii," *Revoliutsiia prava*, no. 1 (1929): 53–54, 49, 57.

7. Shelley provides an overview of the dispute in "The 1929 Dispute on Soviet Criminology," 175–85. A transcript of the dispute proceedings was immediately published in the Communist Academy's legal journal, *Revoliutsiia prava* (see "Disput po voprosu ob izuchenii prestupnosti v SSSR v sektsii prava i gosudarstva," *Revoliutsiia prava*, no. 3 (1929): 47–78). It provides an inside look at the dynamics of a "purge" session.

8. "Disput po voprosu ob izuchenii prestupnosti v SSSR v sektsii prava i gosudarstva," 58.

9. See Shelley, "Soviet Criminology: Its Birth and Demise, 1917–1936," 165–66. Shelley emphasizes that most scholars conformed to the ideas presented at the dispute because a lack of Marxist scholarship in the criminological discipline and a poor understanding of the implications of Marxist ideas for criminal law meant criminologists were not able to defend themselves effectively against the accusations.

10. Ibid., 48.

11. Ibid., 51–54.

12. On psychiatry and its dynamics in Soviet Russia, see Healey, *Homosexual Desire*; Joravsky, *Russian Psychiatry*; and Miller, *Freud and the Bolsheviks*, among others. Of course, the "new" Soviet criminology did not consider the influence of socioeconomic conditions resulting from Soviet and Stalinist policies, seeing the factors of crime derive exclusively from the "remnants" of the capitalist system.

13. Louise Shelley suggests that during the Communist Academy dispute the criminologists failed to present a united defense of criminology because they were more interested in their personal survival. See Shelley, "The 1929 Dispute on Soviet Criminology," 185.

14. Ivanov and Il'ina, *Puti i sud'by otechestvennoi kriminologii*, 10. Evsei Gustavovich Shirvindt (1891–1958), head of the Main Prison Administration (GUMZ) of the NKVD during the 1920s, was arrested in 1937 and released in 1955. See Solomon, *Soviet Criminologists and Criminal Policy*, 180–81. Aleksandr Georgievich Beloborodov (1891–1938) served as People's Commissar of Internal Affairs from 1923 until 1927, when he was removed from his post. No information seems to be available regarding his activities after this point, and his death in 1938 suggests he was a victim of Stalin's purge, posthumously rehabilitated. See *Deiateli Soiuza Sovetskikh Sotsialisticheskikh Respublik i Oktiabr'skoi Revoliutsii (Avtobiografii i biografii)* (Moscow: Izdatel'stvo "Kniga," 1989). Even less information is available for many of the 1920s criminologists. According to his dates, statistician Evgenii Nikitich Tarnovskii (1856–1936) may have perished in the purges or died of old age (his biography is silent on this matter). No information is available on the death of Aleksandr Aleksandrovich Zhizhilenko (born 1873), a Leningrad jurist and law professor.

15. Mikhail Nikolaevich Gernet (1874–1953), for instance, continued to teach at Moscow State University. He turned his research focus to the prerevo-

lutionary era, writing his magnum opus, a five-volume exploration of the tsarist prisons and the fate of the revolutionaries who found themselves locked up in them [*Istoriia tsarskoi tiur'my*, 5 vols. (Moscow: Gosudarstvennoe izdatel'stvo iuridicheskoi literatury, 1951–1956)]. Aron Naumovich Trainin (1883–1957) focused his post-1930 research on international law, crimes against humanity, war crimes, and state intervention, serving as a representative of the USSR at the Nuremberg trials after World War II. On Trainin's involvement at Nuremberg, see Francine Hirsch, "The Soviets at Nuremberg: International Law, Propaganda, and the Making of the Postwar Order," *American Historical Review* 113, no. 3 (June 2008): 701–30. Mikhail Mikhailovich Isaev (Surskii) (1881–1949), an influential jurist and law professor at Moscow State University who had been active among the left-wing criminologists before the revolution, emphasized the study of penal politics in his works. Evgenii Konstantinovich Krasnushkin (1885–1951), a psychiatrist who had helped found the Serbskii Institute of Forensic Psychiatry in 1921, organized a psychiatric clinic for the Moscow region, which he directed throughout the 1940s. After World War II he was involved with the prosecution of the Nuremberg trials. His research after 1930 focused less on the analysis of criminals and more on mental illness and psychiatry. Andrei Andreevich Piontkovskii (1899–1973), a scholar of criminal law and son of the eminent law professor Andrei Antonovich Piontkovskii (1862–1915), remained active in international criminal law circles throughout his later life and focused his studies on the theoretical principles of Soviet criminal law. Boris Samoilovich Utevskii (1887–1970), a penologist who had written extensively about penal policies and recidivists in the 1920s, turned his attention to juvenile crime and to the principles of Soviet correctional labor law.

16. Il'ina and Nad'iarnyi, "Izuchenie lichnosti prestupnika v SSSR," 308–9.

17. See Wimberg, "'Replacing the Shackles'"; and Shelley, "The 1929 Dispute on Soviet Criminology."

18. Solomon, *Soviet Criminologists and Criminal Policy*, 36.

19. Aleksei Adol'fovich Gertsenzon (1902–1970) was born in Kishenev. After finishing school in 1920, he worked as a statistician in the Institute of Current Affairs (Kon'iukturnyi Institut), joining first the construction workers' union and later the enlightenment workers' union. He attended the Law Department of Moscow State University's Faculty of Social Sciences from 1921 to 1925. In the years 1929–1931, he headed the Department of Moral Statistics of the Central Statistical Administration, and served in the statistical department of the Main Administration of Police and Prosecutors of the USSR from 1934 to 1935. Gertsenzon joined the Communist Party in 1940. He earned his doctorate in Soviet legal sciences and received the distinction of Honored Fellow of Sciences in the RSFSR (zasluzhennyi deiatel' nauki RSFSR) in 1962. He published extensively on crime and court statistics, criminal law, and methodologies and theories of criminology, and was the first to rework the theoretical basis of Soviet legal statistics. See V. E. Eminov, ed., *Kriminologiia. Uchebnoe posobie* (Moscow:

Izdatel'stvo gruppa INFRA M-NORMA, 1997), 104; *Bol'shaia Sovetskaia Entsik-lopediia*, 3rd ed., vol. 6 (Moscow: "Sov. entsiklopediia," 1971), 430; V. P. Kornev, *Vidnye deiateli otechestvennoi statistiki, 1686–1990* (Moscow: Finansy i statistika, 1993), 39–40; and Tsentral'nyi Munitsipal'nyi arkhiv g. Moskvy (TsMAM), f. 1609, op. 7, d. 627, ll. 10, 1, 23–23ob.

20. "Disput po voprosu ob izuchenii prestupnosti v SSSR," 61.

21. A. A. Gertsenzon, "Zadachi izucheniia prestupnosti," in *Problema izucheniia prestupnosti*, ed. I. T. Goliakov (Moscow: Iuridicheskoe izdatel'stvo NKIu SSSR, 1945), 17.

22. A. A. Gertsenzon, "Ob izuchenii prestupnosti," in *Sovetskaia kriminal-istika na sluzhebe sledstviia. Sbornik statei* (Moscow: Gosudarstvennoe izdatel'stvo iuridicheskoi literatury, 1958), 6–8; and Gertsenzon, "Protiv biologicheskikh teorii prichin prestupnosti (Ocherk vtoroi)," in *Voprosy bor'by s prestupnost'iu* (Moscow: Izdatel'stvo "Iuridicheskaia literatura," 1967), 51. "The incorrect equation of theories of the factors of crime—theories based on unsound, clearly bourgeois and idealistic (positivistic) methodologies—with the study of concrete factors (causes and conditions) of crime led to the unnecessary study of the immediate causes and conditions of individual types of crimes." Gertsenzon, "Ob izuchenii prestupnosti," 10.

23. Gertsenzon, *Vvedenie v sovetskuiu kriminologiiu*, 94.

24. Gertsenzon, "Protiv biologicheskikh teorii prichin prestupnosti (Ocherk vtoroi)," 53.

25. A. A. Gertsenzon, *Predmet, metod i sistema sovetskoi kriminologii* (Moscow: Akademiia nauk SSSR, 1962), 76.

26. L. V. Il'ina, "Iz istorii razvitiia sovetskoi kriminologii," in *Voprosy bor'by s prestupnost'iu* (Moscow: Izdatel'stvo "Iuridicheskaia literatura," 1968), 34.

27. *Sovetskaia kriminologiia* (Moscow: Izdatel'stvo "Iuridicheskaia literatura," 1966), 27; and Gertsenzon, *Vvedenie v sovetskuiu kriminologiiu*.

28. I. S. Noi, *Metodologicheskie problemy*, 41, 50. Other recent analyses of the history of Soviet criminology include Iu. P. Kasatkin, "Ocherki istorii izucheniia prestupnosti v SSSR," in *Problemy iskoreneniia prestupnosti* (Moscow: Izdatel'stvo "Iuridicheskaia literatura," 1965), 187–225; Ivanov and Il'ina, *Puti i sud'by otechest-vennoi kriminologii*; Luneev, *Prestupnost' XX veka*; Sakharov, *Istoriia kriminologicheskoi nauki*; A. S. Shliapochnikov, *Sovetskaia kriminologiia na sovremennom etape* (Moscow: Vsesoiuznyi institut po izucheniiu prichin i razrabotke mer preduprezhdeniia pre-stupnosti, 1973); Shelley, "Soviet Criminology: Its Birth and Demise, 1917–1936"; Shestakov, "K voprosu ob istorii sovetskoi kriminologii," 74–81; and Solomon, "Soviet Criminology—Its Demise and Rebirth, 1928–1963," 571–93.

29. Noi, *Metodologicheskie problemy*, 36, 55–56. Noi's analysis completely disregards the pernicious influence of the Stalinist state and its cooptation of the discipline for its own needs in the early 1930s.

30. Shestakov, "K voprosu ob istorii sovetskoi kriminologii," 79.

31. Ibid. See also Kuznetsova, "Sovetskaia kriminologiia v usloviiakh per-estroiki," 26, who writes that with the implementation of *glasnost'*, "criminology can become a genuine science that speaks with a full voice to society about its most difficult social calamity—crime, its causes and conditions, and can develop scientific recommendations for the prevention of crime not speculatively but based on the real objective data of legal and social statistics." On Soviet dissidents, mental illness, and psychiatry, see Sidney Bloch and Peter Reddaway, *Russia's Political Hospitals: The Abuse of Psychiatry in the Soviet Union* (London: Victor Gollancz, 1977); and Thomas Smith and Teresa Oleszczuk, *No Asylum: State Psychiatric Repression in the Former USSR* (London: Macmillan Press, 1996).

SELECTED BIBLIOGRAPHY

ARCHIVAL SOURCES

Gosudarstvennyi Arkhiv Rossiiskoi Federatsii (State Archive of the Russian Federation, or GARF)

Fond R-4042: Glavnoe upravlenie mestami zakliucheniia NKVD (Main Prison Administration of the NKVD, or GUMZ)

Fond A-259: Sovet narodnykh komissarov RSFSR (Soviet of People's Commissars, or Sovnarkom)

Fond A-482: Ministerstvo zdravookhraneniia RSFSR (Ministry of Health)

Fond A-2307: Glavnoe upravlenie nauchnymi, nauchno-khudozhestvennymi, museinymi i po okhrane prirody uchrezhdeniiami NKProsa (Main Administration for Scientific, Scientific-Artistic, Museum and Nature Protection Organizations of the Commissariat of Enlightenment)

Fond A-4655: Rossiiskaia assotsiatsiia nauchno-issled. institutov obshchestvennykh nauk (Russian Association of Scientific-Research Institutes of Social Sciences)

Tsentral'nyi Munitsipal'nyi Arkhiv g. Moskvy (Central Municipal Archive of Moscow, or TsMAM)

Fond 1609: 1–yi [Pervyi] Moskovskii Gosudarstvennyi universitet (1st Moscow State University)

Fond 1215: Administrativnyi otdel Mossovet (Administrative Department of the Moscow Soviet)

Tsentral'nyi Gosudarstvennyi Arkhiv Moskovskoi Oblasti (Central State Archive of the Moscow Region, or TsGAMO)

Fond 66: Moskovskii Sovet rabochikh, krest'ianskikh i krasnoarmeiskikh deputatov (Moscow Soviet, or Mossovet)

JOURNALS AND SERIAL PUBLICATIONS

Administrativnyi vestnik (Moscow, 1922–1930)
Arkhiv kriminologii i sudebnoi meditsiny (Khar'kov, 1926–1927)

Biulleten' Tsentral'nogo Statisticheskogo Upravleniia (Moscow, 1919–1926)
Ezhenedel'nik Sovetskoi iustitsii (Moscow, 1922–1929)
Iuridicheskii vestnik (Moscow, 1868–1892)
Pravo i zhizn' (Moscow, 1922–1928)
Prestupnik i prestupnost' (Moscow, 1926–1927)
Problemy prestupnosti (Moscow, 1926–1929)
Proletarskaia revoliutsiia i pravo (Moscow, 1918–1921)
Proletarskii sud (Moscow, 1922–1928)
Rabochii sud (Leningrad, 1923–1930)
Rabotnitsa (Moscow, 1917–)
Rabotnitsa i krest'ianka (Leningrad, 1922–1941)
Revoliutsiia prava (Moscow, 1927–1929)
Sovetskoe gosudarstvo i revoliutsiia prava (Moscow, 1930–1931)
Sovetskoe pravo (Moscow and Leningrad, 1922–1928)
Statisticheskii ezhegodnik (Moscow, 1921–1925)
Statisticheskii obzor deiatel'nosti mestnykh administrativnykh organov NKVD RSFSR (Moscow, 1924–1927)
Statisticheskoe obozrenie (Moscow, 1927–1930)
Sud idet! (Leningrad, 1924–1931)
Sudebnaia praktika RSFSR (Moscow, 1927–1931)
Sudebno-meditsinskaia ekspertiza (Moscow, 1925–1931)
Svod statisticheskikh svedenii po delam ugolovnym (St. Petersburg, 1873–1915)
Vestnik prava (St. Petersburg, 1908–1917)
Vestnik psikhologii, kriminal'noi antropologii i pedologii (St. Petersburg, 1904–1919)
Vestnik Sovetskoi iustitsii (Khar'kov, 1922–1930)
Vestnik statistiki (Moscow, 1919–1929)
Vlast' Sovetov (Moscow, 1919–1938)
Voprosy izucheniia prestupnosti na Severnom Kavkaze (Rostov, 1926–1928)
Voprosy prava (Moscow, 1910–1912)
Zhurnal Ministerstva iustitsii (St. Petersburg, 1897–1917)
Zhurnal psikhologii, nevrologii i psikhiatrii (Moscow, 1922–1924)
Zhurnal ugolovnogo prava i protsessa (St. Petersburg, 1912–1913)

PUBLISHED PRIMARY SOURCES

Aborty v 1925 godu. Moscow: Izdanie TsSU SSSR, 1927.

Akkerman, V. O. "Kriminologicheskaia klinika." *Prestupnik i prestupnost'*, no. 2 (1927): 207–17.

Aliavdin, P. A. "Detoubiistvo v Ivanovo-Voznesenskoi gubernii za 1925 i 1926 g." *Sudebno-meditsinskaia ekspertiza*, no. 7 (1927): 95–99.

———. "Ugolovnye prestupleniia v sviazi s alimentami v Ivanovo-Voznesenskoi gubernii." *Sudebno-meditsinskaia ekspertiza*, no. 11 (1929): 113–15.

Andreev, M. "Detoubiistvo." *Rabochii sud*, no. 2 (1928): 137–44.

Aronovich, A. "Samogonshchiki." In *Prestupnyi mir Moskvy. Sbornik statei*, edited by M. N. Gernet, 174–91. Moscow: Izdatel'stvo "Pravo i zhizn'," 1924.

Arsen'ev, B. Ia. "Ubiistva i sudebnaia bor'ba s nimi." In *Ubiistva i ubiitsy*, edited by E. K. Krasnushkin, G. M. Segal, and Ts. M. Feinberg, 362–70. Moscow: Izdatel'stvo Moszdravotdela, 1928.

Artimenkov, L. "O revoliutsionnoi zakonnosti v derevne." *Ezhenedel'nik Sovetskoi iustitsii*, no. 10 (1925): 241–42.

Aschaffenburg, Gustav. *Prestuplenie i bor'ba s nim. Ugolovnaia psikhologiia dlia vrachei, iuristov i sotsiologov*. Odessa: Paspopov, 1906.

B., Iu. "Prestupnost' goroda i derevni v 1924 g. (Po dannym statisticheskogo biuro NKVD)." *Administrativnyi vestnik*, no. 6 (1925): 23–28.

B., S. "Sovremennaia prestupnost' i sudebnaia praktika." *Revoliutsiia prava*, no. 3 (1928): 110–14.

Bekhterev, Iu. Iu. "Eksperimental'nyi penitentsiarnyi institut." *Sovetskoe pravo*, no. 6 (1926): 119–24.

———. "Gramotnost' zakliuchennykh v sviazi s polom, vozrastom i retsidivom." In *Sovremennaia prestupnost'. Sotsial'nyi sostav, professii, vozrast, gramotnost'*, vol. 2, 52–73. Moscow: Izdatel'stvo Narodnogo Komissariata Vnutrennikh Del RSFSR, 1930.

———. *Izuchenie lichnosti zakliuchennogo (Istoriia, zadachi, metodiki i tekhnika)*. Moscow: Izdatel'stvo NKVD RSFSR, 1928.

Beloborodov, A. G., ed. *Sovremennaia prestupnost' (Prestuplenie, pol, repressiia, retsidiv)*. Moscow: Izdatel'stvo Narodnogo Komissariata Vnutrennikh Del RSFSR, 1927.

Bezpal'ko. "Detoubiistvo." *Ezhenedel'nik Sovetskoi iustitsii*, no. 20 (1927): 603.

Borovitinov, M. M. *Detoubiistvo v ugolovnom prave*. St. Petersburg: Tipo-lit St. Petersb. tiur'my, 1905.

Brailovskii, V. V. *Opyt bio-sotsial'nogo issledovaniia ubiits (Po materialam mest zakliucheniia Severnogo Kavkaza)*. Rostov na Donu: Donskaia pravda, 1929.

———. "Sotsiologicheskii ili biologicheskii uklon v izuchenii prestupnosti?" *Voprosy izucheniia prestupnosti v Severnom Kavkaze*, no. 1 (1926): 1–9.

Brukhanskii, N. P. *Materialy po seksual'noi psikhopatologii. Psikhiatricheskie ekspertizy*. Moscow: M. & S. Sabashnikovykh, 1927.

Bulatov, S. Ia. "Vozrozhdenie Lombrozo v Sovetskoi kriminologii." *Revoliutsiia prava*, no. 1 (1929): 42–61.

Bychkov, I. Ia. *Detoubiistvo v sovremennykh usloviiakh*. Moscow: Gosudarstvennoe meditsinskoe izdatel'stvo, 1929.

———. "Sposoby detoubiistva." *Sudebno-meditsinskaia ekspertiza*, no. 8 (1928): 75–81.

Chalisov, M. "Opyt bio-sotsial'nogo obsledovaniia rastratchikov v Rostove-na-Donu." *Voprosy izucheniia prestupnosti v Severnom Kavkaze*, no. 2 (1927): 45–75.

Cheliapov, N. "Fakul'tet Sovetskogo Prava I Moskovskogo Gos. universiteta." *Revoliutsiia prava*, no. 3 (1928): 96–98.

Chelyshev, M. "Detoubiistvo." *Rabochii sud*, no. 1 (1927): 11–16.

D., O. "Novoe uchrezhdenie." *Rabochii sud*, nos. 9–10 (1925): 412–14.

"Disput k voprosy ob izuchenii prestupnosti v SSSR v sektsii prava i gosudarstva." *Revoliutsiia prava*, no. 3 (1929): 47–78.

Dril', D. A. *Maloletnye prestupniki. Etiud po voprosu o chelovecheskoi prestupnosti, ee faktorakh i sredstvakh bor'by s nei*, 2 vols. Moscow: Tip. A. I. Mamontova i Ko., 1884–1888.

———. "Nauka ugolovnoi antropologii, ee predmet i zadachi." *Vestnik psikhologii, kriminal'noi antropologii i gipnotizma*, no. 1 (1904): 12–20.

Edel'shtein, A. O. "K psikhopatologii detoubiistv." In *Ubiistva i ubiitsy*, edited by E. K. Krasnushkin, G. M. Segal, and Ts. M. Feinberg, 273–82. Moscow: Izdatel'stvo Moszdravotdela, 1928.

Engelgardt, A. N. *Letters from the Country, 1872–1887*. Translated and edited by Cathy A. Frierson. Oxford: Oxford University Press, 1993.

Eratov, L. "Nakazuema li prostitutsiia?" *Ezhenedel'nik Sovetskoi iustitsii*, no. 4 (1922): 4–6.

Ezerskii, N. "Gorodskaia i sel'skaia prestupnost' v byvsh. Leningradskoi gub. (Po dannym statistiki osuzhdennykh za 1925/26 g.)." *Vestnik statistiki*, no. 2 (1928): 219–27.

F., A. "Aborty v gubernskikh gorodakh, prochikh gorodakh i sel'skikh mestnostakh." *Aborty v 1925 godu*, 52–62. Moscow: Izdanie TsSU SSSR, 1927.

Ferri, Enrico. *Criminal Sociology*. Translated by Joseph Kelly and John Lisle. Boston: Little, Brown and Company, 1917.

———. "Printsip legal'noi otvetstvennosti v novom Russkom ugolovnom kodekse." *Pravo i zhizn'*, nos. 2–3 (1928): 33–43.

Foinitskii, I. Ia. "Faktory prestupnosti." *Severnyi vestnik*, no. 10 (1893): 97–119; and no. 11 (1893): 77–94.

———. *Na dosuge. Sbornik iuridicheskikh statei i issledovanii c 1870 goda*. 2 vols. St. Petersburg: Tip. M. M. Stasiulevicha, 1898–1900.

———. "Zhenshchina-prestupnitsa." *Severnyi vestnik. Zhurnal literaturno-nauchnyi i politicheskii*, no. 2 (1893): 123–44; and no. 3 (1893): 111–40.

Fuks, I. B. *Problema prestupnosti plodoizgnaniia*. Khar'kov: Tipo-Litografiia M. Sergeeva i K. Gal'chenka, 1910.

G., A. "Moskovskaia obshcheugolovnaia prestupnost' v period voennogo kommunizma." *Prestupnik i prestupnost'*, no. 2 (1927): 365–87.

G., M. "O detoubiistve." *Arkhiv sudebnoi meditsiny*, no. 1 (1868): 21–55.

Gedeonov, N. N. "Grabiteli i bandity." In *Prestupnyi mir Moskvy. Sbornik statei*, edited by M. N. Gernet, 3–40. Moscow: Izdatel'stvo "Pravo i zhizn'," 1924.

Gens, A. "Abort-sotsial'noe zlo." *Meditsina*, no. 7 (1926): 10–11.

———. "K probleme legalizatsii i statistiki abortov v RSFSR." *Aborty v 1925 godu*, 21–28. Moscow: Izdanie TsSU SSSR, 1927.

Gernet, M. N. "Abort v zakone i statistika abortov." *Aborty v 1925 godu*, 3–20. Moscow: Izdanie TsSU SSSR, 1927.

———. *Detoubiistvo. Sotsiologicheskoe i sravnitel'no-iuridicheskoe issledovanie.* Moscow: Tipografiia Imperatorskogo Moskovskogo universiteta, 1911.

———. "Gosudarstvennyi Institut po izucheniiu prestupnosti." *Administrativnyi vestnik,* no. 11 (1925): 30–36.

———. "Istreblenie ploda s ugolovno-sotsiologicheskoi tochki zreniia." *Vestnik prava,* no. 8 (1914): 233–38.

———. *Izbrannye proizvedeniia.* Moscow: Iuridicheskaia literatura, 1974.

———. "K statistike abortov." *Statisticheskoe obozrenie,* no. 3 (1927): 66–69.

———. *Moral'naia statistika (Ugolovnaia statistika i statistika samoubiistv).* Moscow: Izdanie Tsentral'nogo Statisticheskogo Upravleniia, 1922.

———. *Obshchestvennye prichiny prestupnosti. Sotsialisticheskoe napravlenie v nauke ugolovnogo prava.* Moscow: S. Skirmunt, 1906. Reprinted in *Izbrannye proizvedeniia.* Moscow: Izdatel'stvo "Pravo i zhizn'," 1924.

———. "Pervaia russkaia laboratoriia po izucheniiu prestupnosti." *Pravo i zhizn',* no. 2 (1924): 26–34.

———. "Predislovie." *Prestupnyi mir Moskvy. Sbornik statei,* edited by M. N. Gernet, i–xli. Moscow: Izdatel'stvo "Pravo i zhizn'," 1924.

———. *Prestuplenie i bor'ba s nim v sviazi s evoliutsiei obshchestva.* Moscow: Mir, 1914. Reprinted in *Izbrannye proizvedeniia.* Moscow: Iuridicheskaia literatura, 1974.

———. *Prestupnost' i samoubiistva vo vremia voiny i posle nee. Vtoroi [2nd] vypusk "Moral'noi statistiki."* Moscow: Izdatel'stvo TsSU SSR, 1927.

———. "Prestupnost' v sviazi s klassovo-sotsial'nym sostavom osuzhdennykh v 1922 g." *Vestnik statistiki,* nos. 1–3 (1924): 135–54.

———. *Prestupnosti za granitsei i v SSSR.* Moscow: Sovetskoe zakonodatel'stvo, 1931.

———. "Statistika detoubiistv." *Statisticheskoe obozrenie,* nos. 2 (1928): 102–6.

———. "Statistika gorodskoi i sel'skoi prestupnosti." *Problemy prestupnosti,* no. 2 (1927): 15–24.

———. *Ukazatel' russkoi i inostrannoi literatury po statistike prestuplenii, nakazanii i samoubiistv.* Moscow: Izdanie Tsentral'nogo statisticheskogo upravleniia, 1924.

———. "Zhenshchiny-ubiitsy." *Pravo i zhizn',* nos. 6–7 (1926): 78–91.

———, ed. *Prestupnyi mir Moskvy. Sbornik statei.* Moscow: Izdatel'stvo "Pravo i zhizn'," 1924.

———, and D. P. Rodin. "Statistika osuzhdennykh v 1922 g. i statistika samoubiistv v 1922–23 gg." *Biulleten' Tsentral'nogo Statisticheskogo Upravleniia,* no. 84 (1924): 113–25.

Gertsenzon, A. A. "Bor'ba s prestupnost'iu v RSFSR." *Sovetskoe pravo. Zapiski Instituta Sovetskogo prava,* no. 3 (1929): 95–117.

———. *Bor'ba s prestupnost'iu v RSFSR po materialam obsledovaniia NK RKI SSSR,* edited and with an introduction by V. Radus-Zenkovich. Moscow: Iuridicheskoe izdatel'stvo NKIu RSFSR, 1928.

———. "Izuchenie Moskovskoi prestupnosti (Otchet za 1926 god)." *Proletarskii sud*, nos. 17–18 (1927): 10–12.

———. "Ob izuchenii prestupnosti." In *Sovetskaia kriminalistika na sluzhbe sledstviia. Sbornik statei*, edited by G. B. Karnovich, 3–24. Moscow: Gosudarstvennoe izdatel'stvo iuridicheskoi literatury, 1958.

———. "Osnovnye tendentsii dinamiki prestupnosti za desiat' let." *Sovetskoe pravo*, no. 1 (1928): 69–85.

———. *Predmet, metod i sistema Sovetskoi kriminologii*. Moscow: Akademiia Nauk SSSR, 1962.

———. "Prestupnost' epokhi pervoi russkoi revoliutsii." *Sovetskoe pravo*, no. 3 (1926): 95–103; and no. 4 (1926): 96–107.

———. "Protiv biologicheskikh teorii prichin prestupnosti (Ocherk pervyi)." In *Voprosy preduprezhdeniia prestupnosti*, edited by I. I. Karpets, 3–34. Moscow: Izdatel'stvo "Iuridicheskaia literatura," 1966.

———. "Protiv biologicheskikh teorii prichin prestupnosti (Ocherk vtoroi)." In *Voprosy bor'by s prestupnost'iu*, edited by I. I. Karpets, 3–53. Moscow: Izdatel'stvo "Iuridicheskaia literatura," 1967.

———. *Vvedenie v Sovetskuiu kriminologiiu*. Moscow: Izdatel'stvo "Iuridicheskaia literatura," 1965.

———. "Zadachi izucheniia prestupnosti." In *Problema izucheniia prestupnosti*, edited by I. T. Goliakov, 5–19. Moscow: Iuridicheskoe izdatel'stvo NKIu SSSR, 1945.

———, and N. S. Lapshina. "Ubiistva v R.S.F.S.R. i za granitsei." In *Ubiistva i ubiitsy*, edited by E. K. Krasnushkin, G. M. Segal, and Ts. M. Feinberg, 324–61. Moscow: Izdatel'stvo Moszdravotdela, 1928.

Grodzinskii, M. M. "Gosudarstvennyi Institut po izucheniiu prestupnosti i prestupnika." *Vestnik Sovetskoi iustitsii*, no. 19 (1926): 773–74.

Iakobzon, L. Ia. *Onanizm i bor'ba s nim*. 2nd ed. Moscow: Izd-vo Okhrana materinstva i mladenchestva NKZ, 1928.

Iakubson, V. R. "Repressiia lisheniem svobody." In *Sovremennaia prestupnost' (Prestuplenie, pol, repressiia, retsidiv)*, edited by A. G. Beloborodov, 20–38. Moscow: Izdatel'stvo Narodnogo Komissariata Vnutrennikh Del RSFSR, 1927.

Ianchovskii, B. "Prestuplenie i kara v Sovetskoi Rossii." *Proletarskaia revoliutsiia i pravo*, no. 15 (1921): 14–16.

Itogi Russkoi ugolovnoi statistiki za 20 let (1874–1894 gg.). St. Petersburg: Tip. Pravitel'stvuiushchogo Senata, 1899.

Ivanov, G. "Iz praktiki Saratovskogo gubernskogo kabineta kriminal'noi antropologii i sudebno-psikhiatricheskoi ekspertizy." *Sovetskoe pravo*, no. 1 (1925): 84–95.

Izuchenie lichnosti prestupnika v SSSR i za granitsei. Moscow: Izdanie Moszdravotdela, 1925.

K., K. "Nash kriminologicheskii kabinet." *Rabochii sud*, no. 21 (1927): 1705–8.

Kabinet ugolovnago prava pri Imperatorskom S.-Peterburgskom Universitete. Katalog museia, izd. 3–e [3rd ed.]. St. Petersburg, Senatskaia tipografiia, 1902.

Kandinskii, L. "Zhenshchina-rastratchik." *Proletarskii sud*, nos. 23–24 (1926): 12.

Kessler, M. "Imushchestvennye prestupleniia po dannym perepisi 1926 g." In *Sovremennaia prestupnost' (Prestuplenie, pol, repressiia, retsidiv)*, edited by A. G. Beloborodov, 50–58. Moscow: Izdatel'stvo Narodnogo Komissariata Vnutrennikh Del RSFSR, 1927.

Khalfin, V. "Istreblenie ploda (abort) v Moskve i Moskovskoi gubernii." *Problemy prestupnosti*, no. 2 (1927): 190–211.

———. "Razmery prestupnosti v SSSR po dannym ugolovno-administrativnykh organov na 1923 g. (Po materialam statisticheskogo biuro NKVD)." *Proletarskii sud*, nos. 1–2 (1924): 23–26.

"Kharakter dvizheniia prestupnosti za 1924–1928 gody." *Administrativnyi vestnik*, no. 2 (1930): 52–57.

Khatuntsev, B. N. "O sotsial'no-psikhologicheskom issledovanii lichnosti obviniaemogo na predvaritel'nom sledstvii na sude." *Pravo i sud*, no. 2 (1924): 51–56.

Khodakov, Iu. "Sovremennaia prestupnost' zhenshchin." *Vlast' Sovetov*, nos. 11–12 (1923): 86–94.

Khonin, V. "O detoubiistve." *Rabochii sud*, no. 9 (1926): 615–22.

"Khronika. Gosudarstvennyi Institut po izucheniiu prestupnosti i prestupnika." *Ezhenedel'nik Sovetskoi iustitsii*, no. 32 (1925): 1091.

"Khronika. Institut Sovetskogo prava." *Ezhenedel'nik Sovetskoi iustitsii*, nos. 18 (1922): 12–13.

"Khronika. Iz itogov bor'by s samogonom v Moskve i Moskovskoi gub." *Ezhenedel'nik Sovetskoi iustitsii*, no. 30 (1923): 687.

"Khronika. Klinika po izucheniiu prestupnosti v Moskve." *Ezhenedel'nik Sovetskoi iustitsii*, no. 31 (1923): 711–12.

Khuliganstvo i khuligany. Moscow: Izdatel'stvo NKVD RSFSR, 1929.

Kniazev, D. "Dva mesiatsa raboty osobykh kamer narodnogo suda po delam o samogonkakh v Moskve (s 25–IX po 25–XI 1922 goda)." *Proletarskii sud*, nos. 2–3 (1922): 48–49.

Krasnushkin, E. K. "Chto takoe prestupnik?" *Prestupnik i prestupnost'*, no. 1 (1926): 6–33.

———. *Izbrannye trudy*. Moscow: Medgiz, 1960.

———. "Kriminal'nye psikhopaty sovremennosti i bor'ba s nimi." In *Prestupnyi mir Moskvy. Sbornik statei*, edited by M. N. Gernet, 192–207. Moscow: Izdatel'stvo "Pravo i zhizn'," 1924.

———. "Moskovskii Kabinet po izucheniiu lichnosti prestupnika i prestupnosti i obshchaia kharakteristika Moskovskikh pravonarushitelei." In *Sudebno-meditsinskaia ekspertiza. Trudy II [Vtorogo] Vserossiiskogo s''ezda sudebno-meditsinskikh ekspertov, Moskva 25 fevralia—3 marta 1926*, edited by Ia. L. Leibovich, 157–60. Ul'ianovsk: Ul'ianovsk kombinat PPP, 1926.

———, G. M. Segal, and Ts. M. Feinberg, eds. *Khuliganstvo i ponozhovshchina*. Moscow: Izdatel'stvo Moszdravotdela, 1927.

————, eds. *Nishestvo i besprizornost'*. Moscow: Izdatel'stvo Moszdravotdela, 1929.

————, eds. *Pravonarusheniia v oblasti seksual'nykh otnoshenii*. Moscow: Izdatel'stvo Moszdravotdela, 1927.

————, eds. *Ubiistva i ubiitsy*. Moscow: Izdatel'stvo Moszdravotdela, 1928.

Kremleva, T. "Vory i vorovki bol'shikh magazinov." *Problemy prestupnosti*, no. 4 (1929): 24–38.

Krylenko, N. "Criminal Law in the Soviet Union." *Communist* 2, no. 10 (1927): 173–80; and no. 11 (1927): 274–82.

Krylov, S. "Bor'ba s samogonom (Ivanovo-Voznesenskaia guberniia)." *Administrativnyi vestnik*, no. 4 (1925): 61–62.

Kufaev, V. I. "Retsidivisty (Povtorno-obviniaemye)." In *Prestupnyi mir Moskvy. Sbornik statei*, edited by M. N. Gernet, 102–44. Moscow: Izdatel'stvo "Pravo i zhizn'," 1924.

Kutanin, M. P. "Saratovskii kabinet po izucheniiu prestupnosti i prestupnika." In *Puti Sovetskoi psikho-nevrologii*, 61–66. Samara: Srednevolzhskii kraizdrav, 1931.

L., A. "Detoubiistvo (Po dannym Kostromskogo gubsuda)." *Rabochii sud*, no. 1 (1928): 70–74.

Leibovich, Ia. L. "Itogi deiatel'nosti sudebno-meditsinskoi ekspertisy za 7 let i ee zadachi." *Administrativnyi vestnik*, no. 5 (1926): 20–26.

————. "Sudebno-meditsinskaia ekspertiza pri NEPe." *Ezhenedel'nik Sovetskoi iustitsii*, no. 2 (1923): 36–38.

————. "Tri goda sudebnoi meditsiny." *Ezhenedel'nik Sovetskoi iustitsii*, no. 7 (1922): 7–8.

Levin, D. M. "Bor'ba s prostitutsiei." *Administrativnyi vestnik*, no. 1 (1926): 29–35.

Lindenberg, V. *Materialy k voprosu o detoubiistve i plodoizgnanii v Vitebskoi gubernii (Po dannym Vitebskogo okruzhnogo suda za desiat' let 1897–1906)*. Iuriev: Tip. K. Mattisena, 1910.

Liszt, F. von. "Obshchestvennye faktory prestupnosti." *Zhurnal Ministerstva iustitsii*, no. 2 (1903): 38–54.

Liublinskii, P. I. *Prestupleniia v oblasti polovykh otnoshenii*. Moscow and Leningrad: Izdatel'stvo L. D. Frenkel', 1925.

Lobas, N. S. *Ubiitsy. Nekotorye cherty psikhofiziki prestupnikov*. Moscow: Tip. T-va I. D. Sytina, 1913.

Lombroso, Cesare, and Guglielmo Ferrero. *The Female Offender*. New York and London: D. Appleton and Company, 1895.

Luchaninov, V. "Stat'ia 38–a ugolovnogo kodeksa i alimenty." *Proletarskii sud*, nos. 1–2 (1925): 22–24.

Man'kovskii, B. S. "Detoubiistvo." In *Ubiistva i ubiitsy*, edited by E. K. Krasnushkin, G. M. Segal, and Ts. M. Feinberg, 249–72. Moscow: Izdatel'stvo Moszdravotdela, 1928.

Manns, G. "Derevenskie ubiistva i ubiitsy." *Problemy prestupnosti*, no. 2 (1927): 25–40.

Marriage Laws of Soviet Russia. Complete Text of First Code of Laws of the Russian Socialist Federal Soviet Republic Dealing with Civil Status and Domestic Relations, Marriage, the Family, and Guardianship. New York: The Russian Soviet Government Bureau, 1921.

Men'shagin, V. D. "Pritonoderzhatel'stvo (Sotsiologicheskii ocherki)." In *Pravonarusheniia v oblasti seksual'nykh otnoshenii,* edited by E. K. Krasnushkin, G. M. Segal, and Ts. M. Feinberg, 158–79. Moscow: Izdanie Mozdravotdela, 1927.

———. "Ubiistva." In *Ubiistva i ubiitsy,* edited by E. K. Krasnushkin, G. M. Segal, and Ts. M. Feinberg, 33–86. Moscow: Izdatel'stvo Moszdravotdela, 1928.

Mokeev, V. "Prestupnost' v derevne." *Ezhenedel'nik Sovetskoi iustitsii,* no. 16 (1925): 417–20.

Nemchenkov, I. "Detoubiistvo." *Ezhenedel'nik Sovetskoi iustitsii,* no. 30 (1927): 924–26.

Nemilov, A. V. *Biologicheskaia tragediia zhenshchiny.* Leningrad: Knigoizdatel'stvo "Seiatel'," 1927.

Noi, I. S. *Metodologicheskie problemy Sovetskoi kriminologii.* Saratov: Izdatel'stvo Saratovskogo universiteta, 1975.

Novitskii, R. "Semeinoe polozhenie zakliuchennykh." In *Sovremennaia prestupnost'.* Vol. 2, *Sotsial'nyi sostav, professii, vozrast, gramotnost',* 22–33. Moscow: Izdatel'stvo Narodnogo Komissariata Vnutrennikh Del RSFSR, 1930.

Orshanskii, L. G. "Chto takoe sotsial'naia opasnost'?" *Rabochii sud,* no. 7 (1927): 625–32.

———. "Ubiitsy (Psikhologicheskii ocherk)." In *Ubiitsy. S 75 tablitsami i fotograficheskimi snimkami. Sbornik,* edited by L. G. Orshanskii and A. A. Zhizhilenko, 89–130. Leningrad: Izdatel'stvo "Rabochii sud," 1928.

"Otchet Instituta Sovetskogo prava RANION za 1925/26 g." *Sovetskoe pravo,* no. 2 (1927): 162–70.

Ozeretskii, N. I. "Polovye pravonarusheniia nesovershennoletnikh." In *Pravonarusheniia v oblasti seksual'nykh otnoshenii,* edited by E. K. Krashnushkin, G. M. Segal, and Ts. M. Feinberg, 128–57. Moscow: Izdanie Mosdravotdela, 1927.

Ozerov, I. "Sravnitel'naia prestupnost' polov v zavisimosti ot nekotorykh faktorov." *Zhurnal iuridicheskogo obshchestva pri Imperatorskom S-Peterburgskom universitete,* no. 4 (1896): 45–83.

Paevskii, V. "Aborty v Moskve i Leningrade." In *Aborty v 1925 godu,* 29–51. Moscow: Izdanie TsSU SSSR, 1927.

Pervyi Moskovskii Gosudarstvennyi universitet za pervoe Sovetskoe desiatiletie (1917–1927 gg.). Moscow: Izdatel'stvo 1-go [Pervogo] Moskovskogo Gosudarstvennogo universiteta, 1928.

Petrova, A. E. "Sluchai izuvecheniia muzha." In *Prestupnyi mir Moskvy. Sbornik statei,* edited by M. N. Gernet, 82–101. Moscow: Izdatel'stvo "Pravo i zhizn'," 1924.

Piontkovskii, A. A. *Marksizm i ugolovnoe pravo. O nekotorykh spornykh voprosakh teorii ugolovnogo prava.* Moscow: Iuridicheskoe izdatel'stvo NKIu RSFSR, 1927.

————. "Sistema osobennoi chasti ugolovnogo prava." *Sovetskoe pravo*, no. 2 (1926): 43–63.

Pokrovskaia, Maria I. "Prostitutsiia i alkogolizm." In *Russian Women, 1698–1917: Experience and Expression*, edited by Robin Bisha et al., 361. Bloomington: Indiana University Press, 2002.

Polianskii, N. *Dolzhnostnye rastraty. Ikh ugolovnoe presledovanie.* Moscow: Pravovaia zashchita, 1926.

Portugalov, Iu. V. "Nauchnye problemy kriminologii." *Vestnik psikhologii, kriminal'noi antropologii, i gipnotizma*, no. 7 (1904): 456–77.

Poznyshev, S. V. "Ob izuchenii prestupnika v nauke ugolovnogo prava." *Voprosy prava*, no. 6 (1911): 184–206; no. 7 (1911): 40–71; and no. 8 (1911): 190–231.

————. *Prestupniki iz-za alimentov. Tipy ikh i mery bor'by s nimi.* Moscow and Leningrad: Gosudarstvennoe izdatel'stvo, 1928.

Rapoport, A. M. "K praktike izucheniia lichnosti prestupnika." *Prestupnik i prestupnost'*, no. 1 (1926): 34–48.

————, and A. G. Kharlamova. "O zhenskom khuliganstve." In *Khuliganstvo i ponozhovshchina*, edited by E. K. Krasnushkin, G. M. Segal and Ts. M. Feinberg, 140–49. Moscow: Izdanie Moszdravotdela, 1927.

Rastraty i rastratchiki. Sbornik statei. Moscow: Izdatel'stvo NKVD, 1926.

Razumovskii, I. "Sektsiia prava Kommunisticheskoi Akademii pri TsIK SSSR." *Ezhenedel'nik Sovetskoi iustitsii*, no. 16 (1926): 502–3.

Rodin, D. P. "Gorodskaia i sel'skaia prestupnost'." *Pravo i zhizn'*, nos. 2–3 (1926): 94–101.

————. "Iz dannykh o sovremennoi prostitutsii." *Pravo i zhizn'*, nos. 8–10 (1926): 100–102; and no. 5 (1927): 63–69.

————. "O moral'noi statistiki." *Vestnik statistiki*, nos. 9–12 (1922): 105–16.

————. "Obshchii obzor dannykh perepisi zakliuchennykh." In *Sovremennaia prestupnost' (Prestuplenie, pol, repressiia, retsidiv)*, edited by A. G. Beloborodov, 10–14. Moscow: Izdatel'stvo Narodnogo Komissariata Vnutrennikh Del RSFSR, 1927.

————. "Prestupnost' muzhchin, zhenshchin i nesovershennoletnikh v 1922 godu." *Biulleten' Tsentral'nogo Statisticheskogo upravleniia*, no. 79 (1923): 67–75.

————. "Sotsial'nyi sostav osuzhdennykh v 1923 g." *Biulleten' Tsentral'nogo Statisticheskogo upravleniia*, no. 93 (1924): 124–30.

————. "Statistika prestupnosti vo vremia i posle Evropeiskoi voiny v raznikh stranakh." *Problemy prestupnosti*, no. 1 (1926): 173–91.

Rozanov, Ia. S., ed. *Problema prestupnosti.* Vol. 2, *Problemy Marksizma*. Kiev: Gosudarstvennoe izdatel'stvo Ukrainy, 1924.

Sanchov, V. L. "Toska po domu, kak faktor prestupnosti." *Rabochii sud*, nos. 11–12 (1924): 33–42.

Segalov, T. "Psikhologiia polovykh prestuplenii." *Vestnik prava i notariata*, no. 25 (1910): 806–10.

Semenov, A. "Samogon i Russkaia gor'kaia." *Administrativnyi vestnik*, nos. 9–10 (1925): 38–41.

Semenova Tian-Shanskaia, Olga. *Village Life in Late Tsarist Russia*. Translated by David Ransel. Bloomington: Indiana University Press, 1993.

Shashkov, S. S. *Istoricheskie sud'by zhenshchiny, detoubiistvo, i prostitutsiia*. St. Petersburg: Izdanie N. A. Shigina, 1871.

Shcheglov, A. L. "Prestupnik, kak predmet izucheniia vrachebnoi nauki." *Vestnik psikhologii, kriminal'noi antropologii i pedologii*, no. 1 (1913): 1–21.

Shestakova, A. "Prestuplenie protiv lichnosti." In *Sovremennaia prestupnost' (Prestuplenie, pol, repressiia, retsidiv)*, edited by A. G. Beloborodov, 59–66. Moscow: Izdatel'stva NKVD RSFSR, 1927).

———. "Prestupleniia protiv lichnosti v derevne." *Problemy prestupnosti*, no. 1 (1926): 215–23.

———. "Ubiistvo mater'iu novorozhdennogo rebenka." *Problemy prestupnosti*, no. 3 (1928): 154–63.

Shirvindt, E. G. "Izuchenie problem prestupnosti (K otkrytiiu Gosudarstvennogo Instituta po izucheniiu prestupnosti)." *Rabochii sud*, nos. 47–48 (1925): 1791–94.

———. "K istorii voprosa ob izuchenii prestupnosti i mer bor'by s nei." *Sovetskoe gosudarstvo i pravo*, no. 5 (1958): 137–42.

———. "Udarnye kampanii v svete Vsesoiuznoi perepisi po mestam zakliucheniia." In *Sovremennaia prestupnost' (Prestuplenie, pol, repressiia, retsidiv)*, edited by A. G. Beloborodov, 7–9. Moscow: Izdatel'stvo Narodnogo Komissariata Vnutrennikh Del RSFSR, 1927.

Shmidt. "Detoubiistva." *Proletarskii sud*, no. 5 (1928): 8–9.

Shmukler, I. K. *Onanizm u detei. Ego prichiny, simptomy, posledstviia i lechenie*. Kiev: Tip. L. I. Shliter, 1897.

Skliar, L. "Prestupnost' v RSFSR v pervykh chertvertiakh 1921–1923 g. (Po dannym upravleniia ugolovnogo rozyska respubliki)." *Vlast' Sovetov*, nos. 6–7 (1923): 123–30.

Slupskii, S. N. "Belorusskii kabinet po izucheniiu prestupnosti." *Problemy prestupnosti*, no. 4 (1929): 149–51.

Smirnov, I. "Doklad predsedatelia Moskovskogo Gubsuda tov. I. Smirnova na plenume Mossoveta 3 fevralia 1925 goda." *Proletarskii sud*, no. 3 (1925): 1–6.

Smirnov, I. A. "Rabota suda Moskovskoi gubernii v 1923 goda. Doklad predsedatelia gubsuda I. A. Smirnova plenumu Ispolkoma Moskovskoga Soveta 6 iunia 1924 g." *Proletarskii sud*, nos. 1–2 (1924): 3–10.

Solov'ev, M. "O klassovoi prirode St. 140 ug. kod. v novoi redaktsii." *Ezhenedel'nik Sovetskoi iustitsii*, no. 18 (1924): 424–25.

Sovetskaia Kriminologiia. Moscow: Izdatel'stvo "Iuridicheskaia literatura," 1966.

Sovremennaia prestupnost'. Vol. 2, *Sotsial'nyi sostav, professii, vozrast, gramotnost'*. Moscow: Izdatel'stvo Narodnogo Komissariata Vnutrennikh Del RSFSR, 1930.

Spasokukotskii, N. N. "Deiatel'nost' Gosudarstvennogo Instituta po izucheniiu prestupnosti i prestupnika." *Problemy prestupnosti*, no. 2 (1927): 233–47.

———. "Deiatel'nost' Gosudarstvennogo Instituta po izucheniiu prestupnosti i prestupnika pri NKVD." *Problemy prestupnosti*, no. 4 (1929): 136–45.

———. "Gosudarstvennyi Institut po izucheniiu prestupnosti i prestupnika pri NKVD i ego deiatel'nost'." *Sudebno-meditsinskaia ekspertiza*, no. 9 (1928): 113–18.

———. "Organizatsiia i pervye shagi deiatel'nosti Gosudarstvennogo Instituta po izucheniiu prestupnosti i prestupnika pro NKVD." *Problemy prestupnosti*, no. 1 (1926): 269–76.

Statistika osuzhdennykh v RSFSR za 1926 god. Moscow: Izdanie TsSU RSFSR, 1928.

Statistika osuzhdennykh v SSSR 1923–1924. Moscow: Izdanie TsSU SSSR, 1927.

Statistika osuzhdennykh v SSSR v 1925, 1926 i 1927 gg. Moscow: Izdanie TsSU SSSR, 1930.

Stel'makhovich, A. *Bor'ba s rastratami*. Moscow: Novaia Moskva, 1925.

Strogovich, M. "Bor'ba s prostitutsiei putem ugolovnoi repressii." *Ezhenedel'nik Sovetskoi iustitsii*, no. 37 (1925): 1212–14.

Svod zakonov Rossiiskoi Imperii. 16 vol. St. Petersburg/Petrograd: I. I. Zubkova, 1913–1916.

T., S. "V iuridicheskoi klinike Kievskogo INKh'oza." *Sovetskoe gosudarstvo i pravo*, no. 3 (1927): 104–5.

Tagantsev, N. "O detoubiistve." *Zhurnal Ministerstva iustitsii*, no. 9 (1868): 215–50; and no. 10 (1868): 341–80.

Tarnovskaia, P. N. *Zhenshchiny-ubiitsy. Antropologicheskoe issledovanie*. St. Petersburg: T-vo khudozhestvennoi pechati, 1902.

———. "Zhenskaia prestupnost' v sviazi s rannimi brakami." *Severnyi vestnik*, no. 5 (1898): 133–49.

Tarnovskii, E. N. "Dvizhenie prestupnosti v RSFSR za 1920–23 g.g." *Vlast' Sovetov*, no. 10 (1923): 110–17.

———. "Osnovnye cherty sovremennoi prestupnosti." *Administrativnyi vestnik*, no. 9 (1925): 27–32; and no. 11 (1925): 45–53.

———. "Prestupleniia protiv zhizni po polam, vozrastam i semeinomu sostoianiiu." *Iuridicheskii vestnik*, no. 10 (1886): 276–97.

———. "Statistika prestuplenii za 1924–25 gg." *Ezhenedel'nik Sovetskoi iustitsii*, no. 21 (1926): 646–49; and no. 22 (1926): 674–77.

———. "Vliianie khlebnykh tsen i urozhaev na dvizhenie prestuplenii protiv sobstvennosti v Rossii." *Zhurnal Ministerstva iustitsii*, nos. 8 (1898): 73–106.

———. "Voina i dvizhenie prestupnosti v 1911–1916 gg." *Sbornik statei po proletarskoi revoliutsii i pravu*, nos. 1–4 (1918): 100–22.

Terent'eva, A. N. "Dva sluchaia zhenshchin-rastratchits." *Prestupnik i prestupnost'*, no. 2 (1927): 290–99.

Trainin, A. N. "K kharakteristike zhenskoi prestupnosti." *Vestnik prava i notariata,* no. 14 (1910): 463–66.

———. "Prestupnost' goroda i derevni v Rossii." *Russkaia mysl',* no. 7 (1909): 1–27.

Trakhterov, V. "Vseukrainskii kabinet po izucheniiu lichnosti prestupnika." *Vestnik Sovetskoi iustitsii,* no. 4 (1927): 126–28.

Uchevatov, A. "Bezrabotnye i prestupnost'." *Proletarskii sud,* nos. 1–2 (1925): 48–52.

———. "Itogi za piat' let (Iz materialov registr.-daktiloskopicheskogo biuro MURa)." *Proletarskii sud,* nos. 8–9 (1925): 20–24.

———. "Iz byta prostitutsii nashikh dnei." *Pravo i zhizn',* no. 1(1928): 50–60.

———. "Tainoe vinokurenie v gorode i derevne." *Problemy prestupnosti,* no. 2 (1927): 110–29.

———. "Ugolovnye prestupniki." *Proletarskii sud,* nos. 4–5 (1924): 50–59.

Ugolovnyi kodeks RSFSR. Moscow: Znanie, 1922.

Ugolovnyi kodeks RSFSR redaktsii 1926 g. Moscow: Iuridicheskoe izdatel'stvo NKIu RSFSR, 1926.

Ukshe, S. "Muzheubiitsy." *Pravo i zhizn',* nos. 2–3 (1926): 101–7; and nos. 4–5 (1926): 99–106.

———. "Ubiitsy." In *Prestupnyi mir Moskvy. Sbornik statei,* edited by M. N. Gernet, 41–81. Moscow: Izdatel'stvo "Pravo i zhizn'," 1924.

———. "Zhenshchiny, osuzhdennye za khuliganstvo." In *Khuliganstvo i khuligany,* edited by V. N. Tolmachev, 143–66. Moscow: Izdatel'stvo NKVD RSFSR, 1929.

Utevskii, B. S. "Gosudarstvennyi Institut po izucheniiu prestupnosti i prestupnika." *Ezhenedel'nik Sovetskoi iustitsii,* no. 18 (1926): 569–70.

———. "Gosudarstvennyi Institut po izucheniiu prestupnosti i prestupnika pri NKVD." *Administrativnyi vestnik,* no. 4 (1926): 7–8.

———. "Ob eksperimental'nom penitentsiarnom otdelenii Gosudarstvennogo Instituta po izucheniiu prestupnosti i prestupnika." *Administrativnyi vestnik,* no. 12 (1926): 31–36.

———. "Prestupnost' i retsidiv." In *Sovremennaia prestupnost' (Prestuplenie, pol, repressiia, retsidiv),* edited by A. G. Beloborodov, 39–49. Moscow: Izdatel'stvo Narodnogo Komissariata Vnutrennikh Del RSFSR, 1927.

———. "Prestupnost' v RSFSR po dannym vsesoiuznoi perepisi." *Ezhenedel'nik Sovetskoi iustitsii,* no. 41 (1927): 1280–82.

———. "Sovremennaia prestupnost' po dannym perepisi mest zakliucheniia." *Administrativnyi vestnik,* no. 1 (1928): 37–44.

———. "Vozrast i gramotnost' retsidivistov." In *Sovremennaia prestupnost'.* Vol. 2, *Sotsial'nyi sostav, professii, vozrast, gramotnost',* 74–87. Moscow: Izdatel'stvo Narodnogo Komissariata Vnutrennikh Del RSFSR, 1930.

Varshavskii, I. "Vserossiiskii s"ezd po pedologii, eksperimental'noi pedagogike, i psikhonevrologii v Leningrade." *Rabochii sud,* nos. 1–2 (1924): 53–62; and nos. 3–5 (1924): 29–36.

Vasilevskii, L. A., and L. M. Vasilevskii. *Abort kak sotsial'noe iavlenie. Sotsial'no-gigien-icheskii ocherk.* Moscow and Leningrad: Izdatel'stvo L. D. Frenkel', 1924.

Vasilevskii, L. M. *Prostitutsiia i molodezh'. Sotsialno-gigienicheskii ocherk.* Moscow: Novaia Moskva, 1926.

Verkhovskii, P. V. "Bor'ba s prestupnost'iu v derevne." *Vlast' Sovetov,* no. 43 (1925): 3–4.

Visherskii, N. "Professiia i prestupnost'." In *Sovremennaia prestupnost'.* Vol. 2, *Sotsial'nyi sostav, professii, vozrast, gramotnost',* 34–51. Moscow: Izdatel'stvo Narodnogo Komissariata Vnutrennikh Del RSFSR, 1930.

———. "Raspredelenie zakliuchennykh po polu i prestupleniiam." In *Sovremennaia prestupnost' (Prestuplenie, pol, repressiia, retsidiv),* edited by A. G. Beloborodov, 15–19. Moscow: Izdatel'stvo Narodnogo Komissariata Vnutrennikh Del RSFSR, 1927.

Vnukov, V. A. "Zhenshchiny-ubiitsy." In *Ubiistva i ubiitsy,* edited by E. K. Krasnushkin, G. M. Segal, and Ts. M. Feinberg, 191–248. Moscow: Izdatel'stvo Moszdravotdela, 1928.

Zamengof, M. "Gorod i derevnia v prestupnosti." *Zhurnal ugolovnogo prava i protsessa,* no. 1 (1913): 74–101; and no. 2 (1913): 51–74.

Zhelikhovskii, S. M., and M. V. Solov'eva. "K kazuistike detskikh ubiistv." *Zhurnal nevropatologii i psikhiatrii imeni S. S. Korsakova,* nos. 5–6 (1928): 673–81.

Zhizhilenko, A. A. *Prestupnost' i ee faktory.* Petrograd: Mir znanii, 1922.

———, and L. G. Orshanskii. *Polovaia prestupleniia.* Leningrad: Izdatel'stvo "Rabochii sud," 1927.

Zhukovskii, A. "Detoubiistvo v Poltavskoi gubernii i predovrashchenie ego." *Arkhiv sudebnoi meditsiny,* no. 3 (1870): 1–13.

Zivert, V. "Kievskii Institut nauchno-sudebnoi ekspertizy i ego rabota v oblasti izucheniia prestupnika i prestupnosti." *Sovetskoe gosudarstvo i pravo,* no. 24 (1927): 838–39.

Zmiev, B. N. "Detoubiistvo." *Vestnik Sovetskoi iustitsii Avtonomnoi Tatarskoi Sotsialisticheskoi Sovetskoi Respubliki,* no. 6 (1923): 2–3; and no. 7 (1923): 5–8.

———. "Detoubiistvo (Po dannym sudebnoi statistiki)." *Pravo i zhizn',* nos. 6–7 (1927): 89–96.

———. "Pokhishchenie zhenshchin." *Vestnik Sovetskoi iustitsii Avtonomnoi Tatarskoi Sotsialisticheskoi Sovetskoi Respubliki,* nos. 8–9 (1923): 3–5.

———. "Prestupleniia v oblasti polovykh otnoshenii v gorode i v derevne." *Problemy prestupnosti,* no. 2 (1927): 41–50.

———. "Prestupnost' v Tatrespublike." *Problemy prestupnosti,* no. 4 (1929): 39–57.

Zvonitskaia, A. S. "K voprosu ob izuchenii prestupnika i prestupnosti." *Tekhnika, ekonomika i pravo,* no. 3 (1924): 74–92.

Secondary Sources

Abelson, Elaine S. *When Ladies Go A-Thieving: Middle-Class Shoplifters in the Victorian Department Store.* New York: Oxford University Press, 1989.

Adams, Bruce F. *The Politics of Punishment: Prison Reform in Russia, 1863–1917.* DeKalb: Northern Illinois University Press, 1996.

Adams, Mark B. "Eugenics as Social Medicine in Revolutionary Russia: Prophets, Patrons, and the Dialectics of Discipline-Building." In *Health and Society in Revolutionary Russia*, edited by Susan Gross Solomon and John F. Hutchinson, 200–23. Bloomington: Indiana University Press, 1990.

Alexopoulos, Golfo. *Stalin's Outcasts: Aliens, Citizens, and the Soviet State, 1926–1936.* Ithaca, NY: Cornell University Press, 2003.

Andrews, James T. *Science for the Masses: The Bolshevik State, Public Science, and the Popular Imagination in Soviet Russia, 1917–1934.* College Station: Texas A&M University Press, 2003.

Antonian, Iu. M. *Prestupnost' sredi zhenshchin.* Moscow: Rossiiskoe pravo, 1992.

Attwood, Lynne. *Creating the New Soviet Woman: Women's Magazines as Engineers of Female Identity, 1922–1953.* New York: St. Martin's Press, 1999.

Bailes, Kendall E. *Technology and Society Under Lenin and Stalin: Origins of the Soviet Technical Intelligentsia, 1917–1941.* Princeton, NJ: Princeton University Press, 1978.

Ball, Alan. *And Now My Soul Is Hardened: Abandoned Children in Soviet Russia, 1918–1930.* Berkeley: University of California Press, 1994.

———. *Russia's Last Capitalists: The Nepmen, 1921–1929.* Berkeley: University of California Press, 1987.

Balzer, Harley. "The Problem of Professions in Imperial Russia." In *Between Tsar and People: Educated Society and the Quest for Public Identity in Late Imperial Russia*, edited by Edith W. Clowes, Samuel D. Kassow, and James L. West, 183–98. Princeton, NJ: Princeton University Press, 1991.

Balzer, Harley D., ed. *Russia's Missing Middle Class: The Professions in Russian History.* Armonk, NY: M. E. Sharpe, 1996.

Bauer, R. A. *The New Man in Soviet Psychology.* Cambridge: Harvard University Press, 1952.

Bechtold, Brigitte H., and Donna Cooper Graves, eds. *Killing Infants: Studies in the Worldwide Practice of Infanticide.* Lewiston, NY: The Edwin Mellen Press, 2006.

Becker, Elisa Marielle. "Medicine, Law, and the State: The Emergence of Forensic Psychiatry in Imperial Russia." Ph.D. diss., University of Pennsylvania, 2003.

Beer, Daniel. *Renovating Russia: The Human Sciences and the Fate of Liberal Modernity, 1880–1930.* Ithaca, NY: Cornell University Press, 2008.

Beirne, Piers. "Adolphe Quetelet and the Origins of Positivist Criminology." *American Journal of Sociology* 92, no. 5 (1987): 1140–69.

———. *Inventing Criminology: Essays on the Rise of Homo Criminalis.* Albany: State University of New York Press, 1993.

———, ed. *The Origins and Growth of Criminology: Essays in Intellectual History, 1760–1945.* Aldershot, England: Dartmouth, 1994.

Beirne, Piers, and Alan Hunt. "Lenin, Crime, and Penal Politics, 1917–1924." In *The*

Origins and Growth of Criminology: Essays in Intellectual History, 1760–1945, edited by Piers Beirne, 181–217. Aldershot, England: Dartmouth, 1994.

Belkin, R. S., and A. I. Vinberg. *Istoriia Sovetskoi kriminalistiki. Etap voznikoveniia i stanovleniia nauki (1917–1930-e gody).* Moscow: Akademiia MVD SSSR, 1982.

Bernstein, Frances. *The Dictatorship of Sex: Lifestyle Advice for the Soviet Masses.* DeKalb, IL: Northern Illinois University Press, 2007.

———. "Panic, Potency, and the Crisis of Nervousness in the 1920s." In *Everyday Life in Early Soviet Russia: Taking the Revolution Inside,* edited by Christina Kiaer and Eric Naiman, 153–182. Bloomington: Indiana University Press, 2006.

Bernstein, Laurie. *Sonia's Daughters: Prostitutes and Their Regulation in Imperial Russia.* Berkeley: University of California Press, 1995.

Bialkowski, Zygmunt Ronald, III. "The Transformation of Academic Criminal Jurisprudence into Criminology in Late Imperial Russia." Ph.D. diss., University of California, Berkeley, 2007.

Bonnell, Victoria E. *Iconography of Power: Soviet Political Posters under Lenin and Stalin.* Berkeley: University of California Press, 1997.

———. "The Peasant Woman in Stalinist Political Art of the 1930s." *American Historical Review* 98, no. 1 (1993): 55–82.

———. "The Representation of Women in Early Soviet Political Art." *The Russian Review* 50, no. 3 (1991): 267–89.

Borisova, L. V. "NEP v zerkale pokazatel'nykh protsessov po vziatochnichestvu i khoziaistvennym prestupleniiam." *Otechestvennaia istoriia,* no. 1 (2006): 84–97.

———. "'Tretii vrag revoliutsii.' Bor'ba so vziatochnichestvom i khoziaistvennymi prestupleniami v nachale NEPa." *Soviet and Post-Soviet Review* 30, no. 3 (2003): 245–77.

Boritch, Helen, and John Hagan. "A Century of Crime in Toronto: Gender, Class, and Patterns of Social Control, 1859 to 1955." *Criminology* 28, no. 4 (1990): 567–99.

Bradley, Joseph. *Muzhik and Muscovite: Urbanization in Late Imperial Russia.* Berkeley: University of California Press, 1985.

———. "Patterns of Peasant Migration to Late Nineteenth-Century Moscow: How Much Should We Read into Literacy Rates." *Russian History* 6, no. 1 (1979): 22–38.

———. "Subjects into Citizens: Societies, Civil Society, and Autocracy in Tsarist Russia." *American Historical Review* 107, no. 4 (2002): 1094–123.

———. "Voluntary Organizations, Civic Culture, and *Obshchestvennost'* in Moscow." In *Between Tsar and People: Educated Society and the Quest for Public Identity in Late Imperial Russia,* edited by Edith W. Clowes, Samuel D. Kassow, and James L. West, 131–48. Princeton, NJ: Princeton University Press, 1991.

Brintlinger, Angela, and Ilya Vinitsky, eds. *Madness and the Mad in Russian Culture.* Toronto: University of Toronto Press, 2007.

Brooks, Jeffrey. *Thank You, Comrade Stalin! Soviet Public Culture from Revolution to Cold War*. Princeton, NJ: Princeton University Press, 2000.

———. *When Russia Learned to Read: Literacy and Popular Literature, 1861–1917*. Princeton, NJ: Princeton University Press, 1985.

Brovkin, Vladimir. *Behind the Front Lines in the Civil War: Political Parties and Social Movements in Russia*. Princeton, NJ: Princeton University Press, 1994.

———. *Russia after Lenin: Politics, Culture, and Society, 1921–1929*. London: Routledge, 1998.

Brown, Julie Vail. "Female Sexuality and Madness in Russian Culture: Traditional Values and Psychiatric Theory." *Social Research* 53, no. 2 (1986): 369–85.

———. "Revolution and Psychosis: The Mixing of Science and Politics in Russian Psychiatric Medicine, 1905–13." *The Russian Review* 46, no. 3 (1987): 283–302.

Brown, Kate. "Out of Solitary Confinement: The History of the Gulag." *Kritika* 8, no. 1 (Winter 2007): 67–103.

Buckley, Mary. *Women and Ideology in the Soviet Union*. Ann Arbor: University of Michigan Press, 1989.

Burbank, Jane. *Intelligentsia and Revolution: Russian Views of Bolshevism, 1917–1922*. Oxford: Oxford University Press, 1986.

———. *Russian Peasants Go to Court: Legal Culture in the Countryside, 1905–1917*. Bloomington: Indiana University Press, 2004.

Carleton, Gregory. *Sexual Revolution in Bolshevik Russia*. Pittsburgh, PA: University of Pittsburgh Press, 2005.

Cassidy, Julie A., and Leyla Rouhi. "From Nevskii Prospekt to Zoia's Apartment: Trials of the Russian Procuress," *The Russian Review* 58, no. 3 (1999): 413–31.

Chalidze, Valery. *Criminal Russia: Essays on Crime in the Soviet Union*. Translated by P. S. Falla. New York: Random House, 1977.

Chamberlin, J. Edward, and Sander L. Gilman, eds. *Degeneration: The Dark Side of Progress*. New York: Columbia University Press, 1985.

Chesney-Lind, Meda. "Women and Crime: The Female Offender." *Signs* 12, no. 1 (1986): 78–96.

Chinn, Jeff. *Manipulating Soviet Population Resources*. New York: Holmes & Meier Publishers, 1977.

Clark, Charles E. *Uprooting Otherness: The Literacy Campaign in NEP-Era Russia*. Selinsgrove, PA: Susquehanna University Press/Associated University Presses, 2000.

Clark, Katerina. *Petersburg: Crucible of Cultural Revolution*. Cambridge: Harvard University Press, 1995.

Clements, Barbara. "The Birth of the New Soviet Woman." In *Bolshevik Culture: Experiment and Order in the Russian Revolution*, edited by Abbott Gleason, Peter Kenez, and Richard Stites, 220–37. Bloomington: Indiana University Press, 1985.

Clements, Barbara Evans, Barbara Alpern Engel, and Christine D. Worobec, eds. *Russia's Women: Accommodation, Resistance, Transformation*. Berkeley: University of California Press, 1991.

Clowes, Edith W., Samuel D. Kassow, and James L. West, eds. *Between Tsar and People: Educated Society and the Quest for Public Identity in Late Imperial Russia*. Princeton, NJ: Princeton University Press, 1991.

Cohen, David, and Eric A. Johnson. "French Criminality: Urban-Rural Differences in the Nineteenth Century." *Journal of Interdisciplinary History* 12, no. 3 (1982): 477–501.

Dan'shin, I. N. "Iz istorii kriminologicheskikh uchrezhdenii v Ukrainskoi SSR v 20–30-e gody." *Voprosy bor'by s prestupnost'iu*, 63–70. Moscow: Iuridicheskaia literatura, 1980.

David-Fox, Michael. *Revolution of the Mind: Higher Learning among the Bolsheviks, 1918–1929*. Ithaca, NY: Cornell University Press, 1997.

———. "What Is Cultural Revolution?" *The Russian Review* 58, no. 2 (1999): 181–201.

———, reviewer, I. N. Il'ina, *Obshchestvennye organizatsii Rossii v 1920–e gody*, in *Kritika* 3, no. 1 (Winter 2002): 173–81.

DeHaan, Heather. "Engendering A People: Soviet Women and Socialist Rebirth in Russia." *Canadian Slavonic Papers* 41, nos. 3–4 (1999): 431–55.

Donovan, James M. "Infanticide and the Juries in France, 1825–1913." *Journal of Family History* 16, no. 2 (1991): 157–76.

Dörner, Klaus. *Madmen and the Bourgeoisie: A Social History of Insanity and Psychiatry*. Oxford: Basil Blackwell, 1981.

Dowbiggin, Ian R. *Inheriting Madness: Professionalization and Psychiatric Knowledge in Nineteenth-Century France*. Berkeley: University of California Press, 1991.

Downey, James. "Civil Society and the Campaign against Corporal Punishment in Late Imperial Russia, 1863–1904." Ph.D. diss., Indiana University, 1993.

Drinka, George Frederick. *The Birth of Neurosis: Myth, Malady, and the Victorians*. New York: Simon and Schuster, 1984.

Eklof, Ben. "Peasant Sloth Reconsidered: Strategies of Education and Learning in Rural Russia before the Revolution." *Journal of Social History* 14, no. 3 (1981): 355–85.

———. *Russian Peasant Schools: Officialdom, Village Culture, and Popular Pedagogy, 1861–1914*. Berkeley: University of California Press, 1987.

Eminov, V. E., ed. *Kriminologiia. Uchebnoe posobie*. Moscow: Izdatel'stvo gruppa INFRA M-NORMA, 1997.

Emmons, Terence, and Wayne S. Vucinich, eds. *The Zemstvo in Russia: An Experiment in Local Self-Government*. Cambridge: Cambridge University Press, 1982.

Engel, Barbara Alpern. *Between the Fields and the City: Women, Work, and Family in Russia, 1861–1914*. Cambridge: Cambridge University Press, 1995.

———. "St. Petersburg Prostitutes in the Late Nineteenth Century: A Personal and Social Profile," *The Russian Review* 48, no. 1 (1989): 21–44.

——. *Women in Russia, 1700–2000*. Cambridge: Cambridge University Press, 2004.

Engelstein, Laura. "Gender and the Juridical Subject: Prostitution and Rape in Nineteenth-Century Russian Criminal Codes," *Journal of Modern History* 60, no. 3 (1988): 458–95.

——. *The Keys to Happiness: Sex and the Search for Modernity in Fin-De-Siècle Russia*. Ithaca, NY: Cornell University Press, 1992.

Evans, David J., and David T. Herbert. *The Geography of Crime*. London: Routledge, 1989.

Evans, Janet. "The Communist Party of the Soviet Union and the Women's Question: The Case of the 1936 Decree 'In Defense of Mother and Child.'" *Journal of Contemporary History* 16, no. 4 (October 1981): 757–75.

Farnsworth, Beatrice. "The Litigious Daughter-in-Law: Family Relations in Rural Russia in the Second Half of the Nineteenth Century." In *Russian Peasant Women*, edited by Beatrice Farnsworth and Lynn Viola, 89–106. New York: Oxford University Press, 1992.

——, and Lynn Viola, eds. *Russian Peasant Women*. New York: Oxford University Press, 1992.

Feinman, Clarice. *Women in the Criminal Justice System*. New York: Praeger, 1986.

Finkel, Stuart. "'The Brains of the Nation': The Expulsion of Intellectuals and the Politics of Culture in Soviet Russia, 1920–1924." Ph.D. diss., Stanford University, 2001.

——. "Purging the Public Intellectual: The 1922 Expulsions from Soviet Russia." *The Russian Review* 62, no. 4 (2003): 589–613.

Fitzpatrick, Sheila. "Ascribing Class: The Construction of Social Identity in Soviet Russia." *Journal of Modern History* 65, no. 4 (1993): 745–70.

——. "The Civil War As a Formative Experience." In *Bolshevik Culture: Experiment and Order in the Russian Revolution*, edited by Abbott Gleason, Peter Kenez, and Richard Stites, 57–76. Bloomington: Indiana University Press, 1985.

——. *The Commissariat of Enlightenment: Soviet Organization of Education and the Arts under Lunacharsky, October 1917–1921*. Cambridge: Cambridge University Press, 1970.

——. *The Cultural Front: Power and Culture in Revolutionary Russia*. Ithaca, NY: Cornell University Press, 1992.

——. *Education and Social Mobility in the Soviet Union, 1921–1934*. Cambridge: Cambridge University Press, 1979.

——. "Sex and Revolution: An Examination of Literary and Statistical Data on the Mores of Soviet Students in the 1920s," *Journal of Modern History* 50, no. 2 (June 1978): 252–78.

——. "Stalin and the Making of a New Elite, 1925–1939." *Slavic Review* 38, no. 3 (1979): 377–402.

——. *Tear Off the Masks! Identity and Imposture in Twentieth-Century Russia*. Princeton, NJ: Princeton University Press, 2005.

———, ed. *Cultural Revolution in Russia, 1928–1931*. Bloomington: Indiana University Press, 1978.

———, Alexander Rabinowitch, and Richard Stites, eds. *Russia in the Era of NEP: Explorations in Soviet Society and Culture*. Bloomington: Indiana University Press, 1991.

Forgacs, David. "Imagined Bodies: Rhetorics of Social Investigation in Nineteenth-Century Italy and France," *Journal of the Institute of Romantic Studies* 1 (1992): 375–94.

Foucault, Michel. *Discipline and Punish: The Birth of the Prison*. Translated by Alan Sheridan. 2nd ed. New York: Vintage Books, 1995.

Frank, Stephen P. *Crime, Cultural Conflict, and Justice in Rural Russia, 1856–1914*. Berkeley: University of California Press, 1999.

———. "Cultural Conflict and Criminality in Rural Russia, 1861–1900." Ph.D. diss., Brown University, 1987.

———. "Narratives within Numbers: Women, Crime, and Juridical Statistics in Imperial Russia, 1834–1913." *The Russian Review* 55, no. 4 (1996): 541–66.

———. "Popular Justice, Community and Culture among the Russian Peasantry, 1870–1900." *The Russian Review* 46, no. 3 (1987): 239–65.

Frieden, Nancy Mandelker. *Russian Physicians in an Era of Reform and Revolution, 1856–1905*. Princeton, NJ: Princeton University Press, 1981.

Frierson, Cathy A. "Crime and Punishment in the Russian Village: Rural Concepts of Criminality at the End of the Nineteenth Century." *Slavic Review* 46, no. 1 (1987): 55–69.

———. *Peasant Icons: Representations of Rural People in Late Nineteenth-Century Russia*. Oxford: Oxford University Press, 1993.

Galassi, Silviana. *Kriminologie im deutschen Kaiserreich. Geschichte einer gebrochenen Verwissenschaftlichung*. Stuttgart: Franz Steiner Verland, 2004.

Gallagher, Catherine, and Thomas Laqueur, eds. *The Making of the Modern Body: Sexuality and Society in the Nineteenth Century*. Berkeley: University of California Press, 1987.

Gatrell, Peter. *A Whole Empire Walking: Refugees in Russia during World War I*. Bloomington: Indiana University Press, 1999.

Gaudin, Corinne. *Ruling Peasants: Village and State in Late Imperial Russia*. DeKalb: Northern Illinois University Press, 2007.

Geifman, Anna. *Thou Shalt Kill: Revolutionary Terrorism in Russia, 1894–1917*. Princeton, NJ: Princeton University Press, 1993.

Gibson, Mary. *Born to Crime: Cesare Lombroso and the Origins of Biological Criminology*. Westport, CT: Praeger, 2002.

———. "The 'Female Offender' and the Italian School of Criminal Anthropology." *Journal of European Studies* 12, no. 3 (1982): 155–65.

Gleason, Abbott, Peter Kenez, and Richard Stites, eds. *Bolshevik Culture: Experiment and Order in the Russian Revolution*. Bloomington: Indiana University Press, 1985.

Goldman, Wendy Z. *Women at the Gates: Gender and Industry in Stalin's Russia*. Cambridge: Cambridge University Press, 2002.

———. *Women, the State and Revolution: Soviet Family Policy and Social Life, 1917–1936*. Cambridge: Cambridge University Press, 1993.

Goldsmith, Victor, Philip G. McGuire, John H. Mollenkopf, and Timothy A. Ross, eds. *Analyzing Crime Patterns: Frontiers of Practice*. Thousand Oaks, CA: Sage Publications, Inc., 2000.

Gorham, Michael S. "Tongue-Tied Writers: The Rabsel'kor Movement and the Voice of the 'New Intelligentsia' in Early Soviet Russia." *The Russian Review* 55, no. 3 (1996): 412–29.

Gorsuch, Anne. *Youth in Revolutionary Russia: Enthusiasts, Bohemians, Delinquents*. Bloomington: Indiana University Press, 2000.

Graham, Loren. "The Formation of Soviet Research Institutes: A Combination of Revolutionary Innovation and International Borrowing." *Social Studies of Science* 5, no. 3 (August 1975): 303–29.

———. *Science in Russia and the Soviet Union: A Short History*. Cambridge: Cambridge University Press, 1993.

Groneman, Carol. "Nymphomania: The Historical Construction of Female Sexuality." In *Deviant Bodies: Critical Perspectives on Difference in Science and Popular Culture*, edited by Jennifer Terry and Jacqueline Urla, 219–49. Bloomington: Indiana University Press, 1995.

Guroff, Gregory, and S. Frederick Starr. "A Note on Urban Literacy in Russia, 1890–1914." *Jahrbücher für Geschichte Osteuropas* 19, no. 4 (1971): 520–31.

Halfin, Igal. *From Darkness to Light: Class, Consciousness, and Salvation in Revolutionary Russia*. Pittsburgh, PA: University of Pittsburgh Press, 2000.

Harries, Keith D. *The Geography of Crime and Justice*. New York: McGraw Hill, 1974.

Harris, Ruth. "Melodrama, Hysteria, and Feminine Crimes of Passion in the Fin-de-Siècle." *History Workshop Journal* 25 (1988): 31–63.

———. *Murders and Madness: Medicine, Law, and Society in the Fin-De-Siècle*. Oxford: Oxford University Press, 1989.

Hartnagel, Timothy. "Modernization, Female Social Roles, and Female Crime: A Cross-National Investigation." *Sociological Quarterly* 23, no. 4 (Autumn 1982): 477–90.

Hatchen, Elizabeth A. "In Service to Science and Society: Scientists and the Public in Late-Nineteenth-Century Russia." *Osiris* 17 (2002): 171–209.

Hawthorn, Geoffrey. *Enlightenment and Despair: A History of Social Theory*. 2nd ed. Cambridge: Cambridge University Press, 1987.

Healey, Dan. "Early Soviet Forensic Psychiatric Approaches to Sex Crime, 1917–1934." In *Madness and the Mad in Russian Culture*, edited by Angela Brintlinger and Ilya Vinitsky, 150–72. Toronto: University of Toronto Press, 2007.

———. *Homosexual Desire in Revolutionary Russia: The Regulation of Sexual and*

Gender Dissent. Chicago: University of Chicago Press, 2001.

Heinzen, James W. *Inventing a Soviet Countryside: Soviet State Power and the Transformation of Rural Russia, 1917–1929*. Pittsburgh: University of Pittsburgh Press, 2004.

———. "Professional Identity and the Vision of the Modern Soviet Countryside: Local Agricultural Specialists at the End of the NEP, 1928–1929." *Cahiers du Monde Russe* 39, nos. 1–2 (1998): 9–25.

Hellbeck, Jochen. *Revolution on My Mind: Writing a Diary under Stalin*. Cambridge: Harvard University Press, 2006.

Herbert, David. *The Geography of Urban Crime*. London: Longman, 1982.

Higginbotham, Ann R. "'Sin of the Age': Infanticide and Illegitimacy in Victorian London." *Victorian Studies* 32, no. 3 (1989): 319–37.

Hirsch, Francine. "The Soviets at Nuremberg: International Law, Propaganda, and the Making of the Postwar Order." *American Historical Review* 113, no. 3 (June 2008): 701–30.

Hoffmann, David. *Peasant Metropolis: Social Identities in Moscow, 1929–1941*. Ithaca, NY: Cornell University Press, 1994.

———. "Stalinist Pronatalism in Its Pan-European Context." *Journal of Social History* 34, no. 1 (2000): 35–54.

———. *Stalinist Values: The Cultural Norms of Soviet Modernity, 1917–1941*. Ithaca, NY: Cornell University Press, 2003.

Holquist, Peter. "Information is the Alpha and Omega of Our Work: Bolshevik Surveillance in its Pan-European Context," *Journal of Modern History* 69, no. 3 (1997): 415–50.

———. *Making War, Forging Revolution: Russia's Continuum of Crisis, 1914–1921*. Cambridge: Harvard University Press, 2002.

Hopwood, J. Stanley. "Child Murder and Insanity." *Journal of Mental Science* 73, no. 300 (1927): 95–108.

Horn, David G. *The Criminal Body: Lombroso and the Anatomy of Deviance*. New York: Routledge, 2003.

———. *Social Bodies: Science, Reproduction, and Italian Modernity*. Princeton, NJ: Princeton University Press, 1994.

———. "This Norm Which Is Not One: Reading the Female Body in Lombroso's Anthropology." In *Deviant Bodies: Critical Perspectives on Difference in Science and Popular Culture*, edited by Jennifer Terry and Jacqueline Urla, 109–28. Bloomington: Indiana University Press, 1995.

Huber, Karen. "Sex and Its Consequences: Abortion, Infanticide, and Women's Reproductive Decision-Making in France, 1901–1940." Ph.D. diss., The Ohio State University, 2007.

Hufton, O. H. "The Urban Criminal in Eighteenth-Century France." *Bulletin of the John Rylands University Library of Manchester* 67, no. 1 (1984): 474–99.

Huskey, Eugene. *Russian Lawyers and the Soviet State: The Origins and Development of the Soviet Bar, 1917–1939*. Princeton, NJ: Princeton University Press, 1986.

Hutchinson, John F. *Politics and Public Health in Revolutionary Russia, 1890–1918.* Baltimore, MD: The Johns Hopkins University Press, 1990.

Hutton, Marcelline J. *Russian and West European Women, 1860–1939: Dreams, Struggles, Nightmares.* Lanham, MD: Rowman and Littlefield Publishers, 2001.

Il'ina, I. N. *Obshchestvennye organizatsii Rossii v 1920–e gody.* Moscow: Institut Rossiiskoi istorii RAN, 2000.

Il'ina, L. V. "Iz istorii razvitiia Sovetskoi kriminologii." *Voprosy bor'by s prestupnost'iu,* 29–41. Moscow: Izdatel'stvo "Iuridicheskaia literatura," 1968.

———. "Pervye kriminologicheskie uchrezhdeniia v SSSR." *Ugolovnoe pravo v bor'be s prestupnost'iu,* 150–56. Moscow: Institut gosudarstva i prava Akademii nauk, 1981.

———, and A. V. Nad'iarnyi. "Izuchenie lichnosti prestupnika v SSSR (Istoricheskii obzor)." *Voprosy ugolovnogo prava, prokurorskogo nadzora, kriminalistiki i kriminologii,* 294–310. Dushanbe: Tadzhikskii Gosudarstvennyi universitet, 1968.

Iudin, T. I. *Ocherki istorii otechestvennoi psikhiatrii.* Moscow: Gosudarstvennyi izdatel'stvo meditsinskoi literatury, 1951.

Ivanov, L. O., and L. V. Il'ina. *Puti i sud'by otechestvennoi kriminologii.* Moscow: Nauka, 1991.

Jackson, Mark, ed. *Infanticide: Historical Perspectives on Child Murder and Conceal-ment, 1550–2000.* Aldershot, England: Ashgate, 2002.

———. "Suspicious Infant Deaths: The Statute of 1624 and Medical Evidence at Coroners' Inquests." In *Legal Medicine in History,* edited by Michael Clark and Catherine Crawford, 64–86. Cambridge: Cambridge University Press, 1994.

Jakobson, Michael. *Origins of the Gulag: The Soviet Prison Camp System, 1917–1934.* Lexington: University Press of Kentucky, 1993.

Johnson, Eric A. "Cities Don't Cause Crime: Urban-Rural Differences in Late Nine-teenth- and Early Twentieth-Century German Criminality." *Social Science History* 16, no. 1 (1992): 129–76.

———. "The Roots of Crime in Imperial Germany." *Central European History* 15, no. 4 (1982): 351–76.

———. *Urbanization and Crime: Germany, 1871–1914.* Cambridge: Cambridge University Press, 1995.

———. "Women As Victims and Criminals: Female Homicide and Criminality in Imperial Germany, 1873–1914." *Criminal Justice History* 6 (1985): 151–75.

———, and Eric H. Monkkonen, eds. *The Civilization of Crime: Violence in Town and Country since the Middle Ages.* Urbana: University of Illinois Press, 1996.

Johnson, Robert. *Peasant and Proletariat: The Working Class of Moscow in the Late Nineteenth Century.* New Brunswick, NJ: Rutgers University Press, 1979.

Jones, David A. *History of Criminology: A Philosophical Perspective.* New York: Green-wood Press, 1986.

Jones, Gareth. *Outcast London: A Study in the Relationship between Classes in Victorian Society*. Oxford: Clarendon Press, 1971.

Joravsky, David. "The Construction of the Stalinist Psyche." In *Cultural Revolution in Russia, 1928–1931*, edited by Sheila Fitzpatrick, 105–20. Bloomington: Indiana University Press, 1978.

———. *Russian Psychology: A Critical History*. Oxford: Basil Blackwell, 1989.

Jordanova, Ludmilla. *Sexual Visions: Images of Gender in Science and Medicine between the Eighteenth and Twentieth Centuries*. Madison: University of Wisconsin Press, 1989.

Kasatkin, Iu. P. "Ocherk istorii izucheniia prestupnosti v SSSR." *Problemy iskoreneniia prestupnosti*, 187–225. Moscow: Izdatel'stvo Iuridicheskaia literatura, 1965.

Kassow, Samuel. "Russia's Unrealized Civil Society." In *Between Tsar and People: Educated Society and the Quest for Public Identity in Late Imperial Russia*, edited by Edith W. Clowes, Samuel D. Kassow, and James L. West, 367–71. Princeton, NJ: Princeton University Press, 1991.

Kazantsev, Sergei M. "The Judicial Reform of 1864 and the Procuracy in Russia." In *Reforming Justice in Russia, 1864–1996: Power, Culture, and the Limits of Legal Order*, edited by Peter H. Solomon, 44–60. Armonk, NY: M. E. Sharpe, 1997.

Kenez, Peter. "Liquidating Illiteracy in Revolutionary Russia." *Russian History* 9, nos. 2–3 (1982): 173–86.

Kiaer, Christina, and Eric Naiman, eds. *Everyday Life in Early Soviet Russia: Taking the Revolution Inside*. Bloomington: Indiana University Press, 2006.

Kingston-Mann, Esther. "Statistics, Social Science, and Social Justice: The Zemstvo Statisticians of Pre-Revolutionary Russia." In *Russia in the European Context, 1789–1914: A Member of the Family*, edited by Susan McCaffray and Michael Melancon, 113–40. New York: Palgrave Macmillan, 2005.

Klein, Dorie. "The Etiology of Female Crime: A Review of the Literature." In *The Origins and Growth of Criminology: Essays in Intellectual History, 1760–1945*, edited by Piers Beirne, 265–90. Aldershot, England: Dartmouth, 1994.

Koenker, Diane, William G. Rosenberg, and Ronald Grigor Suny, eds. *Party, State, and Society in the Russian Civil War*. Bloomington: Indiana University Press, 1989.

Kornev, V. P. *Vidnye deiateli otechestvennoi statistiki, 1686–1990*. Moscow: Finansy i statistika, 1993.

Korotkikh, M. G. "Sudebnaia reforma 1864 g. v Rossii." *Voprosy istorii*, no. 12 (1987): 20–34.

Kotkin, Stephen. *Magnetic Mountain: Stalinism As a Civilization*. Berkeley: University of California Press, 1995.

Kowalsky, Sharon A. "Who's Responsible for Female Crime? Gender, Deviance, and the Development of Soviet Social Norms in Revolutionary Russia." *The Russian Review* 62, no. 3 (2003): 366–86.

Krylov, I. F. *Ocherki istorii kriminalistiki i kriminalisticheskoi ekspertizy*. Leningrad: Izdatel'stvo Leningradskogo universiteta, 1975.

Krylova, Anna. "Beyond the Spontaneity-Consciousness Paradigm: 'Class Instinct' As a Promising Category of Historical Analysis." *Slavic Review* 62, no. 1 (Spring 2003): 1–23.

Kumanev, V. A. "Opyt likvidatsii negramotnosti v SSSR." *Vestnik istorii mirovoi kul'tury*, no. 25 (1961): 14–29.

Kushner, Howard I. "Suicide, Gender, and the Fear of Modernity in Nineteenth-Century Medical and Social Thought." *Journal of Social History* 26, no. 3 (1993): 461–90.

Kuznetsova, N. F. "Sovetskaia kriminologiia v usloviiakh perestroiki." *Vestnik Moskovskogo Universiteta*. Seriia 11. *Pravo*, no. 2 (1989): 24–31.

Lampert, Nicholas. *The Technical Intelligentsia and the Soviet State: A Study of Soviet Managers and Technicians, 1928–1935*. London: The MacMillan Press, 1979.

Langer, William L. "Infanticide: A Historical Survey." *History of Childhood Quarterly* 1, no. 3 (1974): 353–65.

Lebina, N. B. *Povsednevnaia zhizn' sovetskogo goroda. Normy i anomalii 1920–1930 gody*. St. Petersburg: Zhurnal "Neva," 1999.

———, and A. N. Chistikov. *Obyvateli i reformy. Kartiny povsednevnoi zhizni gorozhan v gody NEPa i Khrushchevskogo desiatiletiia*. St. Petersburg: Dmitrii Bulanin, 2003.

———, and M. V. Shkarovskii. *Prostitutsiia v Peterburge, 40-e gg XIX–40-e gg XX v.* Moscow: Progress-Akademiia, 1994.

Leboutte, Ren. "Offense against Family Order: Infanticide in Belgium from the Fifteenth to the Early Twentieth Centuries." *Journal of the History of Sexuality* 2, no. 2 (1991): 159–85.

Leibovich, O. L. "Problema prestupnosti v Sovetskoi sotsiologicheskoi literatury 20–kh godov." In *Istoriia stanovleniia Sovetskoi sotsiologicheskoi nauki v 20–30–e gody*, 143–55. Moscow: Institut sotsiologii AN SSSR, 1989.

Leps, Marie-Christine. *Apprehending the Criminal: The Production of Deviance in Nineteenth-Century Discourse*. Durham, NC: Duke University Press, 1992.

Levin, Eve. "Infanticide in Pre-Petrine Russia." *Jahrbücher für Geschichte Osteuropas* 34, no. 2 (1986): 215–24.

———. *Sex and Society in the World of the Orthodox Slavs, 900–1700*. Ithaca, NY: Cornell University Press, 1989.

Lewin, Moshe. "Customary Law and Russian Rural Society in the Post-Reform Era." *The Russian Review* 44, no. 1 (1985): 1–19.

Lindenmeyr, Adele. *Poverty Is Not a Vice: Charity, Society, and the State in Imperial Russia*. Princeton, NJ: Princeton University Press, 1996.

Lindesmith, Alfred, and Yale Levin. "The Lombrosian Myth in Criminology." *American Journal of Sociology* 42, no. 5 (1937): 653–71.

Litvak, K. B. "Samogonovarenie i potreblenie alkogolia v Rossiiskoi derevne 1920–x godov." *Otechestvennaia istoriia*, no. 4 (1992): 74–88.

Lodhi, Abdul Quaiyum, and Charles Tilly. "Urbanization, Crime, and Collective Violence in Nineteenth-Century France." *American Journal of Sociology* 79, no. 2 (1973): 296–318.

Lorimer, Frank. *The Population of the Soviet Union: History and Prospects*. Geneva: League of Nations, 1946.

Luneev, V. V. *Prestupnost' XX [dvadtsatogo] veka. Mirovye, regional'nye i rossiiskie tendentsii*. Moscow: NORMA, 1997.

Mally, Lynn. *Culture of the Future: The Proletkult Movement in Revolutionary Russia*. Berkeley: University of California Press, 1990.

Mannheim, Hermann, ed. *Pioneers in Criminology*. London: Stevens & Sons, 1960.

Martin, Terry. "Interpreting the New Archival Signals: Nationalities Policy and the Nature of the Soviet Bureaucracy." *Cahiers du Monde Russe* 40, nos. 1–2 (1999): 113–24.

Massell, Gregory J. *The Surrogate Proletariat: Moslem Women and Revolutionary Strategies in Soviet Central Asia, 1919–1929*. Princeton, NJ: Princeton University Press, 1974.

Matlock, Jann. *Scenes of Seduction: Prostitution, Hysteria, and Reading Difference in Nineteenth-Century France*. New York: Columbia University Press, 1994.

Maza, Sarah. *Private Lives and Public Affairs: The Causes Célèbres of Prerevolutionary France*. Berkeley: University of California Press, 1993.

McMillan, James. *Housewife or Harlot: The Place of Women in French Society, 1870–1940*. New York: St. Martin's Press, 1981.

McReynolds, Louise. *The News under Russia's Old Regime: The Development of a Mass Circulation Press*. Princeton, NJ: Princeton University Press, 1991.

Medvedev, Zhores. *Soviet Science*. New York: W. W. Norton, 1978.

Mespoulet, Martine. "Statisticiens des *zemstva*. Formation d'une nouvelle profession intellectuelle en Russie dans la periode prerevolutionnaire (1880–1917). Le case de Saratov." *Cahiers du Monde Russe* 40, no. 4 (1999): 573–624.

———. *Statistique et révolution en Russie. Un compromis impossible (1880–1930)*. Rennes, France: Presses Universitaires de Rennes, 2001.

Messerschmidt, James W. *Capitalism, Patriarchy, and Crime: Toward a Socialist Feminist Criminology*. Totowa, NJ: Rowman & Littlefield, 1986.

Miller, Martin A. *Freud and the Bolsheviks: Psychoanalysis in Imperial Russia and the Soviet Union*. New Haven: Yale University Press, 1998.

Mironov, Boris N. "The Development of Literacy in Russia and the USSR from the Tenth to the Twentieth Centuries." *History of Education Quarterly* 31, no. 2 (1991): 229–52.

Morrissey, Susan K. *Suicide and the Body Politic in Imperial Russia*. Cambridge: Cambridge University Press, 2007.

Moscucci, Orvilla. *The Science of Woman: Gynecology and Gender in England, 1800–1929*. Cambridge: Cambridge University Press, 1990.

Mueller, Julie Kay. "Staffing Newspapers and Training Journalists in Early Soviet Russia." *Journal of Social History* 31, no. 4 (1998): 851–73.

Muir, Edward, and Guido Ruggiero, eds. *History from Crime*. Baltimore, MD: The Johns Hopkins University Press, 1994.

Musaev, V. I. *Prestupnost' v Petrograde v 1917–1921 gg.* St. Petersburg: Dmitri Bulanin, 2001.

Naffine, Ngaire. *Feminism and Criminology.* Philadelphia, PA: Temple University Press, 1996.

Naiman, Eric. "The Case of Chubarov Alley: Collective Rape, Utopian Desire, and the Mentality of NEP." *Russian History* 17, no. 1 (1990): 1–30.

———. *Sex in Public: The Incarnation of Early Soviet Ideology.* Princeton, NJ: Princeton University Press, 1997.

Nathans, Benjamin. *Beyond the Pale: The Jewish Encounter with Late Imperial Russia.* Berkeley: University of California Press, 2004.

Nelson, Amy. *Music for the Revolution: Musicians and Power in Early Soviet Russia.* University Park: Pennsylvania State University Press, 2004.

Neuberger, Joan. *Hooliganism: Crime, Culture, and Power in St. Petersburg, 1900–1914.* Berkeley: University of California Press, 1993.

Northrop, Douglas. "Subaltern Dialogues: Subversion and Resistance in Soviet Uzbek Family Law." In *Contending with Stalinism: Soviet Power and Popular Resistance in the 1930s,* edited by Lynn Viola, 109–38. Ithaca, NY: Cornell University Press, 2002.

Nye, Robert A. *Crime, Madness and Politics in Modern France: The Medical Concept of National Decline.* Princeton, NJ: Princeton University Press, 1984.

———. "Heredity or Milieu: The Foundations of Modern European Criminological Theory." *Isis* 67, no. 3 (1976): 335–55.

Organizatsiia nauki v pervye gody Sovetskoi vlasti (1917–1925). Sbornik dokumentov. Edited by K. Ostrovitianov. Leningrad: Izdatel'stvo "Nauka," 1968.

Ostroumov, S. S. *Prestupnost' i ee prichiny v dorevoliutsionnoi Rossii.* Moscow: Izdatel'stvo Moskovskogo universiteta, 1960.

———. *Sovetskaia sudebnaia statistika.* Moscow: Gosudarstvennoe izdatel'stvo iuridicheskoi literatury, 1952.

Paperno, Irina. *Suicide As a Cultural Institution in Dostoevsky's Russia.* Ithaca, NY: Cornell University Press, 1997.

Pelfrey, William V. *The Evolution of Criminology.* Cincinnati, OH: Anderson, 1980.

Pethybridge, Roger. *One Step Backwards, Two Steps Forward: Soviet Society and Politics in the New Economic Policy.* Oxford: Clarendon Press, 1990.

Phillips, Laura L. *Bolsheviks and the Bottle: Drink and Worker Culture in St. Petersburg, 1900–1929.* DeKalb: Northern Illinois University Press, 2000.

Phillipson, Coleman. *Three Criminal Law Reformers: Beccaria, Bentham, Romilly.* London: J. M. Dent and Sons, 1923.

Pick, Daniel. *Faces of Degeneration: A European Disorder, c. 1848–c. 1918.* Cambridge: Cambridge University Press, 1989.

Pinnow, Kenneth M. "Making Suicide Soviet: Medicine, Moral Statistics, and the Politics of Social Science in Bolshevik Russia, 1920–1930." Ph.D. diss., Columbia University, 1998.

Pipes, Richard. *Russia under the Old Regime*. 2nd ed. New York: Macmillan, 1992.

Pomper, Philip. *The Russian Revolutionary Intelligentsia*. 2nd ed. Wheeling, IL: Harlan Davidson, 1993.

Portnov, V. P., and M. M. Slavin. "Iz istorii Sovetskogo ugolovnogo prava (1917–1920 gg.)." In *Ugolovnoe pravo v bor'be s prestupnost'iu*, 140–50. Moscow: Institut gosudarstva i prava Akademii nauk, 1981.

Prozorovskii, V. I., and O. A. Panfilenko. "Razvitie sudebno-meditsinskoi nauki i ekspertizy za gody Sovetskoi vlasti." *Sudebno-meditsinskaia ekspertiza*, no. 3 (1967): 3–10.

Pushkareva, N. L. *Russkaia zhenshchina. Istoriia i sovremennost'*. Moscow: Ladomir, 2002.

———. *Women in Russian History, from the Tenth to the Twentieth Centuries*. Armonk, NY: M. E. Sharpe, 1997.

Radzinowicz, Leon. *Ideology and Crime*. New York: Columbia University Press, 1966.

Raleigh, Donald J. *Experiencing Russia's Civil War: Politics, Society, and Revolutionary Culture in Saratov, 1917–1922*. Princeton, NJ: Princeton University Press, 2002.

Ransel, David L., ed. *The Family in Imperial Russia: New Lines of Historical Research*. Urbana: University of Illinois Press, 1978.

———. *Mothers of Misery: Child Abandonment in Russia*. Princeton, NJ: Princeton University Press, 1988.

Ratcliffe, Barrie M. "Perceptions and Realities of the Urban Margin: The Rag Pickers of Paris in the First Half of the Nineteenth Century." *Canadian Journal of History* 27, no. 2 (1992): 197–233.

Rennie, Ysabel. *The Search for Criminal Man: A Conceptual History of the Dangerous Offender*. Lexington, MA: Lexington Books, 1978.

Roberts, Mary Louise. *Civilization without Sexes: Reconstructing Gender in Postwar France, 1917–1927*. Chicago: University of Chicago Press, 1994.

Rosen, Jeffrey. "The Brain on the Stand: How Neuroscience Is Transforming the Legal System." *The New York Times Magazine*, 11 March 2007.

Rosenberg, Carroll Smith. *Disorderly Conduct: Visions of Gender in Victorian America*. New York: A. A. Knopf, 1985.

Rosenberg, Carroll Smith, and Charles Rosenberg. "The Female Animal: Medical and Biological Views of Woman and Her Role in Nineteenth-Century America." *Journal of American History* 60, no. 2 (1973): 332–56.

Rosenberg, William G. *Bolshevik Visions: First Phase of the Cultural Revolution in Soviet Russia*. Ann Arbor: University of Michigan Press, 1990.

Rothman, David J. *The Discovery of the Asylum: Social Order and Disorder in the New Republic*. Boston, MA: Little Brown, 1971.

Ruane, Christine. *Gender, Class, and the Professionalization of Russian City Teachers, 1860–1914*. Pittsburgh, PA: University of Pittsburgh Press, 1994.

———. "The Vestal Virgins of St. Petersburg: Schoolteachers and the 1897 Marriage Ban." *The Russian Review* 50, no. 2 (1991): 163–82.

Ruggiero, Kristin. "Honor, Maternity, and the Disciplining of Women: Infanticide in Late Nineteenth-Century Buenos Aires." *Hispanic American Historical Review* 72, no. 3 (1992): 353–73.

Russett, Cynthia Eagle. *Sexual Science: The Victorian Construction of Womanhood.* Cambridge: Harvard University Press, 1989.

Sakharov, A. B. *Istoriia kriminologicheskoi nauki.* Moscow: Moskovskaia vysshaia shkola militsii MVD Rossii, 1994.

Schafer, Stephen. *Theories in Criminology: Past and Present Philosophies of the Crime Problem.* New York: Random House, 1969.

Schrader, Abby M. *Languages of the Lash: Corporal Punishment and Identity in Imperial Russia.* DeKalb: Northern Illinois University Press, 2002.

Sellin, Thorsten. "Pioneers in Criminology XV—Enrico Ferri (1856–1929)." *Journal of Criminal Law, Criminology, and Police Science* 48, no. 5 (1958): 481–92.

Shapiro, Ann-Louise. *Breaking the Codes: Female Criminality in Fin-de-Siècle Paris.* Stanford, CA: Stanford University Press, 1996.

Sharlet, Robert. "Pashukanis and the Withering Away of Law in the USSR." In *Cultural Revolution in Russia, 1928–1931*, edited by Sheila Fitzpatrick, 168–88. Bloomington: Indiana University Press, 1978.

Shelley, Louise. "The 1929 Dispute on Soviet Criminology," *Soviet Union* 6, no. 2 (1979): 175–85.

———. *Crime and Modernization: The Impact of Industrialization and Urbanization on Crime.* Carbondale: Southern Illinois University Press, 1981.

———. "Female Criminality in the 1920s: A Consequence of Inadvertent and Deliberate Change." *Russian History* 9, nos. 2–3 (1982): 265–84.

———. "The Geography of Soviet Criminality." *American Sociological Review* 45, no. 1 (1980): 111–22.

———. "Soviet Criminology: Its Birth and Demise 1917–1936." Ph.D. diss., University of Pennsylvania, 1977.

Shestakov, D. A. "K voprosu ob istorii Sovetskoi kriminologii." *Vestnik Leningradskogo Universiteta.* Seriia 6. *Istoriia KPSS, nauchnyi kommunizm, filosofiia, pravo*, no. 2 (1991): 74–81.

Shliapochnikov, A. S. *Sovetskaia kriminologiia na sovremennom etape.* Moscow: Vsesoiuznyi institut po izucheniiu prichin i razrabotke mer preduprezhdeniia prestupnosti, 1973.

Showalter, Elaine. *The Female Malady: Women, Madness, and English Culture, 1830–1980.* New York: Pantheon, 1985.

Simon, Rita J. "American Women and Crime." *Readings in Comparative Criminology*, edited by Louise Shelley, 1–17. Carbondale: Southern Illinois University Press, 1981.

Skultans, Vieda. *English Madness: Ideas on Insanity, 1580–1890.* London: Routledge, 1979.

Smart, Carol. *Women, Crime, and Criminology: A Feminist Critique.* London: Routledge and Kegan Paul, 1977.

Snow, George E. "Perceptions of the Link between Alcoholism and Crime in Pre-Revolutionary Russia." *Criminal Justice History: An International Annual* 8 (1987): 37–51.

Solomon, Peter H., Jr. *Soviet Criminal Justice under Stalin.* Cambridge: Cambridge University Press, 1996.

———. *Soviet Criminologists and Criminal Policy: Specialists in Policy-Making.* New York: Columbia University Press, 1978.

———. "Soviet Criminology—Its Demise and Rebirth, 1928–1963." In *Crime, Criminology, and Public Policy*, edited by Roger Hood, 571–93. New York: The Free Press, 1974.

———. "Soviet Penal Policy, 1917–1934: A Reinterpretation." *Slavic Review* 39, no. 2 (1980): 195–217.

———, ed. *Reforming Justice in Russia, 1864–1996: Power, Culture, and the Limits of Legal Order.* Armonk, NY: M. E. Sharpe, 1997.

Solomon, Susan Gross. "David and Goliath in Soviet Public Health: The Rivalry of Social Hygienists and Psychiatrists for Authority over the Bytovoi Alcoholic." *Soviet Studies* 41, no. 2 (1989): 254–75.

———. "The Limits of Government Patronage of Science: Social Hygiene and the Soviet State, 1920–1930." *Social History of Medicine* 3, no. 3 (1990): 405–35.

———. "Social Hygiene and Soviet Public Health, 1921–1930." In *Health and Society in Revolutionary Russia*, edited by Susan Gross Solomon and John F. Hutchinson, 175–99. Bloomington: Indiana University Press, 1990.

———, ed. *Doing Medicine Together: Germany and Russia between the Wars.* Toronto: University of Toronto Press, 2006.

Soman, Alfred. "Deviance and Criminal Justice in Western Europe, 1300–1800: An Essay in Structure." *Criminal Justice History* 1 (1980): 1–28.

Spagnolo, Rebecca. "When Private Home Meets Public Workplace: Service, Space and the Urban Domestic in 1920s Russia." In *Everyday Life in Early Soviet Russia: Taking the Revolution Inside*, edited by Christina Kiaer and Eric Naiman, 230–55. Bloomington: Indiana University Press, 2006.

Starks, Tricia. *The Body Soviet: Propaganda, Hygiene, and the Revolutionary State.* Madison: University of Wisconsin Press, 2008.

Stites, Richard. "Prostitute and Society in Pre-Revolutionary Russia," *Jahrbücher für Geschichte Osteuropas* 31, no. 3 (1983): 348–64.

———. *Revolutionary Dreams: Utopian Vision and Experimental Life in the Russian Revolution.* Oxford: Oxford University Press, 1991.

———. *The Women's Liberation Movement in Russia: Feminism, Nihilism, and Bolshevism, 1860–1930.* Princeton, NJ: Princeton University Press, 1990.

Sutton, Richard. "Crime and Social Change in Russia after the Great Reforms: Laws, Courts, and Criminals, 1874–1894." Ph.D. diss., Indiana University, 1984.

Talysheva, O. A. "Sovetskie kriminologi o prestupnosti zhenshchin v 1920–1940–e gody." In *Voprosy sovershenstvovaniia zakonodatel'stva i pravoprimenitel'noi deiatel'nosti. Sbornik nauchnykh trudov,* 201–12. Cheliabinsk: Cheliabinsk Gosudarstvennyi universitet, 1998.

Tierney, John. *Criminology: Theory and Context.* London: Prentice Hall, 1996.

Timasheff, Nicholas. *The Great Retreat: The Growth and Decline of Communism in Russia.* New York: E. P. Dutton, 1946.

Todes, Daniel P. *Darwin without Malthus: The Struggle for Existence in Russian Evolutionary Thought.* Oxford: Oxford University Press, 1989.

Tolz, Vera. *Russian Academicians and the Revolution: Combining Professionalism and Politics.* New York: St. Martin's Press, 1997.

Transchel, Kate. *Under the Influence: Working-Class Drinking, Temperance, and Cultural Revolution in Russia, 1895–1932.* Pittsburgh, PA: University of Pittsburgh Press, 2006.

Ulbricht, Otto. "The Debate about Foundling Hospitals in Enlightenment Germany: Infanticide, Illegitimacy, and Infant Mortality Rates." *Central European History* 18, nos. 3–4 (1985): 211–56.

van der Berg, Ger. *The Soviet System of Justice: Figures and Policy.* Dordrecht, Netherlands: Martinus Nijhoff Publishers, 1985.

Viola, Lynn. *Peasant Rebels under Stalin: Collectivization and the Culture of Peasant Resistance.* Oxford: Oxford University Press, 1996.

von Geldern, James. *Bolshevik Festivals, 1917–1920.* Berkeley: University of California Press, 1993.

Vucinich, Alexander. *Empire of Knowledge: The Academy of Sciences of the USSR (1917–1970).* Berkeley: University of California Press, 1984.

Walkowitz, Judith R. *City of Dreadful Delight: Narratives of Sexual Danger in Late-Victorian London.* Chicago: University of Chicago Press, 1992.

———. *Prostitution and Victorian Society: Women, Class, and the Stage.* Cambridge: Cambridge University Press, 1980.

Wartenweiler, David. *Civil Society and Academic Debate in Russia, 1905–1914.* Oxford: Clarendon Press, 1999.

Waters, Elizabeth. "The Modernization of Russian Motherhood, 1917–1937." *Soviet Studies* 44, no. 1 (1992): 123–35.

———. "Victim or Villain? Prostitution in Post-Revolutionary Russia." In *Women and Society in Russia and the Soviet Union,* edited by Linda Edmondson, 160–77. Cambridge: Cambridge University Press, 1992.

Weissman, Neil B. "Prohibition and Alcohol Control in the USSR: The 1920s Campaign against Illegal Spirits." *Soviet Studies* 38, no. 3 (1986): 349–68.

———. "Rural Crime in Tsarist Russia: The Question of Hooliganism, 1905–1914." *Slavic Review* 37, no. 2 (1978): 228–40.

Wessling, Mary Nagle. "Infanticide Trials and Forensic Medicine: Württemberg 1757–93." In *Legal Medicine in History,* edited by Michael Clark, and Catherine Crawford, 117–44. Cambridge: Cambridge University Press, 1994.

Wetzell, Richard F. *Inventing the Criminal: A History of German Criminology, 1880–1945.* Chapel Hill: University of North Carolina Press, 2000.

Wilson, Stephen. "Infanticide, Child Abandonment, and Female Honour in Nineteenth-Century Corsica." *Comparative Studies in Society and History* 30, no. 4 (1988): 762–83.

Wimberg, Ellen Mary. "'Replacing the Shackles': Soviet Penal Theory, Policy, and Practice, 1917–1930." Ph.D. diss., University of Pittsburgh, 1996.

Wolfgang, Marvin E. "Cesare Lombroso." In *Pioneers in Criminology*, edited by Hermann Mannheim, 168–228. London: Stevens & Sons, 1960.

———. "Pioneers in Criminology: Cesare Lombroso (1835–1909)." *Journal of Criminal Law, Criminology, and Police Science* 52, no. 4 (1961): 361–91.

Wood, Elizabeth A. *The Baba and the Comrade: Gender and Politics in Revolutionary Russia*. Bloomington: Indiana University Press, 1997.

Worobec, Christine D. *Peasant Russia: Family and Community in the Post-Emancipation Period*. Princeton, NJ: Princeton University Press, 1991.

———. "Temptress or Virgin? The Precarious Sexual Position of Women in Postemancipation Ukrainian Peasant Society." In *Russian Peasant Women*, edited by Beatrice Farnsworth and Lynn Viola, 41–53. Oxford: Oxford University Press, 1992.

Wortman, Richard S. *The Development of a Russian Legal Consciousness*. Chicago: University of Chicago Press, 1976.

Wrightson, Keith. "Infanticide in European History." *Criminal Justice History* 3 (1982): 1–20.

Zedner, Lucia. *Women, Crime, and Custody in Victorian England*. Oxford: Clarendon Press, 1991.

Zehr, Howard. *Crime and the Development of Modern Society*. London: Croom Helm, 1976.

———. "The Modernization of Crime in Germany and France, 1830–1913." *Journal of Social History* 8 (1975): 117–41.

Zelitch, Judah. *Soviet Administration of Criminal Law*. Philadelphia: University of Pennsylvania Press, 1931.

INDEX